UQ HOLDER!

D0103627

KEN AKAMATSU

vol.23

CHARACTERS

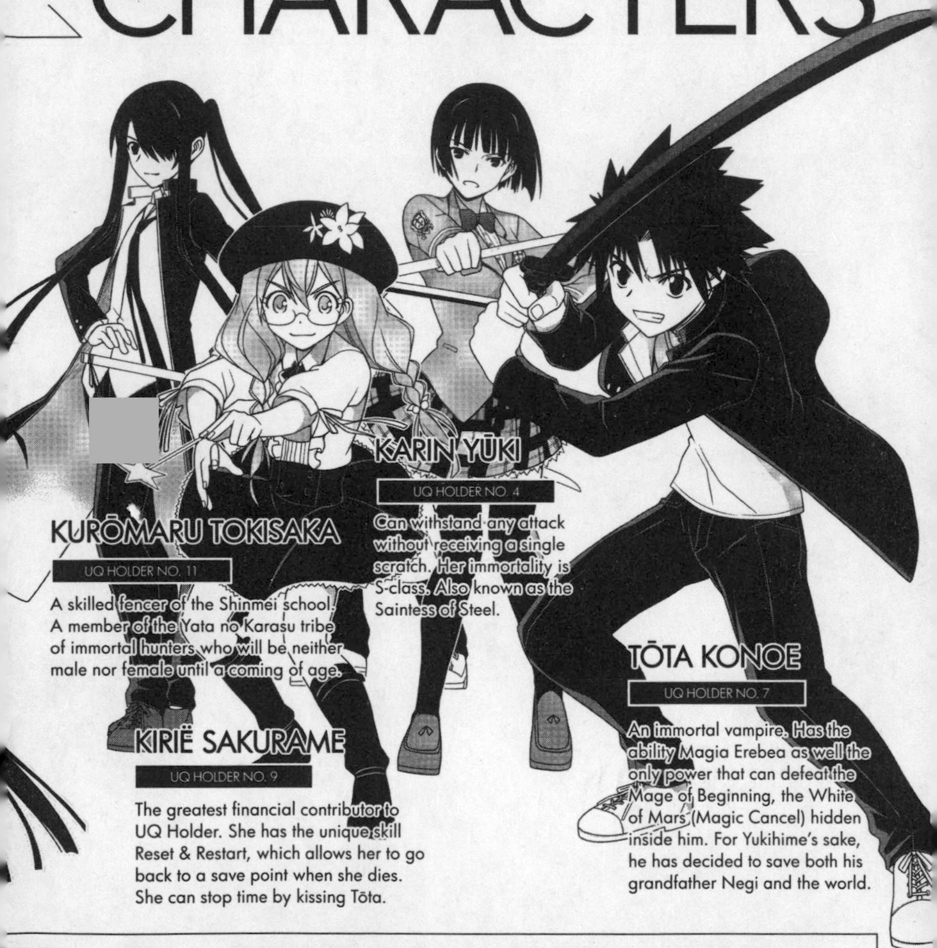

KARIN YŪKI

UQ HOLDER NO. 4

Can withstand any attack without receiving a single scratch. Her immortality is S-class. Also known as the Saintess of Steel.

KURŌMARU TOKISAKA

UQ HOLDER NO. 11

A skilled fencer of the Shinmei school. A member of the Yata no Karasu tribe of immortal hunters who will be neither male nor female until a coming of age.

TŌTA KONOE

UQ HOLDER NO. 7

An immortal vampire. Has the ability Magia Erebea as well the only power that can defeat the Mage of Beginning, the White of Mars (Magic Cancel) hidden inside him. For Yukihime's sake, he has decided to save both his grandfather Negi and the world.

KIRIË SAKURAME

UQ HOLDER NO. 9

The greatest financial contributor to UQ Holder. She has the unique skill Reset & Restart, which allows her to go back to a save point when she dies. She can stop time by kissing Tōta.

UQ HOLDER IMMORTAL NUMBERS

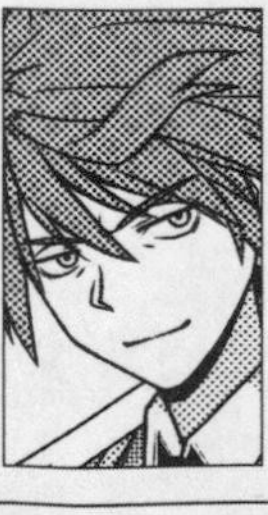

JINBEI SHISHIDO

UQ HOLDER NO. 2

UQ Holder's oldest member. Became an immortal in the middle ages, when he ate mermaid flesh in the Muromachi Period. Has the "Switcheroo" skill that switches the locations of physical objects.

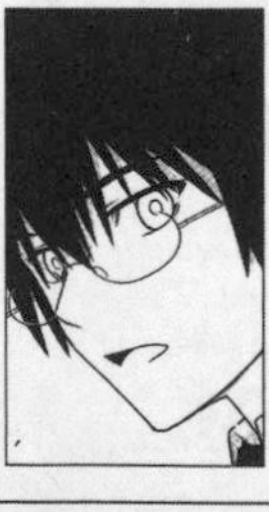

GENGORŌ MAKABE

UQ HOLDER NO. 6

Manages the business side of UQ Holder's hideout and inn. He has a skill known as "multiple lives," so when he dies, another Gengorō appears.

UQ HOLDER!

Ken Akamatsu Presents

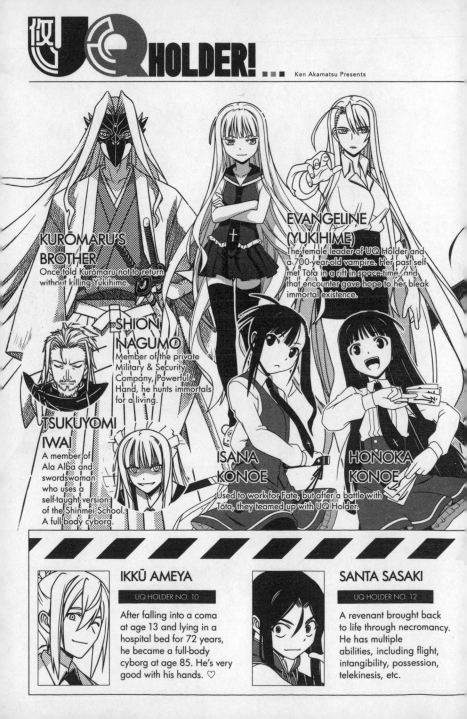

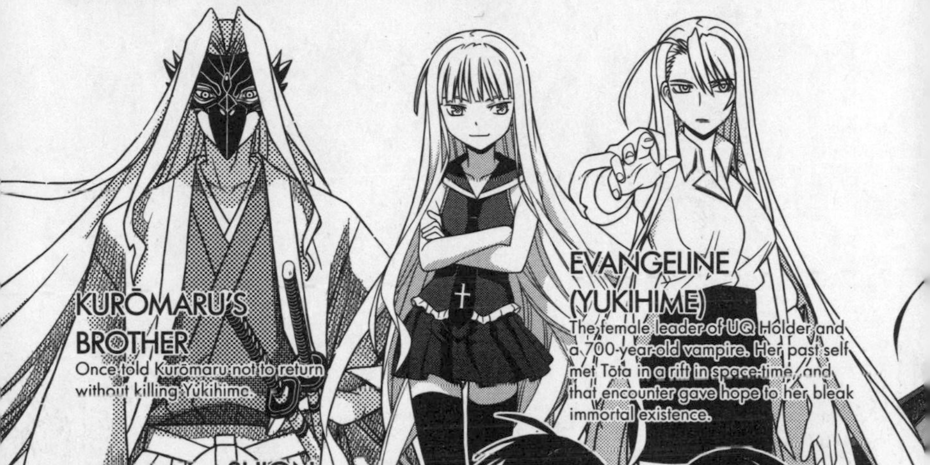
EVANGELINE (YUKIHIME)
The female leader of UQ Holder and a 700-year-old vampire. Her past self met Tōta in a rift in space-time, and that encounter gave hope to her bleak immortal existence.
KURŌMARU'S BROTHER
Once told Kurōmaru not to return without killing Yukihime.
SHION NAGUMO
Member of the private Military & Security Company, Powerful Hand, he hunts immortals for a living.
TSUKUYOMI IWAI
A member of Ala Alba and swordswoman who uses a self-taught version of the Shinmei School. A full-body cyborg.
HONOKA KONOE
ISANA KONOE
Used to work for Fate, but after a battle with Tōta, they teamed up with UQ Holder.

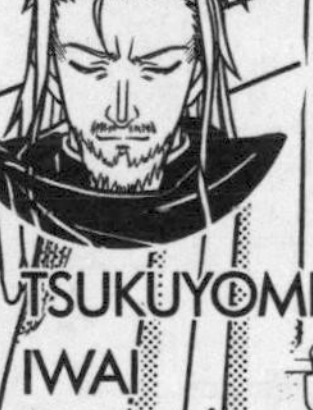

IKKŪ AMEYA

UQ HOLDER NO. 10

After falling into a coma at age 13 and lying in a hospital bed for 72 years, he became a full-body cyborg at age 85. He's very good with his hands. ♡

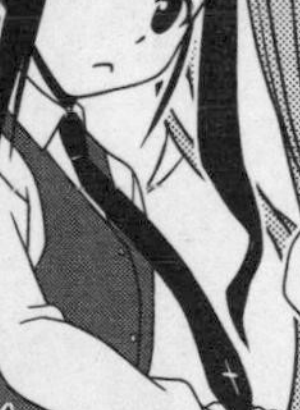

SANTA SASAKI

UQ HOLDER NO. 12

A revenant brought back to life through necromancy. He has multiple abilities, including flight, intangibility, possession, telekinesis, etc.

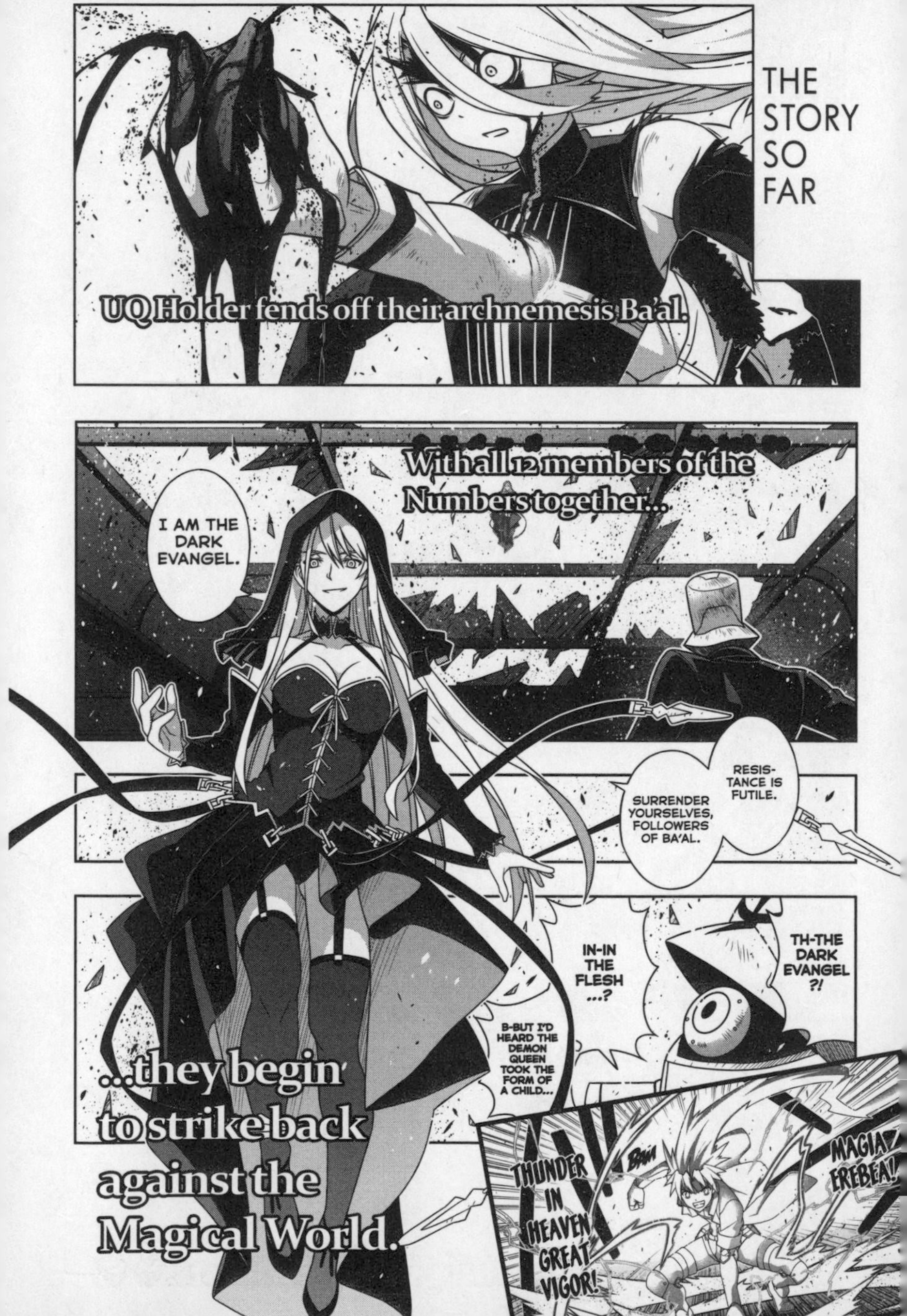
THE STORY SO FAR
UQ Holder fends off their archnemesis Ba'al.
With all 12 members of the Numbers together...
I AM THE DARK EVANGEL.
RESISTANCE IS FUTILE.
SURRENDER YOURSELVES, FOLLOWERS OF BA'AL.
TH-THE DARK EVANGEL ?!
IN-IN THE FLESH ...?
B-BUT I'D HEARD THE DEMON QUEEN TOOK THE FORM OF A CHILD...
...they begin to strike back against the Magical World.
MAGIA EREBEA!
BAM
THUNDER IN HEAVEN GREAT VIGOR!

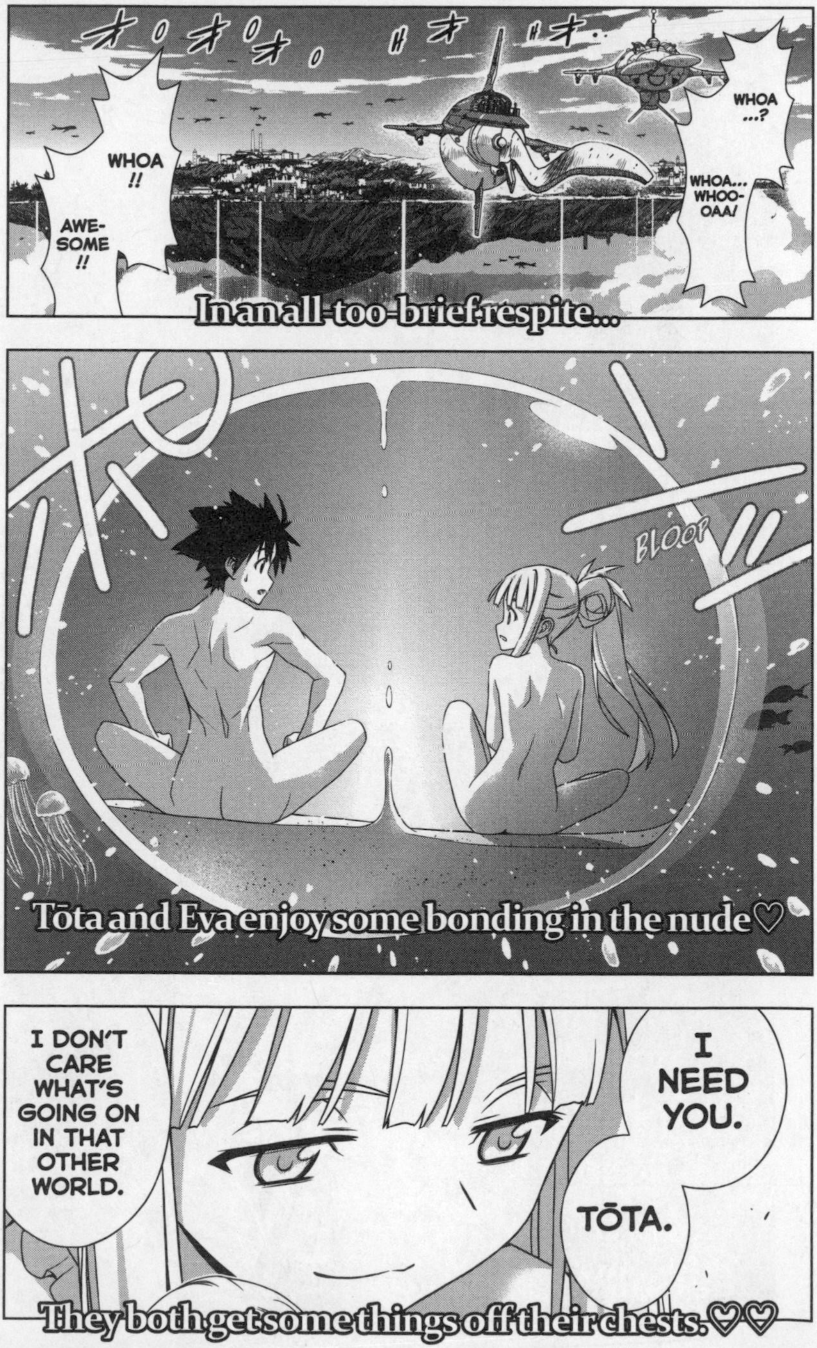
WHOA ...?
WHOA... WHOO-OAA!
WHOA !!
AWE-SOME !!
In an all-too-brief respite...
BLOOP
Tōta and Eva enjoy some bonding in the nude♡
I NEED YOU.
TŌTA.
I DON'T CARE WHAT'S GOING ON IN THAT OTHER WORLD.
They both get some things off their chests.♡♡

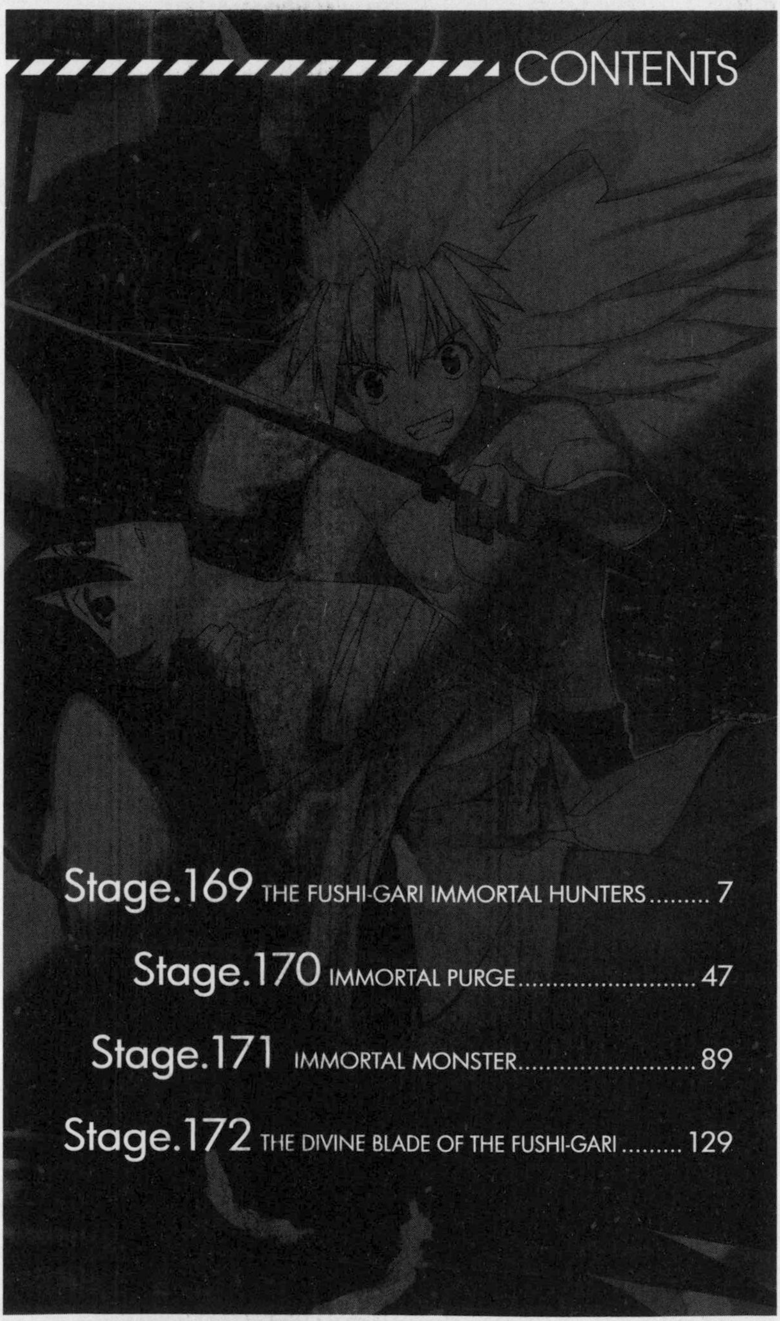

CONTENTS

Stage.169 THE FUSHI-GARI IMMORTAL HUNTERS 7

Stage.170 IMMORTAL PURGE 47

Stage.171 IMMORTAL MONSTER 89

Stage.172 THE DIVINE BLADE OF THE FUSHI-GARI 129

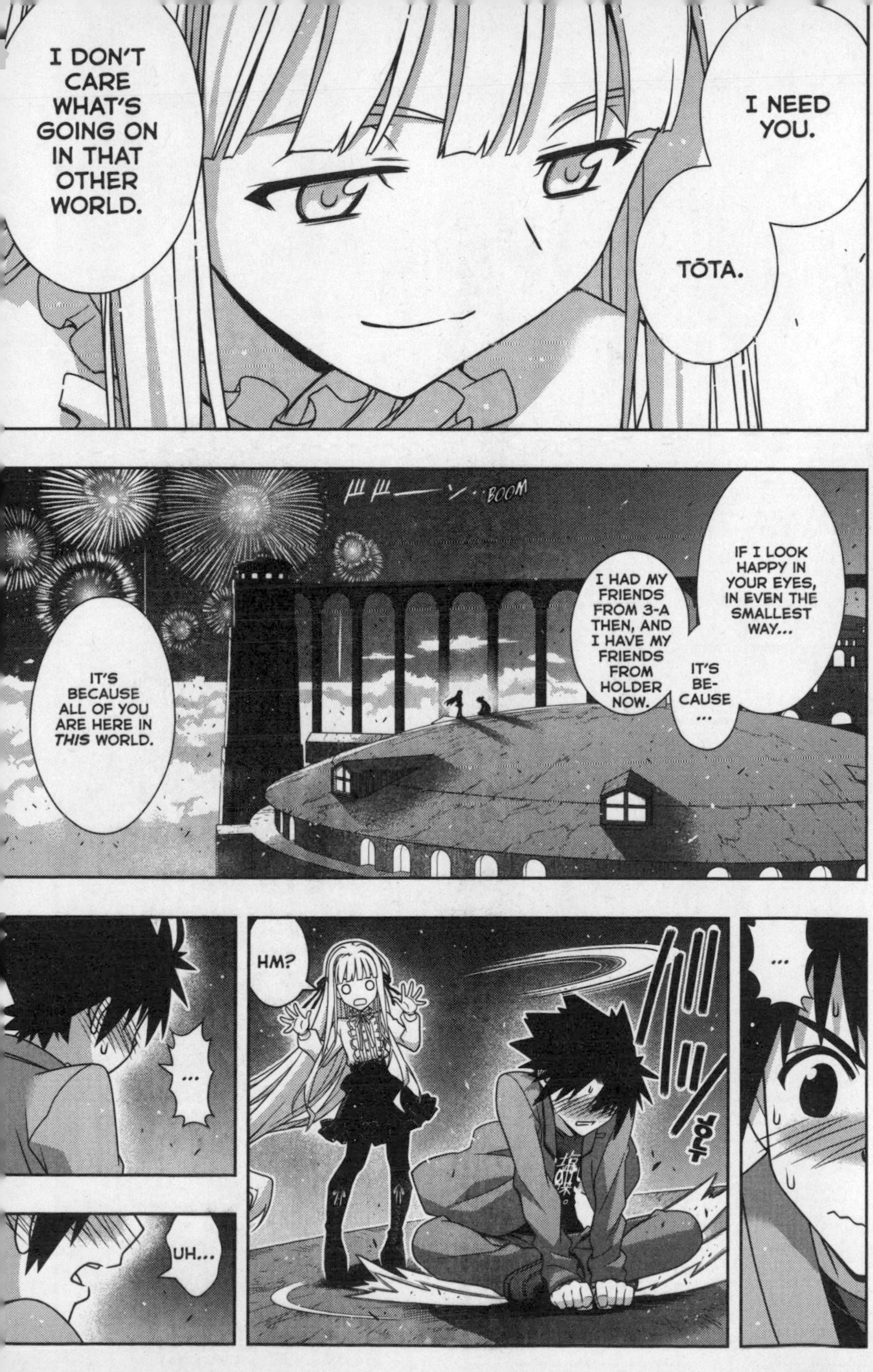
I NEED YOU.
TŌTA.
I DON'T CARE WHAT'S GOING ON IN THAT OTHER WORLD.
BOOM
IF I LOOK HAPPY IN YOUR EYES, IN EVEN THE SMALLEST WAY...
IT'S BE-CAUSE ...
I HAD MY FRIENDS FROM 3-A THEN, AND I HAVE MY FRIENDS FROM HOLDER NOW.
IT'S BECAUSE ALL OF YOU ARE HERE IN *THIS* WORLD.
...
HM?
JOLT
...
UH...

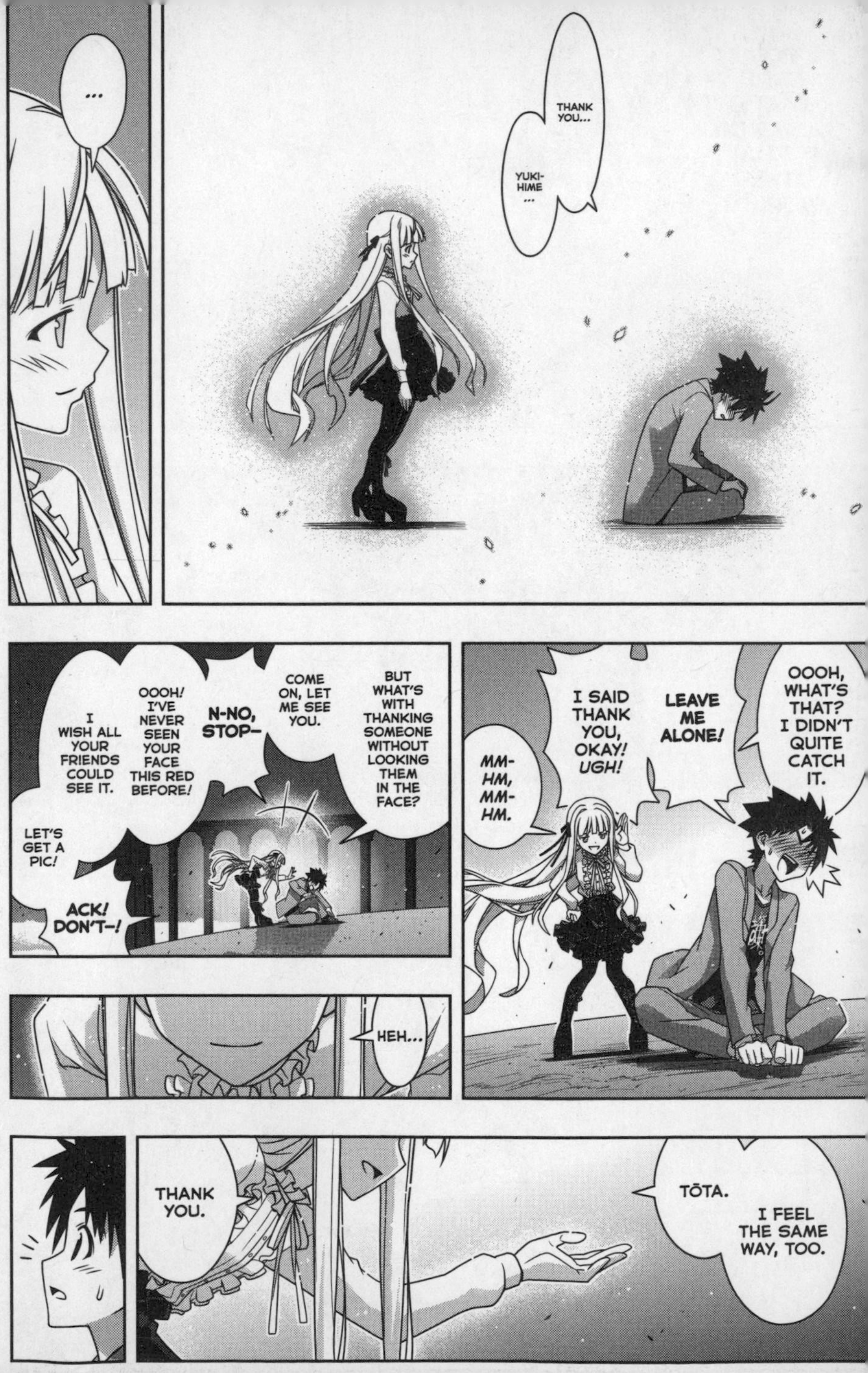
THANK YOU...
YUKI-HIME ...
...
OOOH, WHAT'S THAT? I DIDN'T QUITE CATCH IT.
LEAVE ME ALONE!
I SAID THANK YOU, OKAY! UGH!
MM-HM, MM-HM.
BUT WHAT'S WITH THANKING SOMEONE WITHOUT LOOKING THEM IN THE FACE?
COME ON, LET ME SEE YOU.
N-NO, STOP–
OOOH! I'VE NEVER SEEN YOUR FACE THIS RED BEFORE!
I WISH ALL YOUR FRIENDS COULD SEE IT.
LET'S GET A PIC!
ACK! DON'T–!
HEH...
TŌTA.
I FEEL THE SAME WAY, TOO.
THANK YOU.

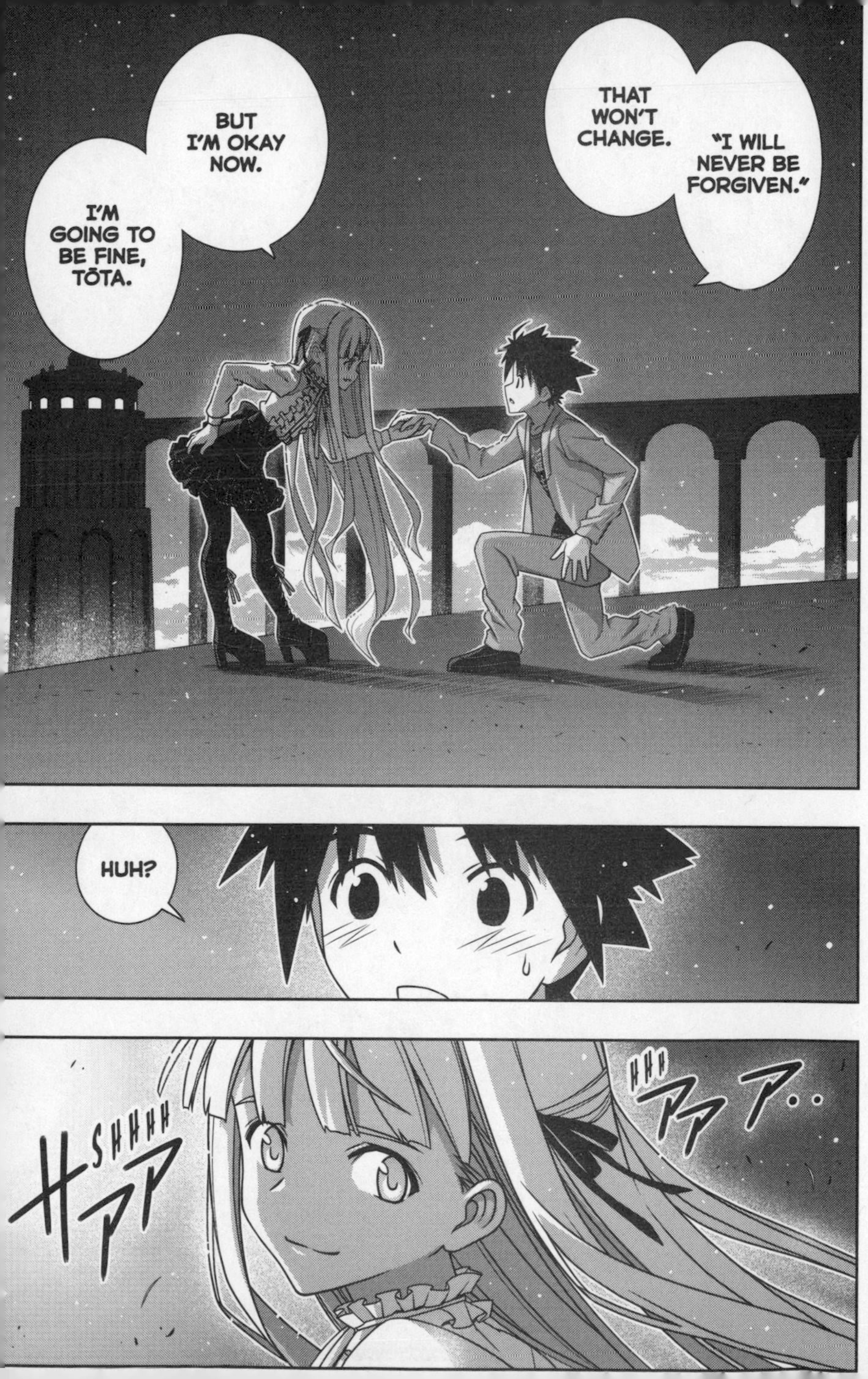
"I WILL NEVER BE FORGIVEN."
THAT WON'T CHANGE.
BUT I'M OKAY NOW.
I'M GOING TO BE FINE, TŌTA.
HUH?
HHH
ァァア..
SHHHH
サアア

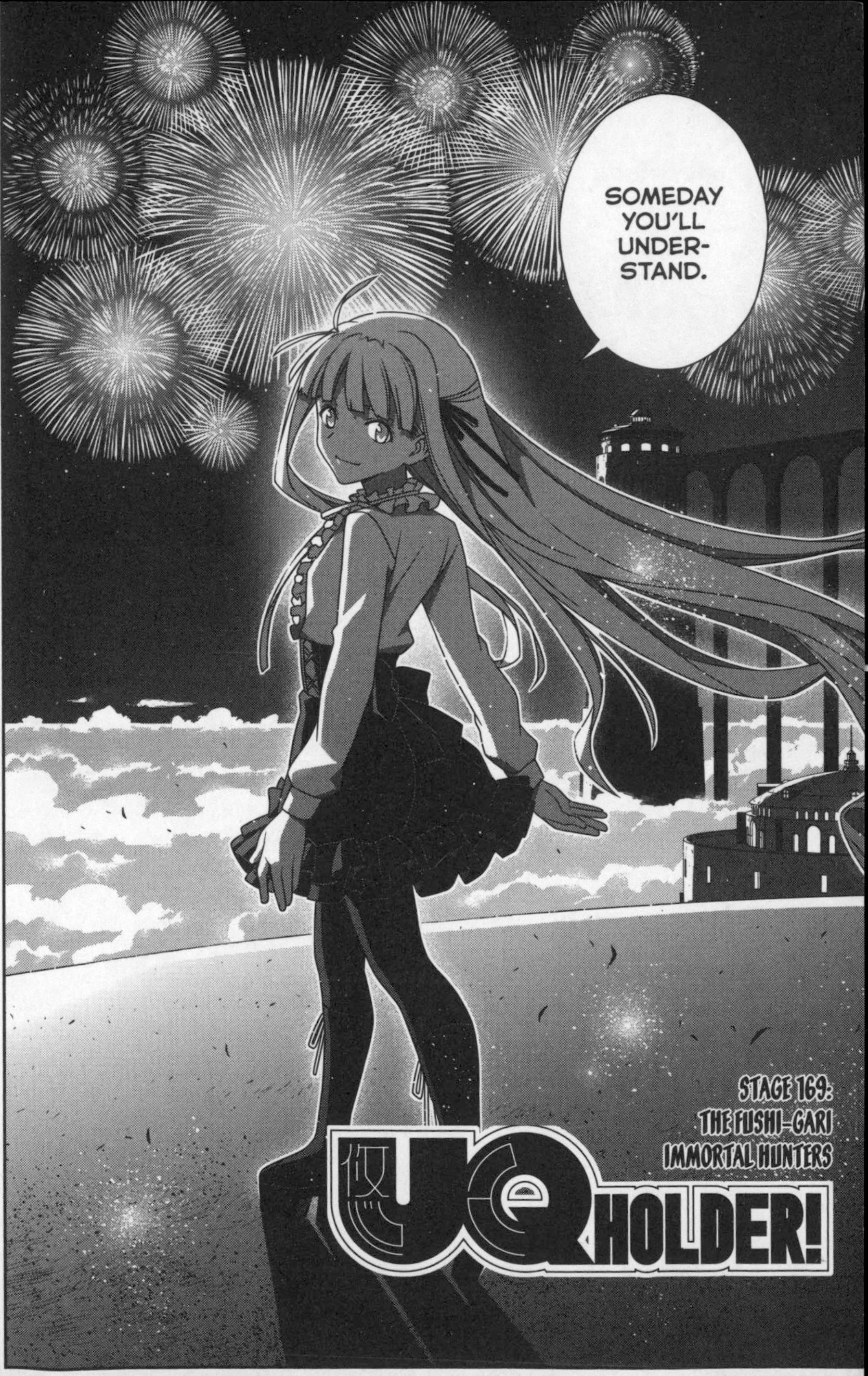
SOMEDAY YOU'LL UNDER-STAND.
STAGE 169: THE FUSHI-GARI IMMORTAL HUNTERS
UQ HOLDER!

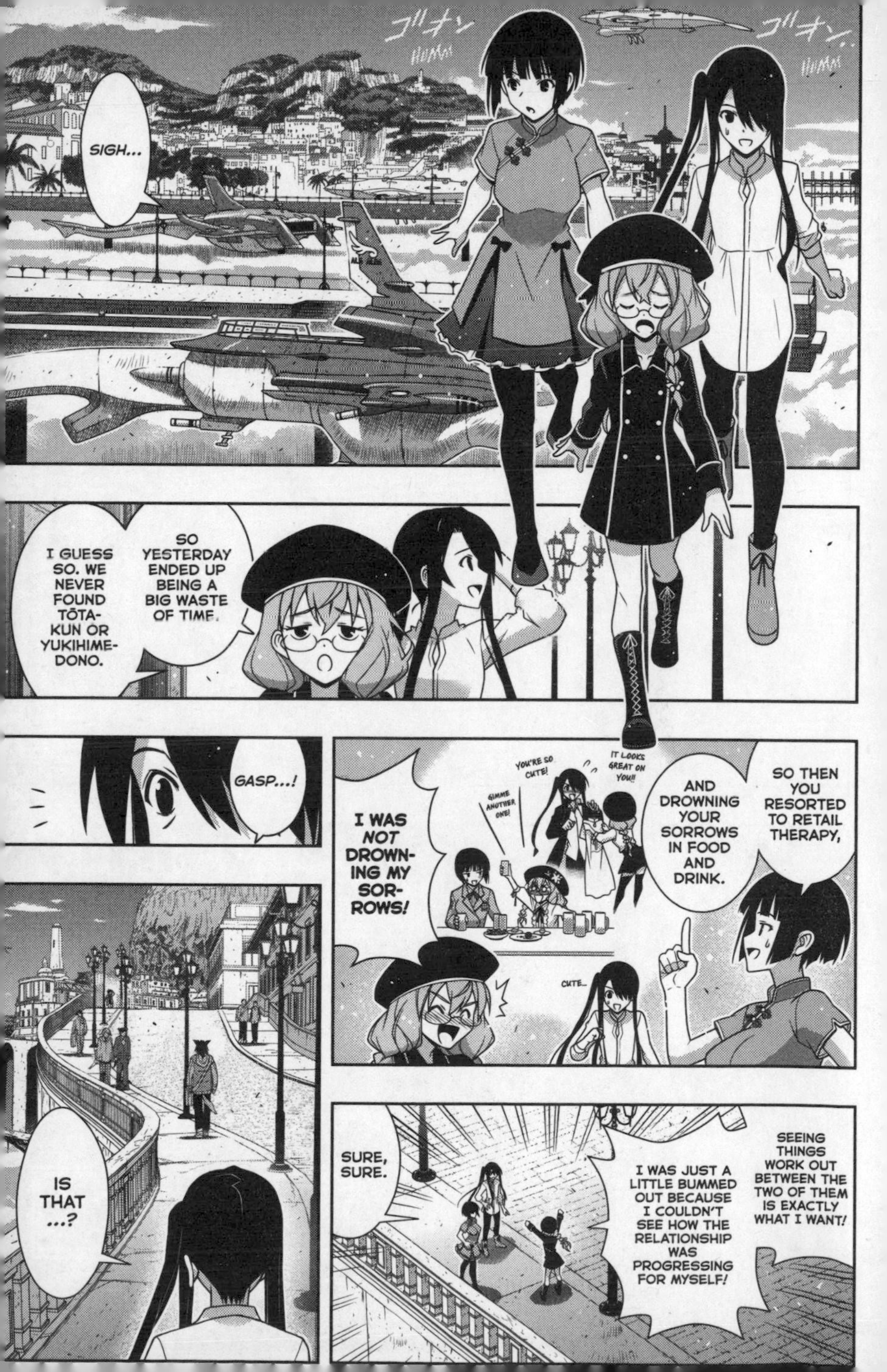
ゴオン
HUMM
ゴオン
HUMM
SIGH...
SO YESTERDAY ENDED UP BEING A BIG WASTE OF TIME.
I GUESS SO. WE NEVER FOUND TŌTA-KUN OR YUKIHIME-DONO.
SO THEN YOU RESORTED TO RETAIL THERAPY,
AND DROWNING YOUR SORROWS IN FOOD AND DRINK.
IT LOOKS GREAT ON YOU!!
YOU'RE SO CUTE!
GIMME ANOTHER ONE!
I WAS *NOT* DROWNING MY SORROWS!
CUTE...
SEEING THINGS WORK OUT BETWEEN THE TWO OF THEM IS EXACTLY WHAT I WANT!
I WAS JUST A LITTLE BUMMED OUT BECAUSE I COULDN'T SEE HOW THE RELATIONSHIP WAS PROGRESSING FOR MYSELF!
SURE, SURE.
GASP...!
IS THAT ...?

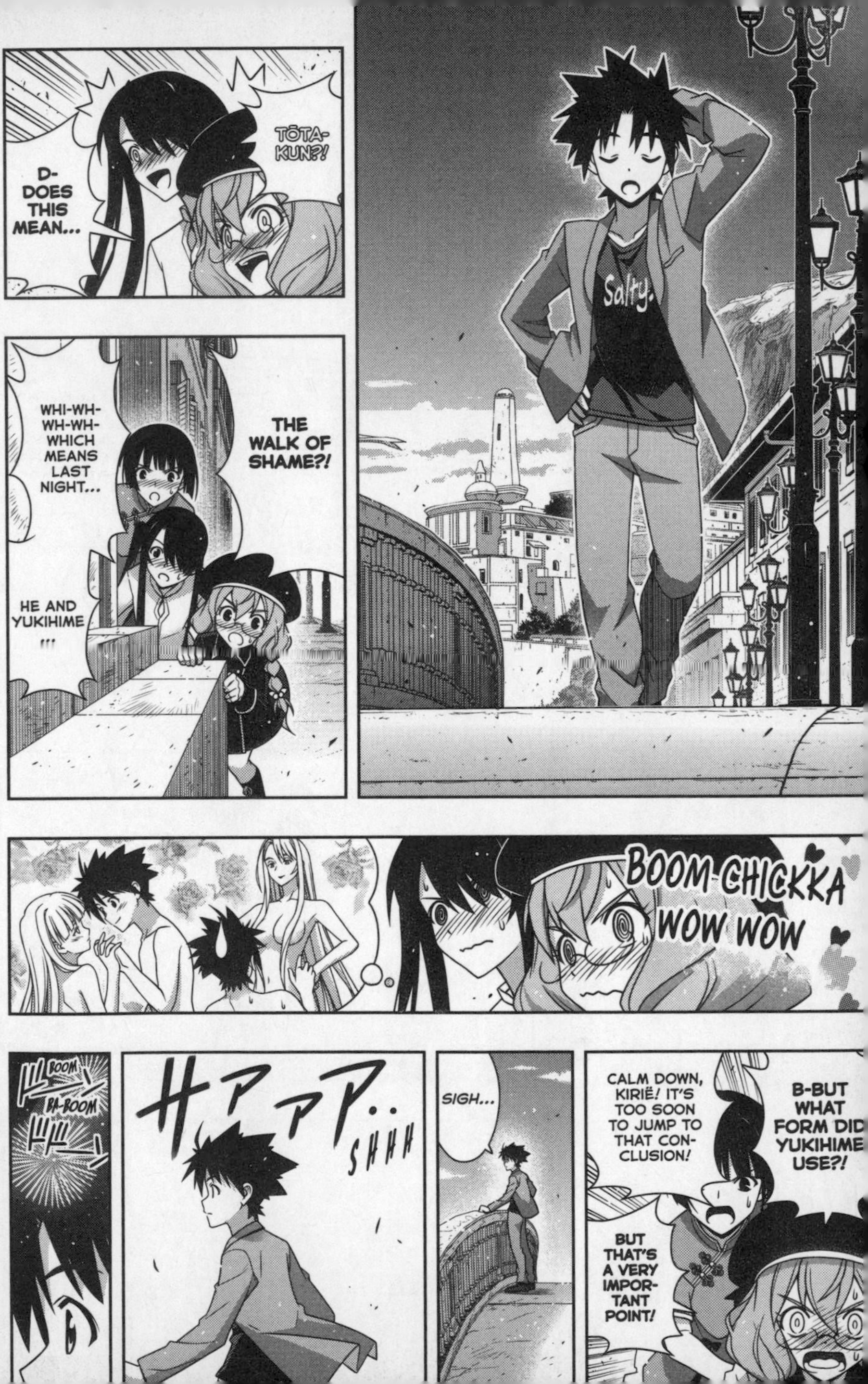
Salty.
TŌTA-KUN?!
D-DOES THIS MEAN...
THE WALK OF SHAME?!
WHI-WH-WH-WH-WHICH MEANS LAST NIGHT...
HE AND YUKIHIME ...
BOOM CHICKKA WOW WOW
B-BUT WHAT FORM DID YUKIHIME USE?!
CALM DOWN, KIRIË! IT'S TOO SOON TO JUMP TO THAT CONCLUSION!
BUT THAT'S A VERY IMPORTANT POINT!
SIGH...
サァァア..
SHHH
BOOM
BA-BOOM

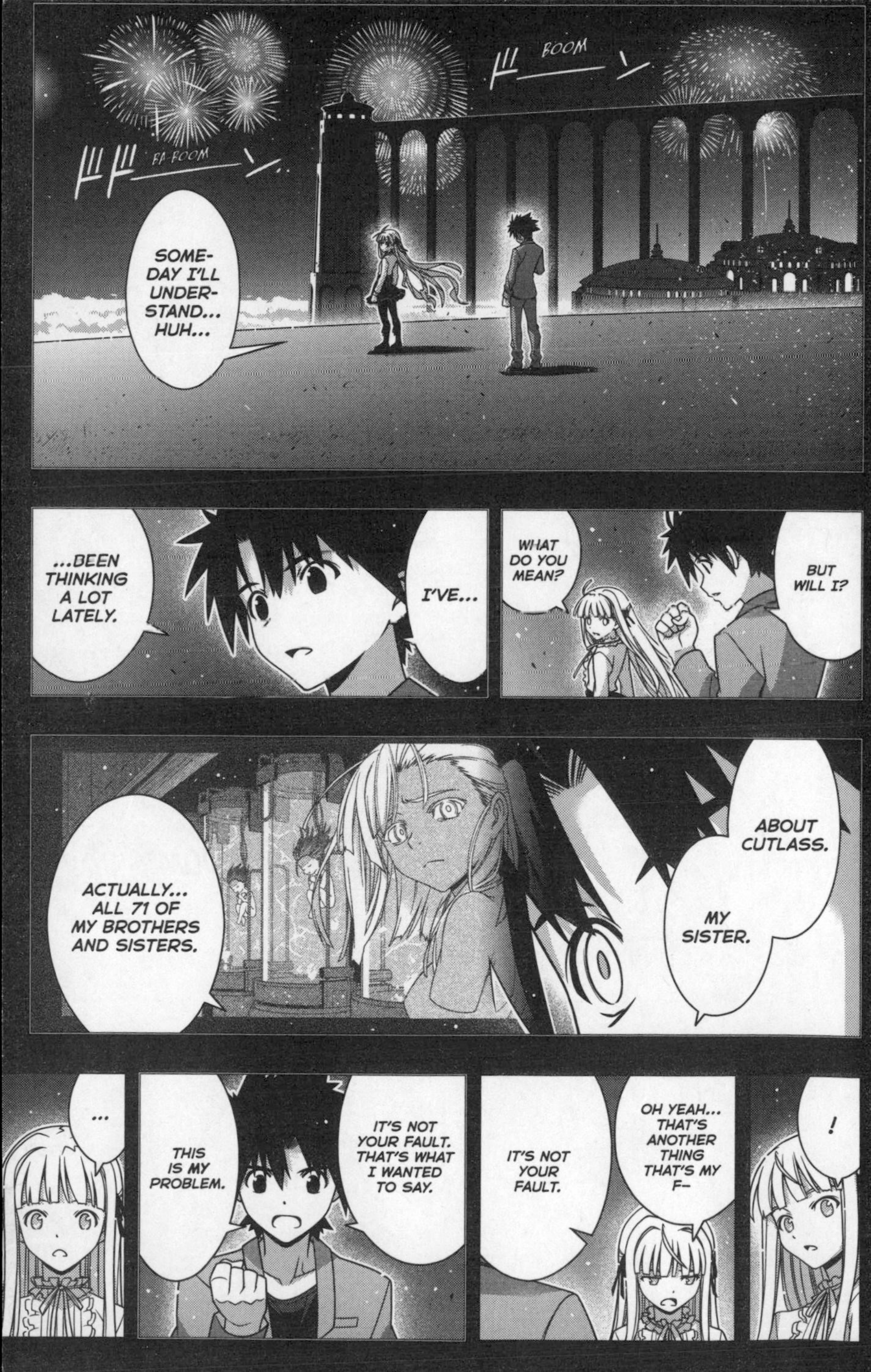
BOOM
BA-BOOM
SOME-DAY I'LL UNDER-STAND... HUH...
BUT WILL I?
WHAT DO YOU MEAN?
I'VE...
...BEEN THINKING A LOT LATELY.
ABOUT CUTLASS.
MY SISTER.
ACTUALLY... ALL 71 OF MY BROTHERS AND SISTERS.
!
OH YEAH... THAT'S ANOTHER THING THAT'S MY F—
IT'S NOT YOUR FAULT.
IT'S NOT YOUR FAULT. THAT'S WHAT I WANTED TO SAY.
THIS IS MY PROBLEM.
...

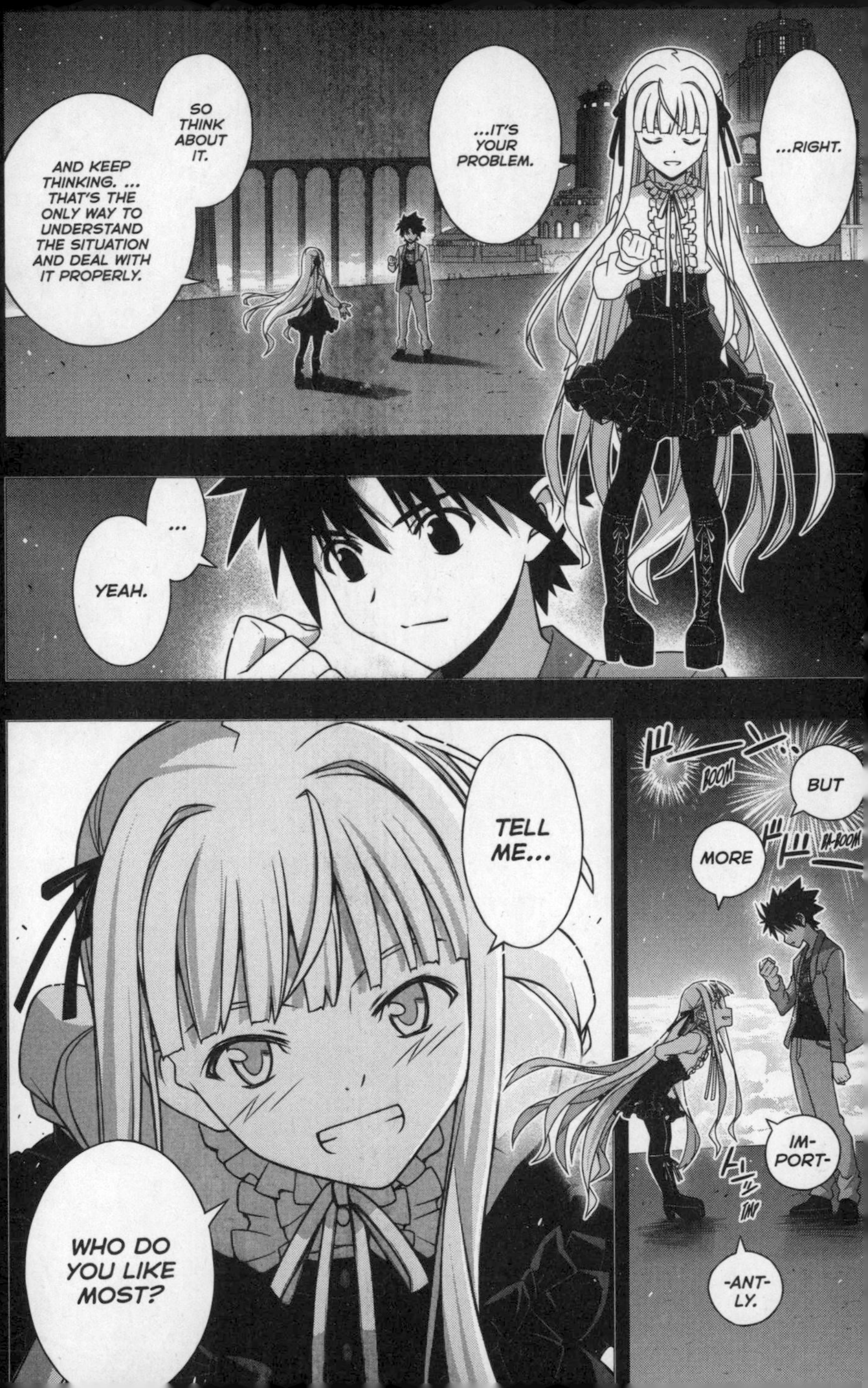
...RIGHT.
...IT'S YOUR PROBLEM.
SO THINK ABOUT IT.
AND KEEP THINKING. ... THAT'S THE ONLY WAY TO UNDERSTAND THE SITUATION AND DEAL WITH IT PROPERLY.
...
YEAH.
BOOM
BUT
KA-BOOM
MORE
IM-PORT-
-ANT-LY.
TELL ME...
WHO DO YOU LIKE MOST?

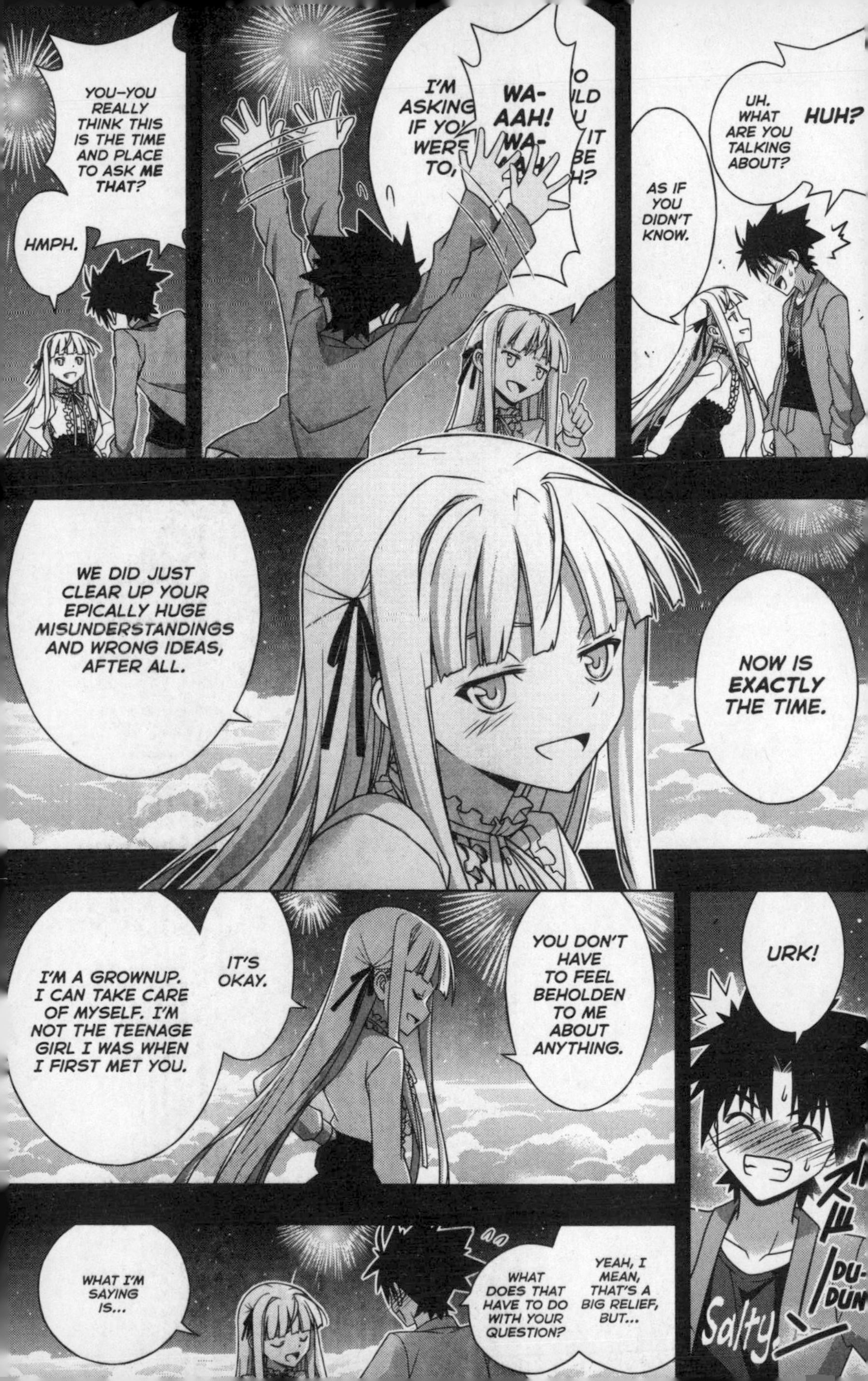
HUH?
UH. WHAT ARE YOU TALKING ABOUT?
AS IF YOU DIDN'T KNOW.
I'M ASKING IF YO WERE TO,
WA-AAH! WA-
YOU–YOU REALLY THINK THIS IS THE TIME AND PLACE TO ASK ME THAT?
HMPH.
NOW IS EXACTLY THE TIME.
WE DID JUST CLEAR UP YOUR EPICALLY HUGE MISUNDERSTANDINGS AND WRONG IDEAS, AFTER ALL.
URK!
DU-DUN
Salty
YOU DON'T HAVE TO FEEL BEHOLDEN TO ME ABOUT ANYTHING.
IT'S OKAY.
I'M A GROWNUP. I CAN TAKE CARE OF MYSELF. I'M NOT THE TEENAGE GIRL I WAS WHEN I FIRST MET YOU.
YEAH, I MEAN, THAT'S A BIG RELIEF, BUT...
WHAT DOES THAT HAVE TO DO WITH YOUR QUESTION?
WHAT I'M SAYING IS...

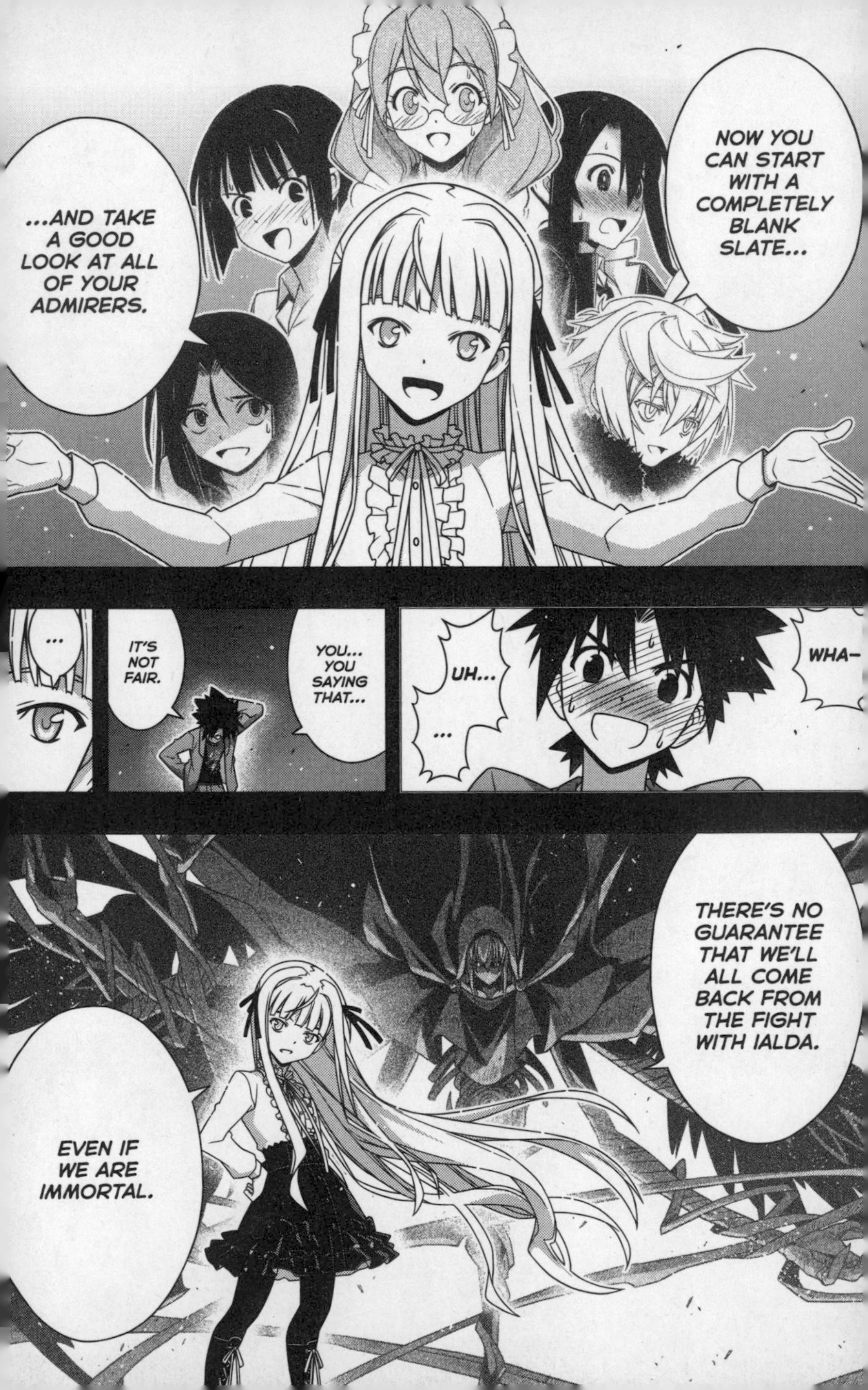
NOW YOU CAN START WITH A COMPLETELY BLANK SLATE...
...AND TAKE A GOOD LOOK AT ALL OF YOUR ADMIRERS.
WHA-
UH...
...
YOU... YOU SAYING THAT...
IT'S NOT FAIR.
...
THERE'S NO GUARANTEE THAT WE'LL ALL COME BACK FROM THE FIGHT WITH IALDA.
EVEN IF WE ARE IMMORTAL.

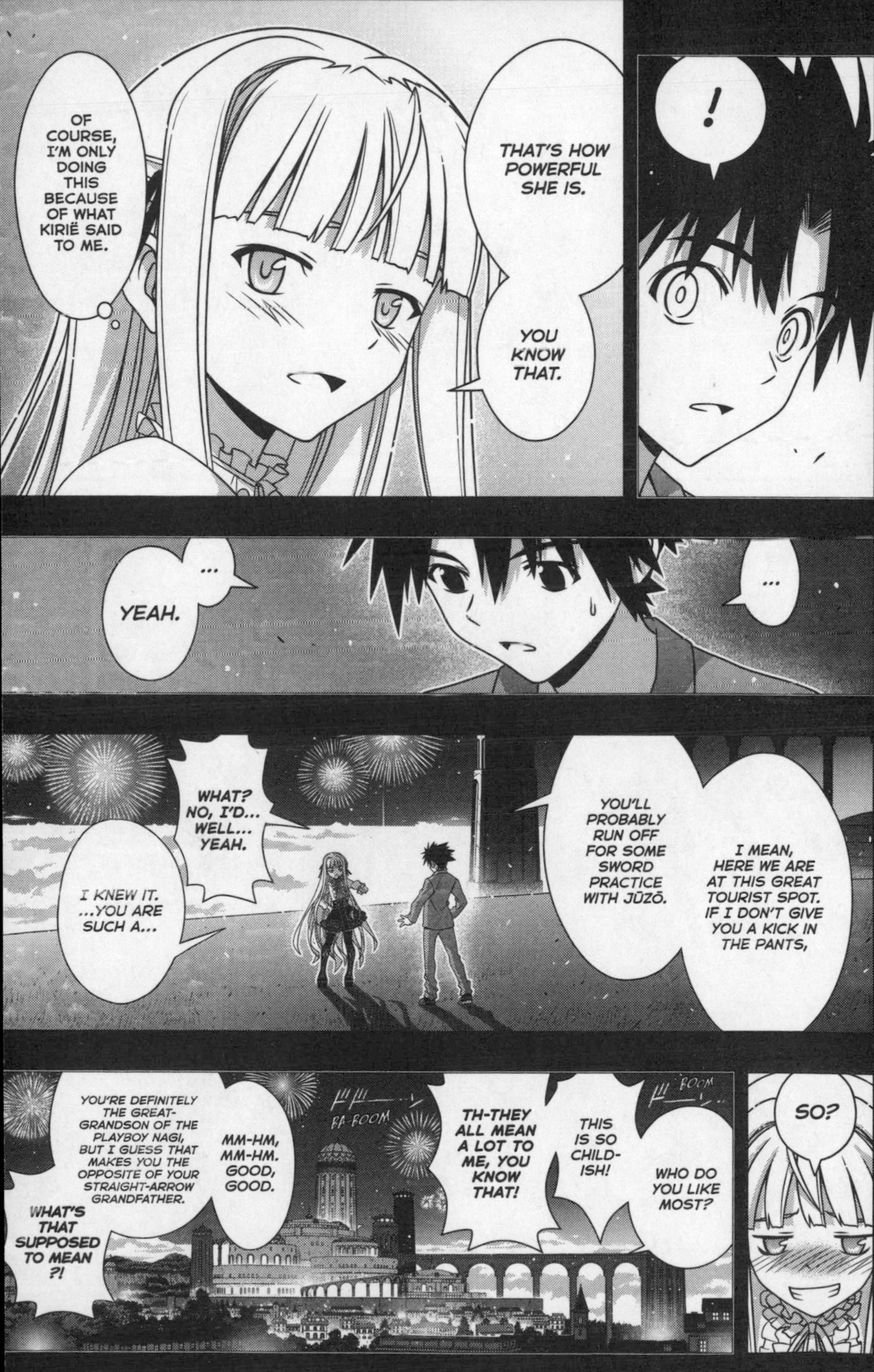
!
THAT'S HOW POWERFUL SHE IS.
YOU KNOW THAT.
OF COURSE, I'M ONLY DOING THIS BECAUSE OF WHAT KIRIË SAID TO ME.
...
... YEAH.
I MEAN, HERE WE ARE AT THIS GREAT TOURIST SPOT. IF I DON'T GIVE YOU A KICK IN THE PANTS,
YOU'LL PROBABLY RUN OFF FOR SOME SWORD PRACTICE WITH JŪZŌ.
WHAT? NO, I'D... WELL... YEAH.
I KNEW IT. ...YOU ARE SUCH A...
SO?
WHO DO YOU LIKE MOST?
BOOM
THIS IS SO CHILD-ISH!
TH-THEY ALL MEAN A LOT TO ME, YOU KNOW THAT!
BA-BOOM
MM-HM, MM-HM. GOOD, GOOD.
YOU'RE DEFINITELY THE GREAT-GRANDSON OF THE PLAYBOY NAGI, BUT I GUESS THAT MAKES YOU THE OPPOSITE OF YOUR STRAIGHT-ARROW GRANDFATHER.
WHAT'S THAT SUPPOSED TO MEAN ?!

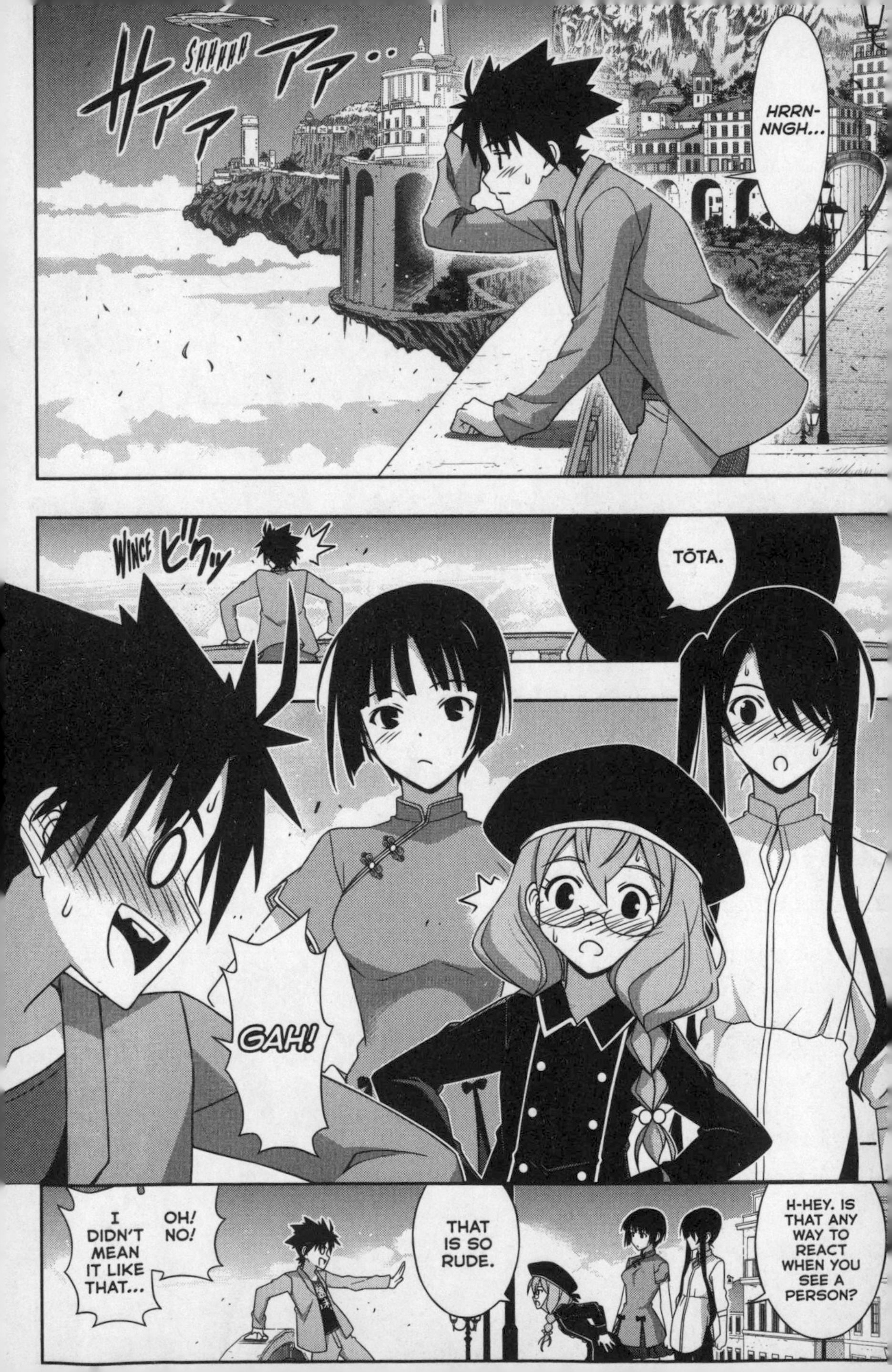
HRRN-NNGH...
SHHHHH
サァァァ‥
TŌTA.
WINCE ビクッ
GAH!
H-HEY. IS THAT ANY WAY TO REACT WHEN YOU SEE A PERSON?
THAT IS SO RUDE.
OH! NO!
I DIDN'T MEAN IT LIKE THAT...

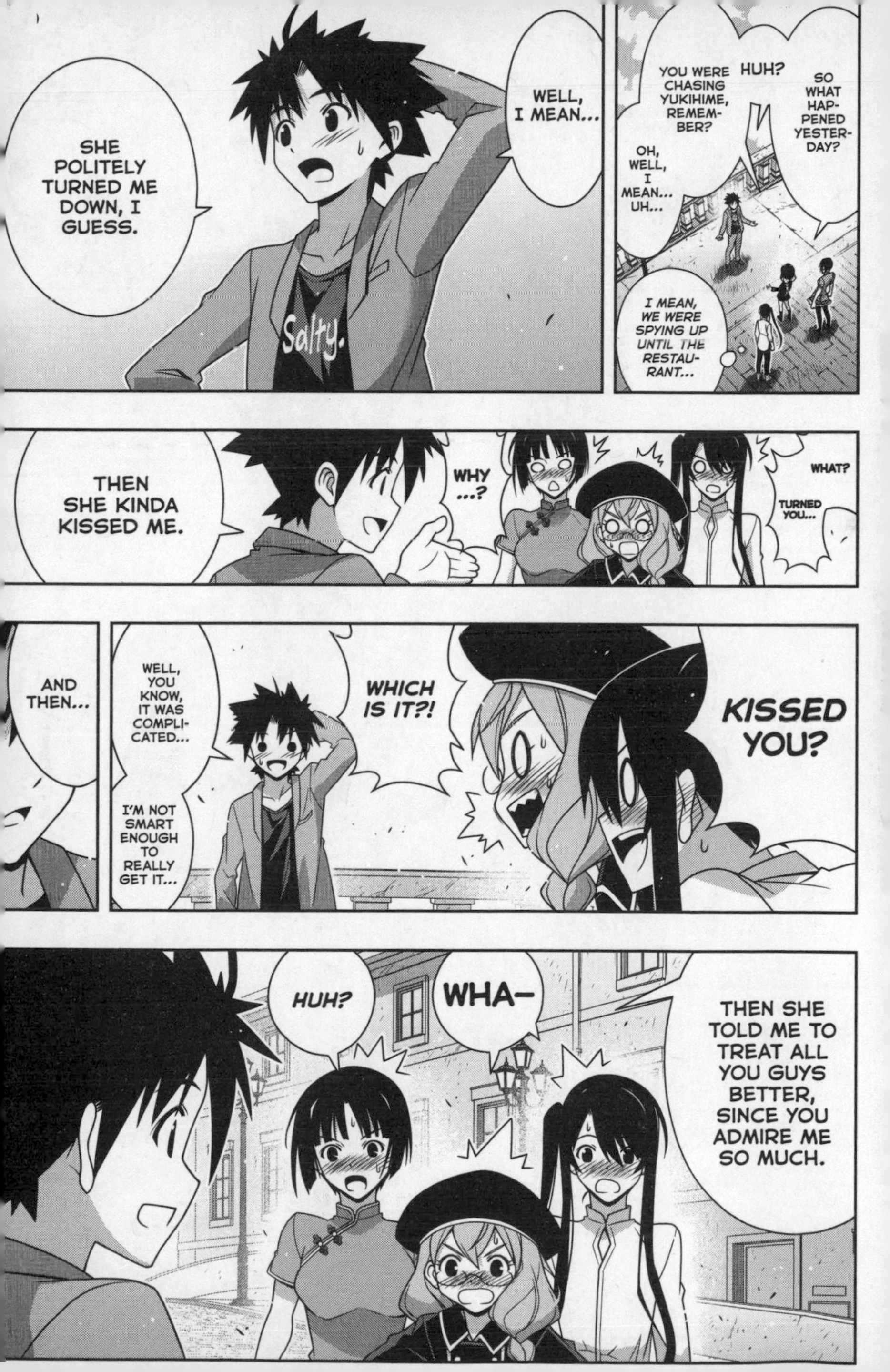
SO WHAT HAPPENED YESTERDAY?
HUH?
YOU WERE CHASING YUKIHIME, REMEMBER?
OH, WELL, I MEAN... UH...
I MEAN, WE WERE SPYING UP UNTIL THE RESTAURANT...
WELL, I MEAN...
SHE POLITELY TURNED ME DOWN, I GUESS.
Salty.
WHAT?
TURNED YOU...
WHY ...?
THEN SHE KINDA KISSED ME.
KISSED YOU?
WHICH IS IT?!
WELL, YOU KNOW, IT WAS COMPLICATED...
I'M NOT SMART ENOUGH TO REALLY GET IT...
AND THEN...
THEN SHE TOLD ME TO TREAT ALL YOU GUYS BETTER, SINCE YOU ADMIRE ME SO MUCH.
WHA-
HUH?

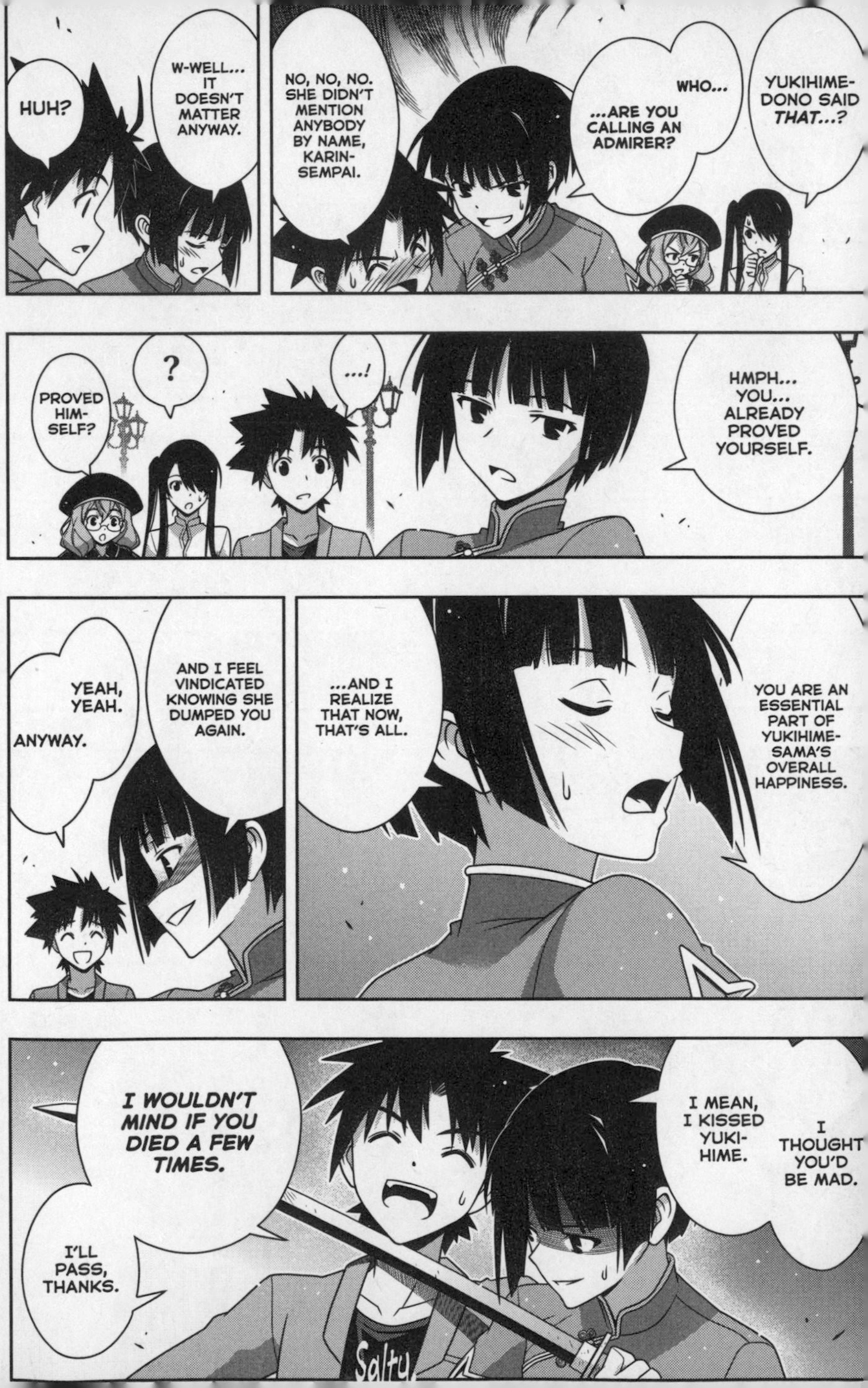
YUKIHIME-DONO SAID *THAT...?*
WHO...
...ARE YOU CALLING AN ADMIRER?
NO, NO, NO. SHE DIDN'T MENTION ANYBODY BY NAME, KARIN-SEMPAI.
W-WELL... IT DOESN'T MATTER ANYWAY.
HUH?
HMPH... YOU... ALREADY PROVED YOURSELF.
...!
?
PROVED HIM-SELF?
YOU ARE AN ESSENTIAL PART OF YUKIHIME-SAMA'S OVERALL HAPPINESS.
...AND I REALIZE THAT NOW, THAT'S ALL.
AND I FEEL VINDICATED KNOWING SHE DUMPED YOU AGAIN.
YEAH, YEAH.
ANYWAY.
I THOUGHT YOU'D BE MAD.
I MEAN, I KISSED YUKI-HIME.
I WOULDN'T MIND IF YOU DIED A FEW TIMES.
I'LL PASS, THANKS.
Salty

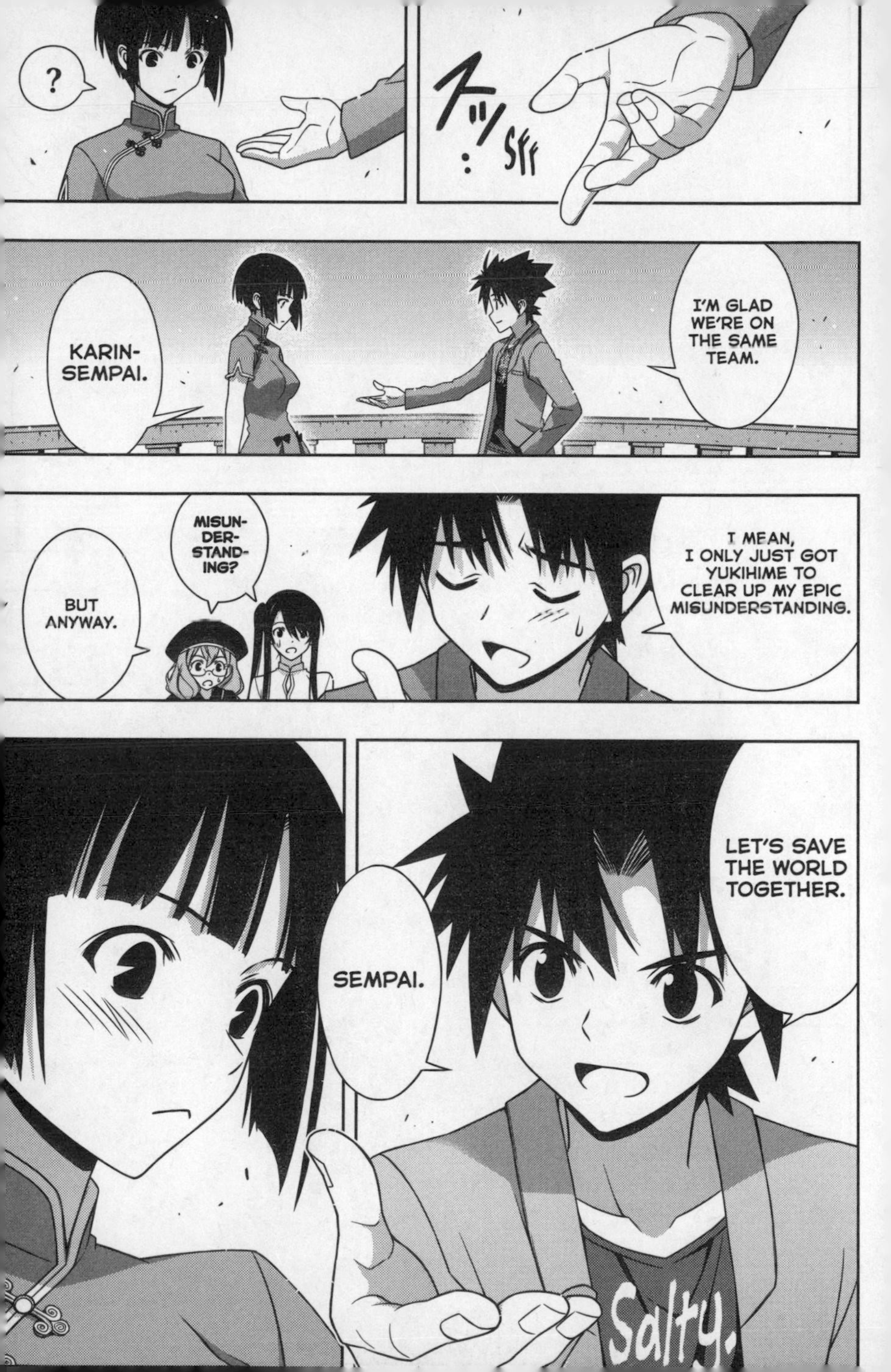
スッ
SFF
?
I'M GLAD WE'RE ON THE SAME TEAM.
KARIN-SEMPAI.
I MEAN, I ONLY JUST GOT YUKIHIME TO CLEAR UP MY EPIC MISUNDERSTANDING.
MISUN-DER-STAND-ING?
BUT ANYWAY.
LET'S SAVE THE WORLD TOGETHER.
SEMPAI.
Salty.

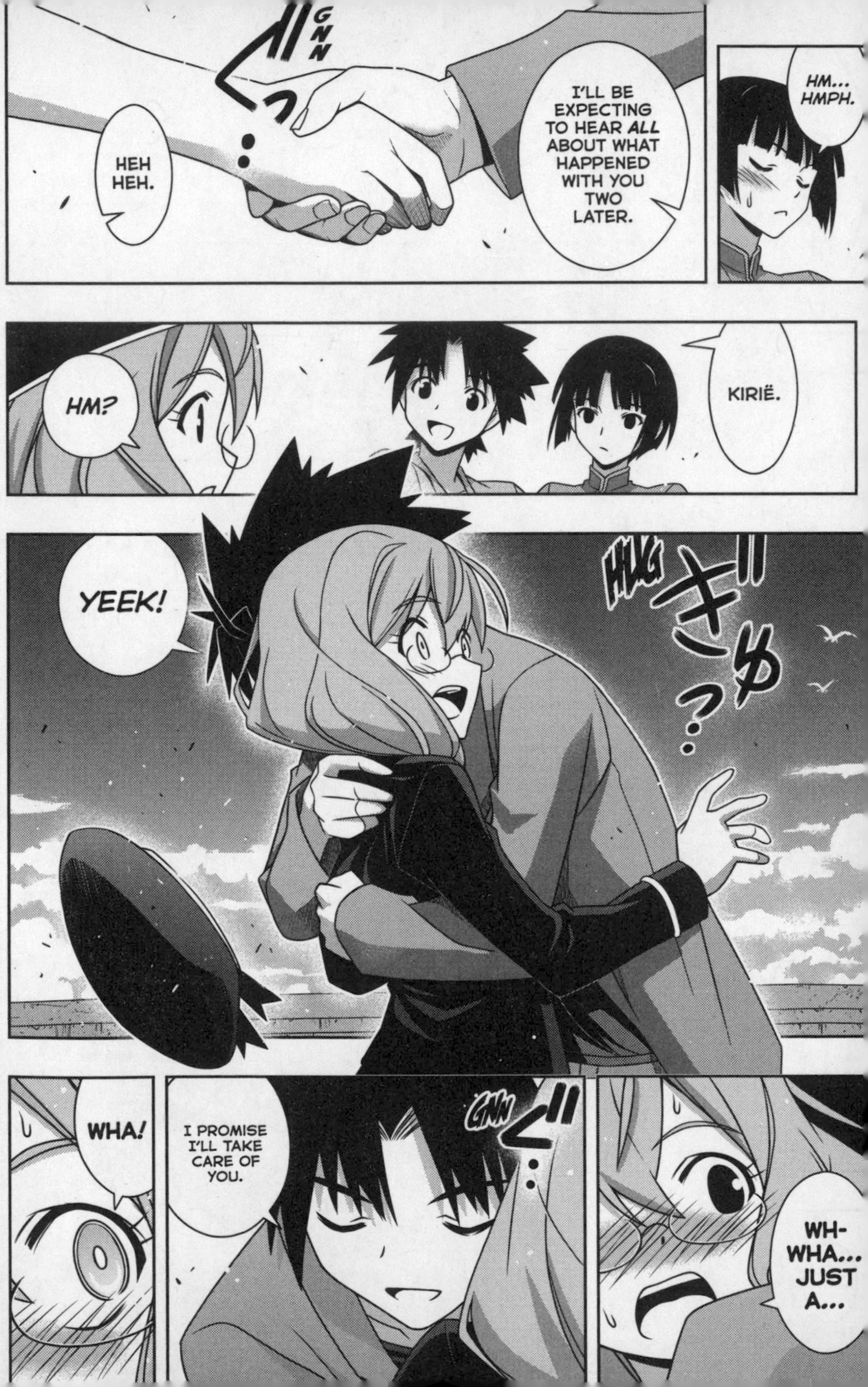
HM... HMPH.
I'LL BE EXPECTING TO HEAR ALL ABOUT WHAT HAPPENED WITH YOU TWO LATER.
GNN
HEH HEH.
KIRIË.
HM?
HUG
きゅっ
YEEK!
WH- WHA... JUST A...
GNN
I PROMISE I'LL TAKE CARE OF YOU.
WHA!

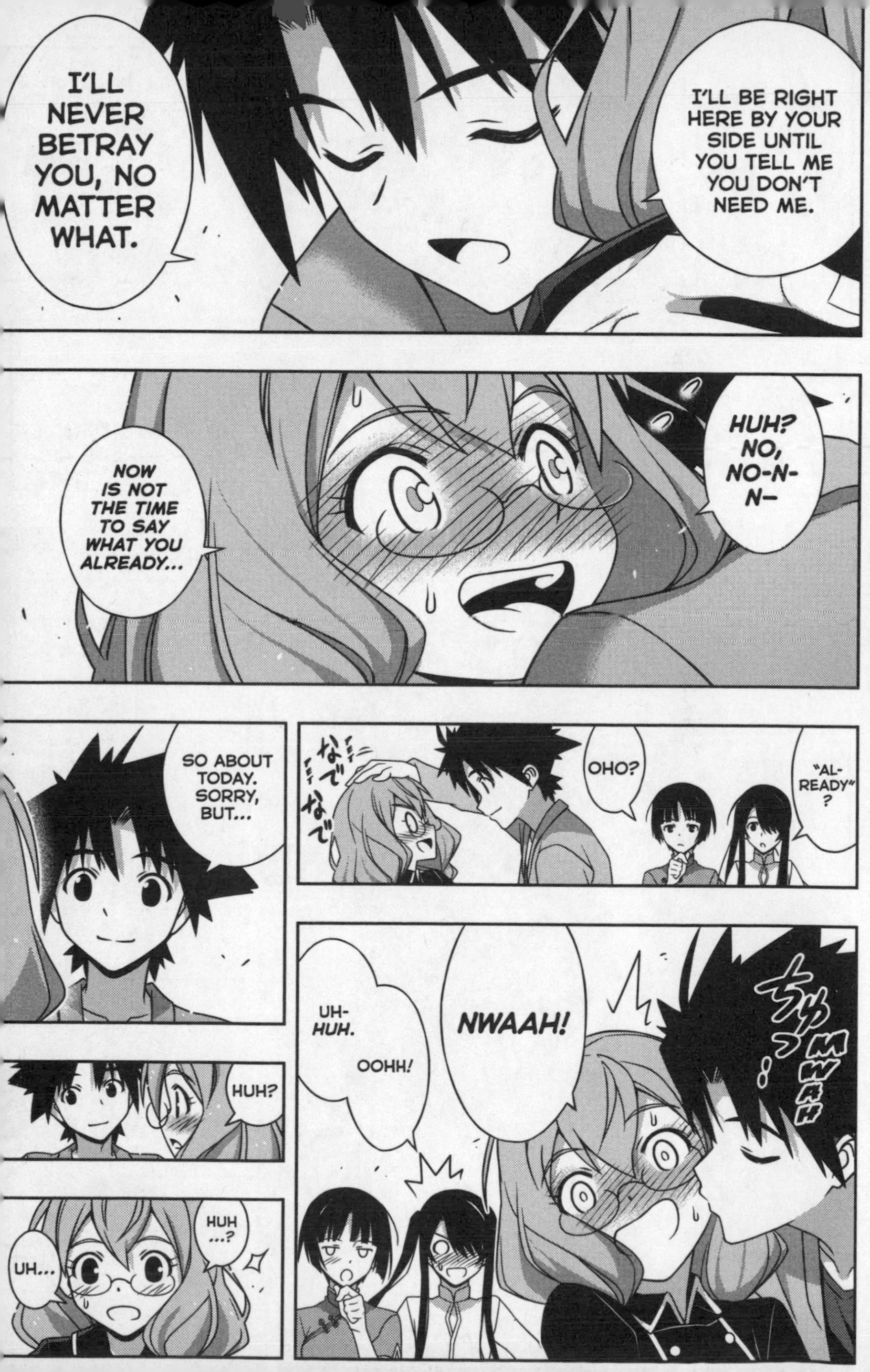
I'LL BE RIGHT HERE BY YOUR SIDE UNTIL YOU TELL ME YOU DON'T NEED ME.
I'LL NEVER BETRAY YOU, NO MATTER WHAT.
HUH? NO, NO-N-N-
NOW IS NOT THE TIME TO SAY WHAT YOU ALREADY...
"AL-READY"?
OHO?
なでなで
SO ABOUT TODAY. SORRY, BUT...
HUH?
HUH ...?
UH...
ちゅっ
MWAH
NWAAH!
UH-HUH.
OOHH!

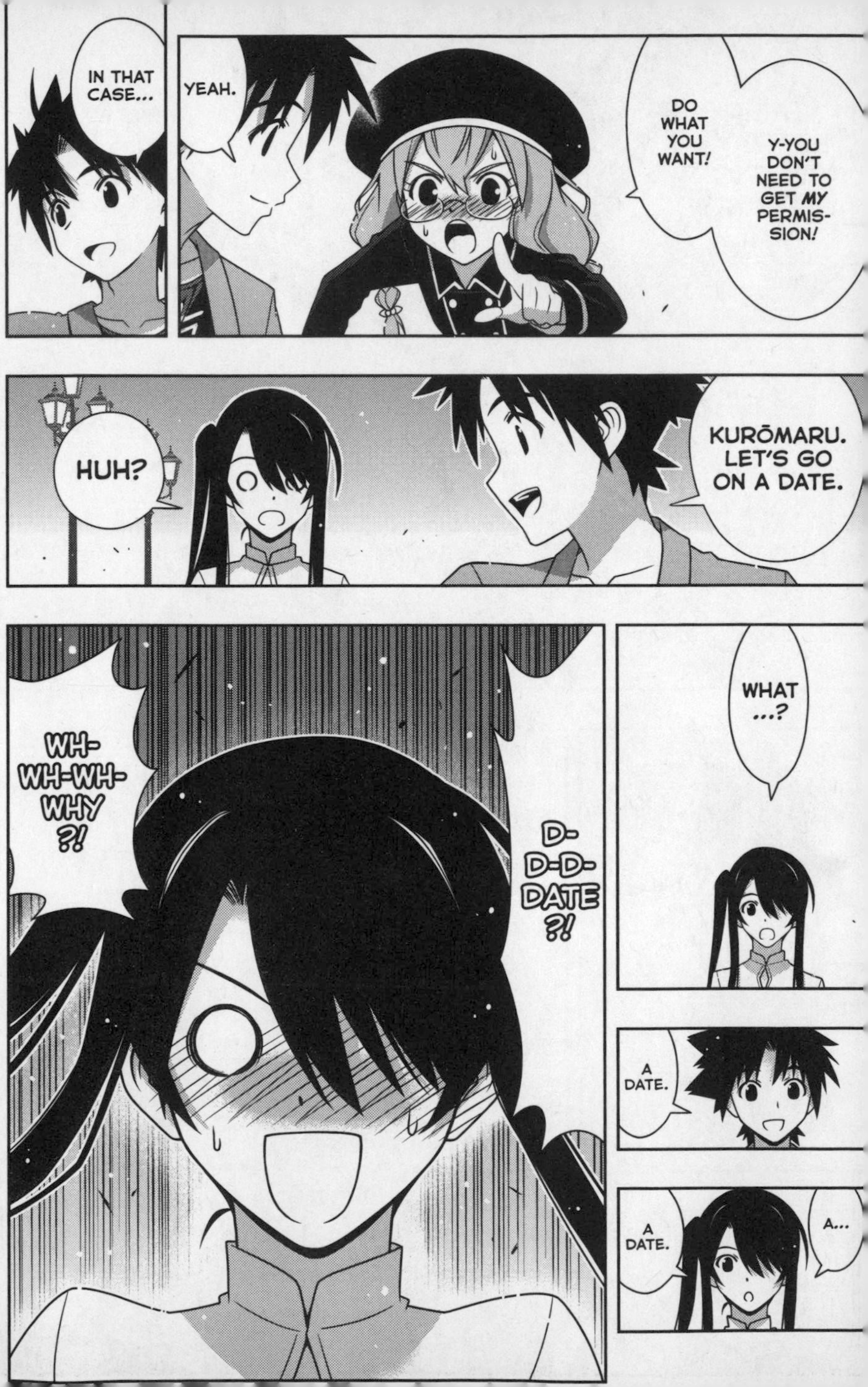
Y-YOU DON'T NEED TO GET MY PERMISSION!
DO WHAT YOU WANT!
YEAH.
IN THAT CASE...
KURŌMARU. LET'S GO ON A DATE.
HUH?
WHAT ...?
A DATE.
A...
A DATE.
D-D-D-DATE?!
WH-WH-WH-WHY?!

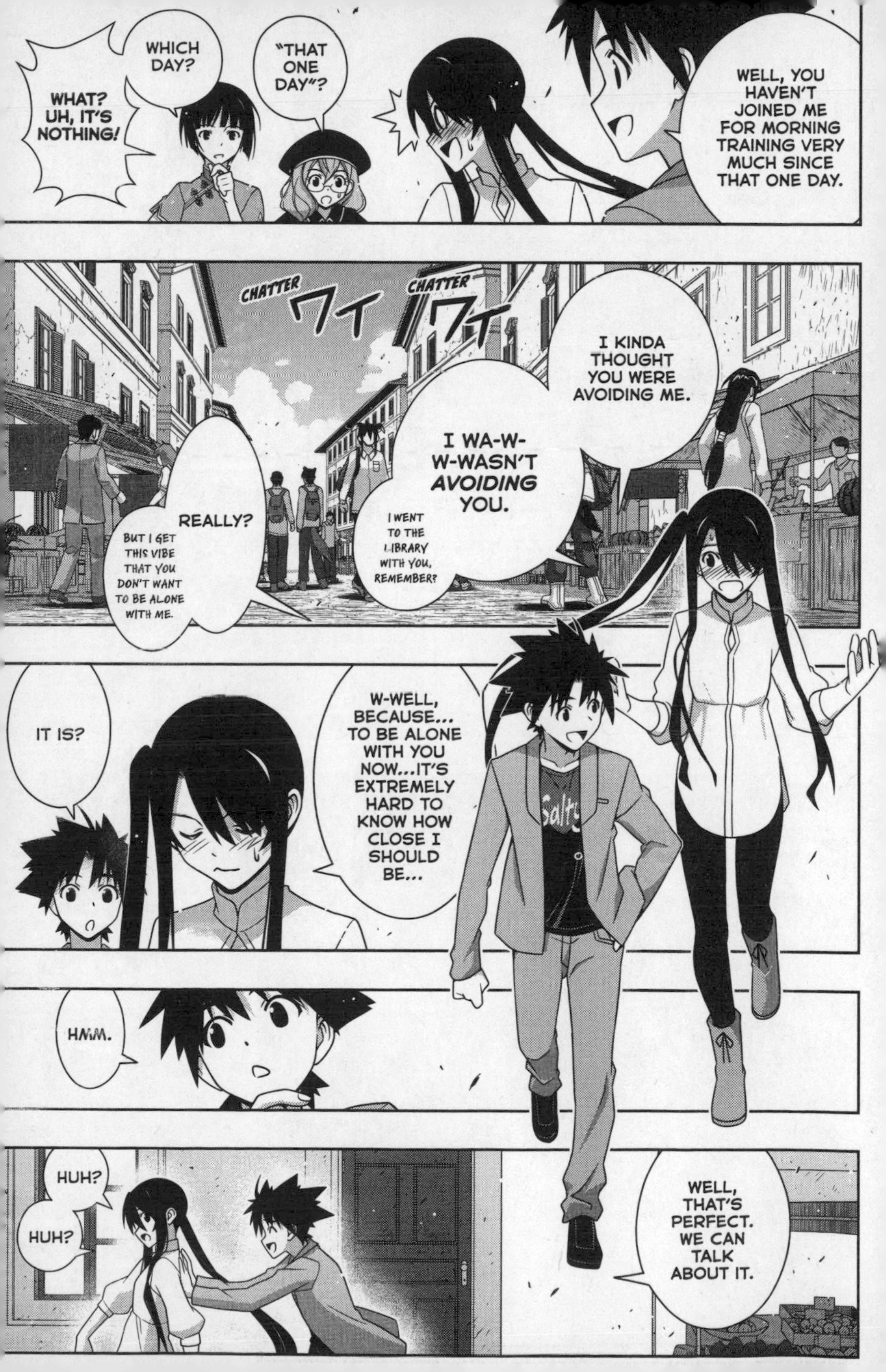
WELL, YOU HAVEN'T JOINED ME FOR MORNING TRAINING VERY MUCH SINCE THAT ONE DAY.
"THAT ONE DAY"?
WHICH DAY?
WHAT? UH, IT'S NOTHING!
CHATTER
ワイ
CHATTER
ワイ
I KINDA THOUGHT YOU WERE AVOIDING ME.
I WA-W-W-WASN'T AVOIDING YOU.
I WENT TO THE LIBRARY WITH YOU, REMEMBER?
REALLY?
BUT I GET THIS VIBE THAT YOU DON'T WANT TO BE ALONE WITH ME.
W-WELL, BECAUSE... TO BE ALONE WITH YOU NOW...IT'S EXTREMELY HARD TO KNOW HOW CLOSE I SHOULD BE...
IT IS?
HMM.
WELL, THAT'S PERFECT. WE CAN TALK ABOUT IT.
HUH?
HUH?

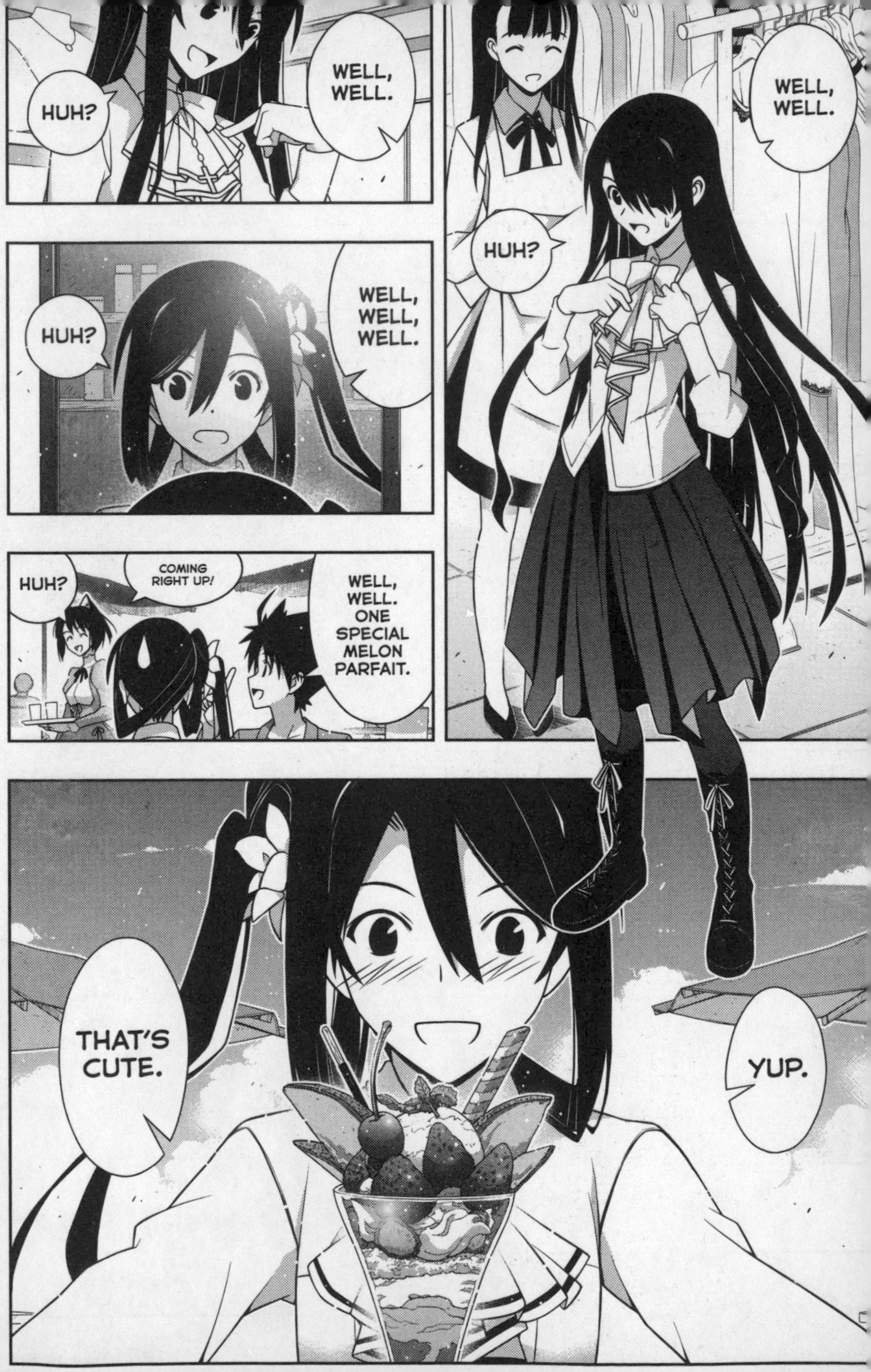
WELL, WELL.
HUH?
WELL, WELL.
HUH?
WELL, WELL, WELL.
HUH?
WELL, WELL. ONE SPECIAL MELON PARFAIT.
COMING RIGHT UP!
HUH?
YUP.
THAT'S CUTE.

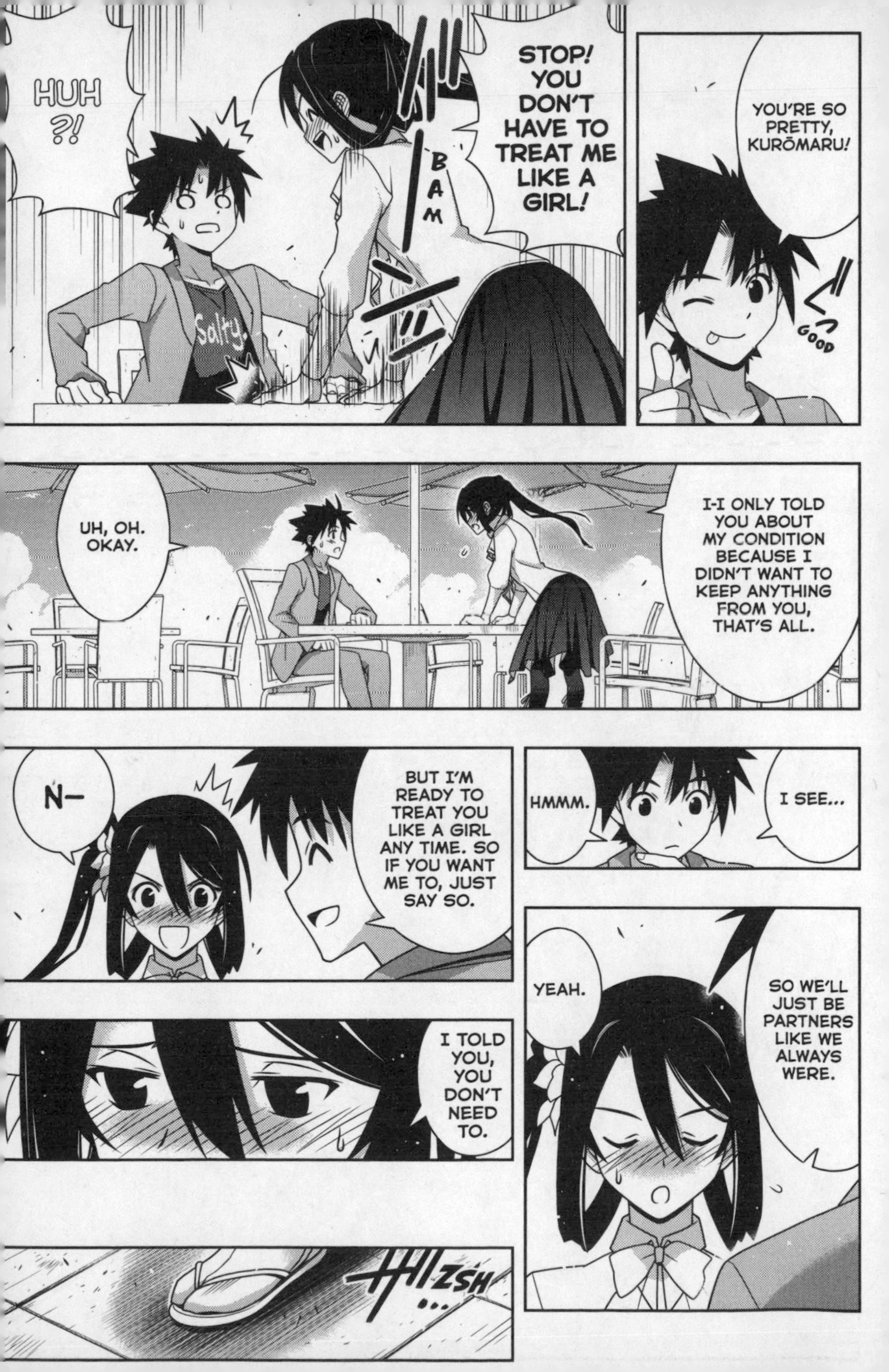
YOU'RE SO PRETTY, KURŌMARU!
GOOD
STOP! YOU DON'T HAVE TO TREAT ME LIKE A GIRL!
BAM
HUH ?!
I-I ONLY TOLD YOU ABOUT MY CONDITION BECAUSE I DIDN'T WANT TO KEEP ANYTHING FROM YOU, THAT'S ALL.
UH, OH. OKAY.
I SEE...
HMMM.
BUT I'M READY TO TREAT YOU LIKE A GIRL ANY TIME. SO IF YOU WANT ME TO, JUST SAY SO.
N–
SO WE'LL JUST BE PARTNERS LIKE WE ALWAYS WERE.
YEAH.
I TOLD YOU, YOU DON'T NEED TO.
HHZSH...

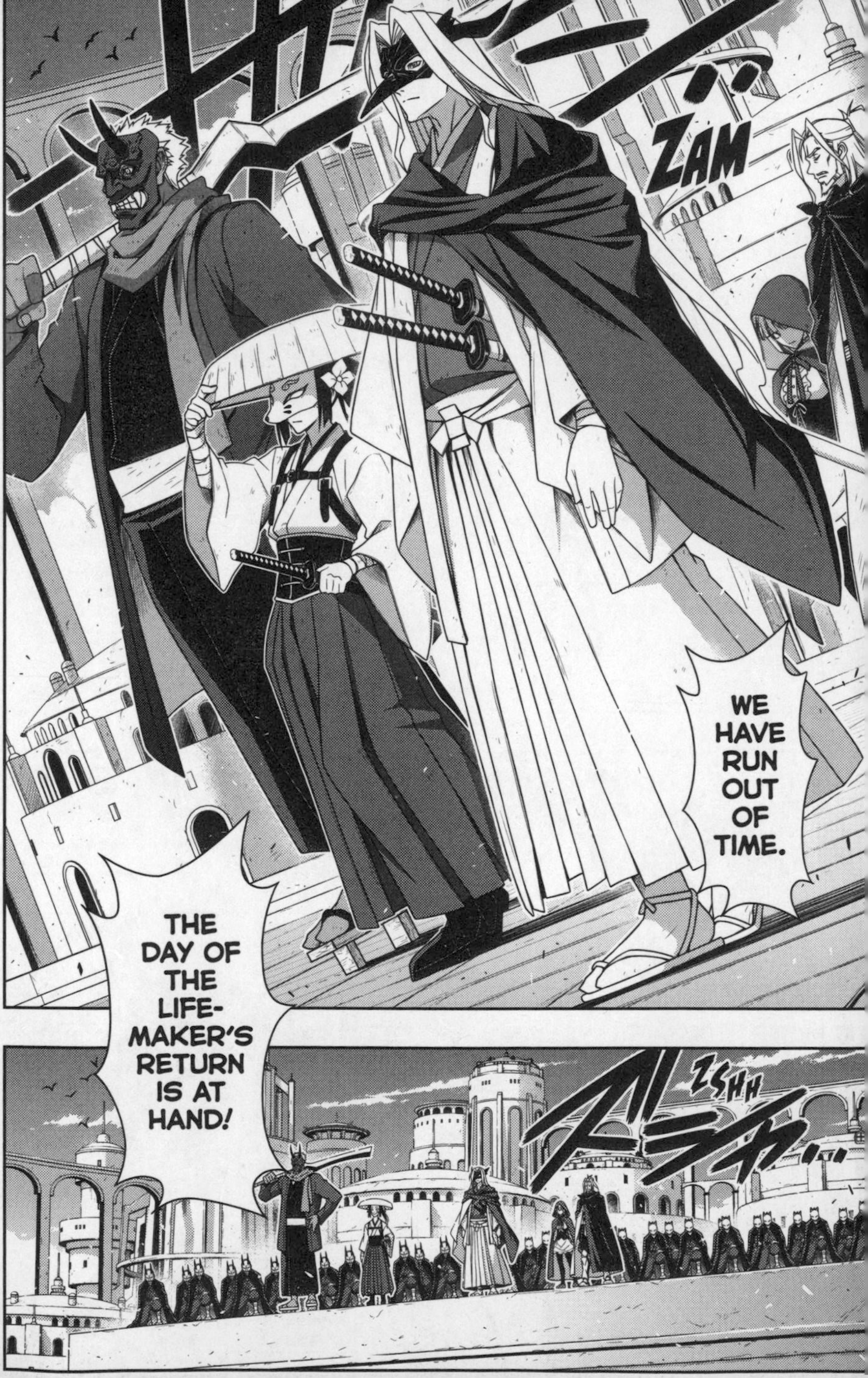
ZAM
WE HAVE RUN OUT OF TIME.
THE DAY OF THE LIFE-MAKER'S RETURN IS AT HAND!
ZSHH

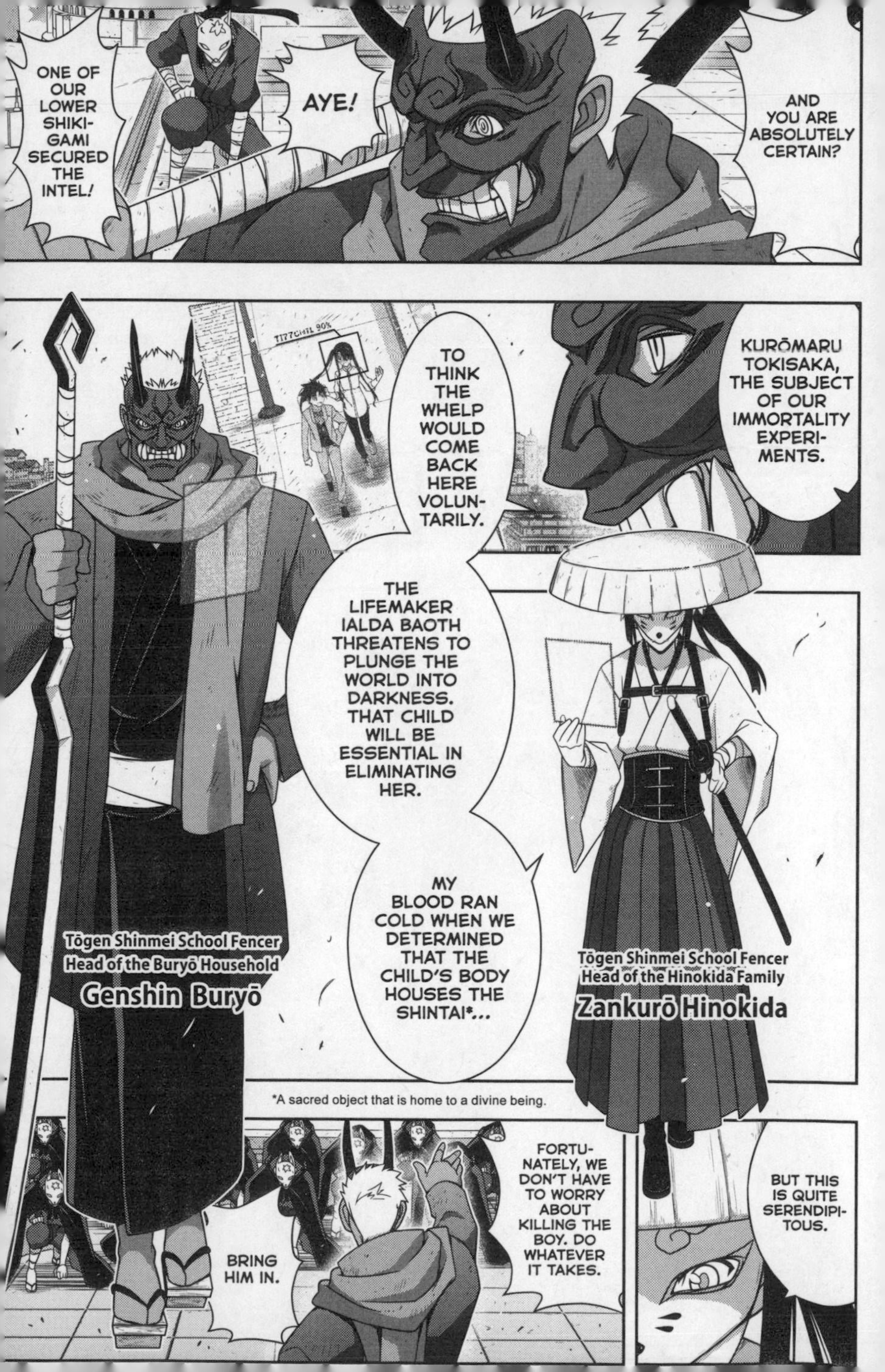
AND YOU ARE ABSOLUTELY CERTAIN?
AYE!
ONE OF OUR LOWER SHIKIGAMI SECURED THE INTEL!
KURŌMARU TOKISAKA, THE SUBJECT OF OUR IMMORTALITY EXPERIMENTS.
TO THINK THE WHELP WOULD COME BACK HERE VOLUNTARILY.
THE LIFEMAKER IALDA BAOTH THREATENS TO PLUNGE THE WORLD INTO DARKNESS. THAT CHILD WILL BE ESSENTIAL IN ELIMINATING HER.
MY BLOOD RAN COLD WHEN WE DETERMINED THAT THE CHILD'S BODY HOUSES THE SHINTAI*...
Tōgen Shinmei School Fencer
Head of the Hinokida Family
Zankurō Hinokida
Tōgen Shinmei School Fencer
Head of the Buryō Household
Genshin Buryō
BUT THIS IS QUITE SERENDIPITOUS.
FORTUNATELY, WE DON'T HAVE TO WORRY ABOUT KILLING THE BOY. DO WHATEVER IT TAKES.
BRING HIM IN.

*A sacred object that is home to a divine being.

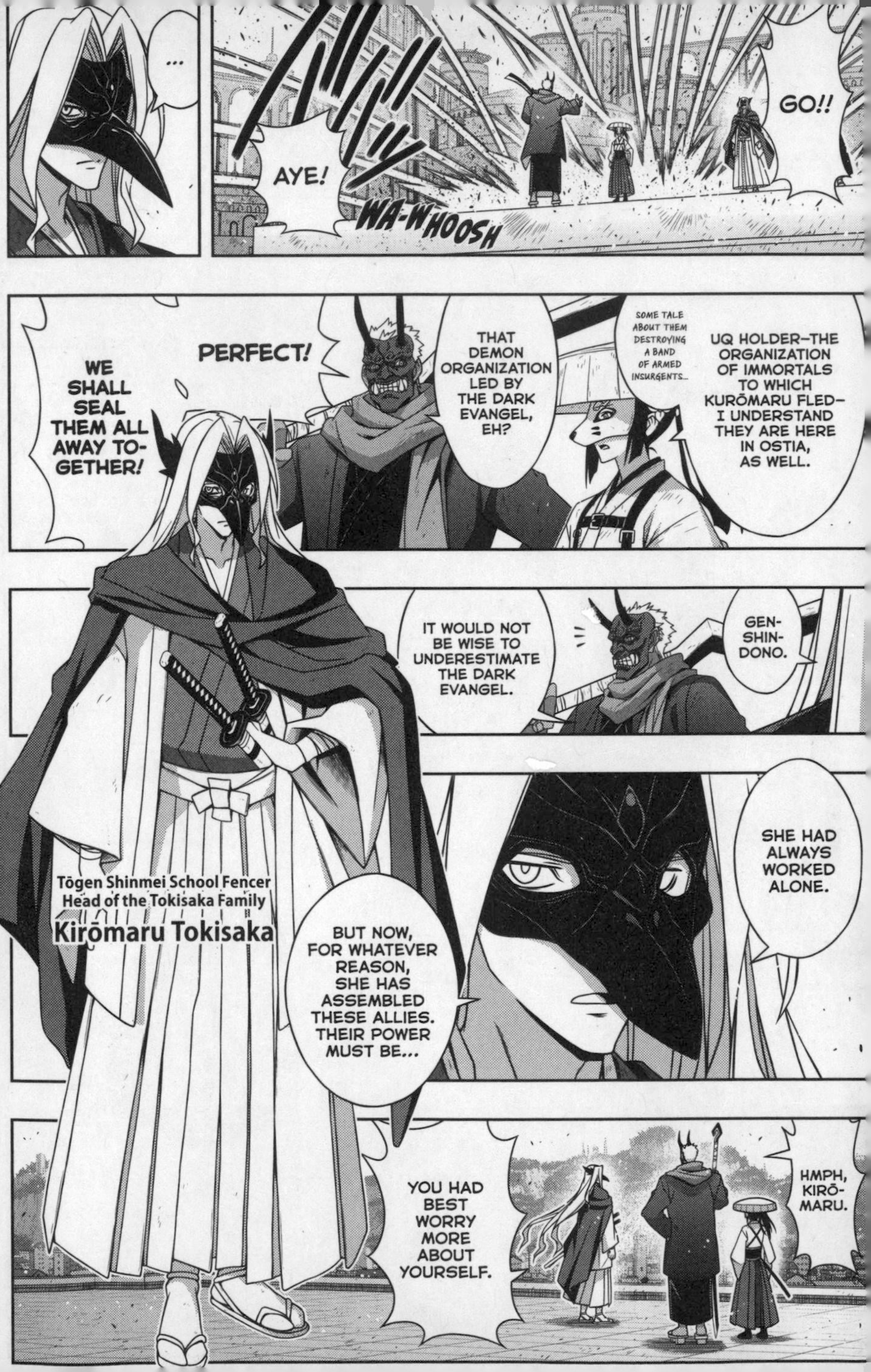
GO!!
AYE!
WA-WHOOSH
...
UQ HOLDER—THE ORGANIZATION OF IMMORTALS TO WHICH KURŌMARU FLED—I UNDERSTAND THEY ARE HERE IN OSTIA, AS WELL.
SOME TALE ABOUT THEM DESTROYING A BAND OF ARMED INSURGENTS...
THAT DEMON ORGANIZATION LED BY THE DARK EVANGEL, EH?
PERFECT!
WE SHALL SEAL THEM ALL AWAY TO-GETHER!
GEN-SHIN-DONO.
IT WOULD NOT BE WISE TO UNDERESTIMATE THE DARK EVANGEL.
SHE HAD ALWAYS WORKED ALONE.
BUT NOW, FOR WHATEVER REASON, SHE HAS ASSEMBLED THESE ALLIES. THEIR POWER MUST BE...
HMPH, KIRŌ-MARU.
YOU HAD BEST WORRY MORE ABOUT YOURSELF.
Tōgen Shinmei School Fencer
Head of the Tokisaka Family
Kirōmaru Tokisaka

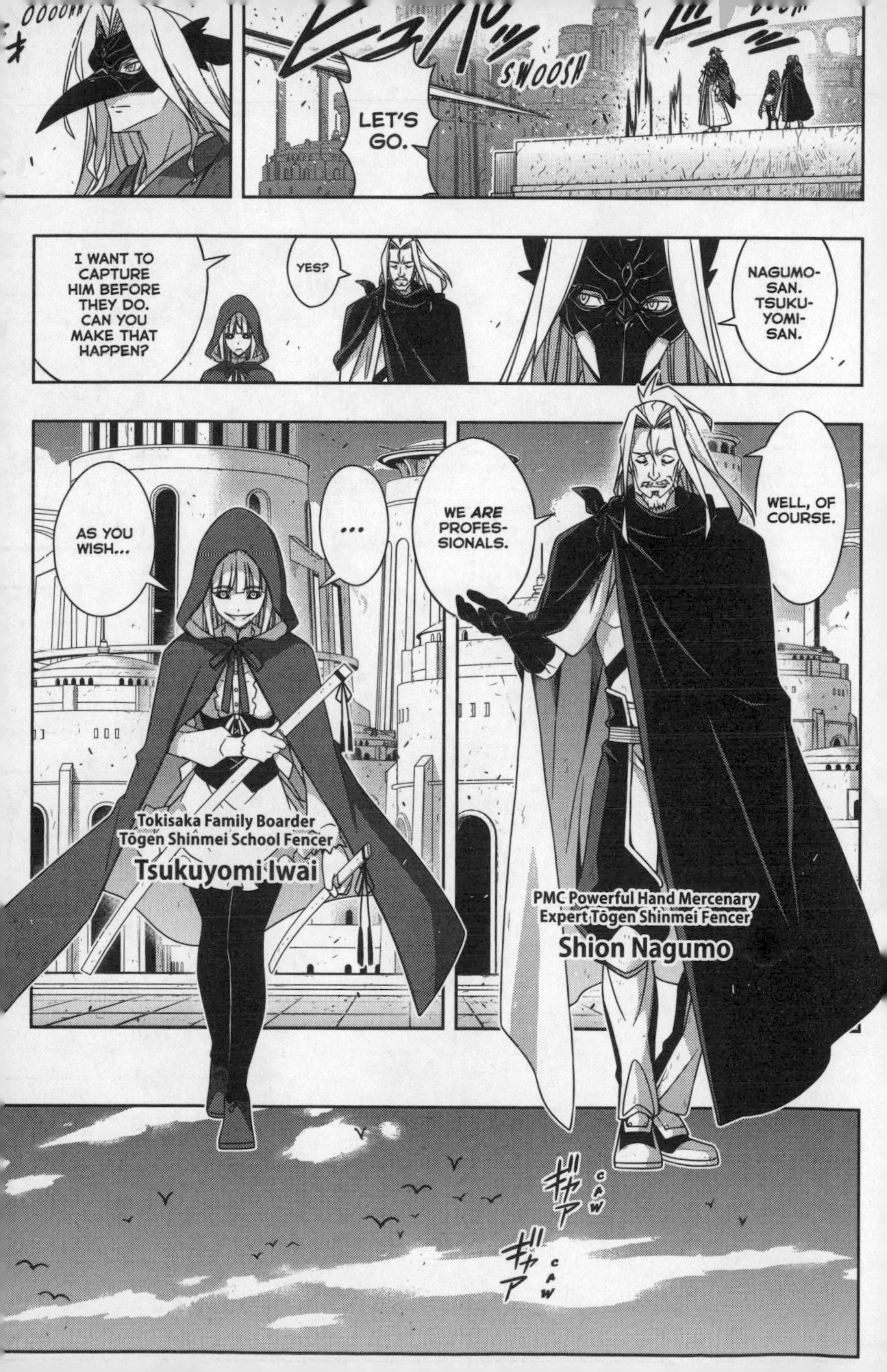
DOOM
SWOOSH
LET'S GO.
OOOOWN
NAGUMO-SAN. TSUKUYOMI-SAN.
YES?
I WANT TO CAPTURE HIM BEFORE THEY DO. CAN YOU MAKE THAT HAPPEN?
WELL, OF COURSE.
WE *ARE* PROFESSIONALS.
PMC Powerful Hand Mercenary
Expert Tōgen Shinmei Fencer
Shion Nagumo
...
AS YOU WISH...
Tokisaka Family Boarder
Tōgen Shinmei School Fencer
Tsukuyomi Iwai
CAW
CAW

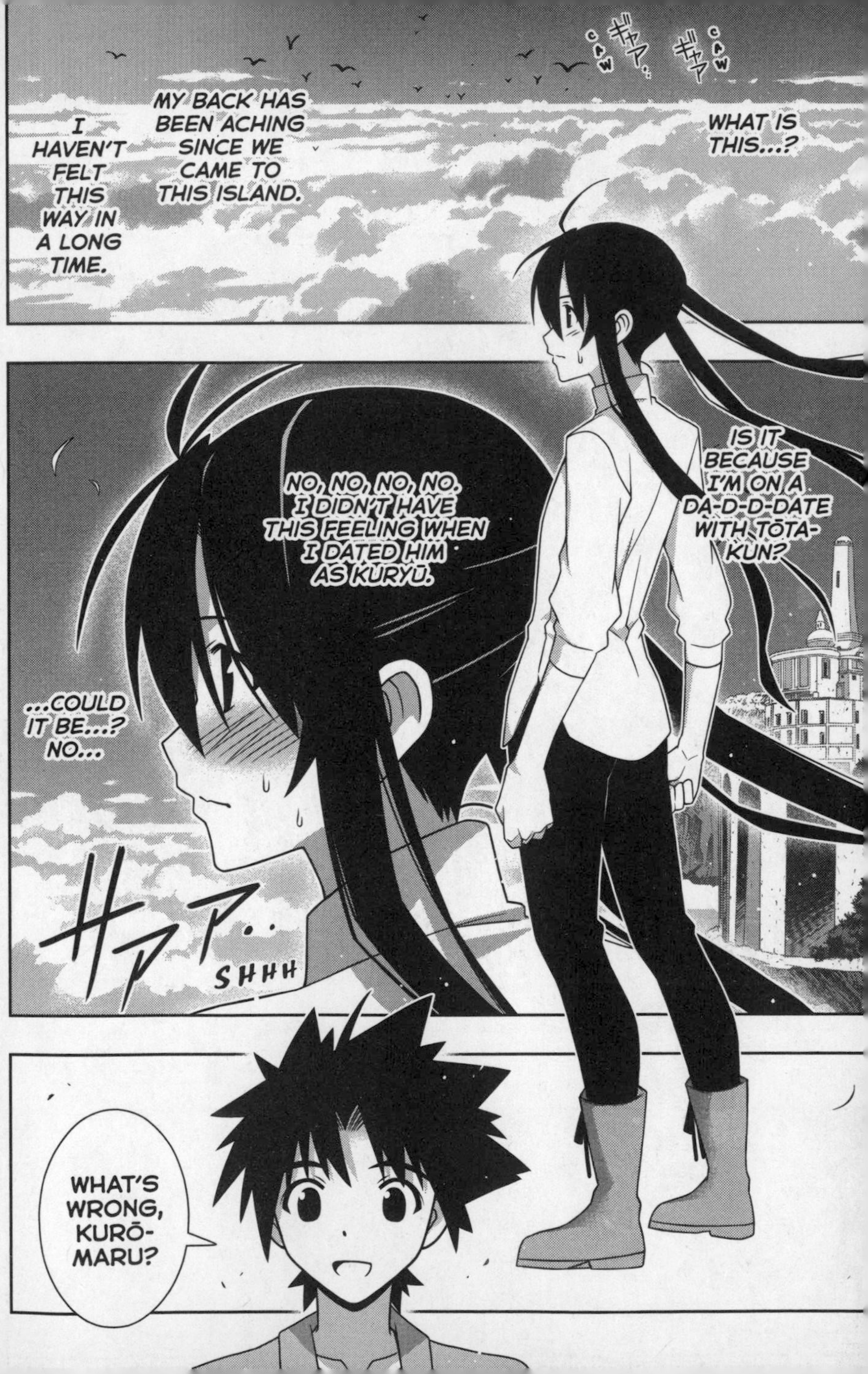
ギャア CAW
ギャア.. CAW
WHAT IS THIS...?
MY BACK HAS BEEN ACHING SINCE WE CAME TO THIS ISLAND.
I HAVEN'T FELT THIS WAY IN A LONG TIME.
IS IT BECAUSE I'M ON A DA-D-D-DATE WITH TŌTA-KUN?
NO, NO, NO, NO. I DIDN'T HAVE THIS FEELING WHEN I DATED HIM AS KURYŪ.
...COULD IT BE...? NO...
ハァ.. SHHH
WHAT'S WRONG, KURŌ-MARU?

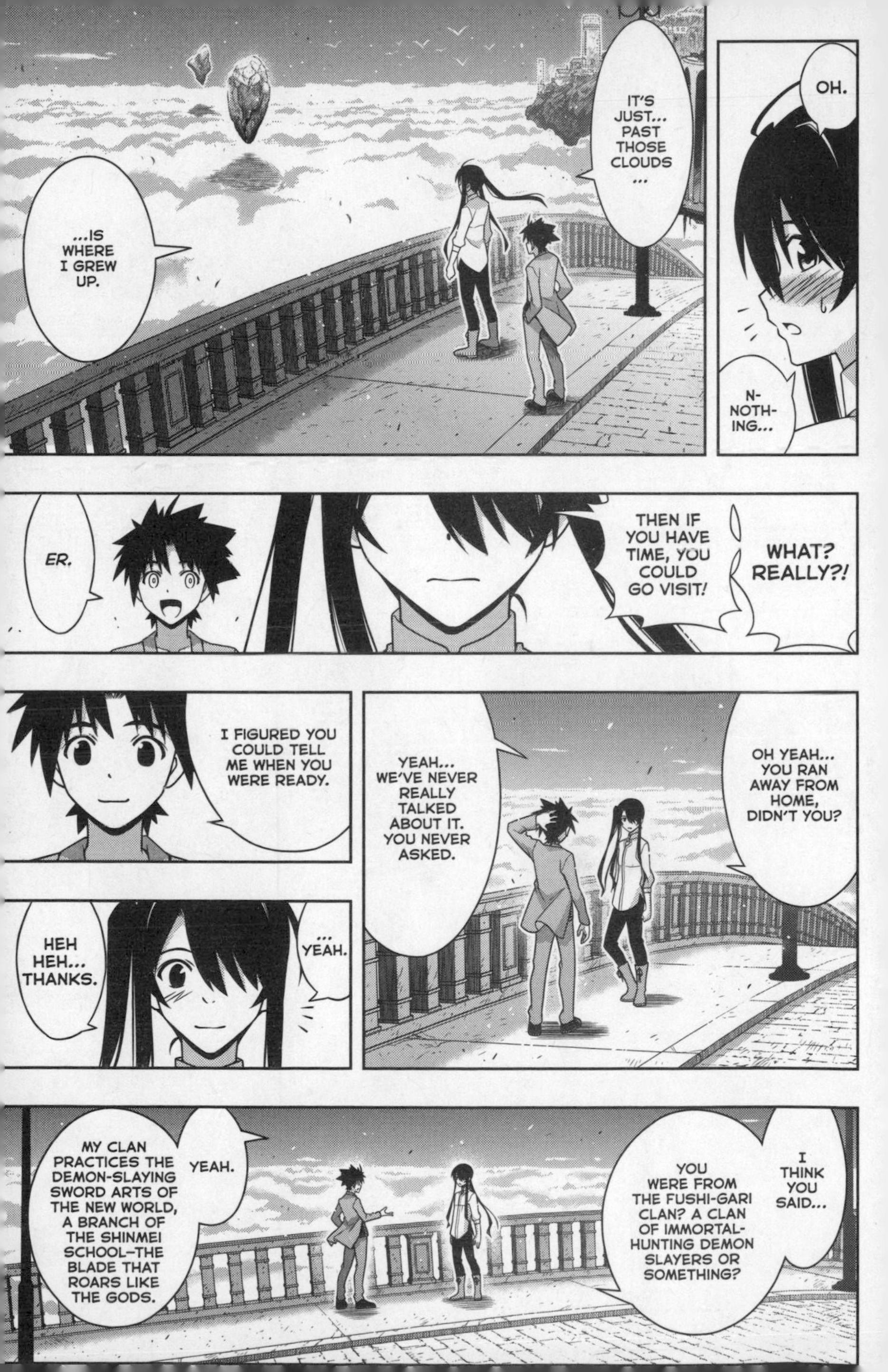
OH.
N-NOTHING...
IT'S JUST... PAST THOSE CLOUDS ...
...IS WHERE I GREW UP.
WHAT? REALLY?!
THEN IF YOU HAVE TIME, YOU COULD GO VISIT!
ER.
OH YEAH... YOU RAN AWAY FROM HOME, DIDN'T YOU?
YEAH... WE'VE NEVER REALLY TALKED ABOUT IT. YOU NEVER ASKED.
I FIGURED YOU COULD TELL ME WHEN YOU WERE READY.
...YEAH.
HEH HEH... THANKS.
I THINK YOU SAID...
YOU WERE FROM THE FUSHI-GARI CLAN? A CLAN OF IMMORTAL-HUNTING DEMON SLAYERS OR SOMETHING?
YEAH.
MY CLAN PRACTICES THE DEMON-SLAYING SWORD ARTS OF THE NEW WORLD, A BRANCH OF THE SHINMEI SCHOOL—THE BLADE THAT ROARS LIKE THE GODS.

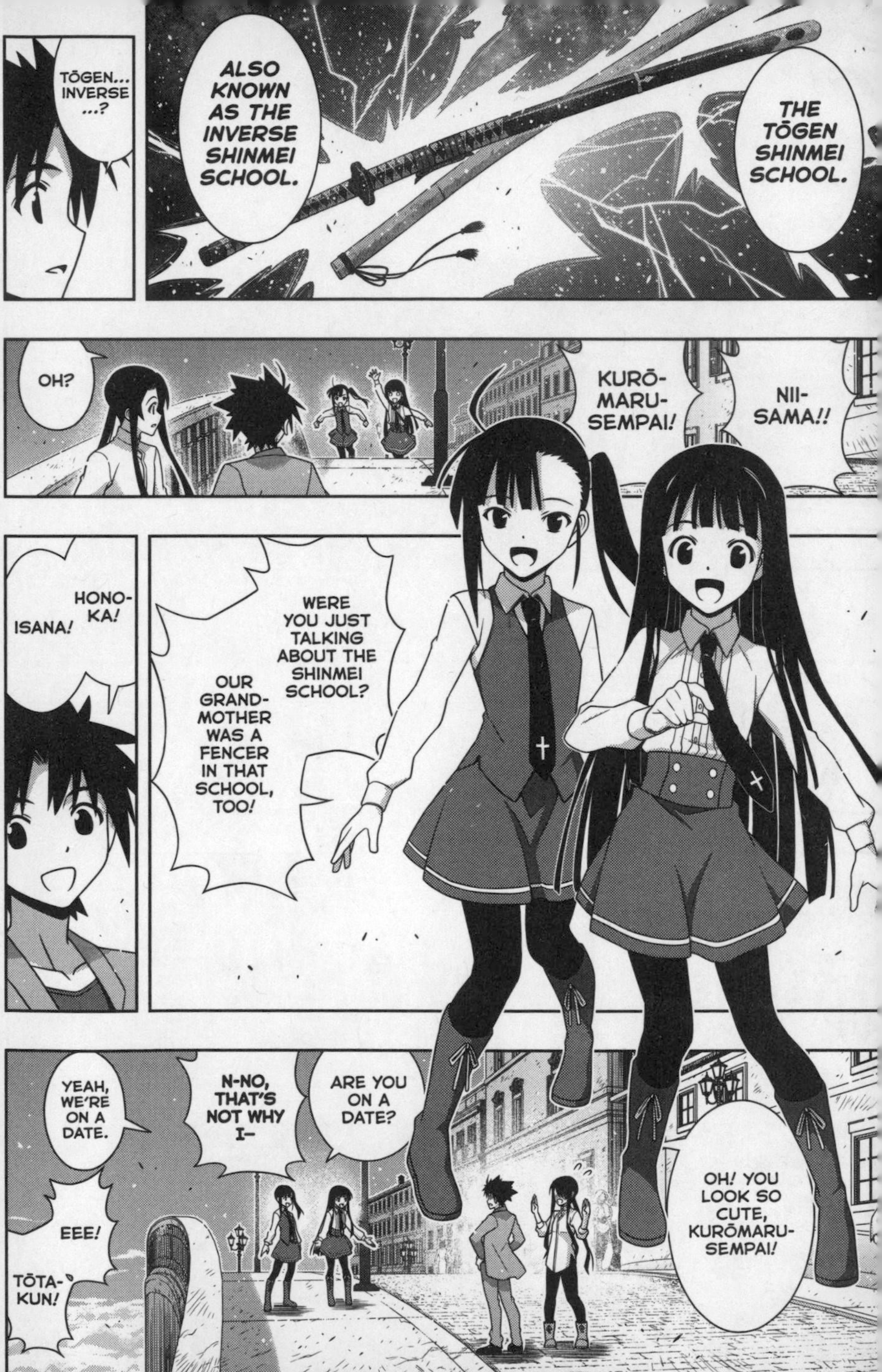
THE TŌGEN SHINMEI SCHOOL.
ALSO KNOWN AS THE INVERSE SHINMEI SCHOOL.
TŌGEN... INVERSE ...?
NII-SAMA!!
KURŌ-MARU-SEMPAI!
OH?
WERE YOU JUST TALKING ABOUT THE SHINMEI SCHOOL?
OUR GRAND-MOTHER WAS A FENCER IN THAT SCHOOL, TOO!
HONO-KA!
ISANA!
OH! YOU LOOK SO CUTE, KURŌMARU-SEMPAI!
ARE YOU ON A DATE?
N-NO, THAT'S NOT WHY I—
YEAH, WE'RE ON A DATE.
EEE!
TŌTA-KUN!

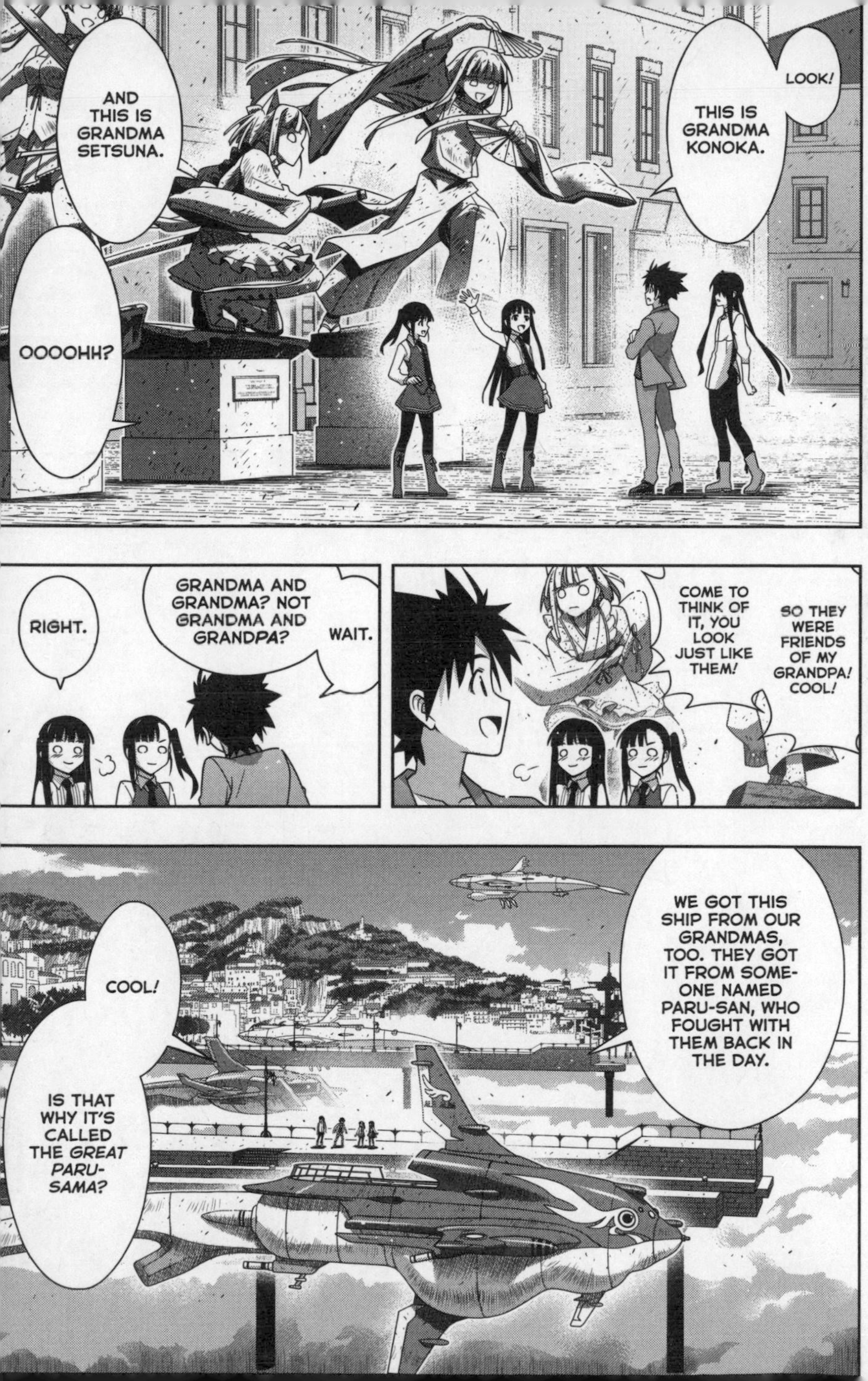
LOOK!
THIS IS GRANDMA KONOKA.
AND THIS IS GRANDMA SETSUNA.
OOOOHH?
SO THEY WERE FRIENDS OF MY GRANDPA! COOL!
COME TO THINK OF IT, YOU LOOK JUST LIKE THEM!
WAIT.
GRANDMA AND GRANDMA? NOT GRANDMA AND GRANDPA?
RIGHT.
WE GOT THIS SHIP FROM OUR GRANDMAS, TOO. THEY GOT IT FROM SOME-ONE NAMED PARU-SAN, WHO FOUGHT WITH THEM BACK IN THE DAY.
COOL!
IS THAT WHY IT'S CALLED THE *GREAT PARU-SAMA*?

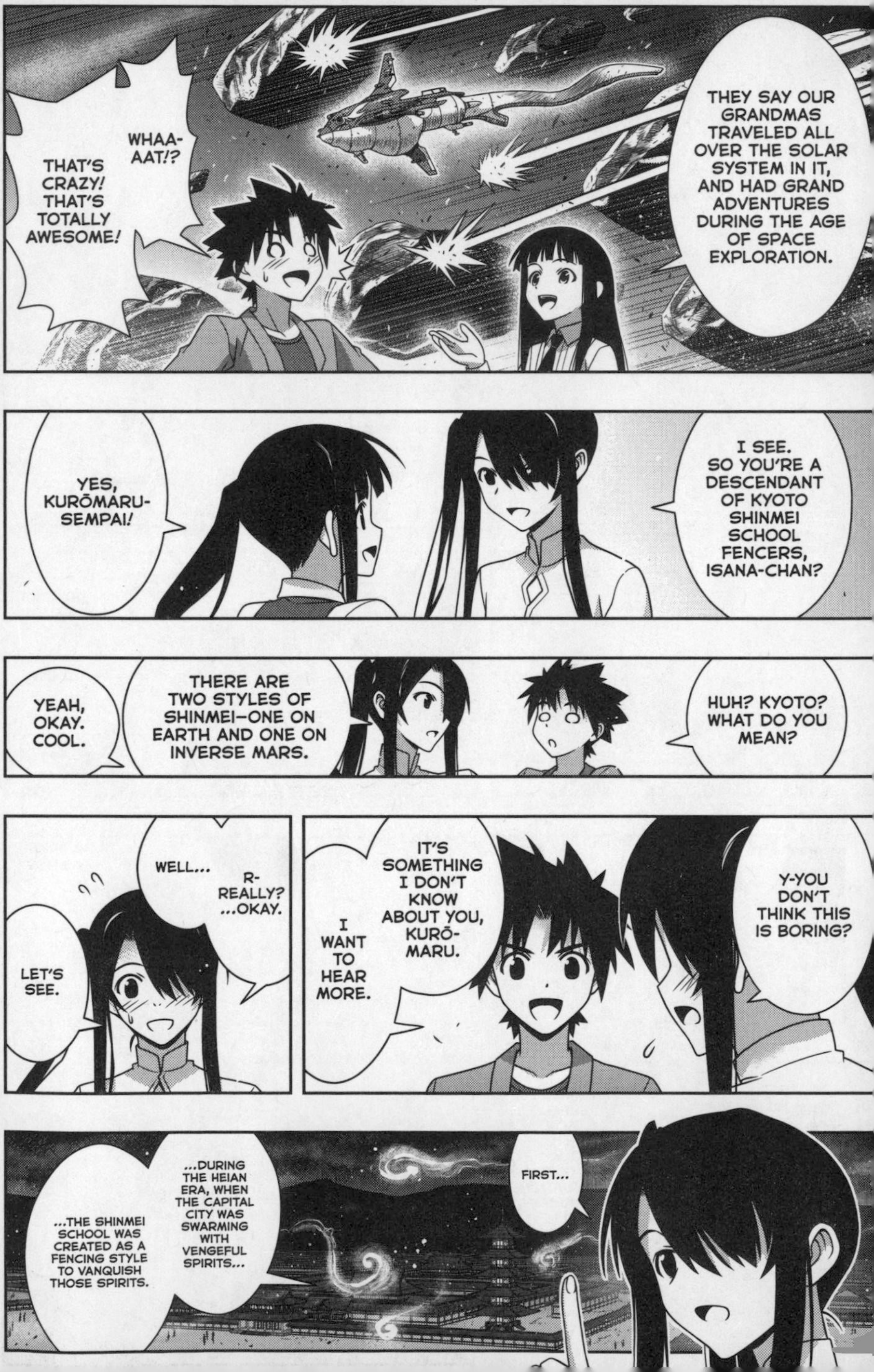
THEY SAY OUR GRANDMAS TRAVELED ALL OVER THE SOLAR SYSTEM IN IT, AND HAD GRAND ADVENTURES DURING THE AGE OF SPACE EXPLORATION.
WHAA-AAT!?
THAT'S CRAZY! THAT'S TOTALLY AWESOME!
I SEE. SO YOU'RE A DESCENDANT OF KYOTO SHINMEI SCHOOL FENCERS, ISANA-CHAN?
YES, KURŌMARU-SEMPAI!
HUH? KYOTO? WHAT DO YOU MEAN?
THERE ARE TWO STYLES OF SHINMEI—ONE ON EARTH AND ONE ON INVERSE MARS.
YEAH, OKAY. COOL.
Y-YOU DON'T THINK THIS IS BORING?
IT'S SOMETHING I DON'T KNOW ABOUT YOU, KURŌ-MARU.
I WANT TO HEAR MORE.
R-REALLY? ...OKAY.
WELL...
LET'S SEE.
FIRST...
...DURING THE HEIAN ERA, WHEN THE CAPITAL CITY WAS SWARMING WITH VENGEFUL SPIRITS...
...THE SHINMEI SCHOOL WAS CREATED AS A FENCING STYLE TO VANQUISH THOSE SPIRITS.

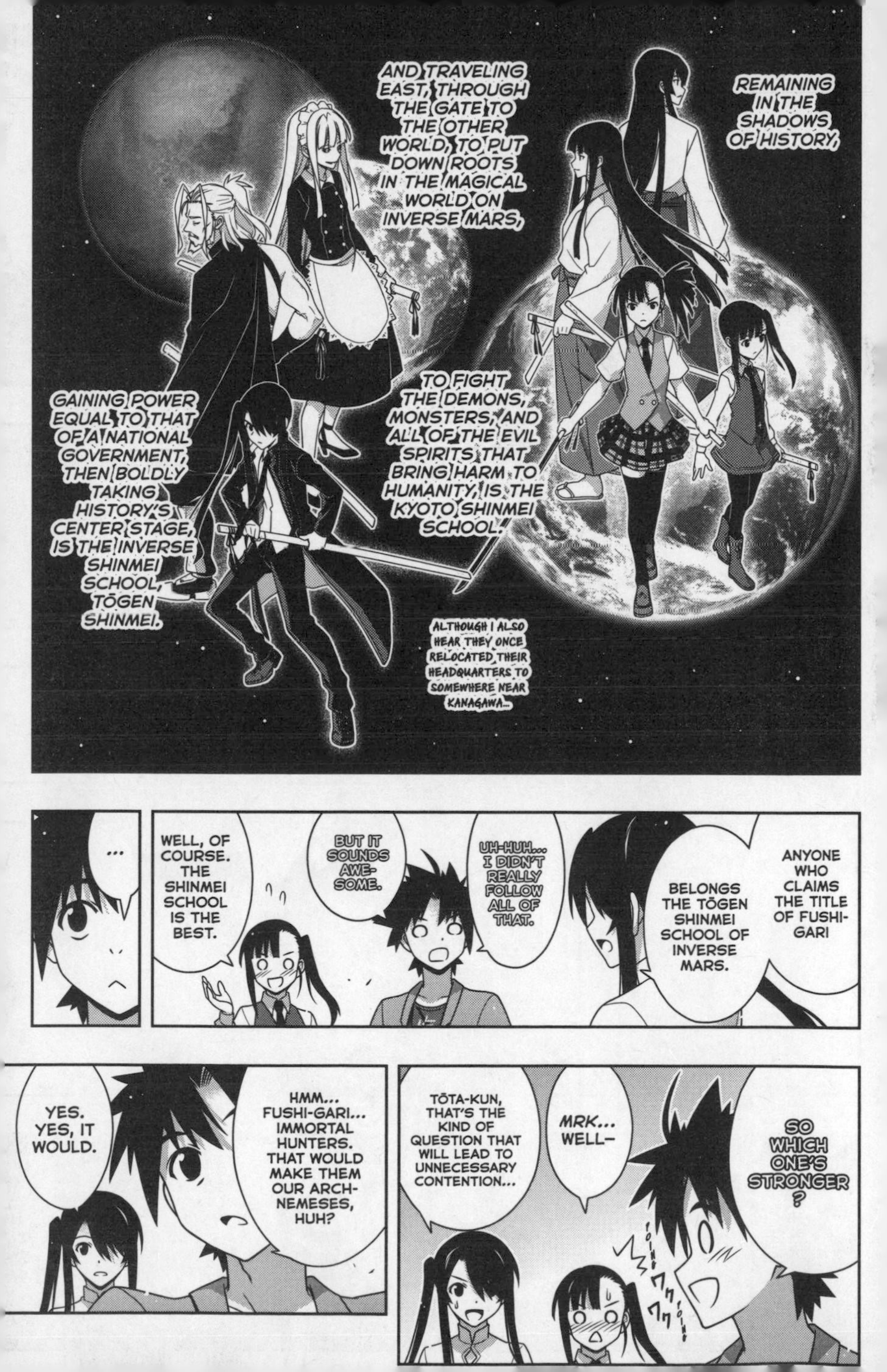
REMAINING IN THE SHADOWS OF HISTORY,
TO FIGHT THE DEMONS, MONSTERS, AND ALL OF THE EVIL SPIRITS THAT BRING HARM TO HUMANITY, IS THE KYOTO SHINMEI SCHOOL.
AND TRAVELING EAST, THROUGH THE GATE TO THE OTHER WORLD, TO PUT DOWN ROOTS IN THE MAGICAL WORLD ON INVERSE MARS,
GAINING POWER EQUAL TO THAT OF A NATIONAL GOVERNMENT, THEN BOLDLY TAKING HISTORY'S CENTER STAGE, IS THE INVERSE SHINMEI SCHOOL, TŌGEN SHINMEI.
ALTHOUGH I ALSO HEAR THEY ONCE RELOCATED THEIR HEADQUARTERS TO SOMEWHERE NEAR KANAGAWA...
ANYONE WHO CLAIMS THE TITLE OF FUSHI-GARI
BELONGS THE TŌGEN SHINMEI SCHOOL OF INVERSE MARS.
UH-HUH... I DIDN'T REALLY FOLLOW ALL OF THAT.
BUT IT SOUNDS AWESOME.
WELL, OF COURSE. THE SHINMEI SCHOOL IS THE BEST.
...
SO WHICH ONE'S STRONGER?
MRK... WELL—
TŌTA-KUN, THAT'S THE KIND OF QUESTION THAT WILL LEAD TO UNNECESSARY CONTENTION...
HMM... FUSHI-GARI... IMMORTAL HUNTERS. THAT WOULD MAKE THEM OUR ARCH-NEMESES, HUH?
YES. YES, IT WOULD.

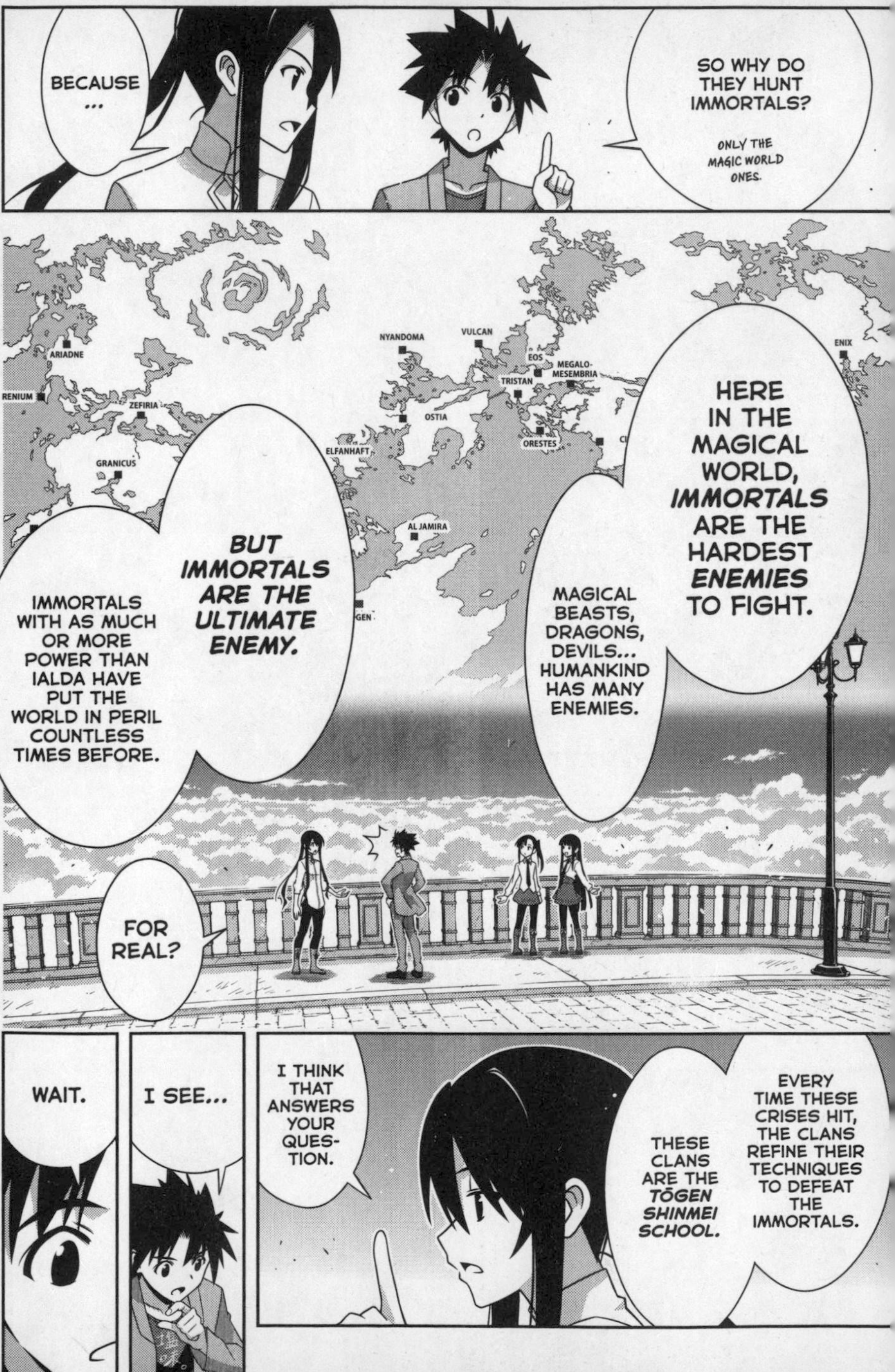
SO WHY DO THEY HUNT IMMORTALS?
ONLY THE MAGIC WORLD ONES.
BECAUSE ...
HERE IN THE MAGICAL WORLD, IMMORTALS ARE THE HARDEST ENEMIES TO FIGHT.
ENIX
MEGALO-MESEMBRIA
EOS
TRISTAN
VULCAN
NYANDOMA
OSTIA
ORESTES
ELFANHAFT
AL JAMIRA
ARIADNE
ZEFIRIA
GRANICUS
MAGICAL BEASTS, DRAGONS, DEVILS... HUMANKIND HAS MANY ENEMIES.
BUT IMMORTALS ARE THE ULTIMATE ENEMY.
IMMORTALS WITH AS MUCH OR MORE POWER THAN IALDA HAVE PUT THE WORLD IN PERIL COUNTLESS TIMES BEFORE.
FOR REAL?
EVERY TIME THESE CRISES HIT, THE CLANS REFINE THEIR TECHNIQUES TO DEFEAT THE IMMORTALS.
THESE CLANS ARE THE TŌGEN SHINMEI SCHOOL.
I THINK THAT ANSWERS YOUR QUESTION.
I SEE...
WAIT.

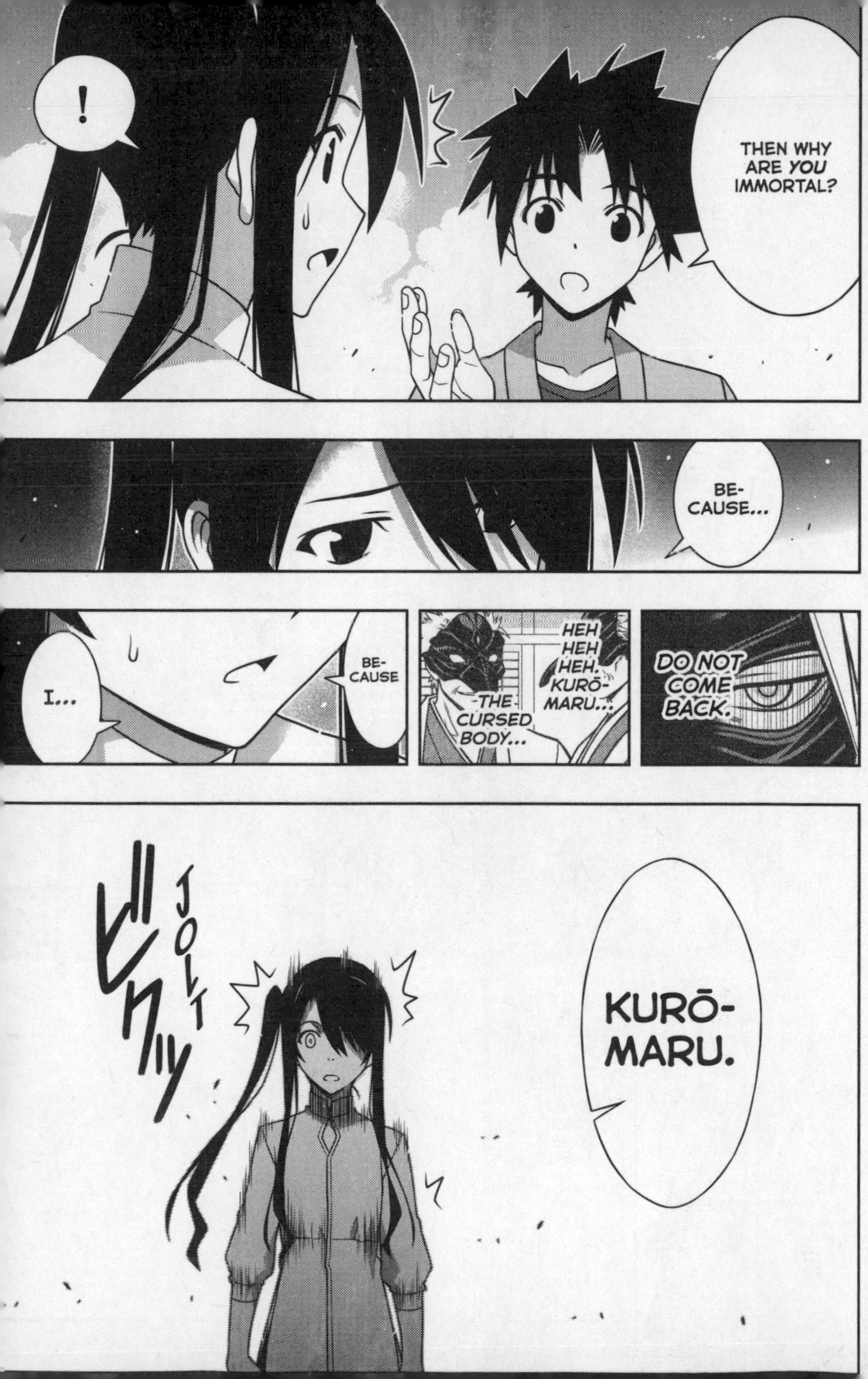
THEN WHY ARE *YOU* IMMORTAL?
!
BE-CAUSE...
DO NOT COME BACK.
HEH HEH HEH. KURŌ-MARU...
THE CURSED BODY...
BE-CAUSE
I...
KURŌ-MARU.
JOLT
ビクッ

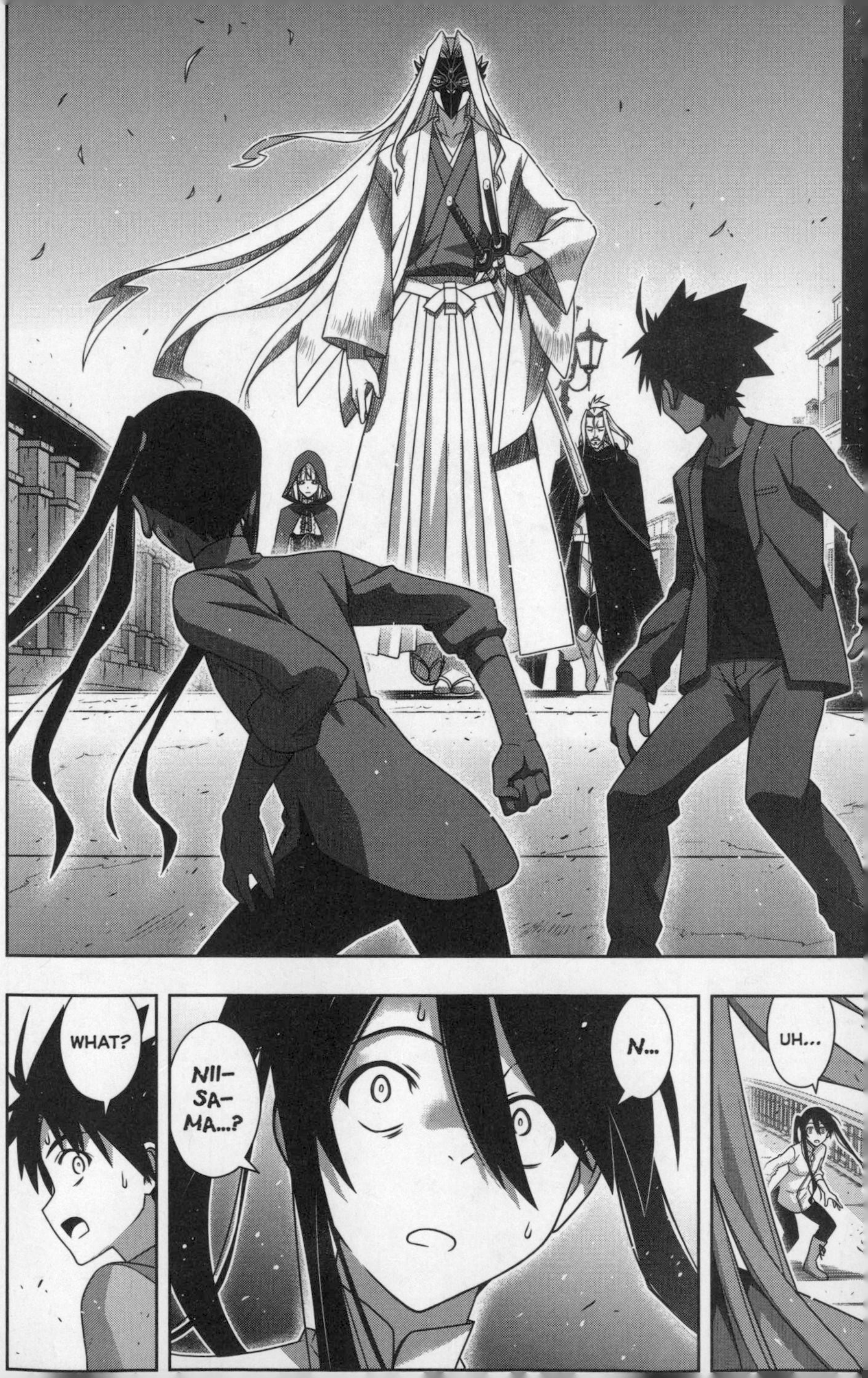
UH...
N...
NII-SA-MA...?
WHAT?

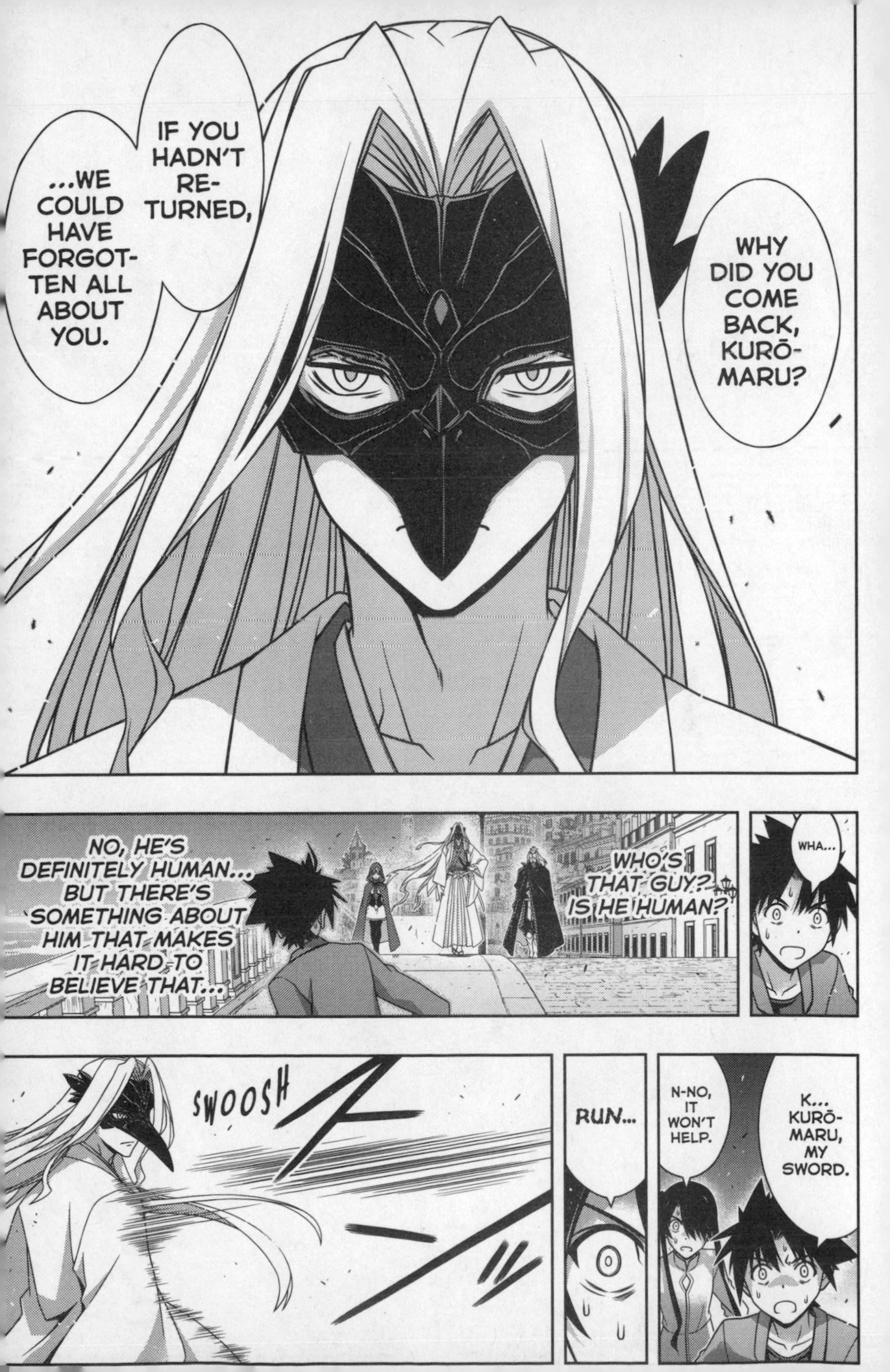

WHY DID YOU COME BACK, KURŌMARU?
IF YOU HADN'T RETURNED,
...WE COULD HAVE FORGOTTEN ALL ABOUT YOU.
WHA...
WHO'S THAT GUY? IS HE HUMAN?
NO, HE'S DEFINITELY HUMAN... BUT THERE'S SOMETHING ABOUT HIM THAT MAKES IT HARD TO BELIEVE THAT...
K... KURŌMARU, MY SWORD.
N-NO, IT WON'T HELP.
RUN...
SWOOSH

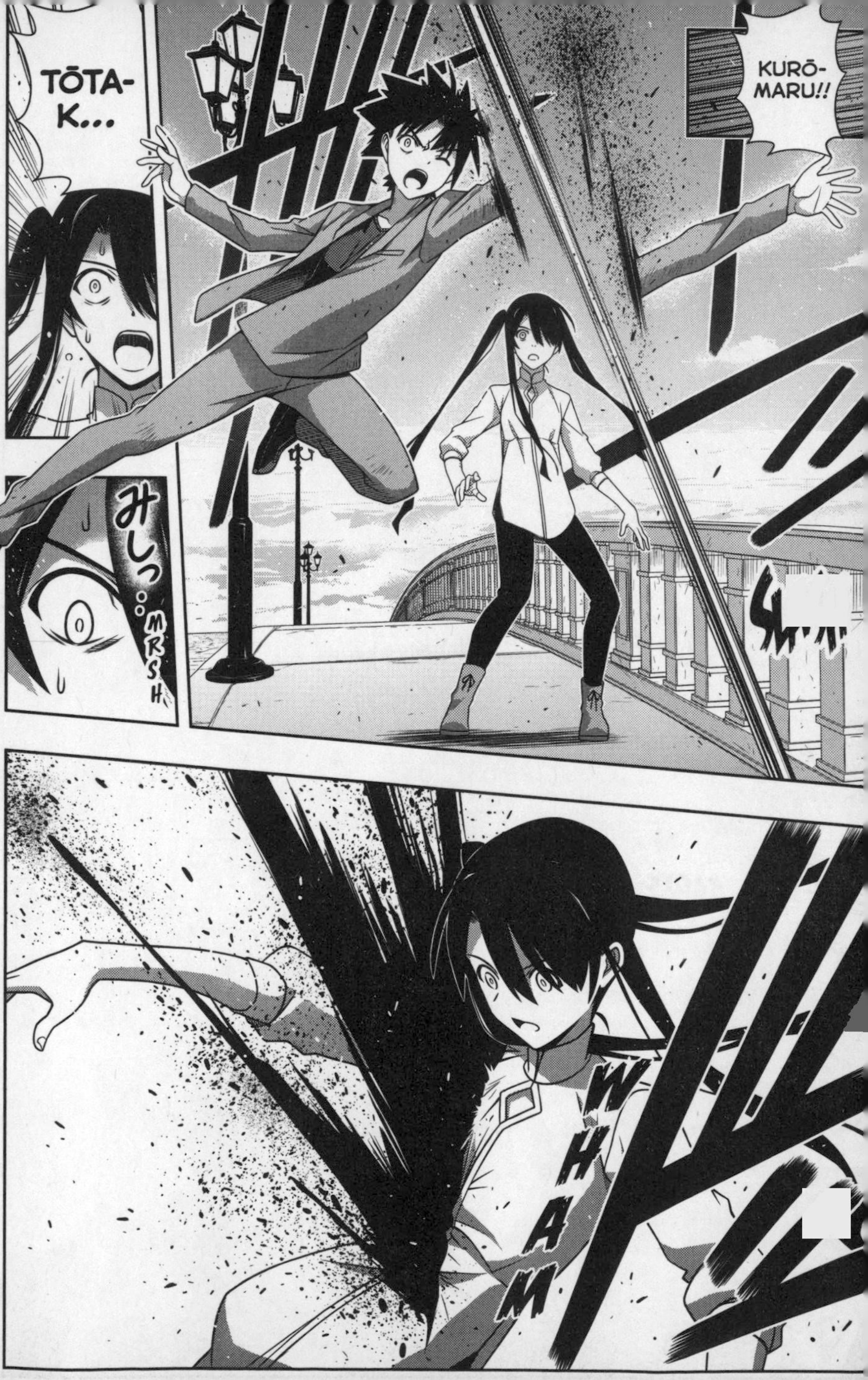
KURŌ-MARU!!
TŌTA-K...
みしっ
MRSH
WHAM

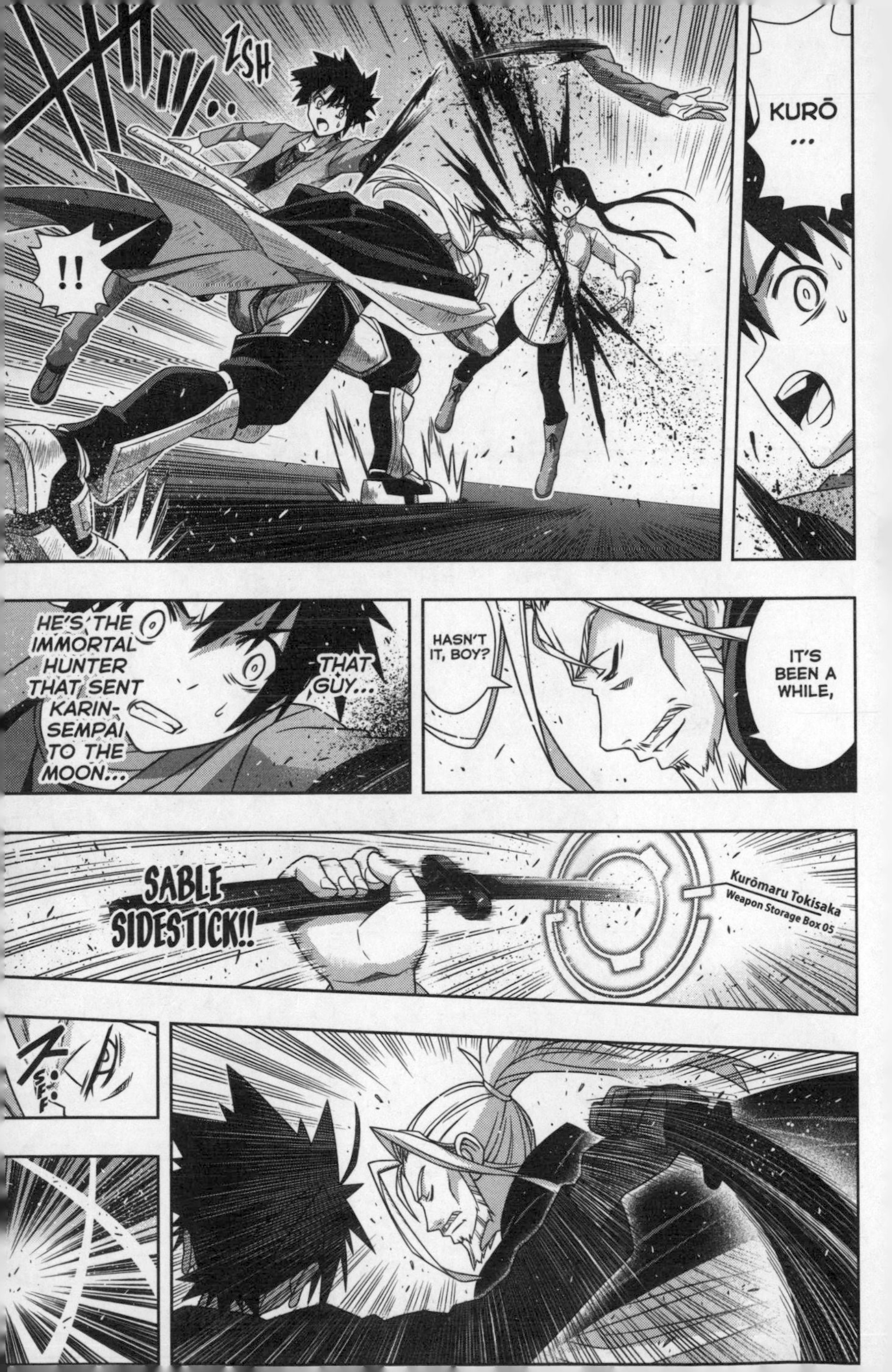
KURŌ ...
ZSH
!!
IT'S BEEN A WHILE,
HASN'T IT, BOY?
THAT GUY...
HE'S THE IMMORTAL HUNTER THAT SENT KARIN-SEMPAI TO THE MOON...
Kurōmaru Tokisaka
Weapon Storage Box 05
SABLE SIDESTICK!!

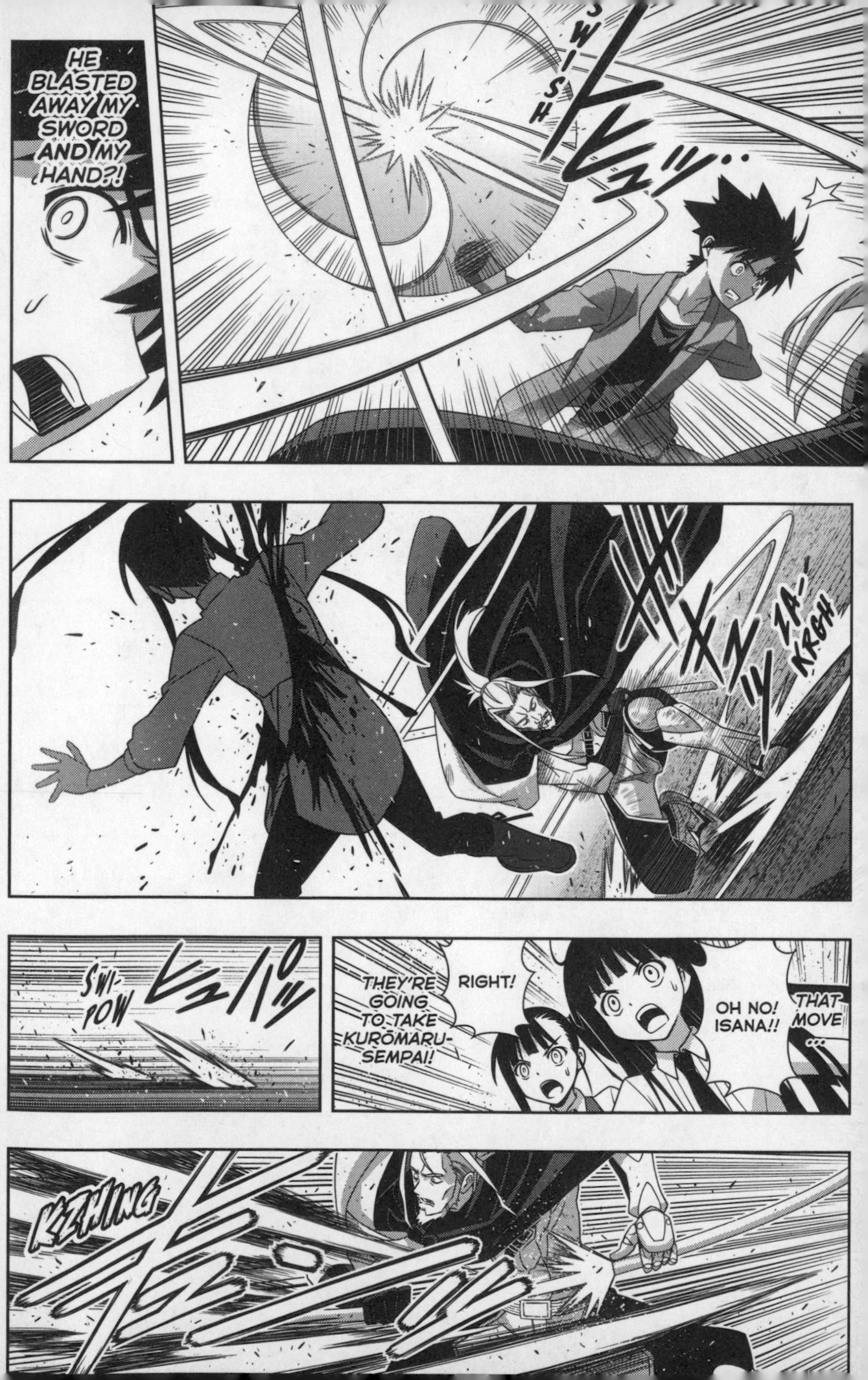
SWISH
HE BLASTED AWAY MY SWORD AND MY HAND?!
ZA-KRGH
THAT MOVE...
OH NO! ISANA!!
RIGHT!
THEY'RE GOING TO TAKE KUROMARU-SEMPAI!
SWI-POW
KZHING

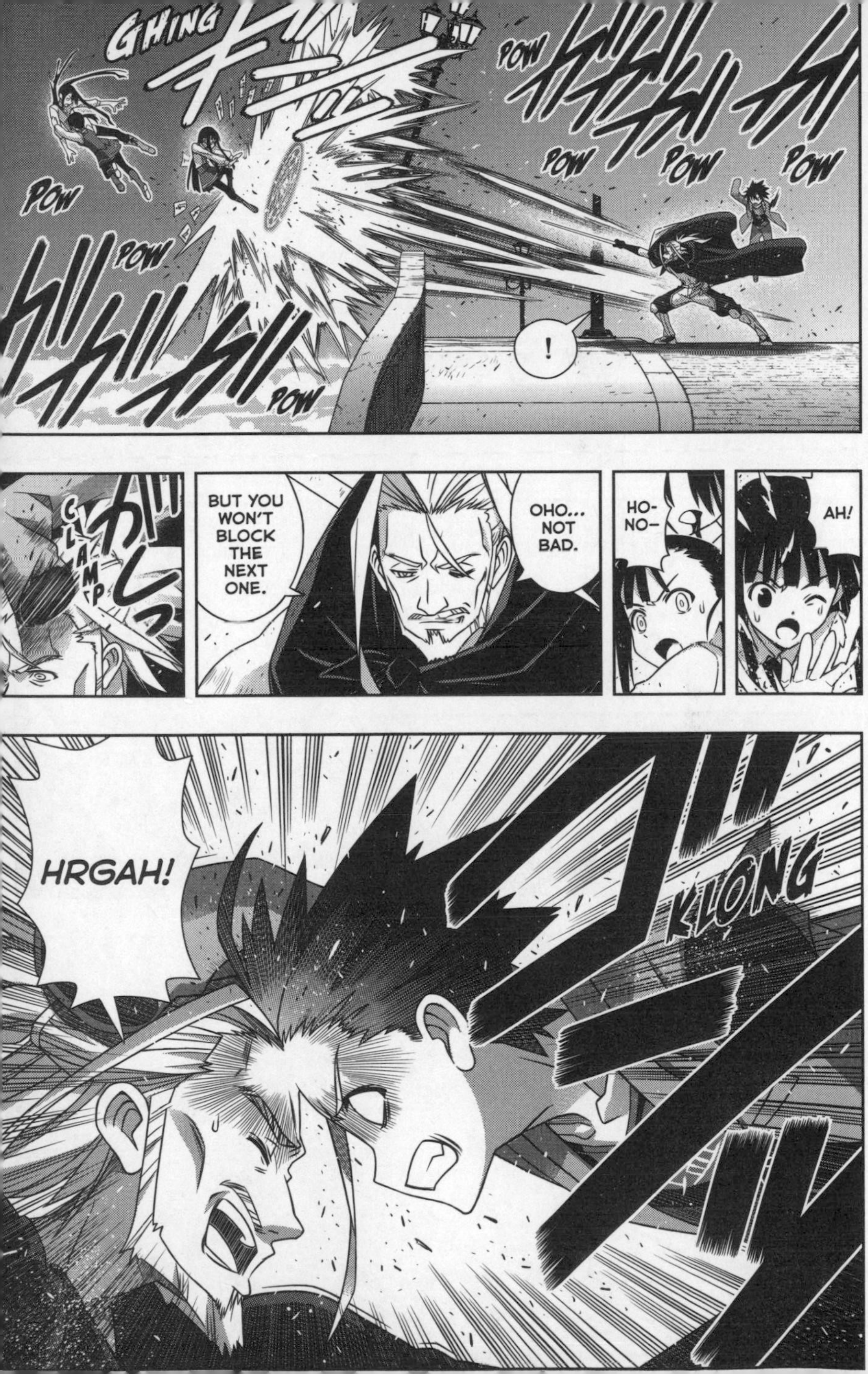
POW
POW
POW
POW
!
GHING
POW
POW
POW
AH!
HO-NO-
OHO... NOT BAD.
BUT YOU WON'T BLOCK THE NEXT ONE.
CLAMP
KLONG
HRGAH!

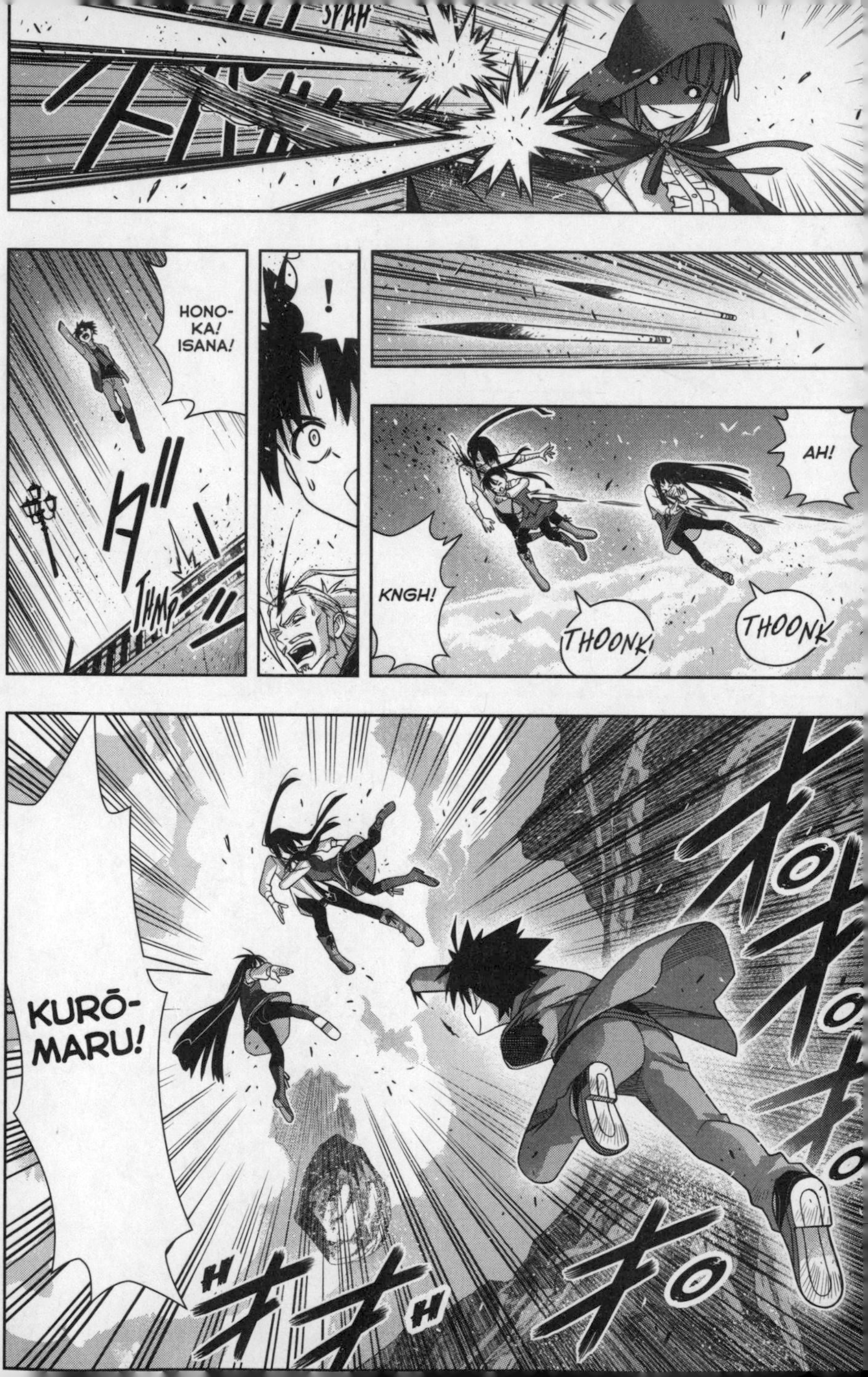

SPAH
AH!
THOONK
KNGH!
THOONK
!
HONO-KA! ISANA!
THMP
KURŌ-MARU!
H
H

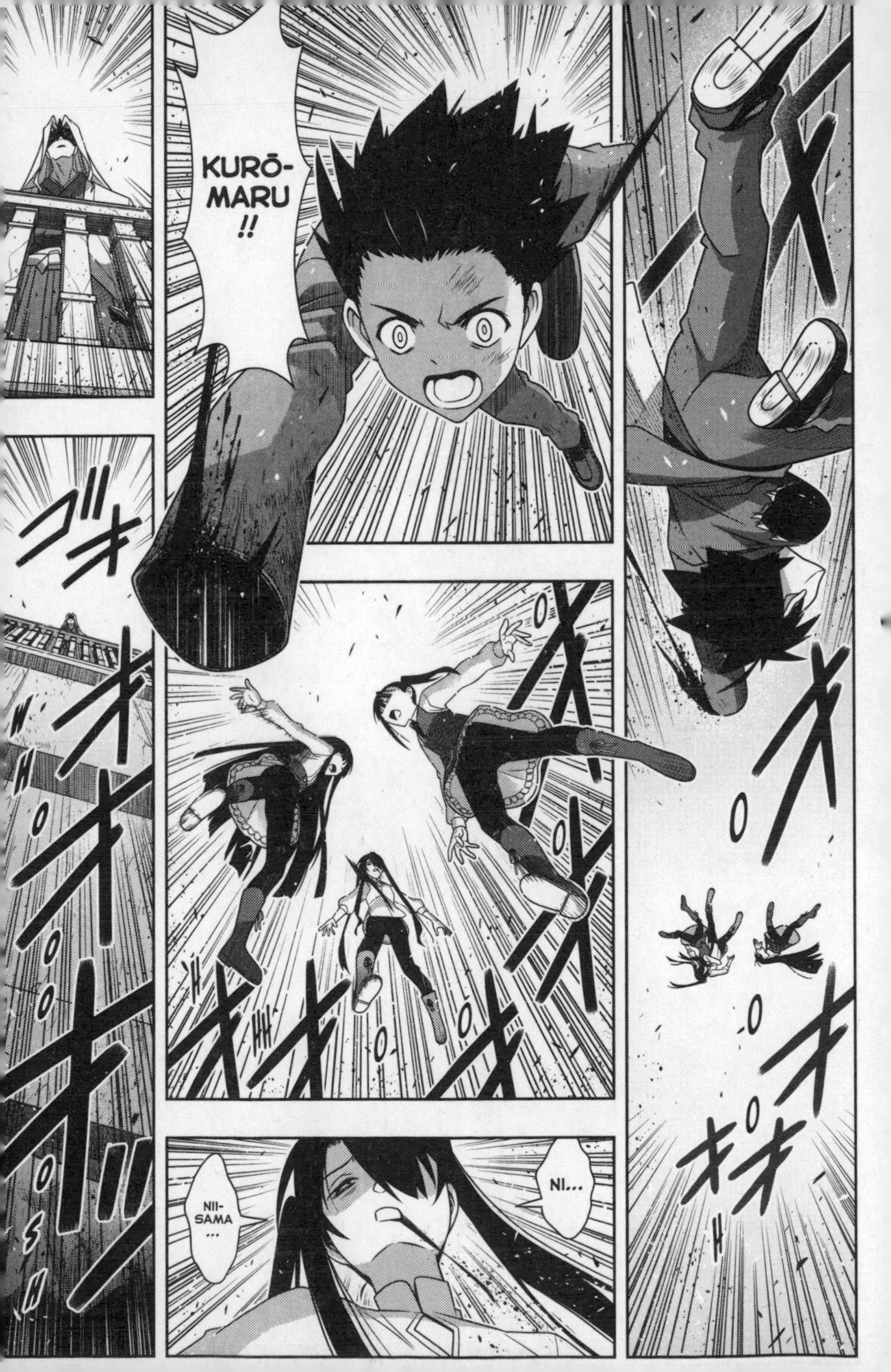
KURŌ-
MARU
!!
NI...
NII-
SAMA
...
WHOOOOSH

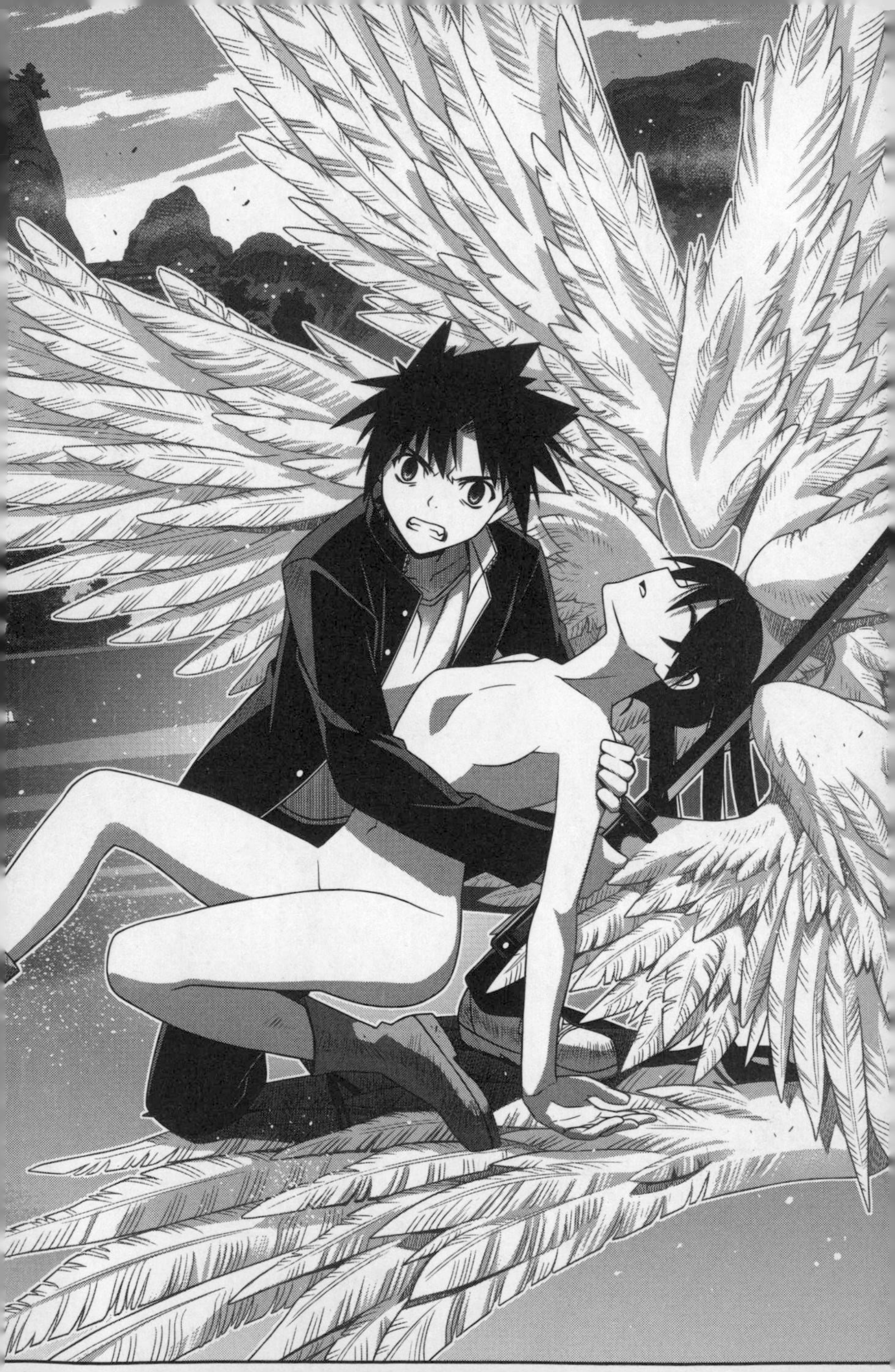

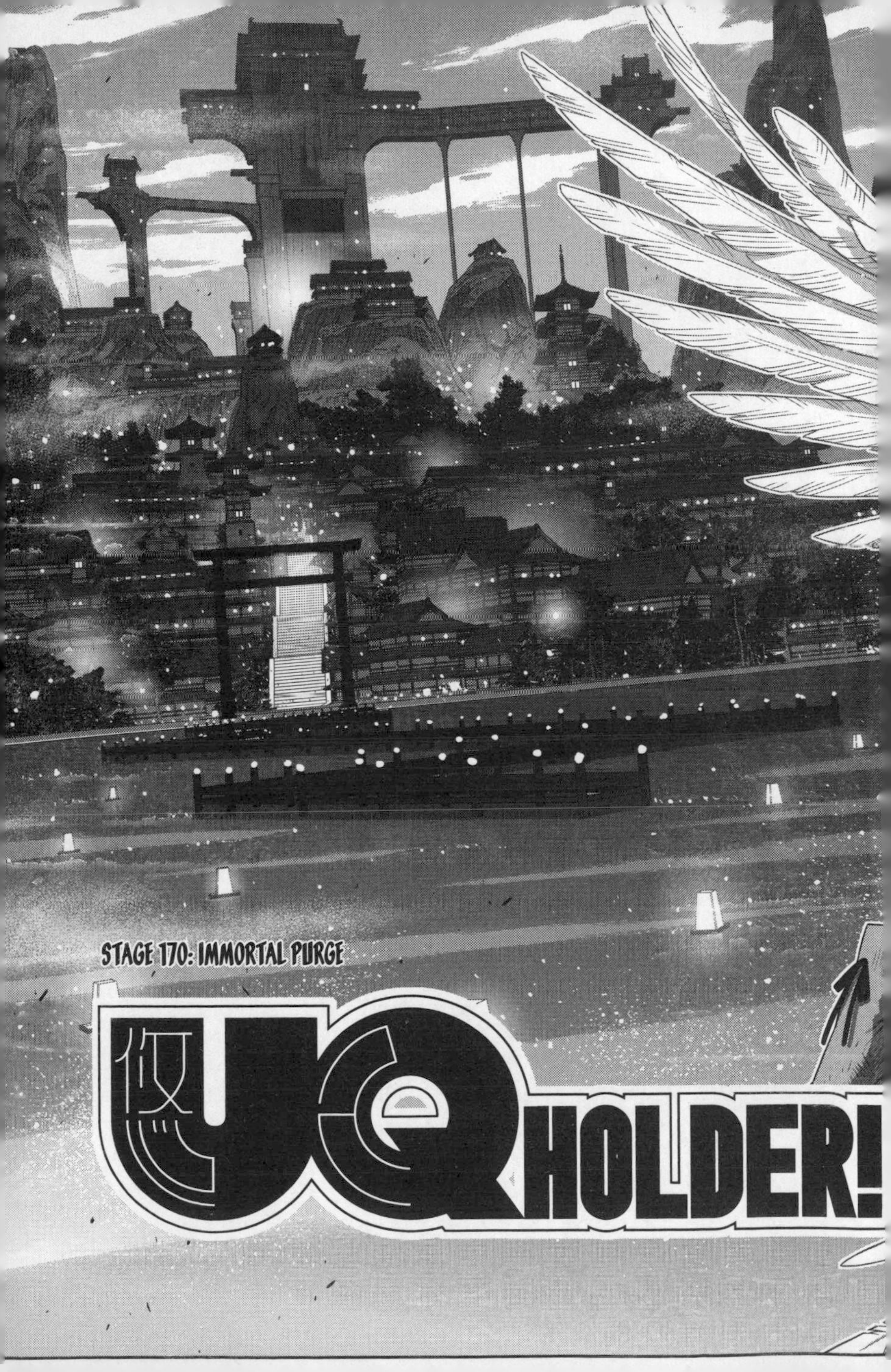
STAGE 170: IMMORTAL PURGE
UQ HOLDER!

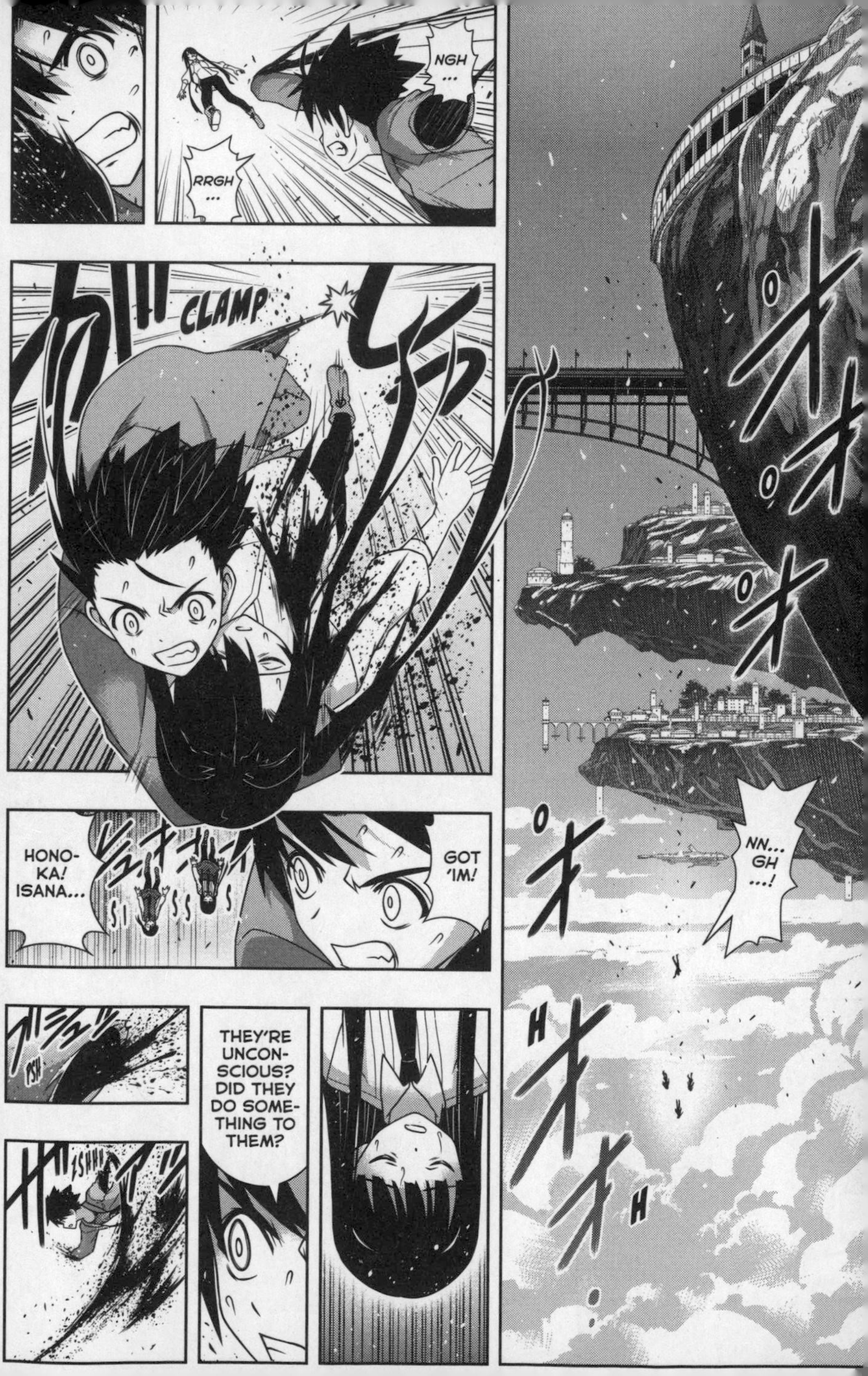
NN... GH ...!
NGH ...
RRGH ...
CLAMP
GOT 'IM!
HONO-KA! ISANA...
THEY'RE UNCON-SCIOUS? DID THEY DO SOME-THING TO THEM?
PSH

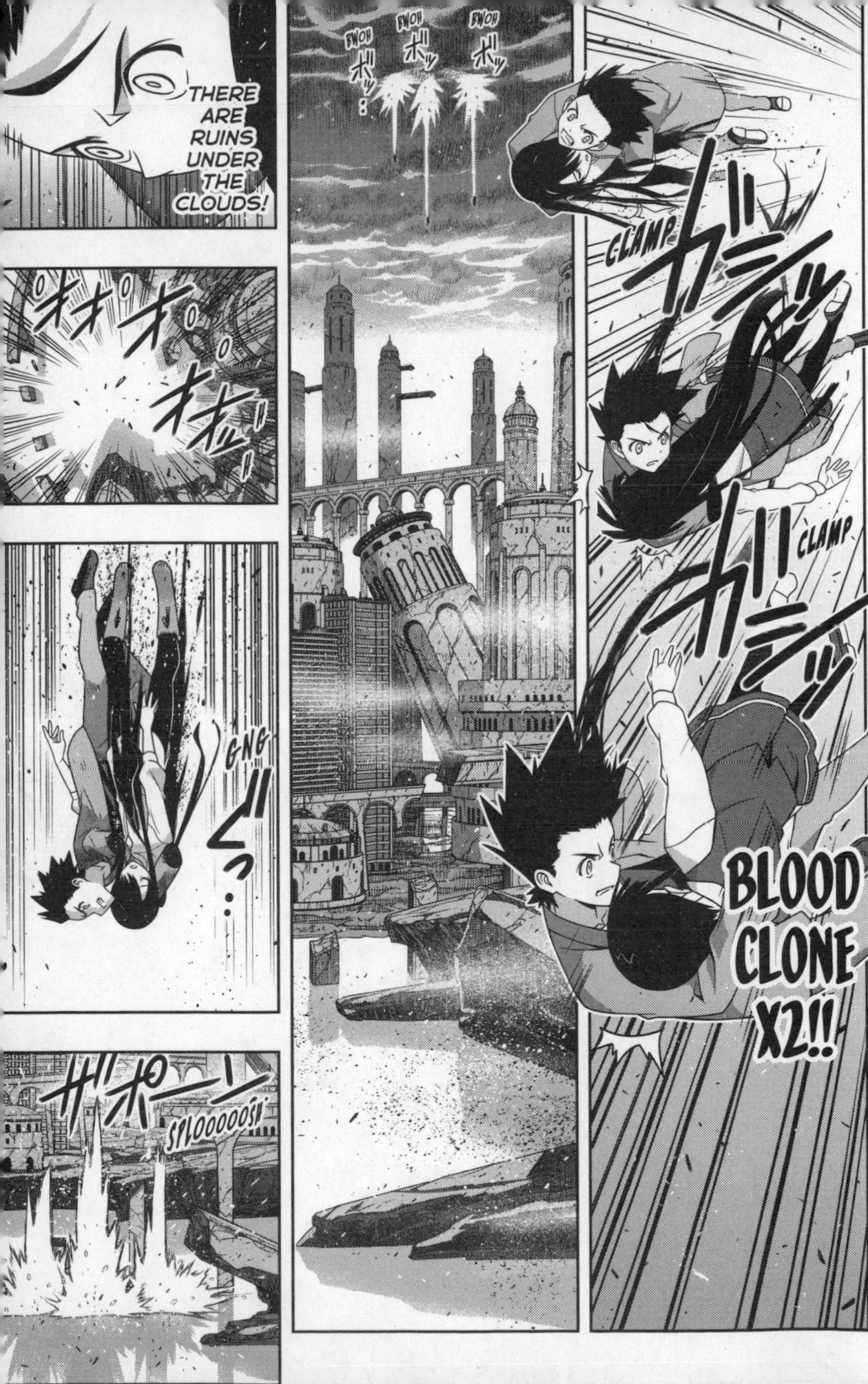
CLAMP
ガシッ
CLAMP
ガシッ
BLOOD CLONE X2!!
BWOH
ボッ
BWOH
ボッ
BWOH
ボッ…
THERE ARE RUINS UNDER THE CLOUDS!
GNG
ぐっ…
SPLOOOOOSH
ザポーン

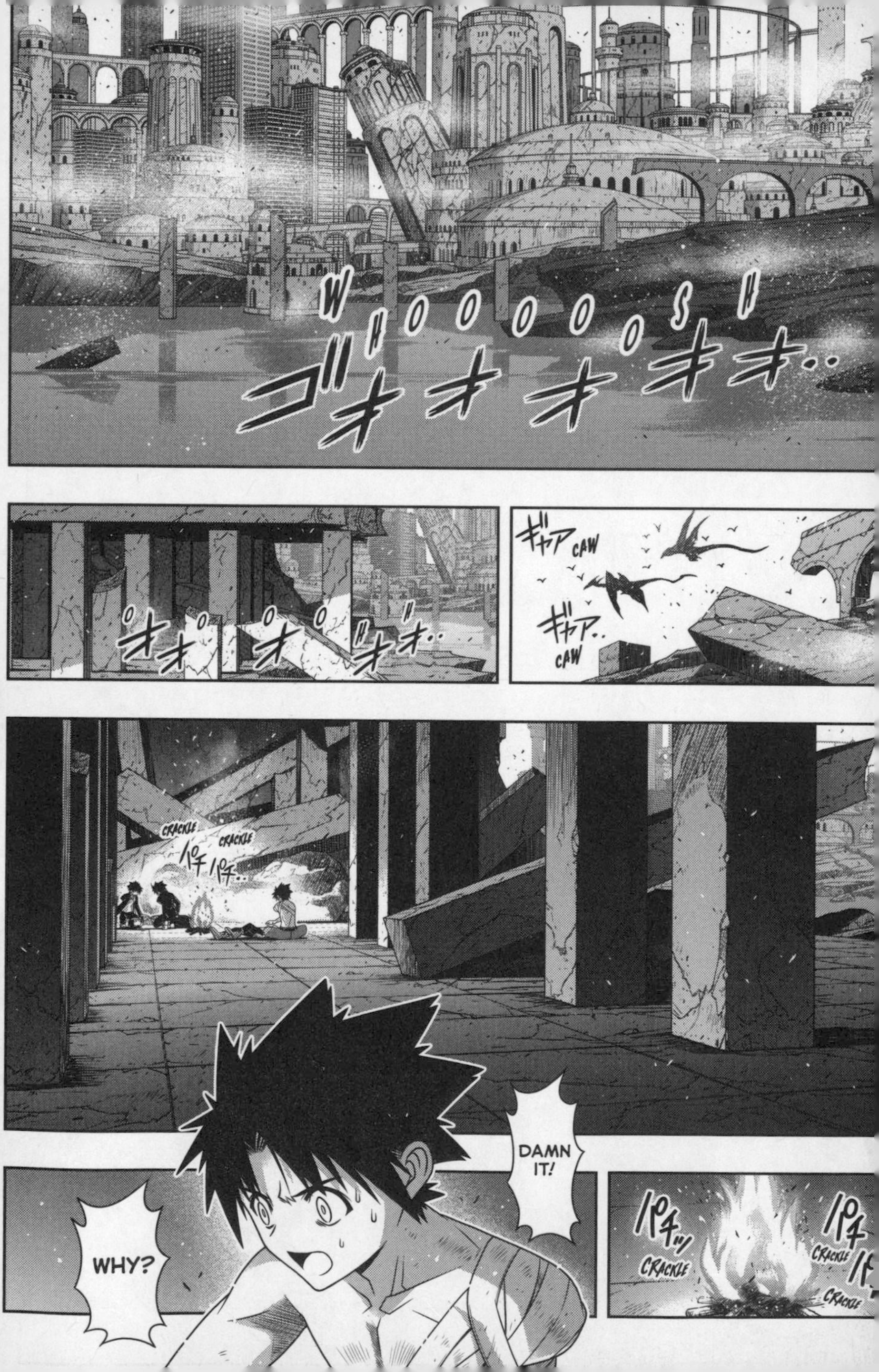
WHOOOOOOSH
ゴオオオオオ..
ギャア CAW
ギャア.. CAW
オオオオォ..
CRACKLE
CRACKLE
パチパチ..
パチ CRACKLE パ
CRACKLE
パチッ CRACKLE
DAMN IT!
WHY?

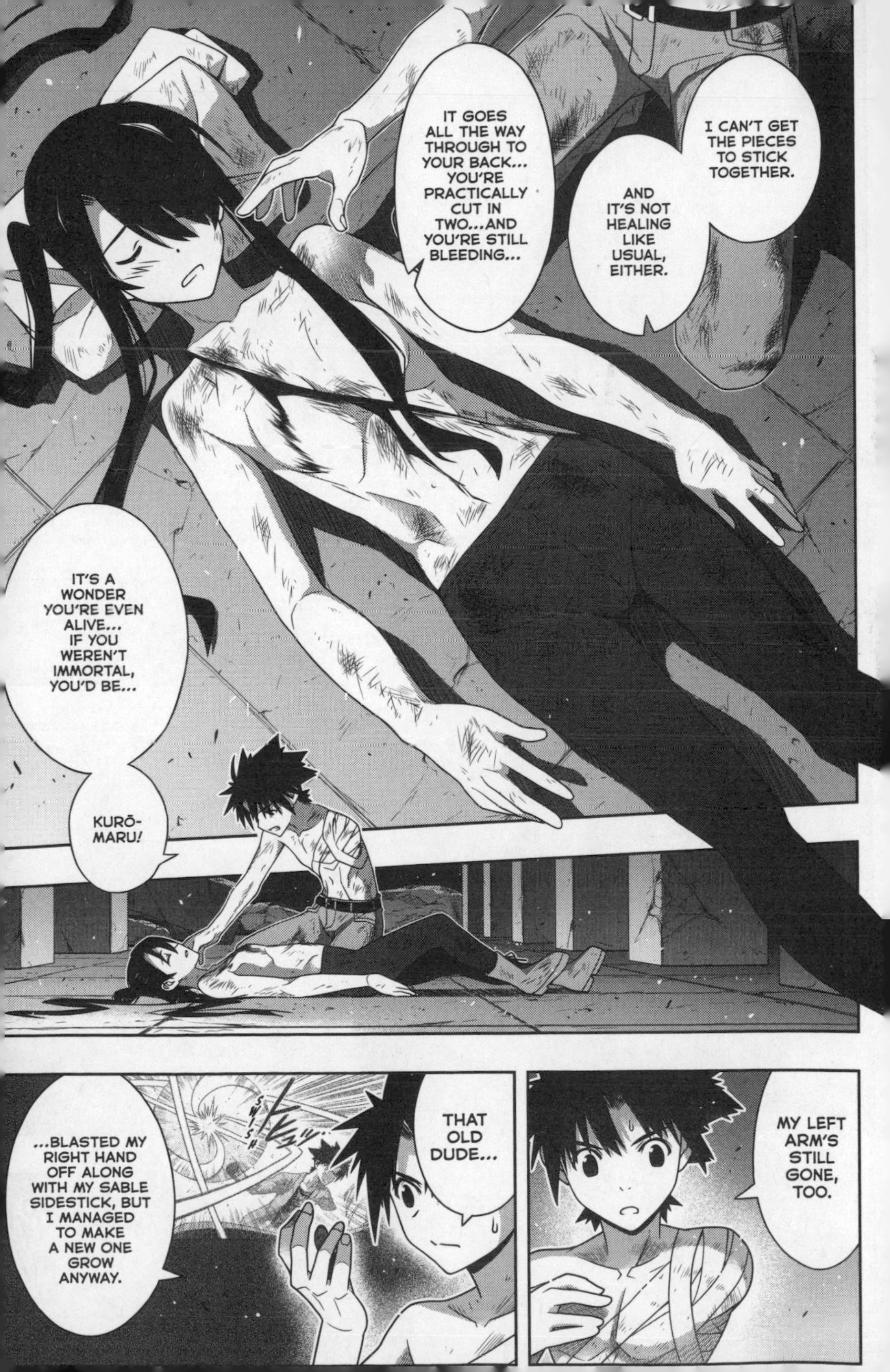
I CAN'T GET THE PIECES TO STICK TOGETHER.
AND IT'S NOT HEALING LIKE USUAL, EITHER.
IT GOES ALL THE WAY THROUGH TO YOUR BACK... YOU'RE PRACTICALLY CUT IN TWO...AND YOU'RE STILL BLEEDING...
IT'S A WONDER YOU'RE EVEN ALIVE... IF YOU WEREN'T IMMORTAL, YOU'D BE...
KURŌ-MARU!
MY LEFT ARM'S STILL GONE, TOO.
THAT OLD DUDE...
SWISH
...BLASTED MY RIGHT HAND OFF ALONG WITH MY SABLE SIDESTICK, BUT I MANAGED TO MAKE A NEW ONE GROW ANYWAY.

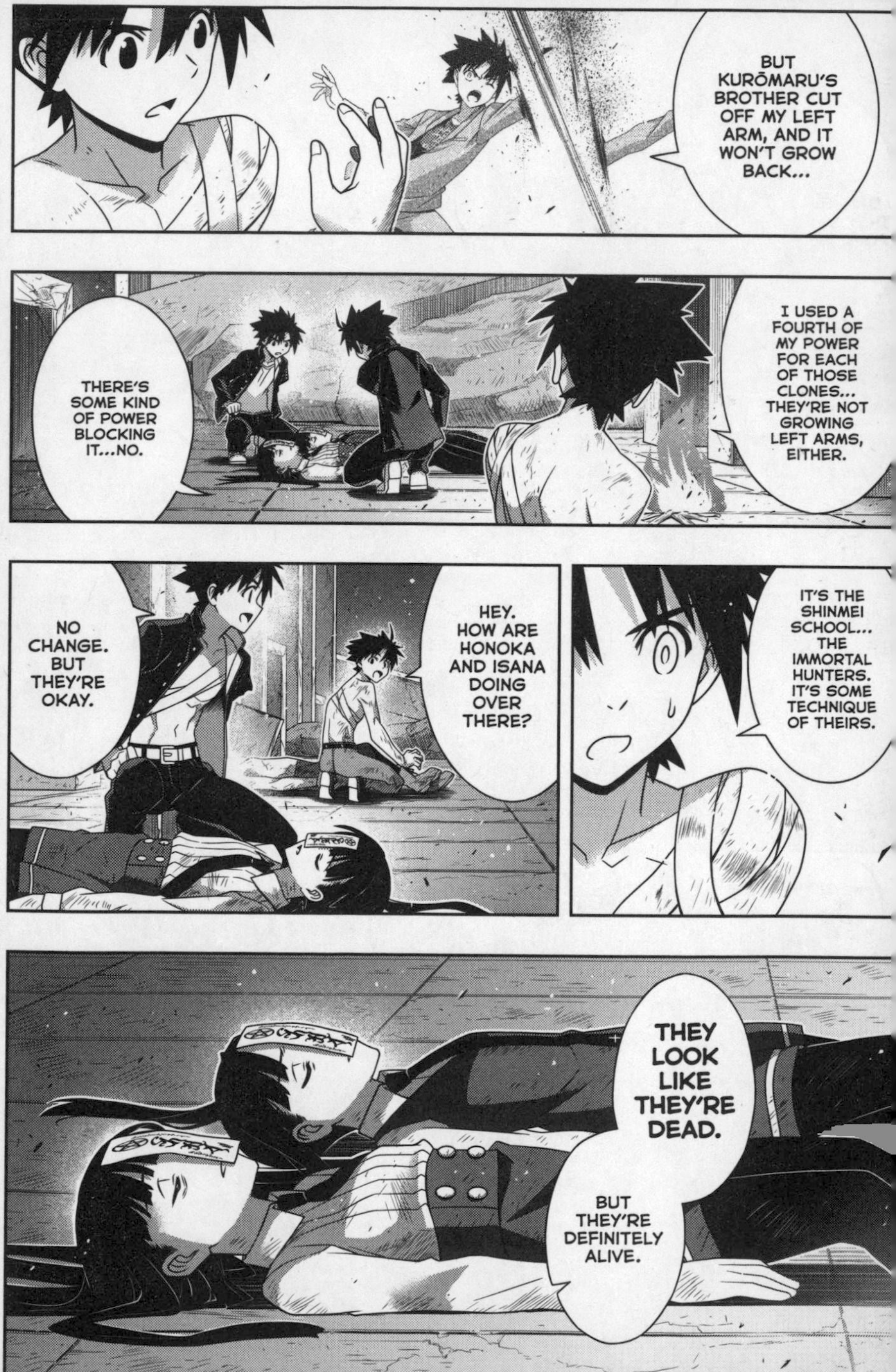
BUT KURŌMARU'S BROTHER CUT OFF MY LEFT ARM, AND IT WON'T GROW BACK...
I USED A FOURTH OF MY POWER FOR EACH OF THOSE CLONES... THEY'RE NOT GROWING LEFT ARMS, EITHER.
THERE'S SOME KIND OF POWER BLOCKING IT...NO.
IT'S THE SHINMEI SCHOOL... THE IMMORTAL HUNTERS. IT'S SOME TECHNIQUE OF THEIRS.
HEY. HOW ARE HONOKA AND ISANA DOING OVER THERE?
NO CHANGE. BUT THEY'RE OKAY.
THEY LOOK LIKE THEY'RE DEAD.
BUT THEY'RE DEFINITELY ALIVE.

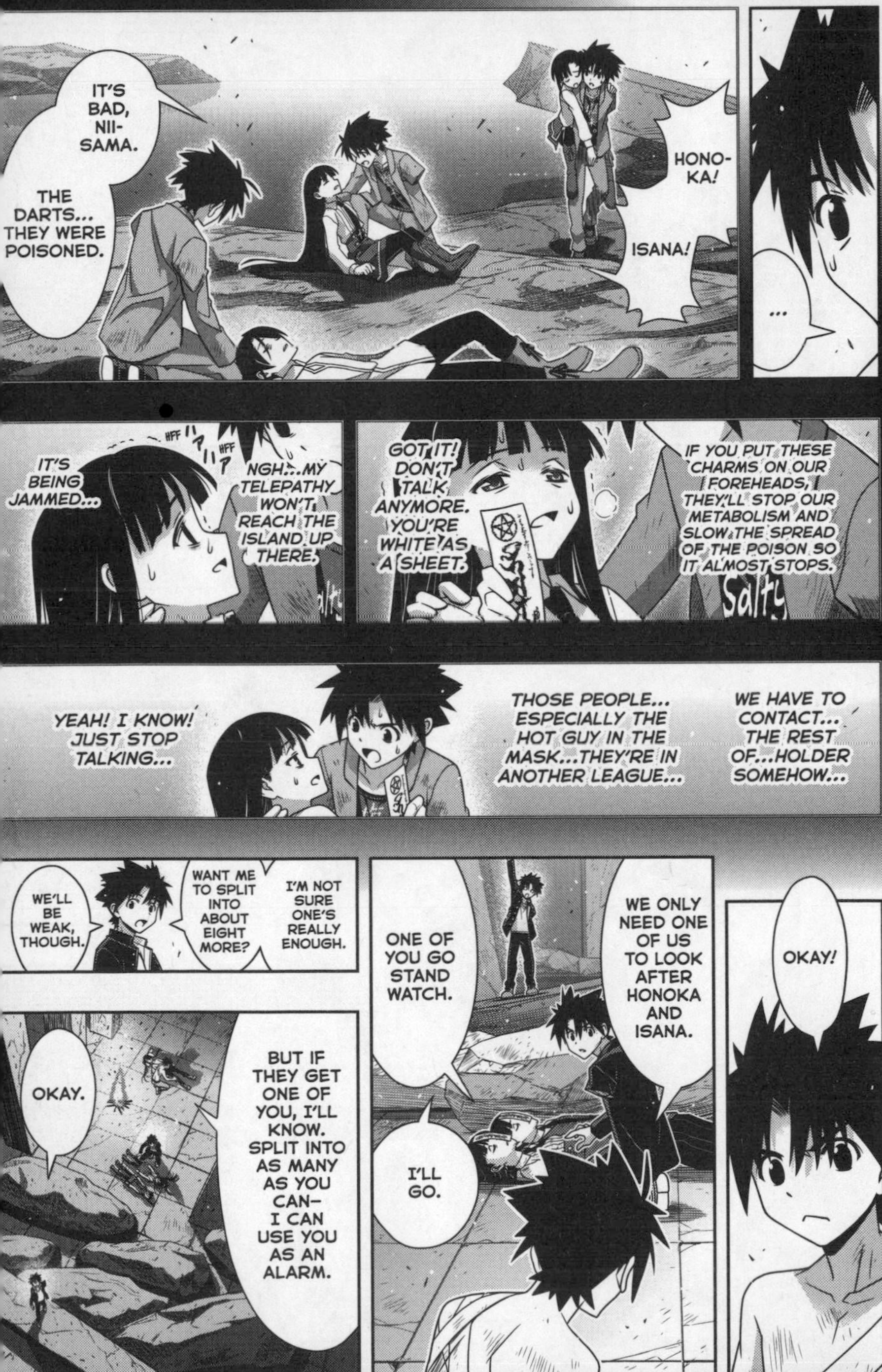

...
HONOKA!
ISANA!
IT'S BAD, NII-SAMA.
THE DARTS... THEY WERE POISONED.
IF YOU PUT THESE CHARMS ON OUR FOREHEADS, THEY'LL STOP OUR METABOLISM AND SLOW THE SPREAD OF THE POISON SO IT ALMOST STOPS.
GOT IT! DON'T TALK ANYMORE. YOU'RE WHITE AS A SHEET.
HFF HFF
NGH...MY TELEPATHY WON'T REACH THE ISLAND UP THERE.
IT'S BEING JAMMED...
WE HAVE TO CONTACT... THE REST OF...HOLDER SOMEHOW...
THOSE PEOPLE... ESPECIALLY THE HOT GUY IN THE MASK...THEY'RE IN ANOTHER LEAGUE...
YEAH! I KNOW! JUST STOP TALKING...
OKAY!
WE ONLY NEED ONE OF US TO LOOK AFTER HONOKA AND ISANA.
ONE OF YOU GO STAND WATCH.
I'LL GO.
I'M NOT SURE ONE'S REALLY ENOUGH.
WANT ME TO SPLIT INTO ABOUT EIGHT MORE?
WE'LL BE WEAK, THOUGH.
BUT IF THEY GET ONE OF YOU, I'LL KNOW. SPLIT INTO AS MANY AS YOU CAN— I CAN USE YOU AS AN ALARM.
OKAY.

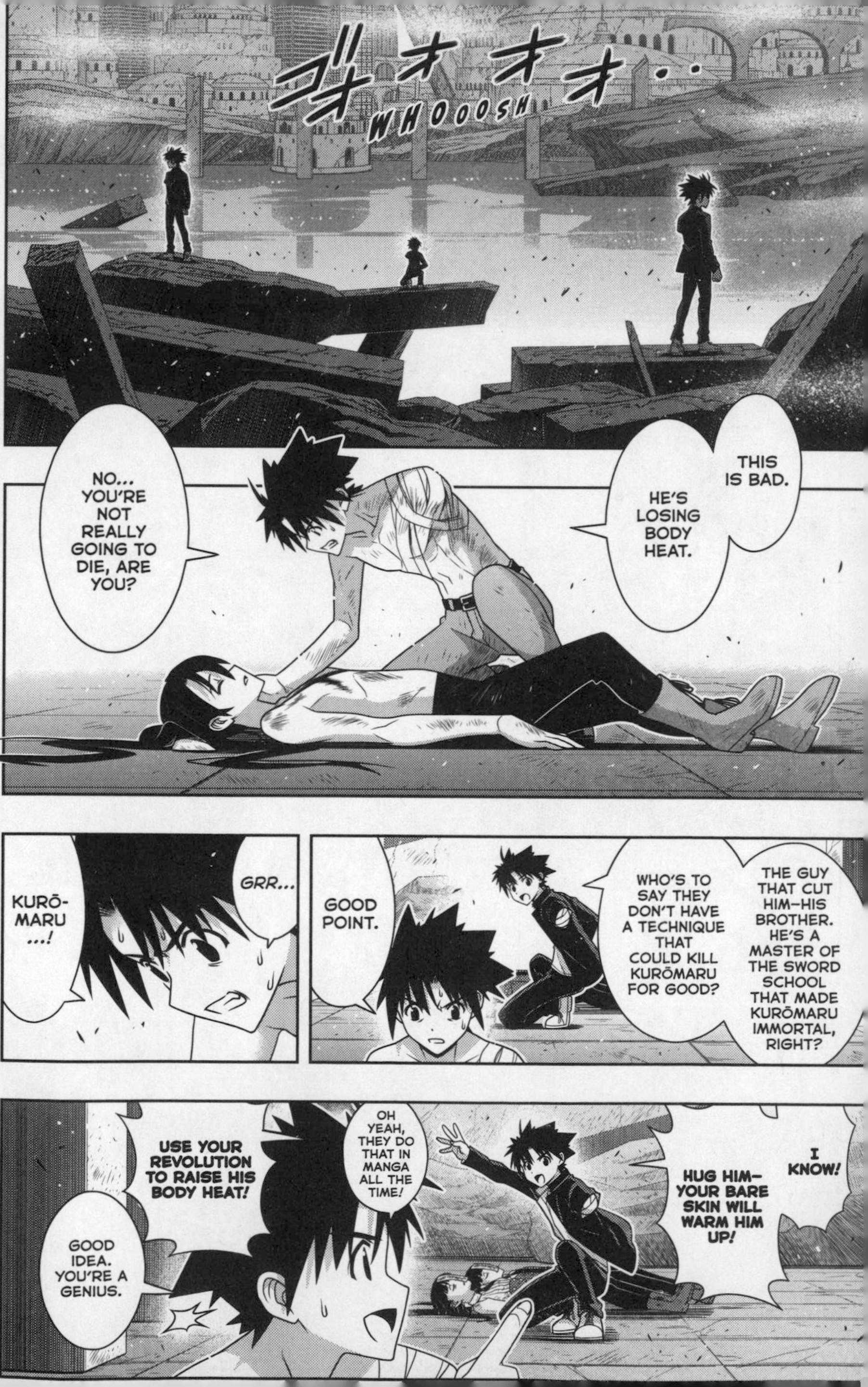
ゴオオオオ..
WHOOOSH
THIS IS BAD.
HE'S LOSING BODY HEAT.
NO... YOU'RE NOT REALLY GOING TO DIE, ARE YOU?
THE GUY THAT CUT HIM—HIS BROTHER. HE'S A MASTER OF THE SWORD SCHOOL THAT MADE KURŌMARU IMMORTAL, RIGHT?
WHO'S TO SAY THEY DON'T HAVE A TECHNIQUE THAT COULD KILL KURŌMARU FOR GOOD?
GOOD POINT.
GRR...
KURŌ-MARU ...!
I KNOW!
HUG HIM—YOUR BARE SKIN WILL WARM HIM UP!
OH YEAH, THEY DO THAT IN MANGA ALL THE TIME!
USE YOUR REVOLUTION TO RAISE HIS BODY HEAT!
GOOD IDEA. YOU'RE A GENIUS.

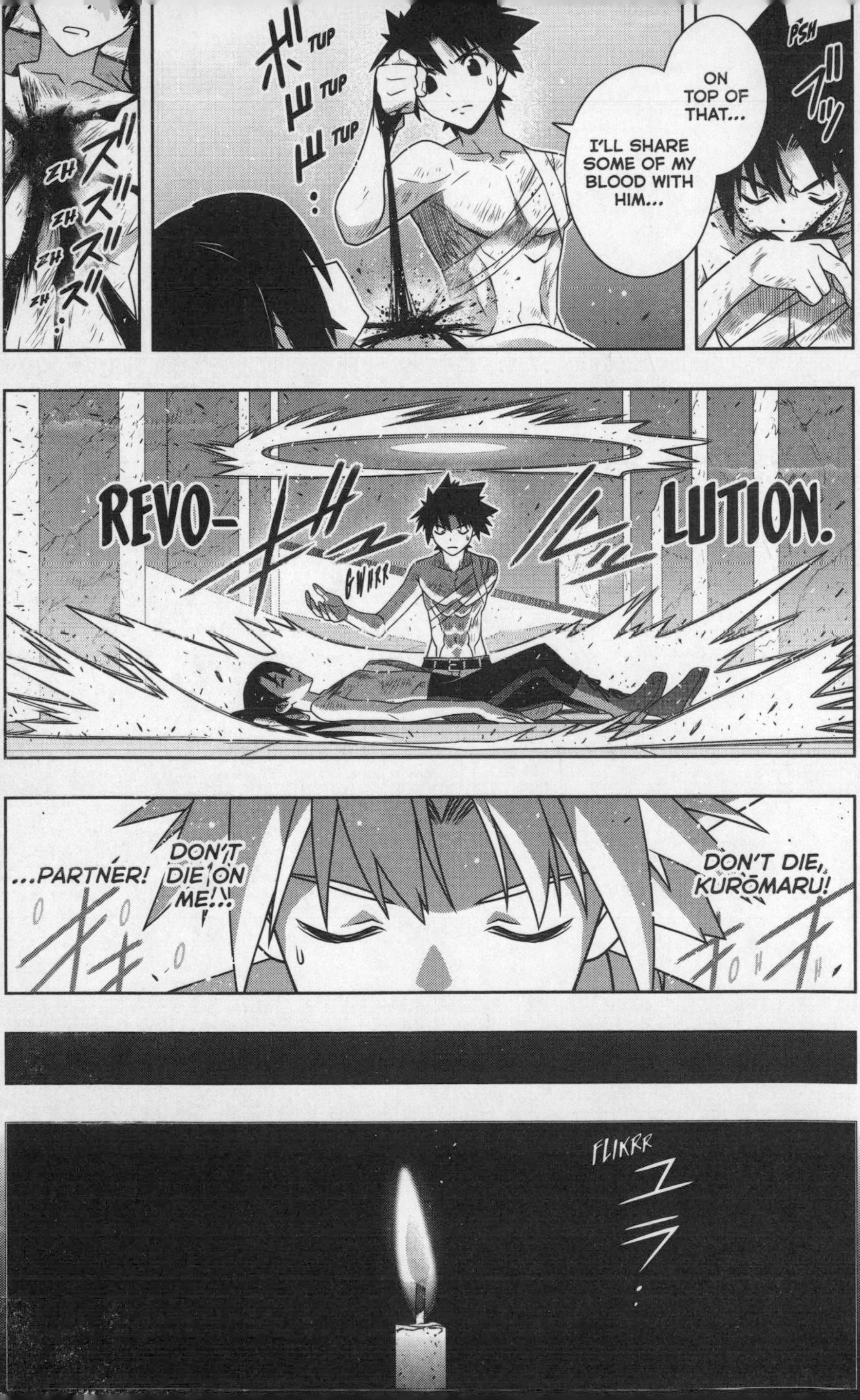
PSH
ON TOP OF THAT...
I'LL SHARE SOME OF MY BLOOD WITH HIM...
TUP
TUP
TUP
ZH
ZH
ZH
ZH
REVO- LUTION.
GWHRR
DON'T DIE, KUROMARU!
DON'T DIE ON ME!!
...PARTNER!
FLIKRR

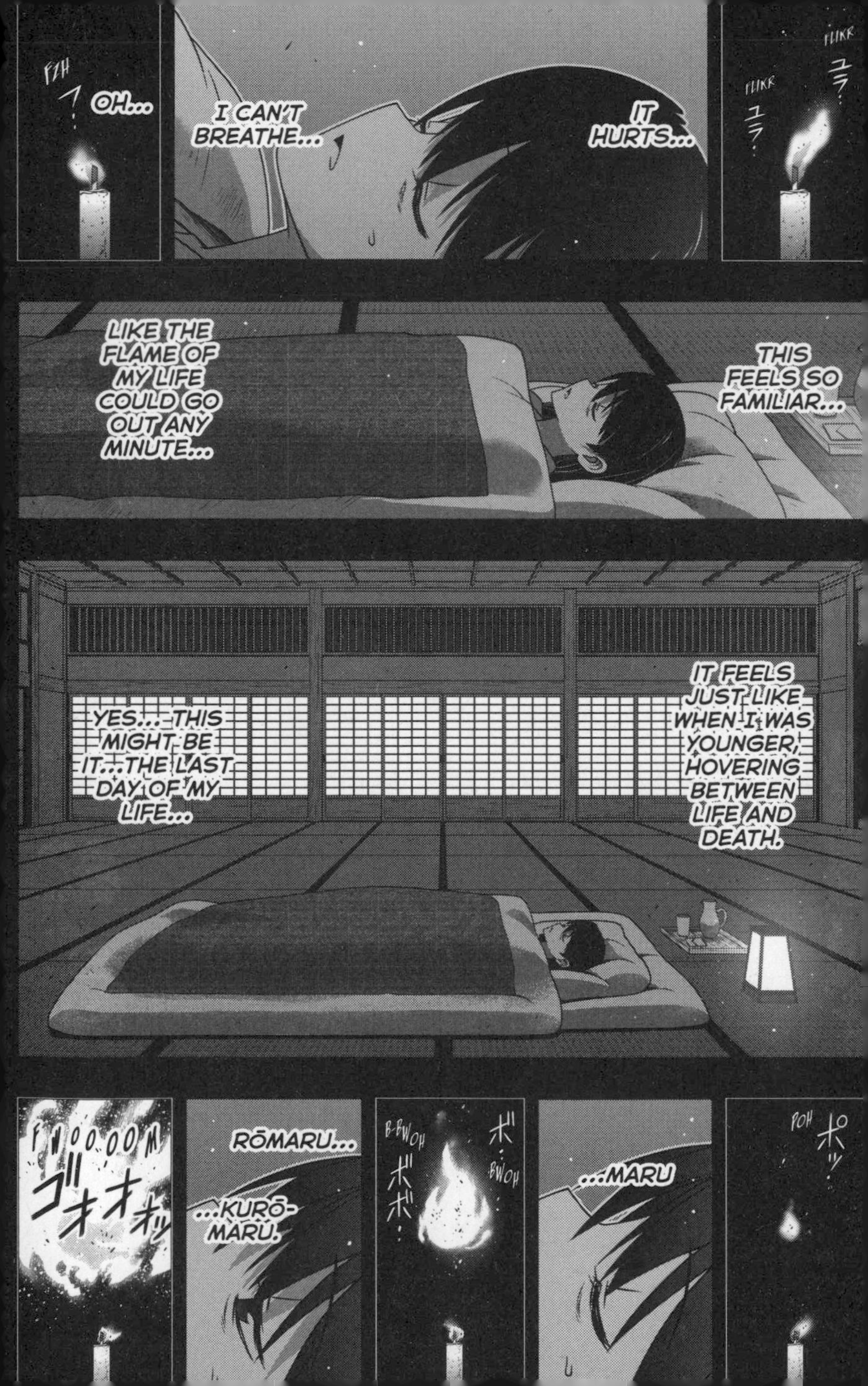
FLIKR
ユラ…
FLIKR
ユラ…
IT HURTS…
I CAN'T BREATHE…
FZH
フ…
OH…
THIS FEELS SO FAMILIAR…
LIKE THE FLAME OF MY LIFE COULD GO OUT ANY MINUTE…
IT FEELS JUST LIKE WHEN I WAS YOUNGER, HOVERING BETWEEN LIFE AND DEATH.
YES… THIS MIGHT BE IT… THE LAST DAY OF MY LIFE…
POH
ポッ…
…MARU
ボ…
BWOH
B-BWOH
ボボ…
RŌMARU…
…KURŌ-MARU.
FWOOOOM
ゴォオオッ

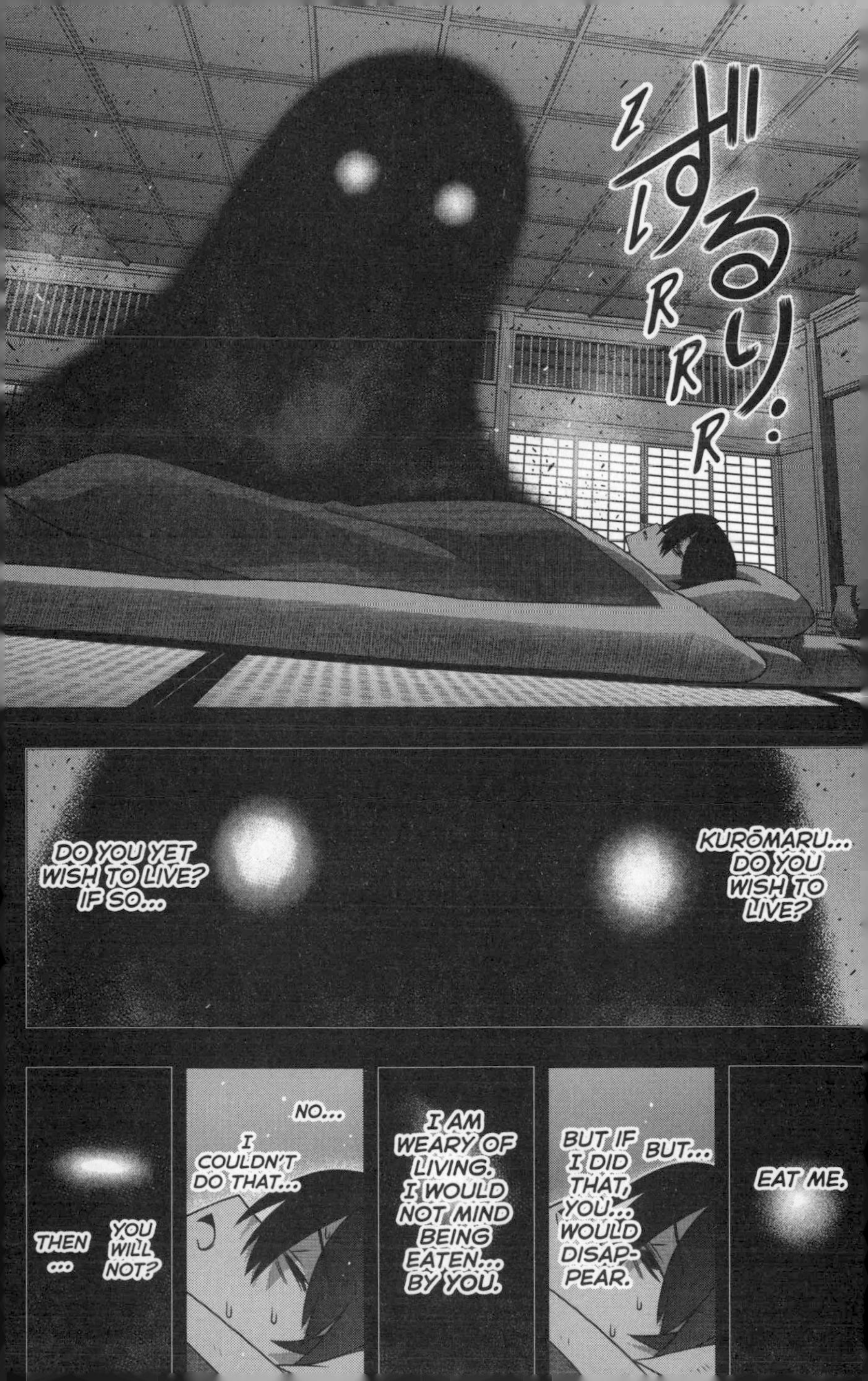
ずるり…
ZURRR
KURŌMARU… DO YOU WISH TO LIVE?
DO YOU YET WISH TO LIVE? IF SO…
EAT ME.
BUT…
BUT IF I DID THAT, YOU… WOULD DISAP-PEAR.
I AM WEARY OF LIVING. I WOULD NOT MIND BEING EATEN… BY YOU.
NO…
I COULDN'T DO THAT…
YOU WILL NOT?
THEN …

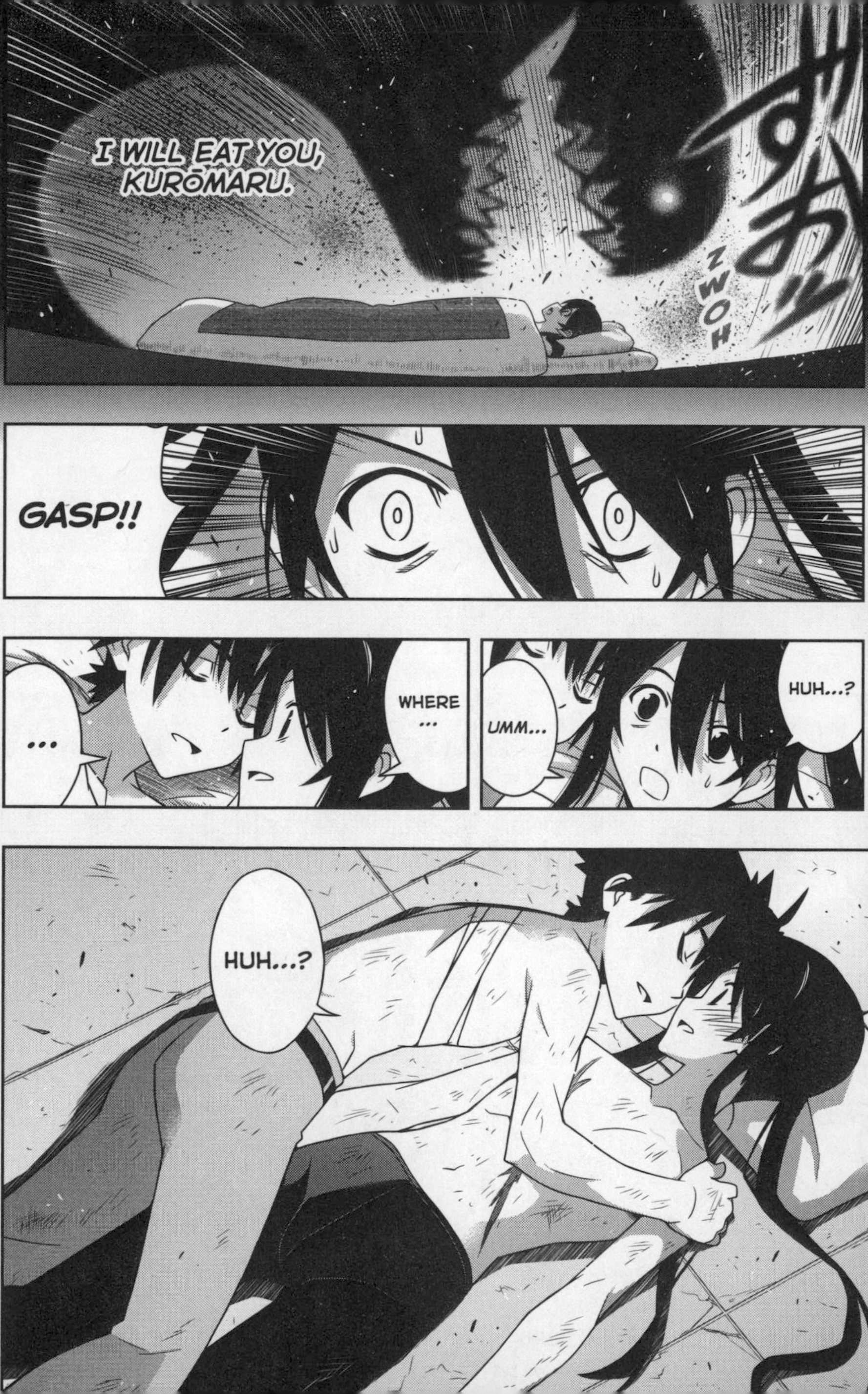
I WILL EAT YOU, KURŌMARU.
ZWOH
GASP!!
HUH...?
UMM...
WHERE ...
...
HUH...?

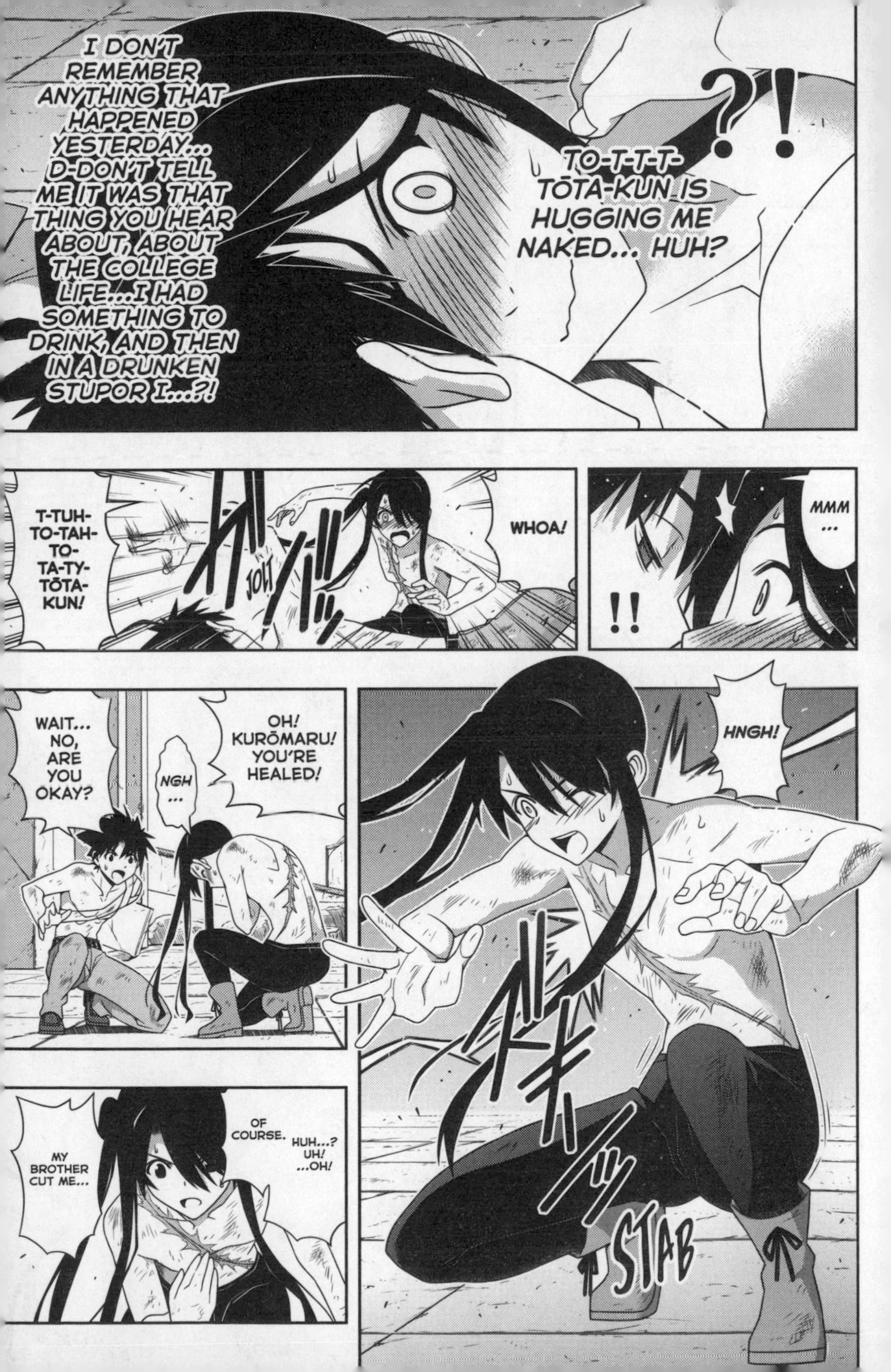
?!
TO-T-T-T-TŌTA-KUN IS HUGGING ME NAKED... HUH?
I DON'T REMEMBER ANYTHING THAT HAPPENED YESTERDAY... D-DON'T TELL ME IT WAS THAT THING YOU HEAR ABOUT, ABOUT THE COLLEGE LIFE...I HAD SOMETHING TO DRINK, AND THEN IN A DRUNKEN STUPOR I...?!
MMM ...
!!
WHOA!
JOLT
T-TUH-TO-TAH-TO-TA-TY-TŌTA-KUN!
HNGH!
STAB
OH! KURŌMARU! YOU'RE HEALED!
NGH ...
WAIT... NO, ARE YOU OKAY?
HUH...? UH! ...OH!
OF COURSE.
MY BROTHER CUT ME...

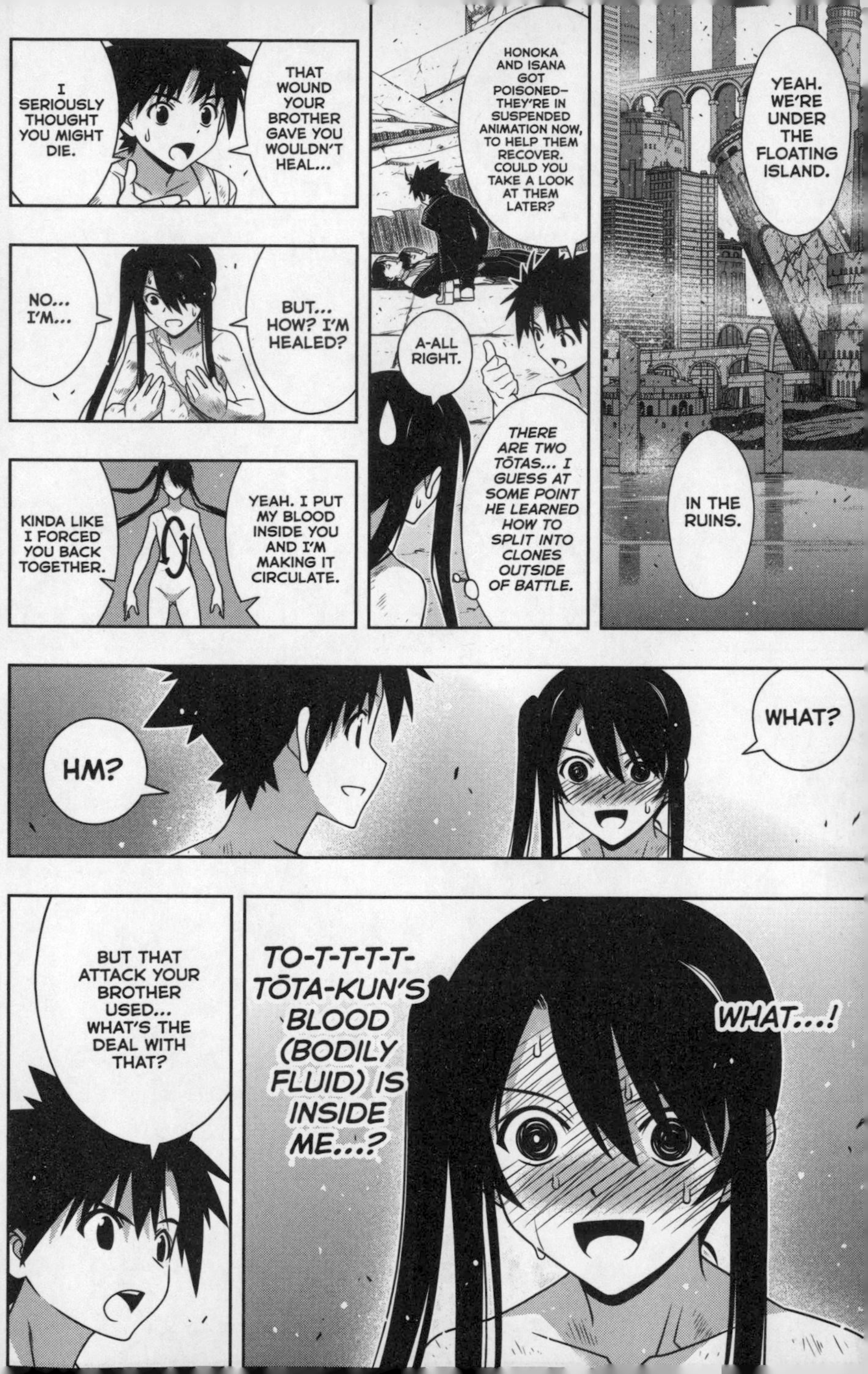
YEAH. WE'RE UNDER THE FLOATING ISLAND.
IN THE RUINS.
HONOKA AND ISANA GOT POISONED— THEY'RE IN SUSPENDED ANIMATION NOW, TO HELP THEM RECOVER. COULD YOU TAKE A LOOK AT THEM LATER?
A-ALL RIGHT.
THERE ARE TWO TŌTAS... I GUESS AT SOME POINT HE LEARNED HOW TO SPLIT INTO CLONES OUTSIDE OF BATTLE.
THAT WOUND YOUR BROTHER GAVE YOU WOULDN'T HEAL...
I SERIOUSLY THOUGHT YOU MIGHT DIE.
BUT... HOW? I'M HEALED?
NO... I'M...
YEAH. I PUT MY BLOOD INSIDE YOU AND I'M MAKING IT CIRCULATE.
KINDA LIKE I FORCED YOU BACK TOGETHER.
WHAT?
HM?
WHAT...!
TO-T-T-T-T-TŌTA-KUN'S BLOOD (BODILY FLUID) IS INSIDE ME...?
BUT THAT ATTACK YOUR BROTHER USED... WHAT'S THE DEAL WITH THAT?

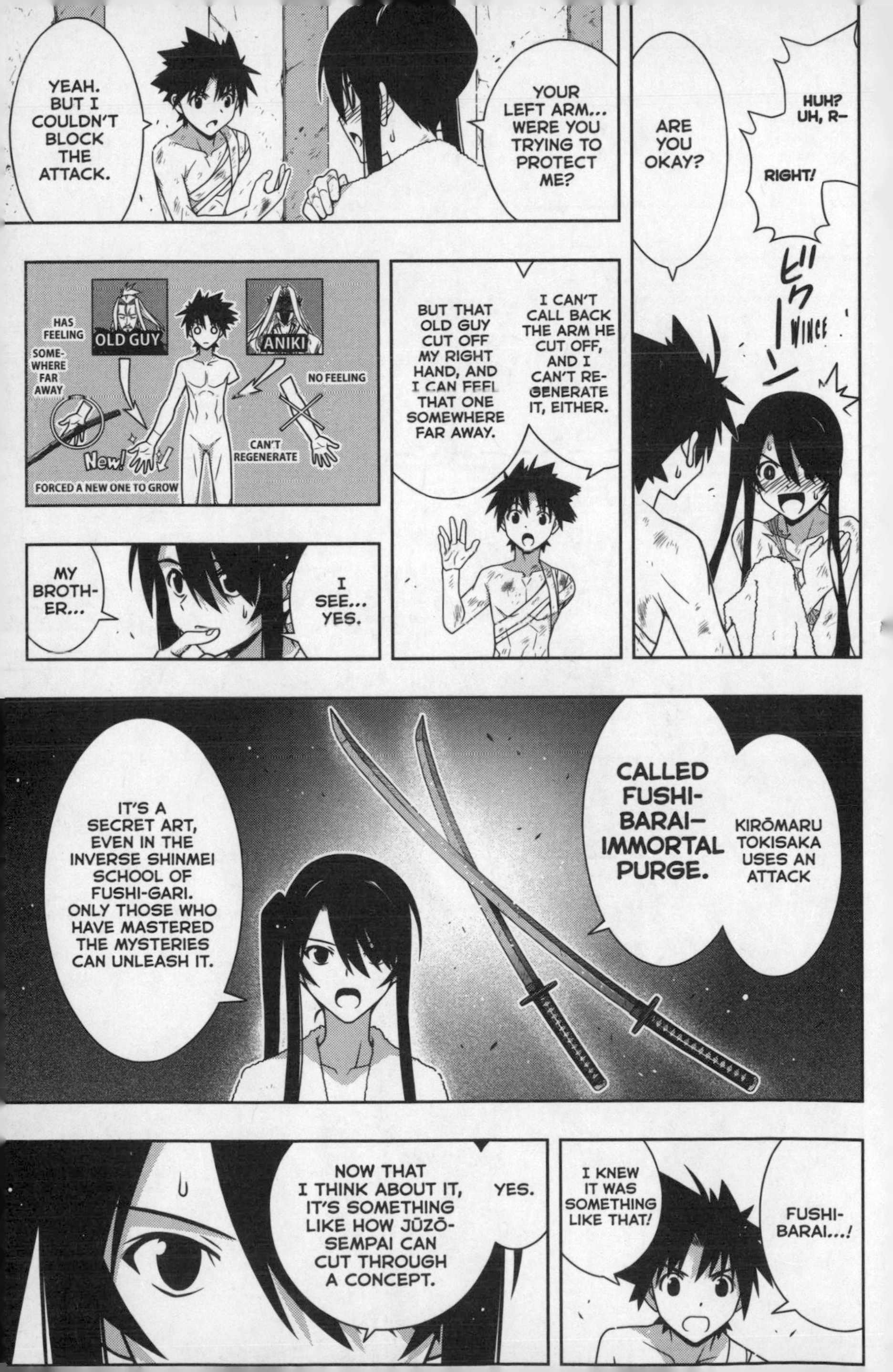

ARE YOU OKAY?
HUH? UH, R- RIGHT!
WINCE
YOUR LEFT ARM... WERE YOU TRYING TO PROTECT ME?
YEAH. BUT I COULDN'T BLOCK THE ATTACK.
I CAN'T CALL BACK THE ARM HE CUT OFF, AND I CAN'T REGENERATE IT, EITHER.
BUT THAT OLD GUY CUT OFF MY RIGHT HAND, AND I CAN FEEL THAT ONE SOMEWHERE FAR AWAY.
ANIKI
NO FEELING
CAN'T REGENERATE
OLD GUY
HAS FEELING SOMEWHERE FAR AWAY
New!
FORCED A NEW ONE TO GROW
I SEE... YES.
MY BROTHER-ER...
KIRŌMARU TOKISAKA USES AN ATTACK
CALLED FUSHI-BARAI—IMMORTAL PURGE.
IT'S A SECRET ART, EVEN IN THE INVERSE SHINMEI SCHOOL OF FUSHI-GARI. ONLY THOSE WHO HAVE MASTERED THE MYSTERIES CAN UNLEASH IT.
FUSHI-BARAI...!
I KNEW IT WAS SOMETHING LIKE THAT!
YES.
NOW THAT I THINK ABOUT IT, IT'S SOMETHING LIKE HOW JŪZŌ-SEMPAI CAN CUT THROUGH A CONCEPT.

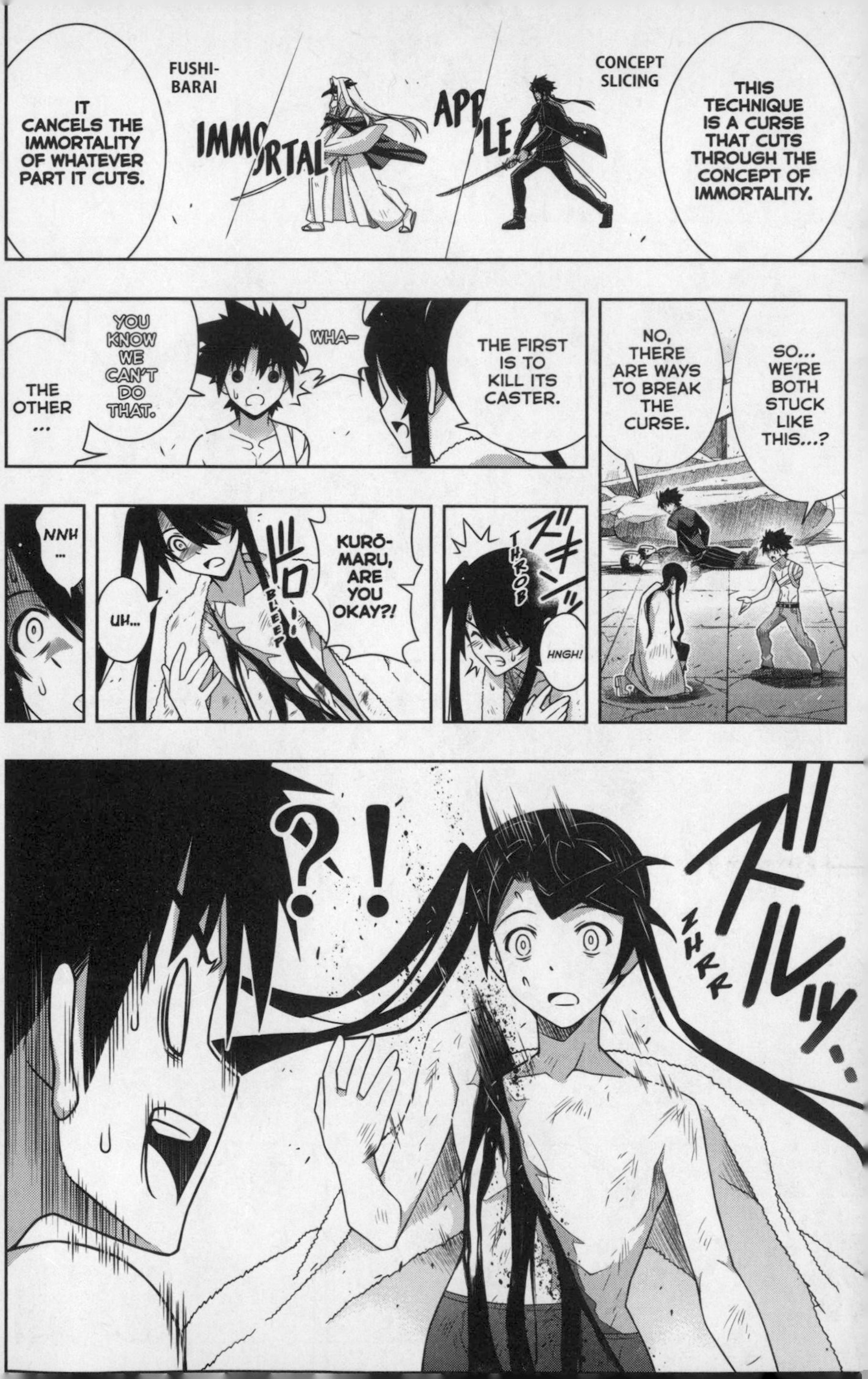
THIS TECHNIQUE IS A CURSE THAT CUTS THROUGH THE CONCEPT OF IMMORTALITY.
CONCEPT SLICING
APPLE
IMMORTAL
FUSHI-BARAI
IT CANCELS THE IMMORTALITY OF WHATEVER PART IT CUTS.
SO... WE'RE BOTH STUCK LIKE THIS...?
NO, THERE ARE WAYS TO BREAK THE CURSE.
THE FIRST IS TO KILL ITS CASTER.
WHA-
YOU KNOW WE CAN'T DO THAT.
THE OTHER ...
THROB
HNGH!
KURŌ-MARU, ARE YOU OKAY?!
BLEEP
UH...
NNH ...
?!
ZHRR

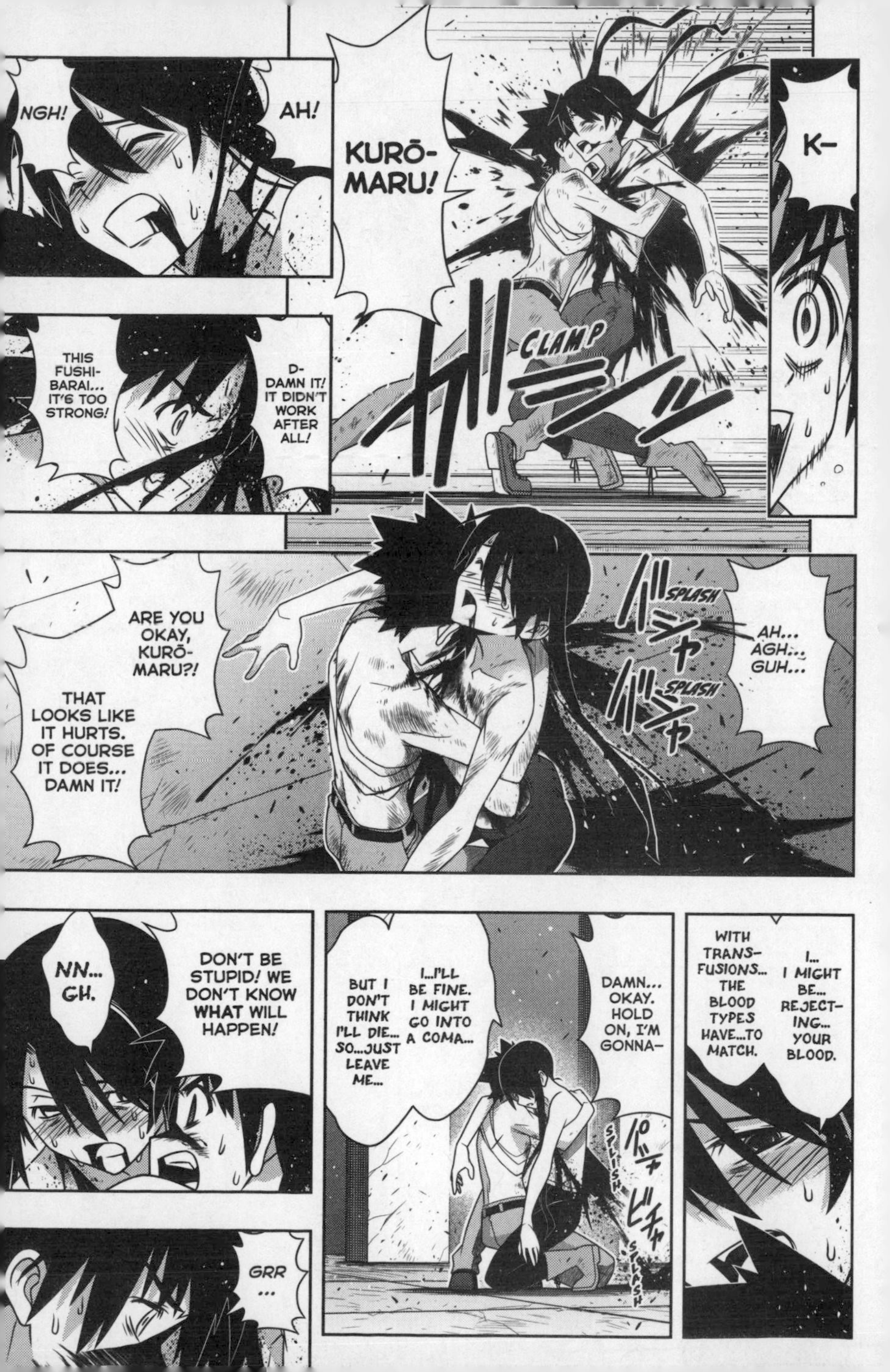
K–
KURŌ-MARU!
CLAMP
AH!
NGH!
D-DAMN IT! IT DIDN'T WORK AFTER ALL!
THIS FUSHIBARAI... IT'S TOO STRONG!
AH... AGH... GUH...
SPLASH
SPLASH
ARE YOU OKAY, KURŌ-MARU?!
THAT LOOKS LIKE IT HURTS. OF COURSE IT DOES... DAMN IT!
I... I MIGHT BE... REJECTING... YOUR BLOOD.
WITH TRANSFUSIONS... THE BLOOD TYPES HAVE...TO MATCH.
DAMN... OKAY. HOLD ON, I'M GONNA–
I...I'LL BE FINE. I MIGHT GO INTO A COMA...
BUT I DON'T THINK I'LL DIE... SO...JUST LEAVE ME...
SPLASH
SPLASH
DON'T BE STUPID! WE DON'T KNOW WHAT WILL HAPPEN!
NN... GH.
GRR...

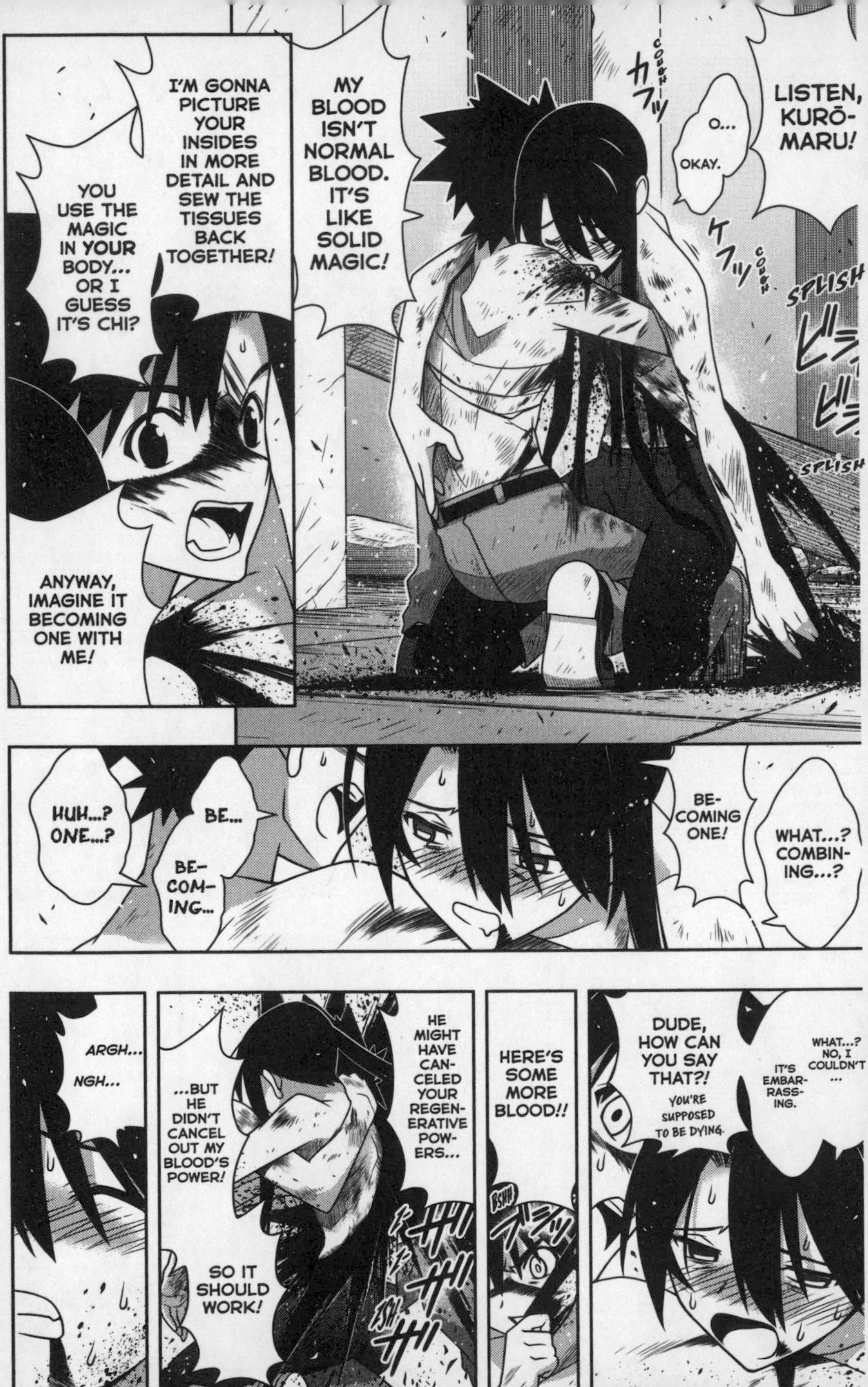

LISTEN, KURŌ-MARU!
O... OKAY.
COUGH
COUGH
MY BLOOD ISN'T NORMAL BLOOD. IT'S LIKE SOLID MAGIC!
SPLISH
SPLISH
I'M GONNA PICTURE YOUR INSIDES IN MORE DETAIL AND SEW THE TISSUES BACK TOGETHER!
YOU USE THE MAGIC IN YOUR BODY... OR I GUESS IT'S CHI?
ANYWAY, IMAGINE IT BECOMING ONE WITH ME!
WHAT...? COMBINING...?
BE-COMING ONE!
BE...
BE-COMING...
HUH...? ONE...?
WHAT...? NO, I COULDN'T ...
IT'S EMBARRASSING.
DUDE, HOW CAN YOU SAY THAT?!
YOU'RE SUPPOSED TO BE DYING.
HERE'S SOME MORE BLOOD!!
BSHH
HE MIGHT HAVE CANCELED YOUR REGENERATIVE POWERS...
...BUT HE DIDN'T CANCEL OUT MY BLOOD'S POWER!
SO IT SHOULD WORK!
ARGH...
NGH...

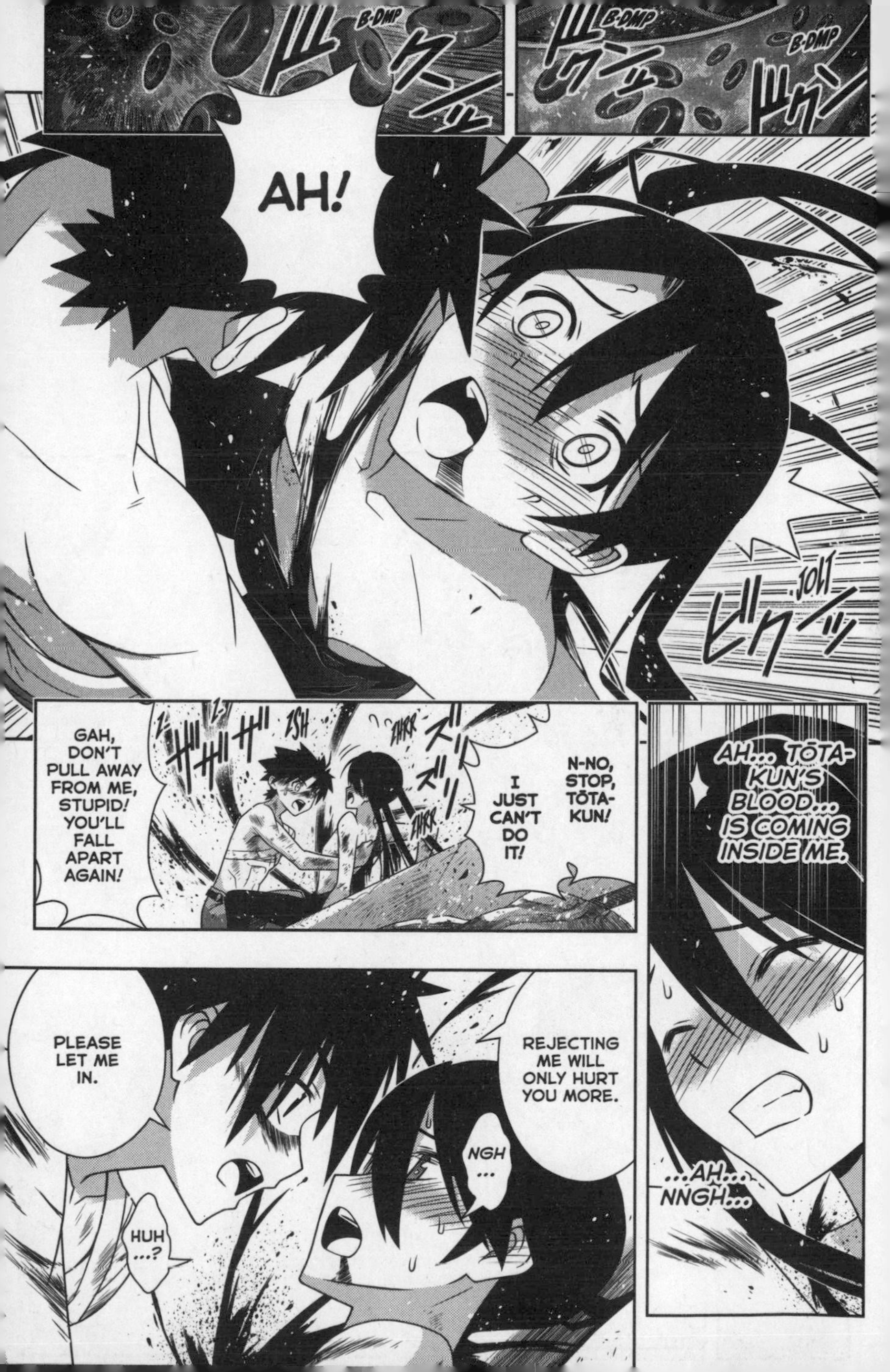
B-DMP
B-DMP
B-DMP
AH!
JOLT
AH... TŌTA-KUN'S BLOOD... IS COMING INSIDE ME.
...AH... NNGH...
ZHRR
N-NO, STOP, TŌTA-KUN!
I JUST CAN'T DO IT!
ZHRR
ZSH
GAH, DON'T PULL AWAY FROM ME, STUPID! YOU'LL FALL APART AGAIN!
REJECTING ME WILL ONLY HURT YOU MORE.
NGH ...
PLEASE LET ME IN.
HUH ...?

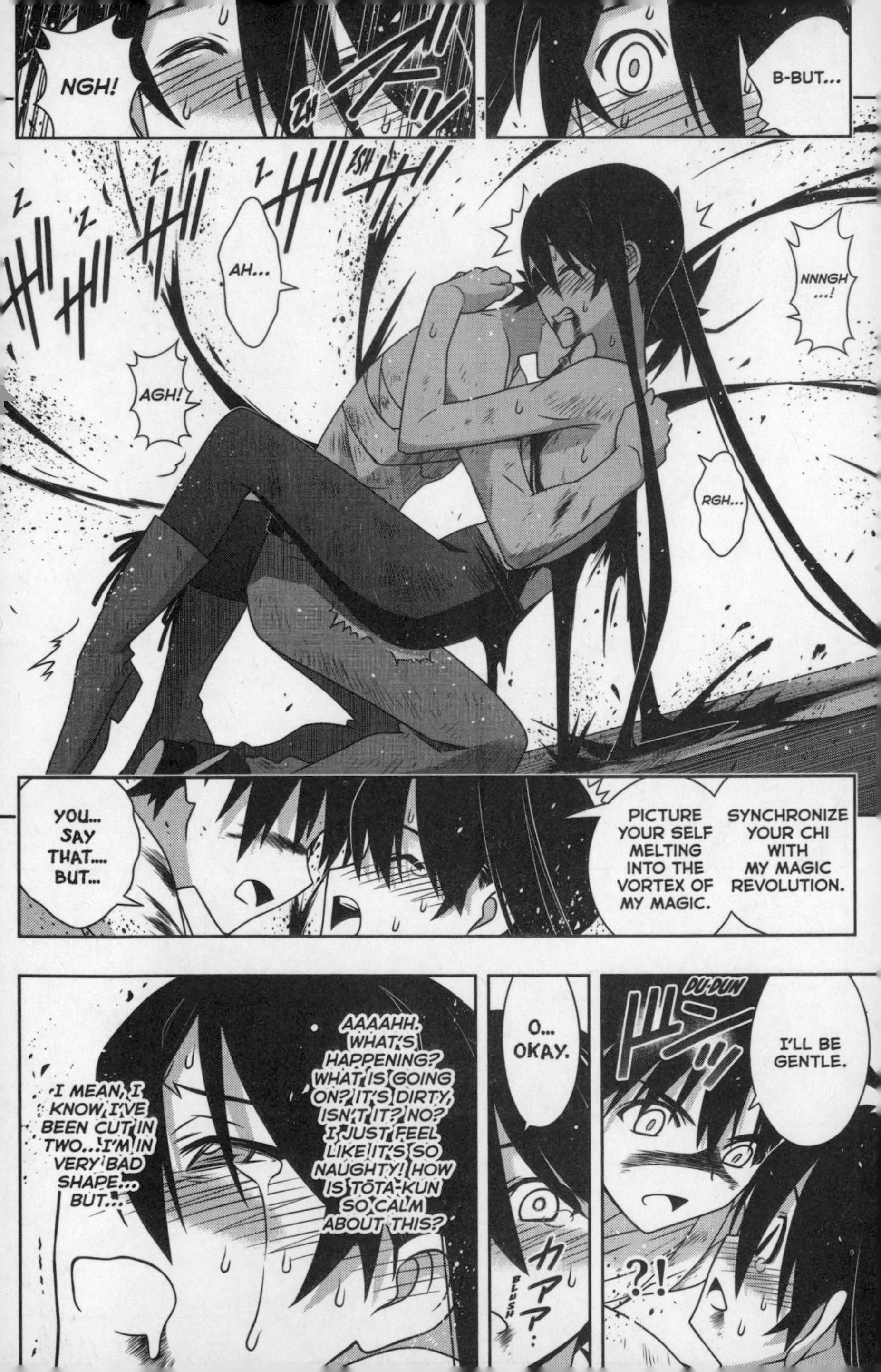

B-BUT...
NGH!
ZH
ZSH
NNNGH ...!
AH...
RGH...
AGH!
SYNCHRONIZE YOUR CHI WITH MY MAGIC REVOLUTION.
PICTURE YOUR SELF MELTING INTO THE VORTEX OF MY MAGIC.
YOU... SAY THAT.... BUT...
DU-DUN
I'LL BE GENTLE.
?!
O... OKAY.
BLUSH
AAAAHH. WHAT'S HAPPENING? WHAT IS GOING ON? IT'S DIRTY, ISN'T IT? NO? I JUST FEEL LIKE IT'S SO NAUGHTY! HOW IS TŌTA-KUN SO CALM ABOUT THIS?
I MEAN, I KNOW I'VE BEEN CUT IN TWO... I'M IN VERY BAD SHAPE... BUT...

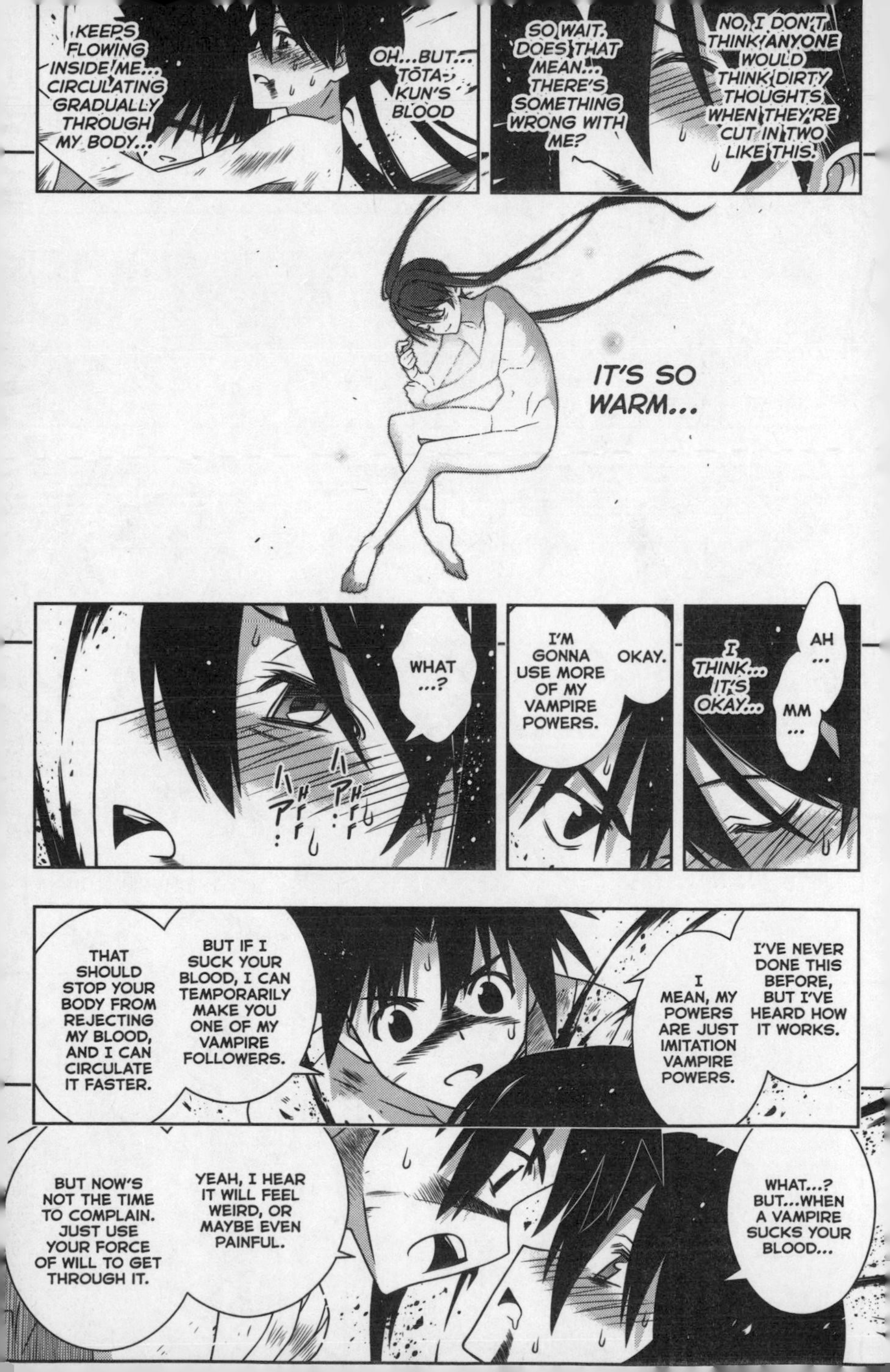
NO, I DON'T THINK ANYONE WOULD THINK DIRTY THOUGHTS WHEN THEY'RE CUT IN TWO LIKE THIS.
SO WAIT. DOES THAT MEAN... THERE'S SOMETHING WRONG WITH ME?
OH...BUT... TŌTA-KUN'S BLOOD
KEEPS FLOWING INSIDE ME... CIRCULATING GRADUALLY THROUGH MY BODY...
IT'S SO WARM...
AH ...
I THINK... IT'S OKAY...
MM ...
OKAY.
I'M GONNA USE MORE OF MY VAMPIRE POWERS.
WHAT ...?
HAH
HAH
I'VE NEVER DONE THIS BEFORE, BUT I'VE HEARD HOW IT WORKS.
I MEAN, MY POWERS ARE JUST IMITATION VAMPIRE POWERS.
BUT IF I SUCK YOUR BLOOD, I CAN TEMPORARILY MAKE YOU ONE OF MY VAMPIRE FOLLOWERS.
THAT SHOULD STOP YOUR BODY FROM REJECTING MY BLOOD, AND I CAN CIRCULATE IT FASTER.
WHAT...? BUT...WHEN A VAMPIRE SUCKS YOUR BLOOD...
YEAH, I HEAR IT WILL FEEL WEIRD, OR MAYBE EVEN PAINFUL.
BUT NOW'S NOT THE TIME TO COMPLAIN. JUST USE YOUR FORCE OF WILL TO GET THROUGH IT.

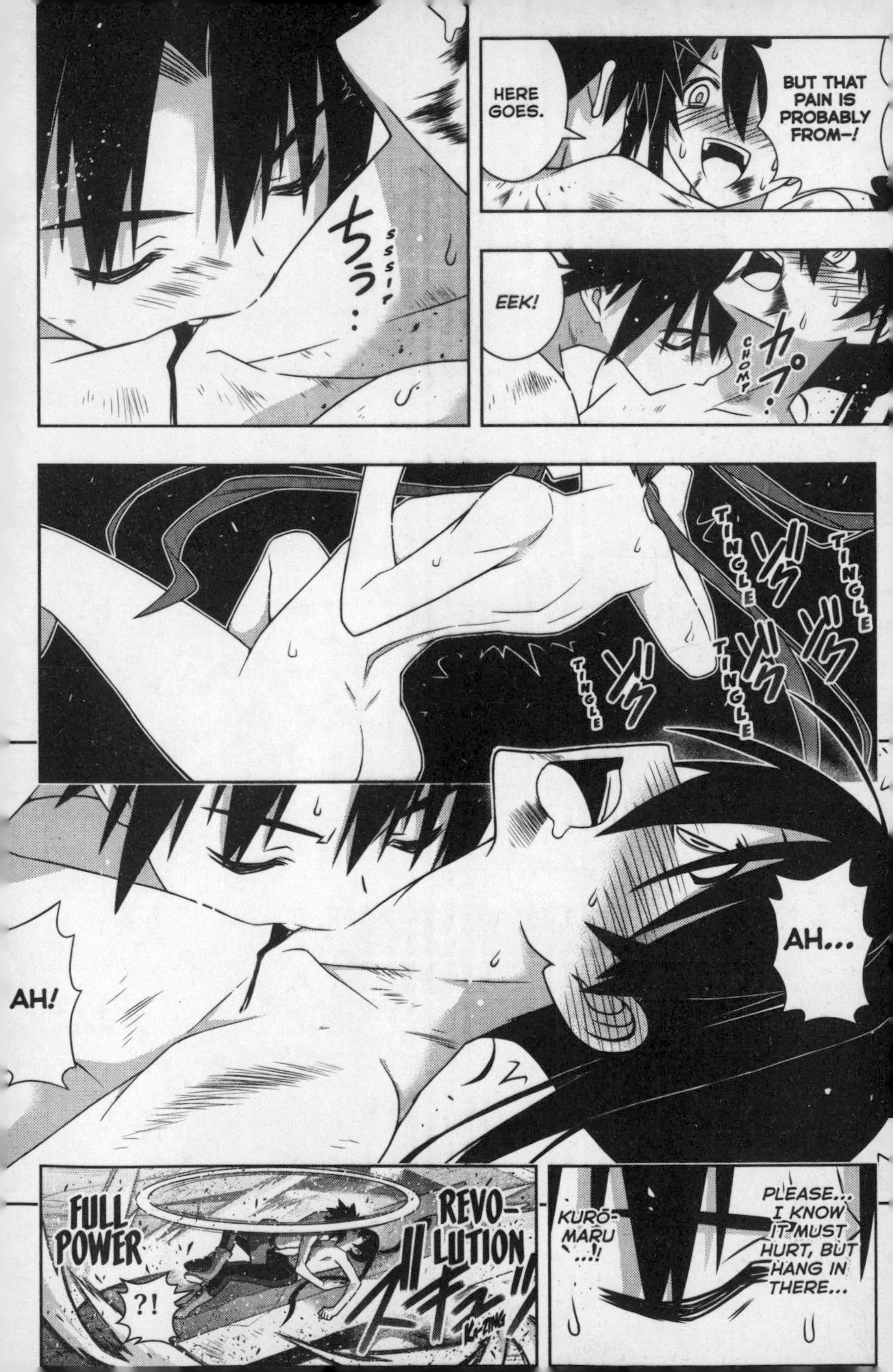
BUT THAT PAIN IS PROBABLY FROM–!
HERE GOES.
EEK!
カプ・・
CHOMP
ちう・・
SSSIP
ゾク
TINGLE
ゾク
TINGLE
ゾク
TINGLE
ゾク
TINGLE
AH...
AH!
PLEASE... I KNOW IT MUST HURT, BUT HANG IN THERE...
KURŌ-MARU ...!!
FULL POWER
REVO-LUTION
Ka-ZING
?!

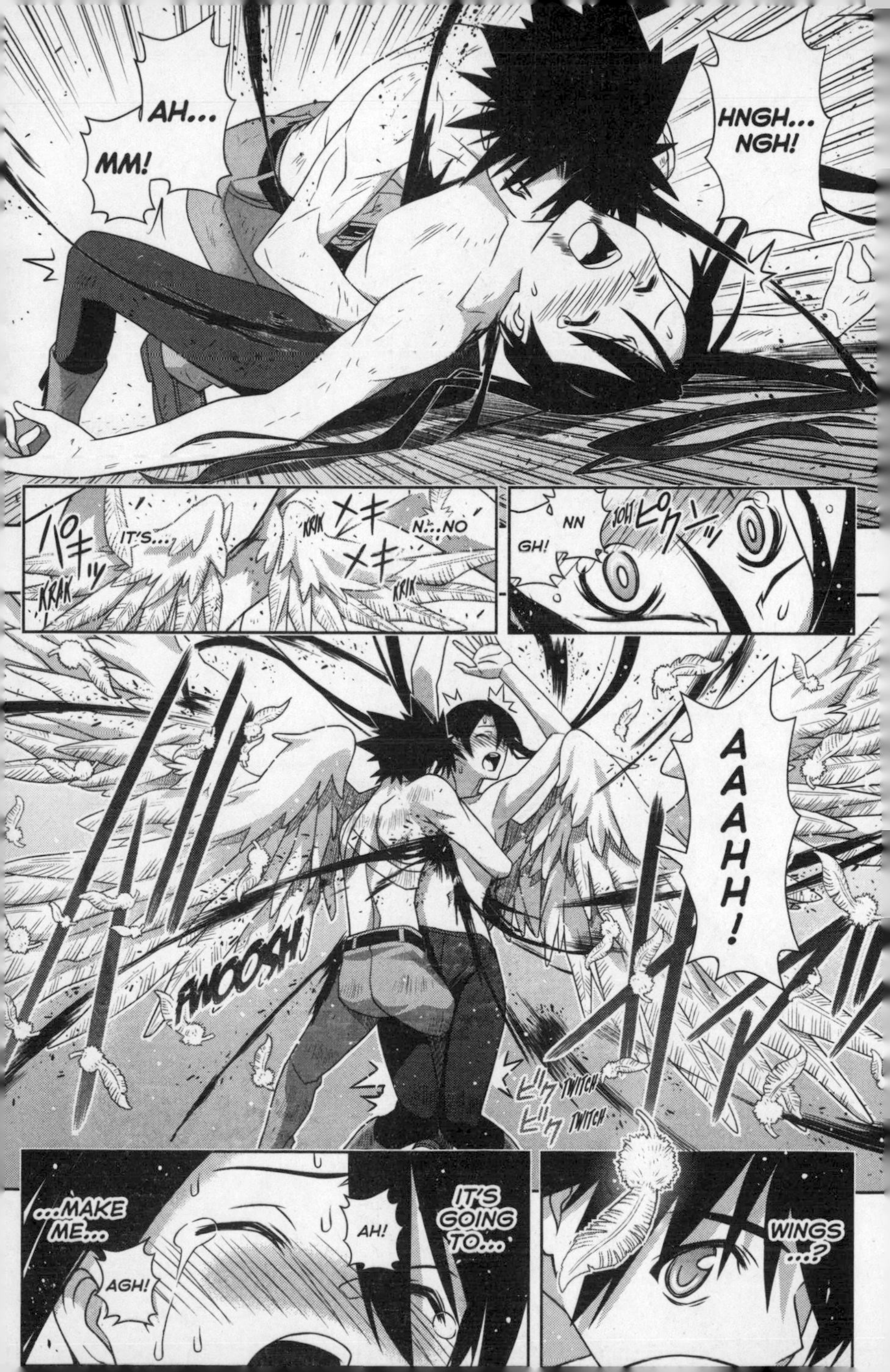
HNGH... NGH!
AH... MM!
NN GH!
ピクンッ JOLT
N...NO
メキメキ KRIK KRIK
IT'S...
パキッ KRAK
AAAAHH!
FWOOSH
ビクッ TWITCH
ビクッ TWITCH
WINGS ...?
IT'S GOING TO...
AH!
...MAKE ME...
AGH!

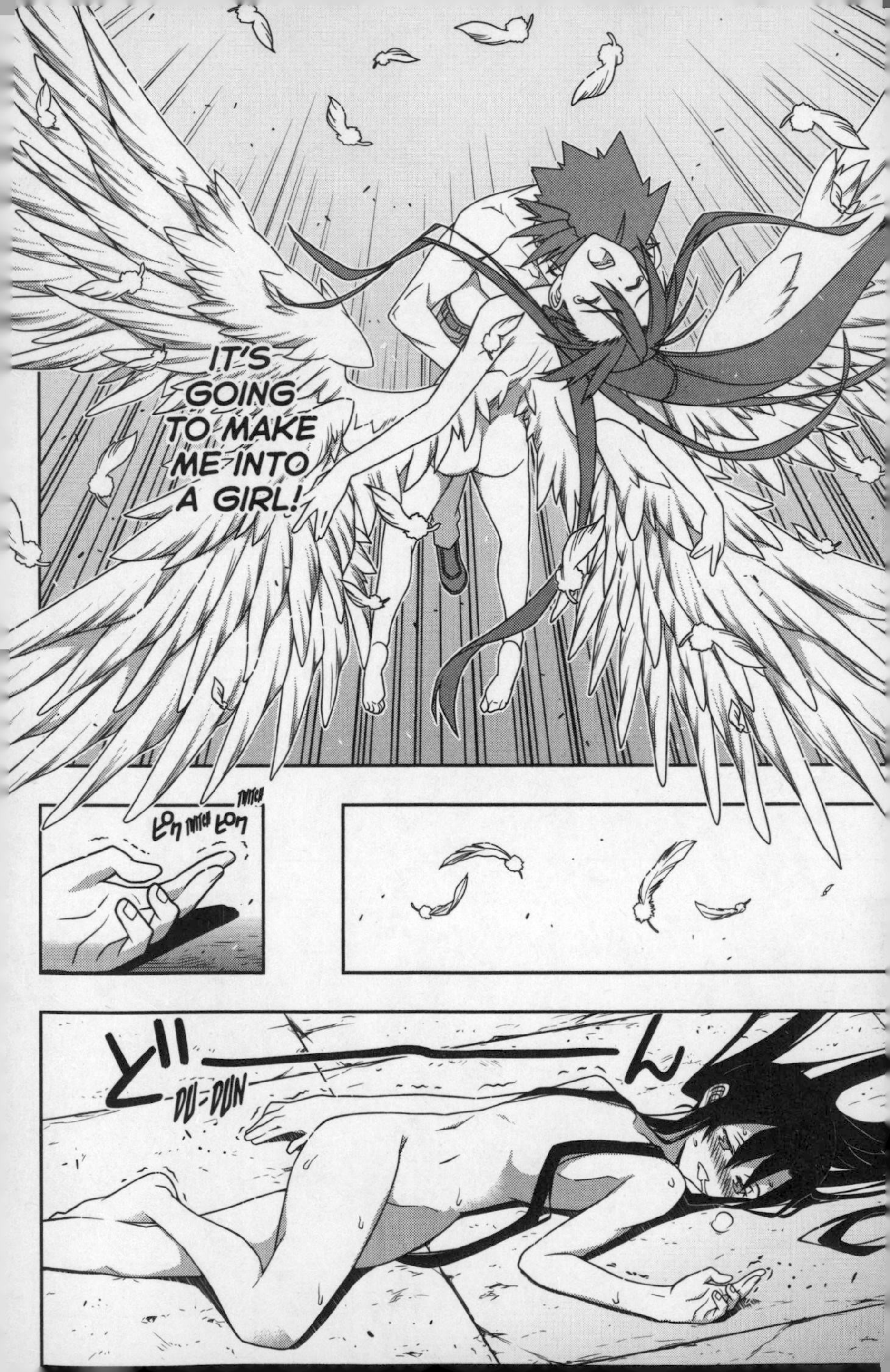
IT'S GOING TO MAKE ME INTO A GIRL!
ピクッ TWITCH
ピクッ TWITCH
どーーーん
DU-DUN

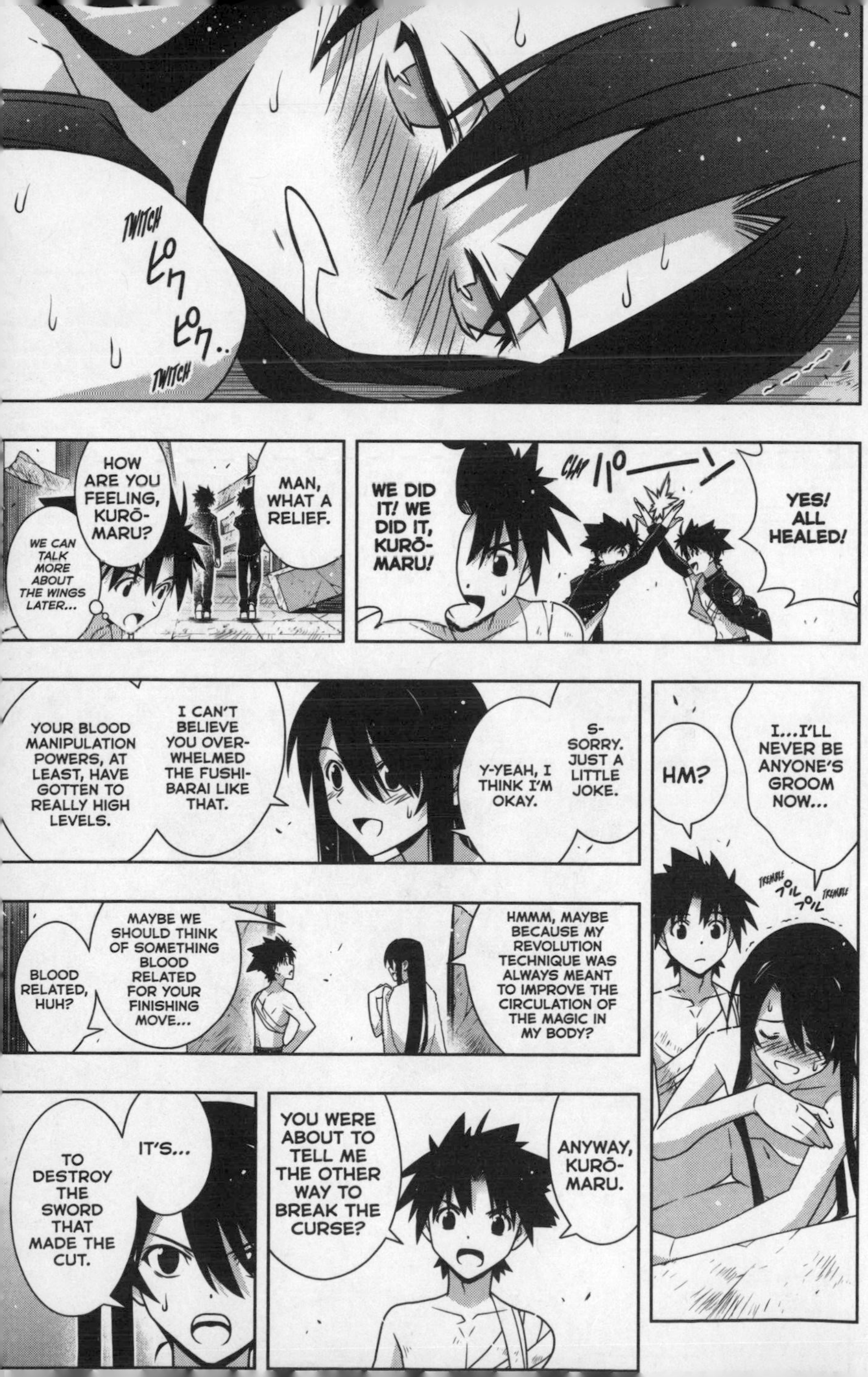
TWITCH
ピク
ピク..
TWITCH
YES! ALL HEALED!
CLAP
パーーン
WE DID IT! WE DID IT, KURŌ-MARU!
MAN, WHAT A RELIEF.
HOW ARE YOU FEELING, KURŌ-MARU?
WE CAN TALK MORE ABOUT THE WINGS LATER...
I...I'LL NEVER BE ANYONE'S GROOM NOW...
HM?
TREMBLE
プルプル
TREMBLE
S-SORRY. JUST A LITTLE JOKE.
Y-YEAH, I THINK I'M OKAY.
I CAN'T BELIEVE YOU OVER-WHELMED THE FUSHI-BARAI LIKE THAT.
YOUR BLOOD MANIPULATION POWERS, AT LEAST, HAVE GOTTEN TO REALLY HIGH LEVELS.
HMMM, MAYBE BECAUSE MY REVOLUTION TECHNIQUE WAS ALWAYS MEANT TO IMPROVE THE CIRCULATION OF THE MAGIC IN MY BODY?
MAYBE WE SHOULD THINK OF SOMETHING BLOOD RELATED FOR YOUR FINISHING MOVE...
BLOOD RELATED, HUH?
ANYWAY, KURŌ-MARU.
YOU WERE ABOUT TO TELL ME THE OTHER WAY TO BREAK THE CURSE?
IT'S...
TO DESTROY THE SWORD THAT MADE THE CUT.

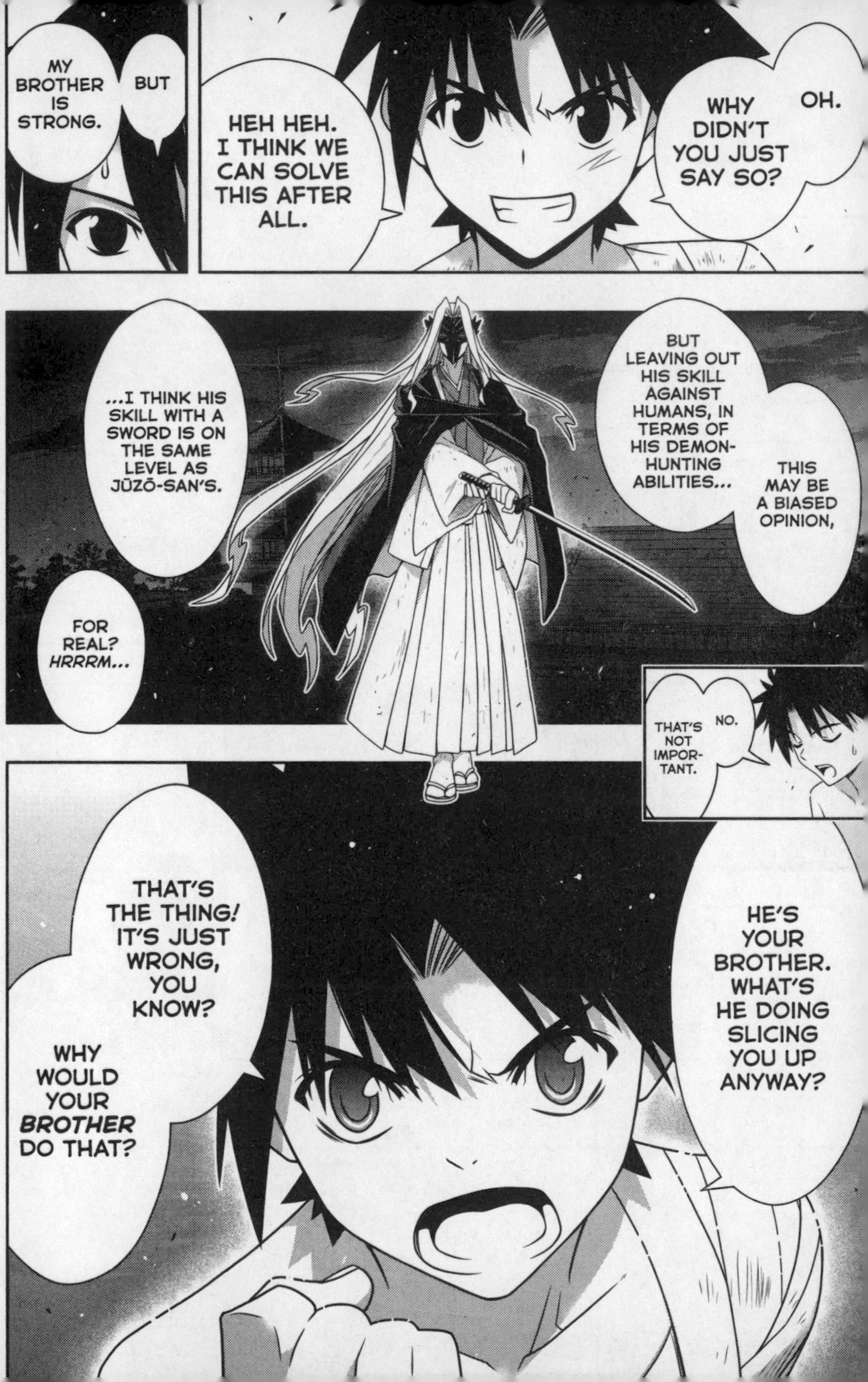
OH.
WHY DIDN'T YOU JUST SAY SO?
HEH HEH. I THINK WE CAN SOLVE THIS AFTER ALL.
BUT
MY BROTHER IS STRONG.
THIS MAY BE A BIASED OPINION,
BUT LEAVING OUT HIS SKILL AGAINST HUMANS, IN TERMS OF HIS DEMON-HUNTING ABILITIES...
...I THINK HIS SKILL WITH A SWORD IS ON THE SAME LEVEL AS JŪZŌ-SAN'S.
FOR REAL? *HRRRM...*
NO.
THAT'S NOT IMPORTANT.
HE'S YOUR BROTHER. WHAT'S HE DOING SLICING YOU UP ANYWAY?
THAT'S THE THING! IT'S JUST WRONG, YOU KNOW?
WHY WOULD YOUR *BROTHER* DO THAT?

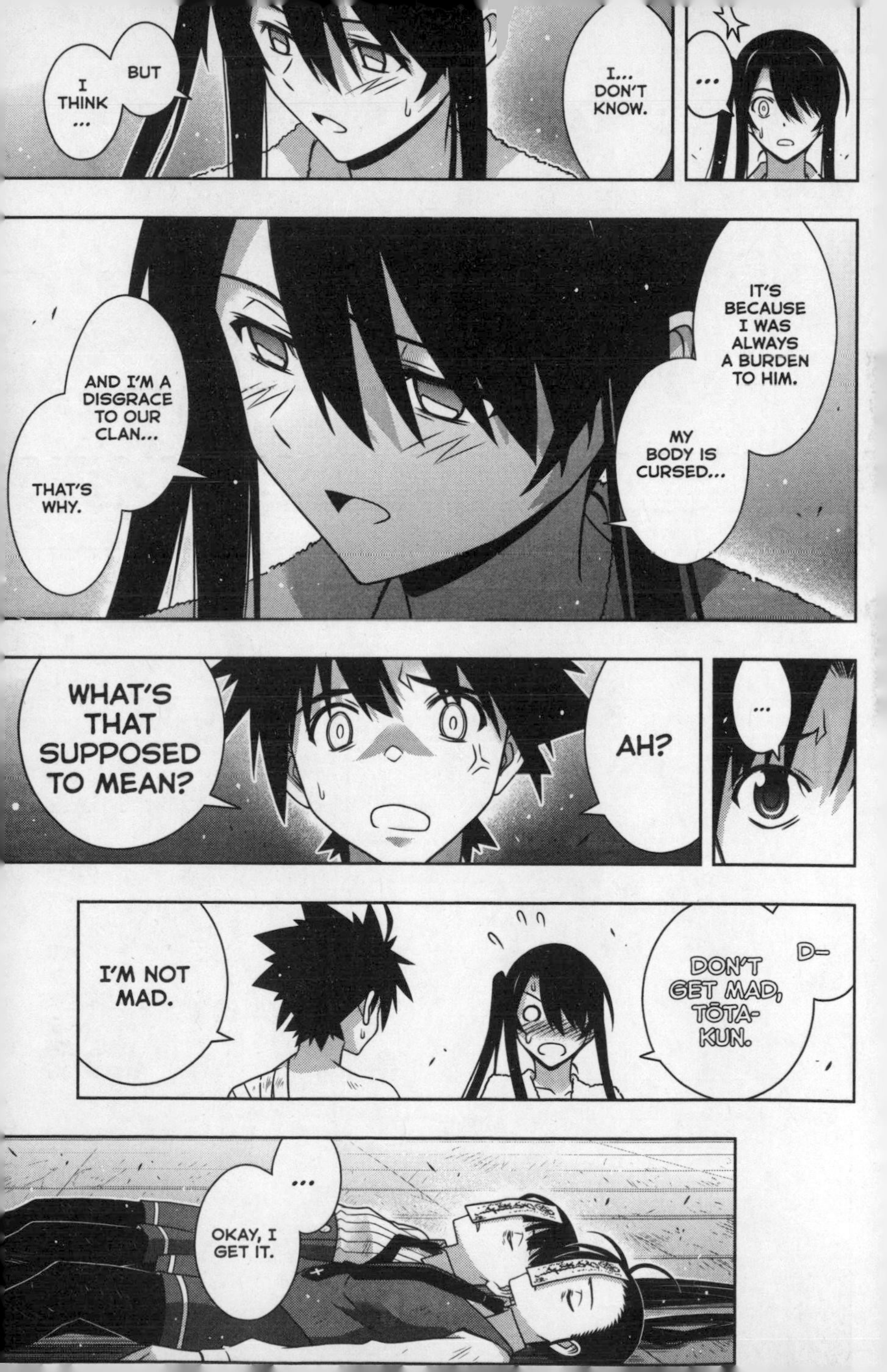
...
I... DON'T KNOW.
BUT I THINK ...
IT'S BECAUSE I WAS ALWAYS A BURDEN TO HIM.
MY BODY IS CURSED...
AND I'M A DISGRACE TO OUR CLAN...
THAT'S WHY.
...
AH?
WHAT'S THAT SUPPOSED TO MEAN?
D- DON'T GET MAD, TŌTA-KUN.
I'M NOT MAD.
...
OKAY, I GET IT.

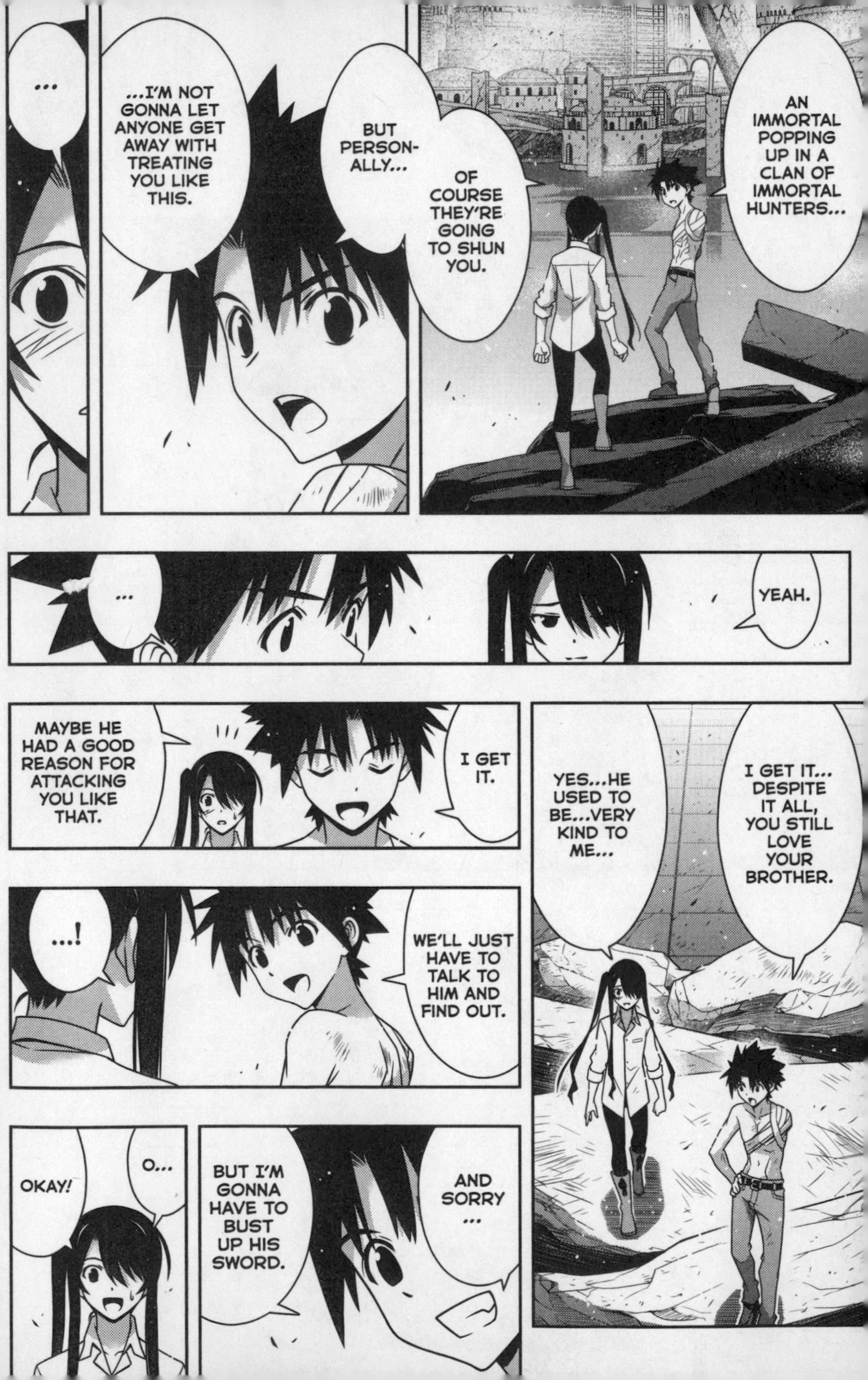
AN IMMORTAL POPPING UP IN A CLAN OF IMMORTAL HUNTERS...
OF COURSE THEY'RE GOING TO SHUN YOU.
BUT PERSON-ALLY...
...I'M NOT GONNA LET ANYONE GET AWAY WITH TREATING YOU LIKE THIS.
...
YEAH.
...
I GET IT... DESPITE IT ALL, YOU STILL LOVE YOUR BROTHER.
YES...HE USED TO BE...VERY KIND TO ME...
I GET IT.
MAYBE HE HAD A GOOD REASON FOR ATTACKING YOU LIKE THAT.
WE'LL JUST HAVE TO TALK TO HIM AND FIND OUT.
...!
AND SORRY ...
BUT I'M GONNA HAVE TO BUST UP HIS SWORD.
O...
OKAY!

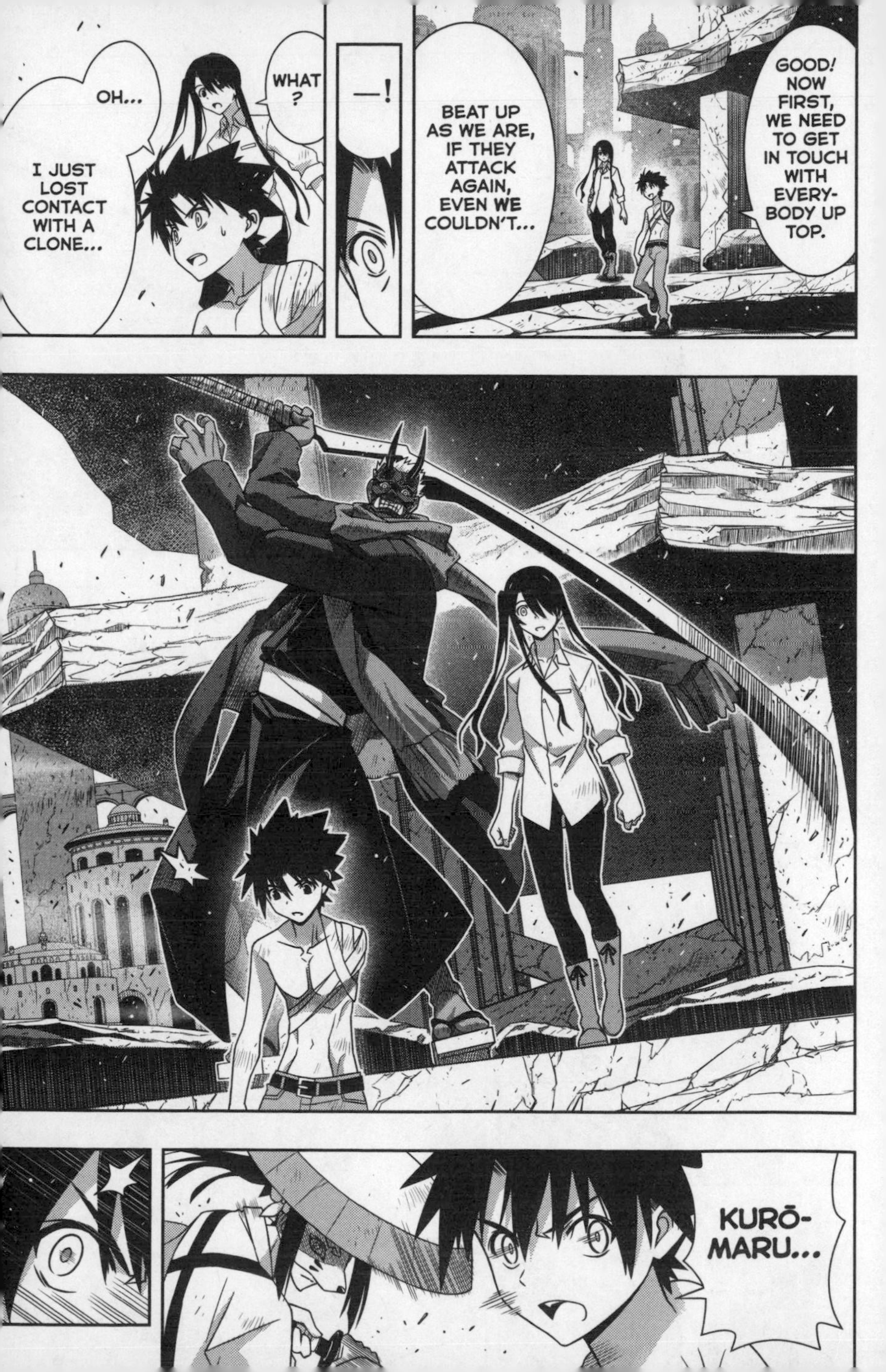
GOOD! NOW FIRST, WE NEED TO GET IN TOUCH WITH EVERY-BODY UP TOP.
BEAT UP AS WE ARE, IF THEY ATTACK AGAIN, EVEN WE COULDN'T...
—!
WHAT?
OH...
I JUST LOST CONTACT WITH A CLONE...
KURŌ-MARU...

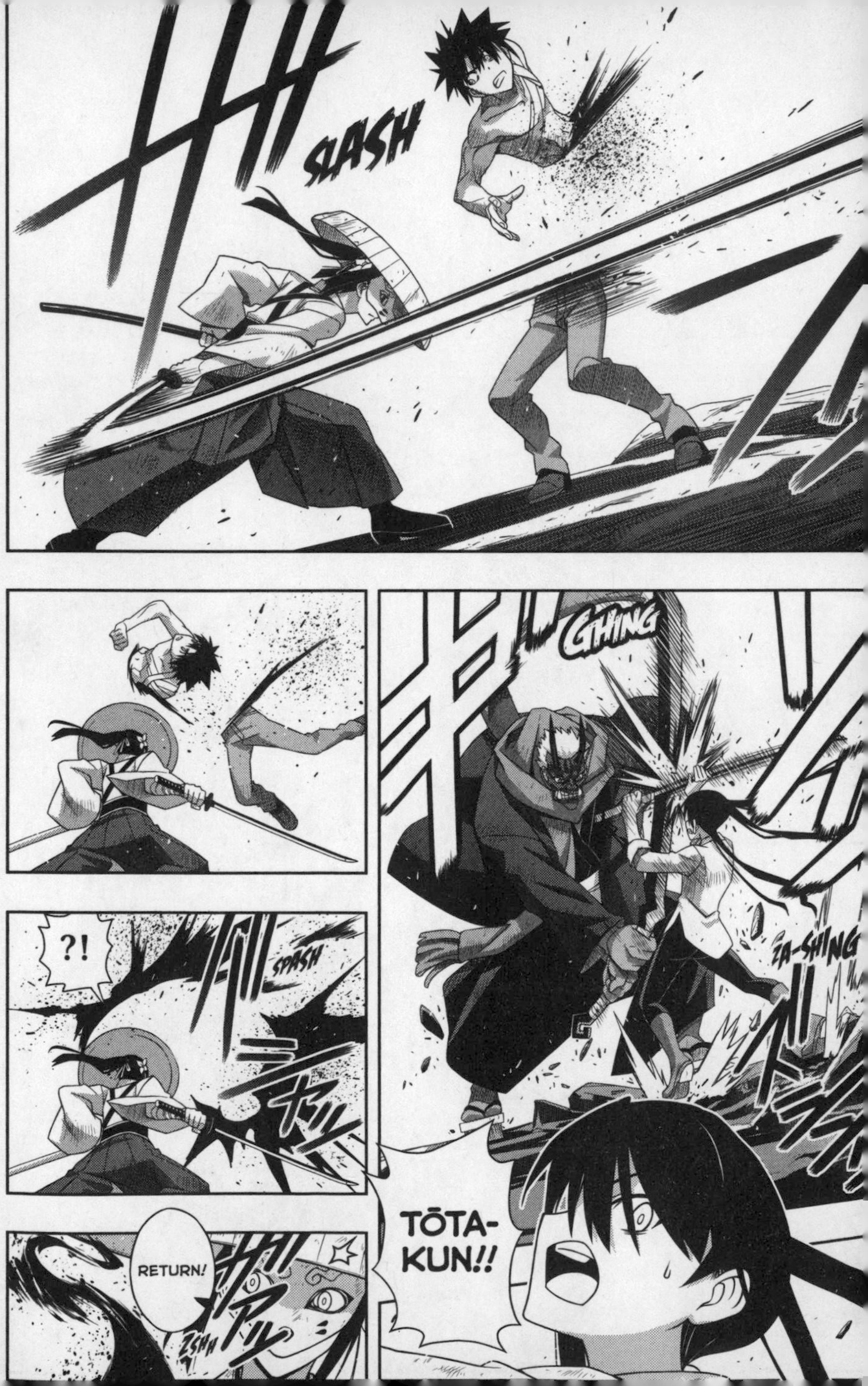
SLASH
GCHING
ZA-SHING
TŌTA-KUN!!
?!
SPASH
RETURN!
ZSHH

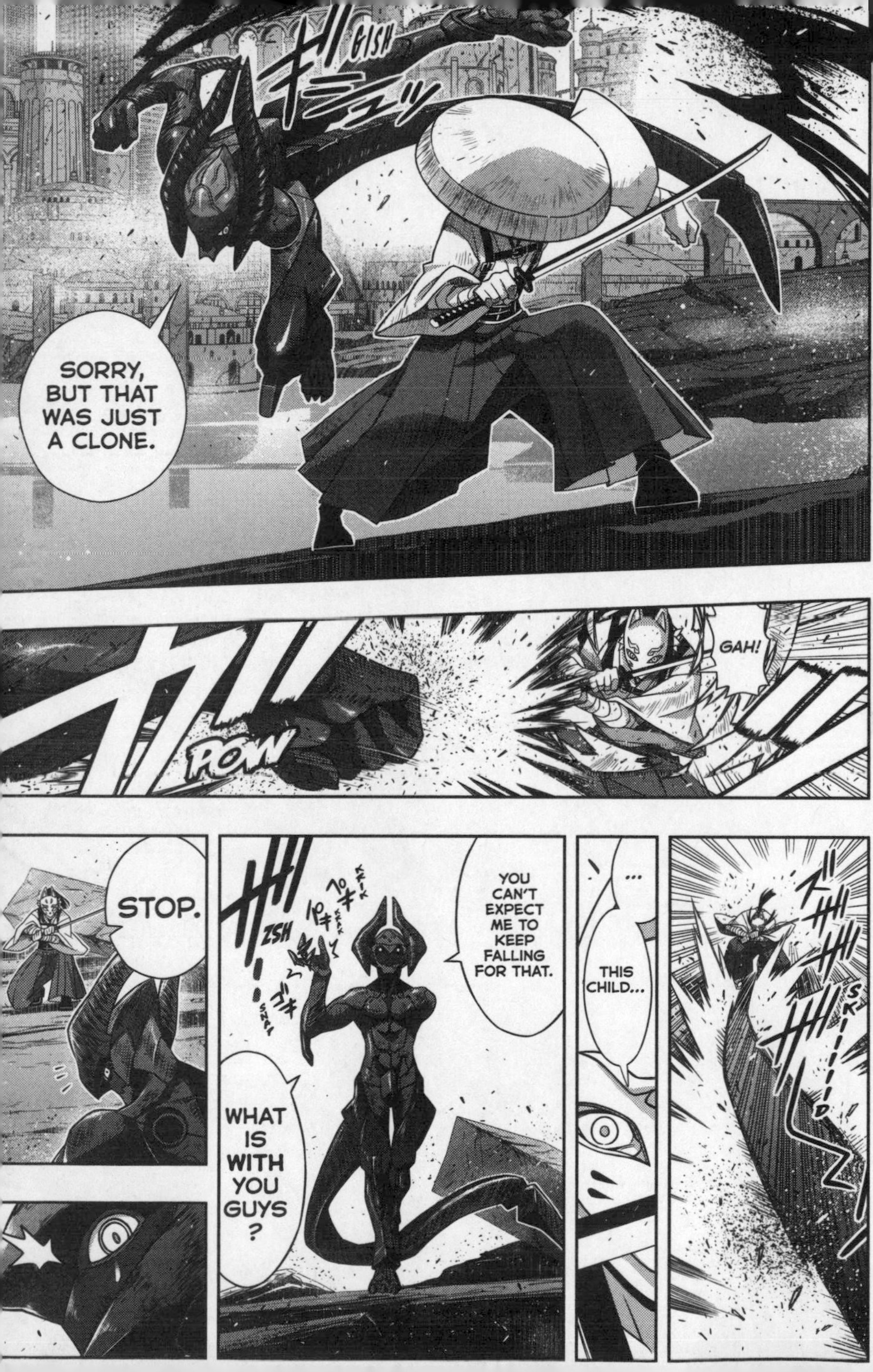
GISH
SORRY, BUT THAT WAS JUST A CLONE.
GAH!
POW
...
THIS CHILD...
YOU CAN'T EXPECT ME TO KEEP FALLING FOR THAT.
ZSH
WHAT IS WITH YOU GUYS?
STOP.

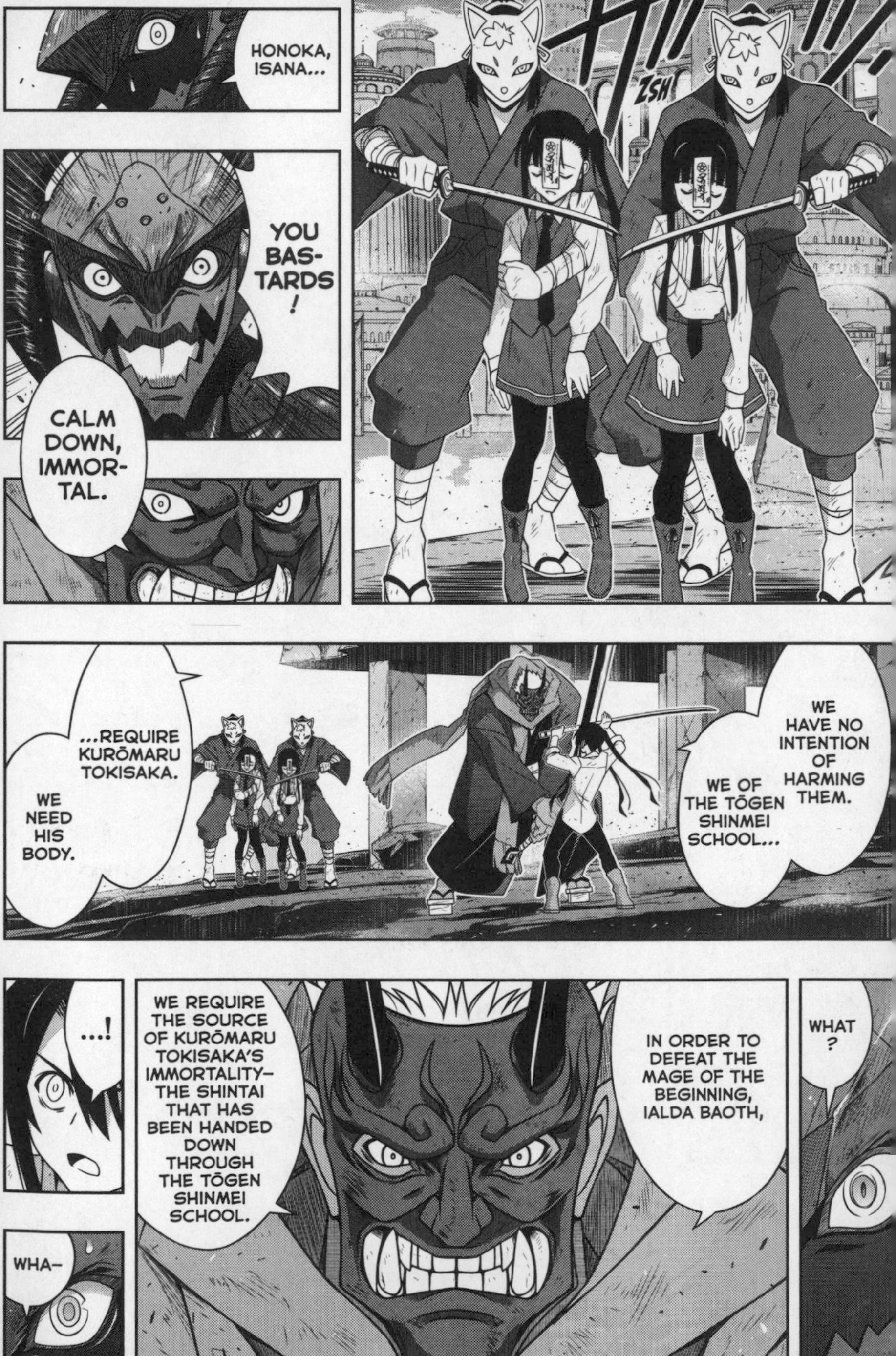
ZSH
HONOKA, ISANA...
YOU BASTARDS!
CALM DOWN, IMMORTAL.
WE HAVE NO INTENTION OF HARMING THEM.
WE OF THE TŌGEN SHINMEI SCHOOL...
...REQUIRE KURŌMARU TOKISAKA.
WE NEED HIS BODY.
WHAT?
IN ORDER TO DEFEAT THE MAGE OF THE BEGINNING, IALDA BAOTH,
WE REQUIRE THE SOURCE OF KURŌMARU TOKISAKA'S IMMORTALITY–THE SHINTAI THAT HAS BEEN HANDED DOWN THROUGH THE TŌGEN SHINMEI SCHOOL.
...!
WHA–

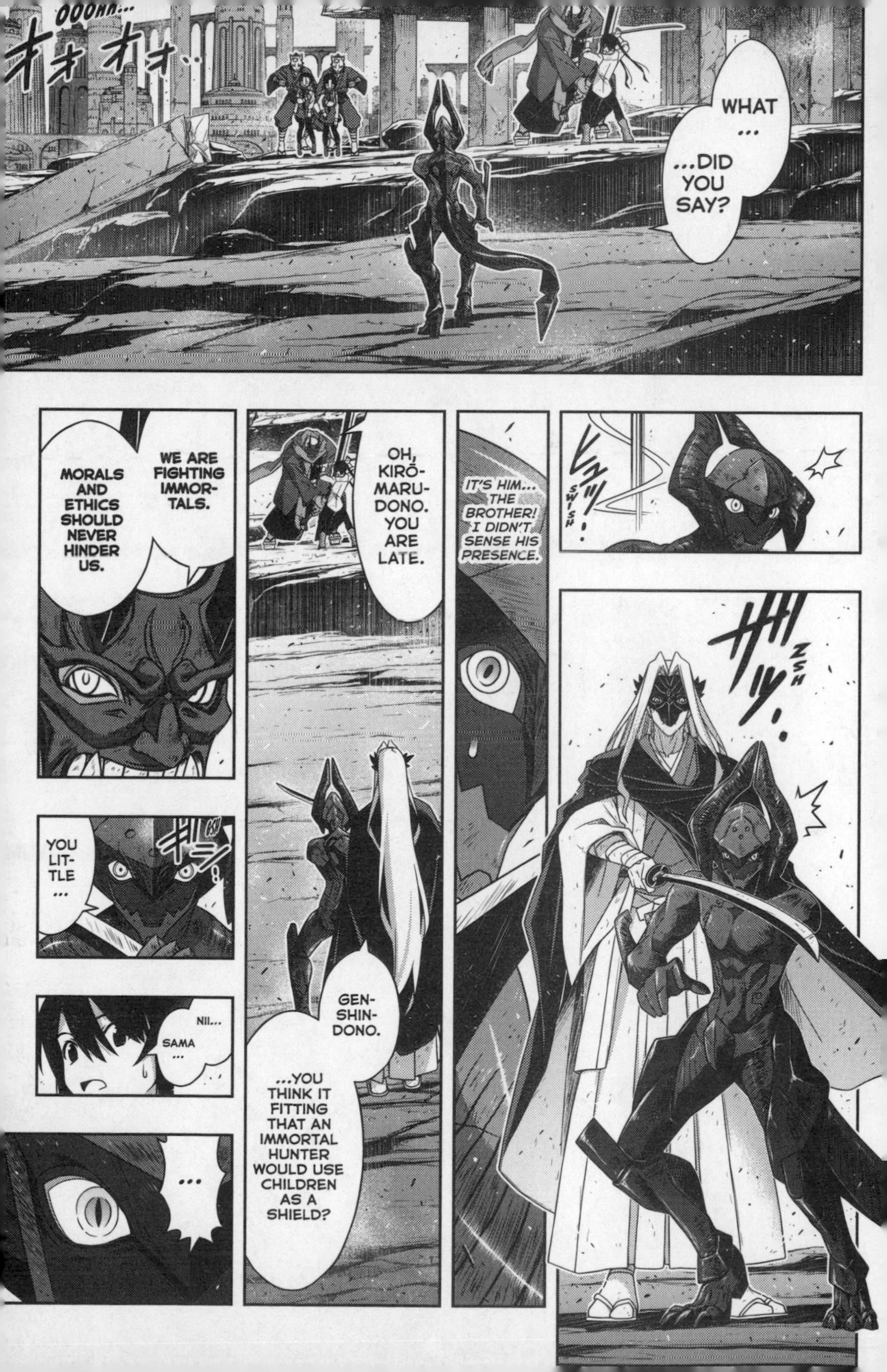
OOOHH...
WHAT ... ...DID YOU SAY?
SWISH
ZSH
IT'S HIM... THE BROTHER! I DIDN'T SENSE HIS PRESENCE.
OH, KIRŌ-MARU-DONO. YOU ARE LATE.
GEN-SHIN-DONO.
...YOU THINK IT FITTING THAT AN IMMORTAL HUNTER WOULD USE CHILDREN AS A SHIELD?
WE ARE FIGHTING IMMOR-TALS.
MORALS AND ETHICS SHOULD NEVER HINDER US.
YOU LIT-TLE ...
NII... SAMA ...
...

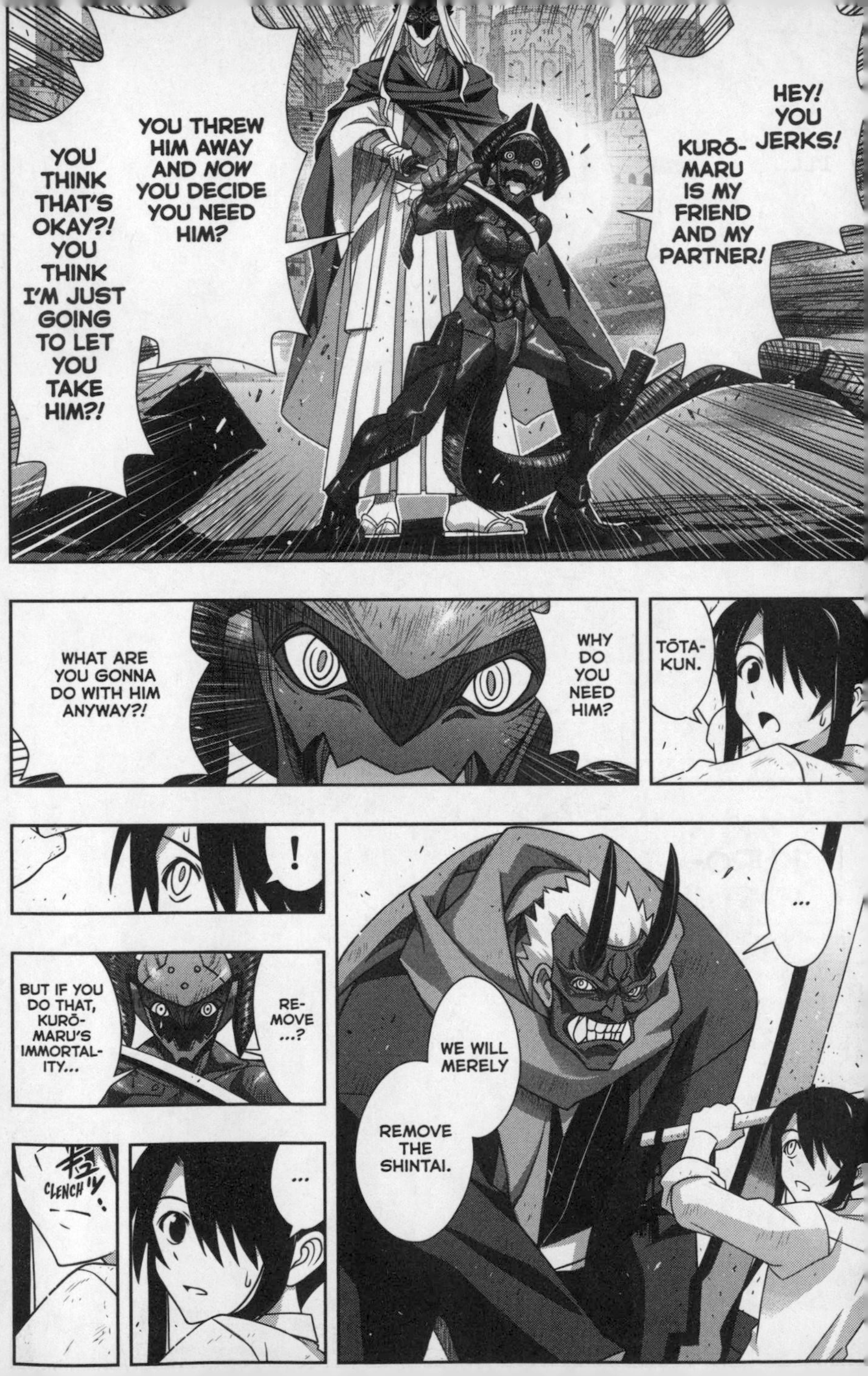
HEY! YOU JERKS!
KURŌ-MARU IS MY FRIEND AND MY PARTNER!
YOU THREW HIM AWAY AND *NOW* YOU DECIDE YOU NEED HIM?
YOU THINK THAT'S OKAY?! YOU THINK I'M JUST GOING TO LET YOU TAKE HIM?!
TŌTA-KUN.
WHY DO YOU NEED HIM?
WHAT ARE YOU GONNA DO WITH HIM ANYWAY?!
...
WE WILL MERELY
REMOVE THE SHINTAI.
!
RE-MOVE...?
BUT IF YOU DO THAT, KURŌ-MARU'S IMMORTAL-ITY...
...
CLENCH

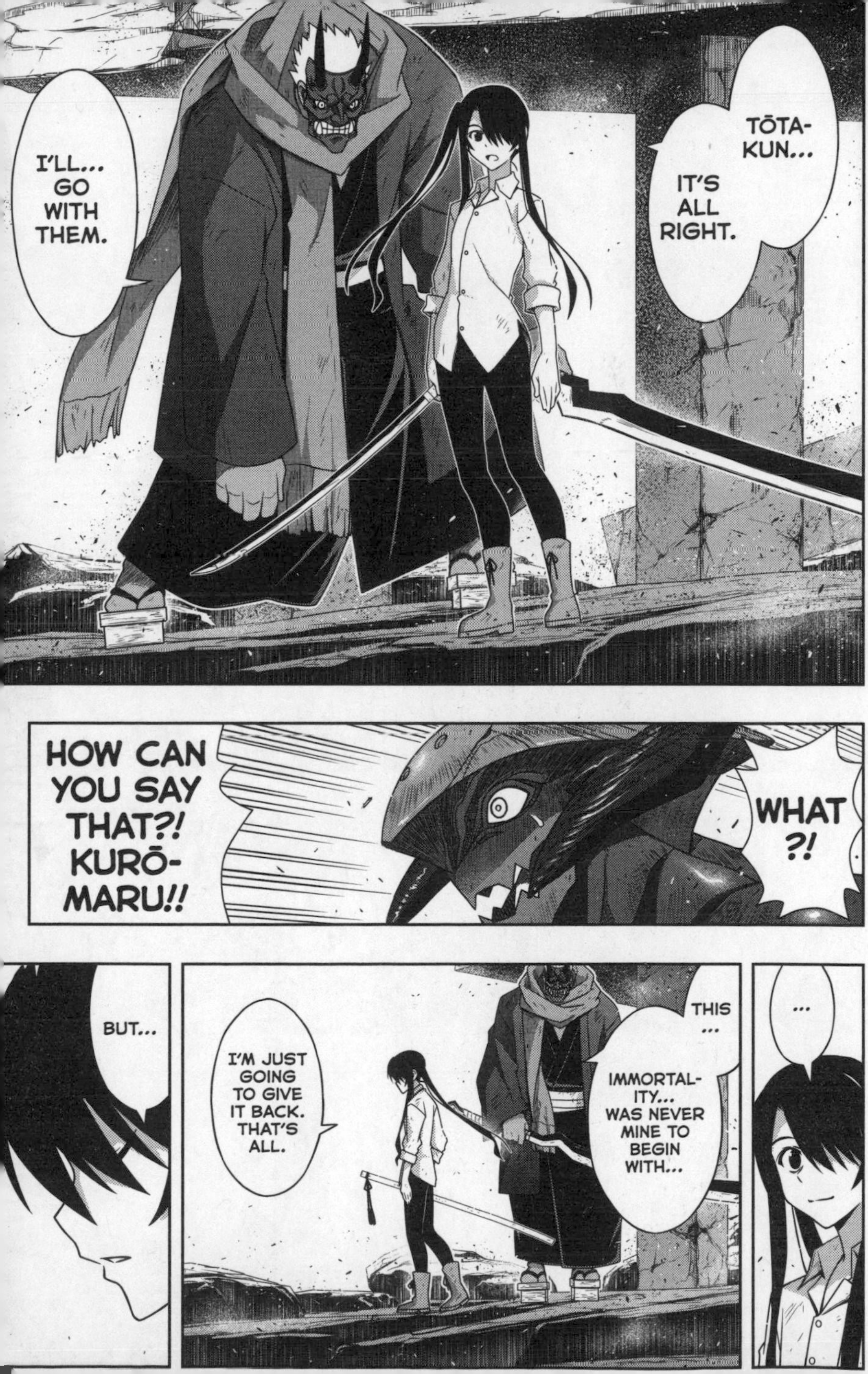
TŌTA-KUN... IT'S ALL RIGHT.
I'LL... GO WITH THEM.
WHAT?!
HOW CAN YOU SAY THAT?! KURŌ-MARU!!
...
THIS... IMMORTALITY... WAS NEVER MINE TO BEGIN WITH...
I'M JUST GOING TO GIVE IT BACK. THAT'S ALL.
BUT...

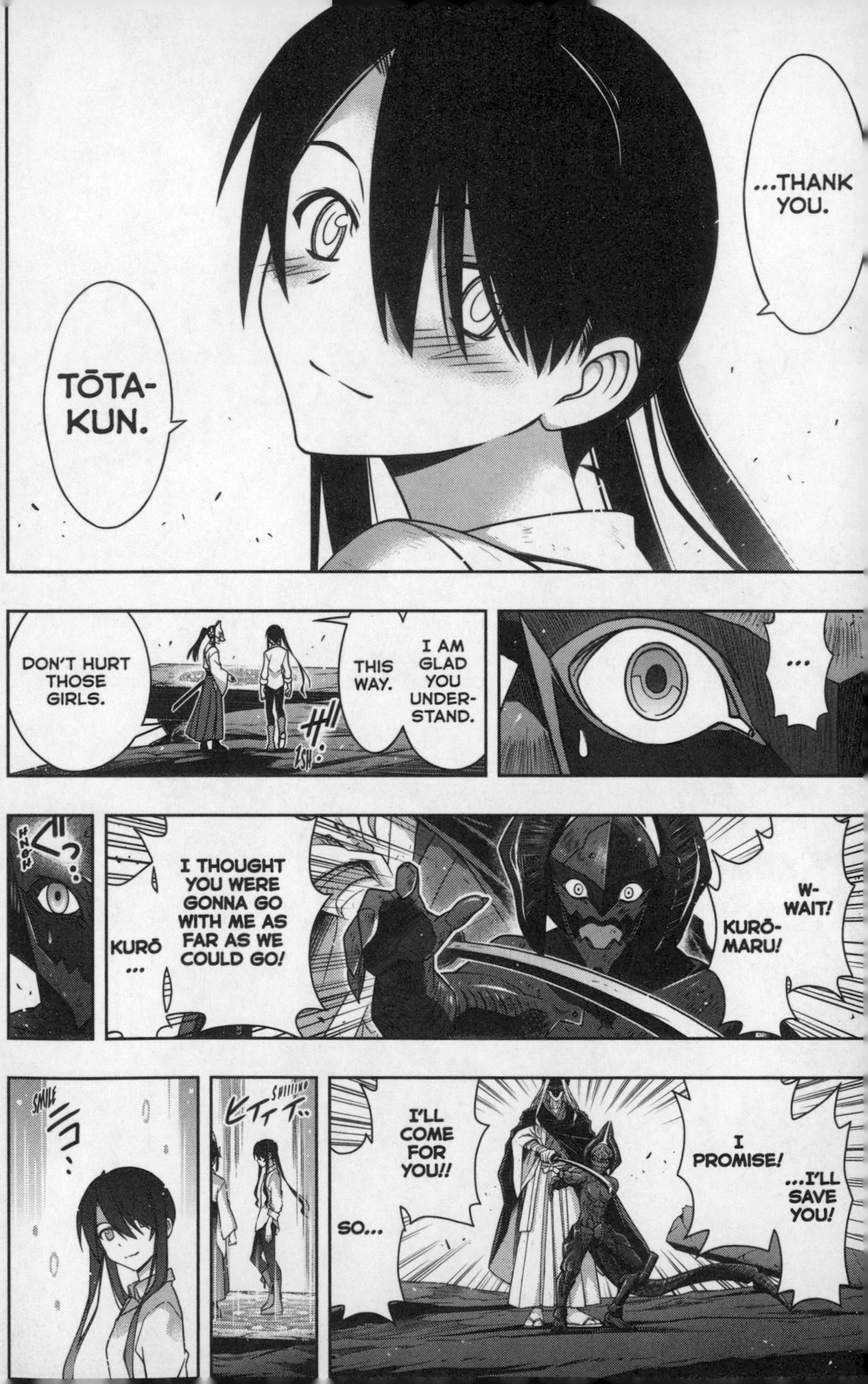
...THANK YOU.
TŌTA-KUN.
...
I AM GLAD YOU UNDERSTAND.
THIS WAY.
DON'T HURT THOSE GIRLS.
TSH
W-WAIT!
KURŌ-MARU!
I THOUGHT YOU WERE GONNA GO WITH ME AS FAR AS WE COULD GO!
KURŌ...
HNGH
I PROMISE!
...I'LL SAVE YOU!
I'LL COME FOR YOU!!
SO...
SHIIIING
SMILE

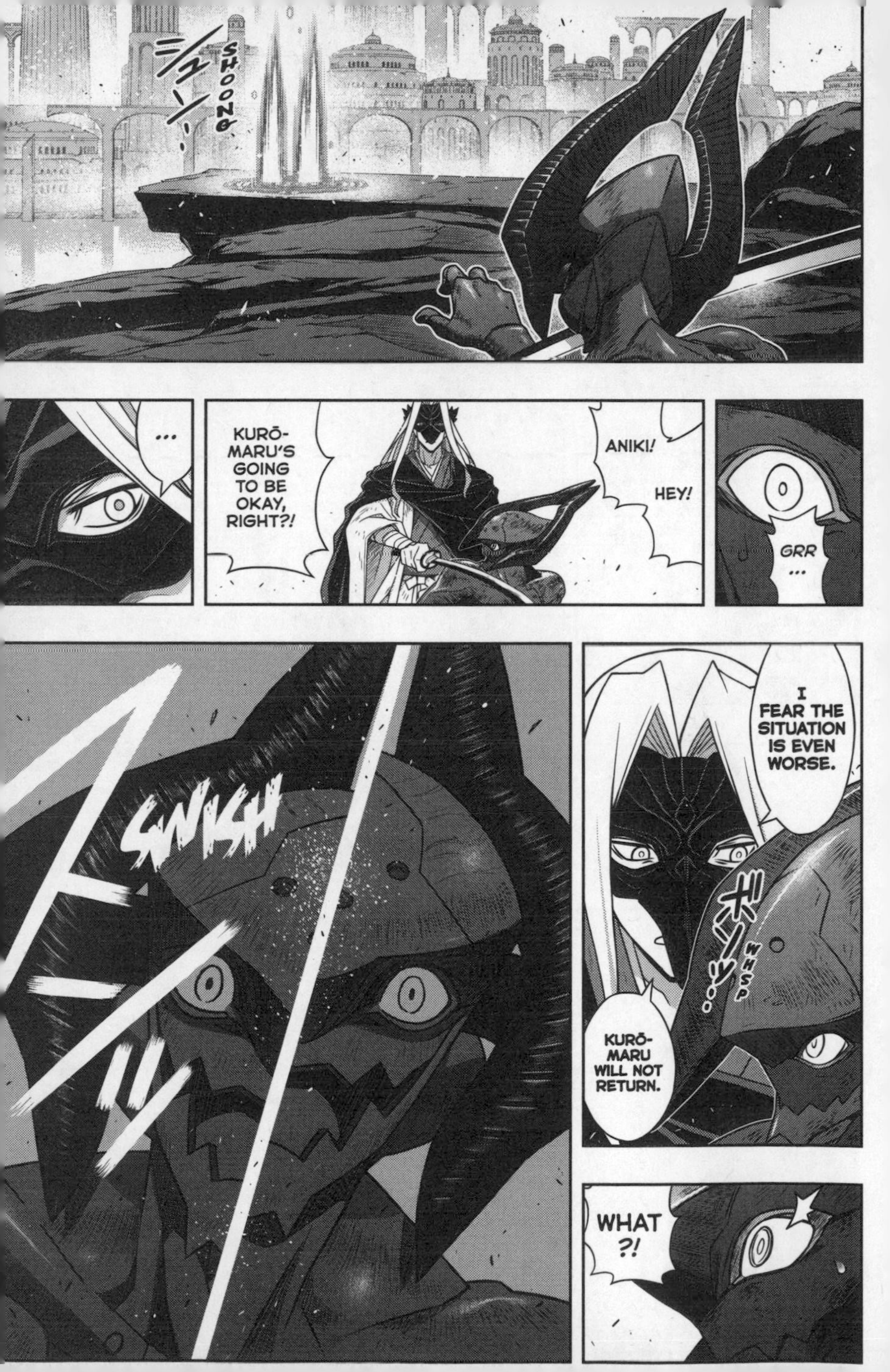
SHOONG
GRR ...
ANIKI!
HEY!
KURŌ-MARU'S GOING TO BE OKAY, RIGHT?!
...
I FEAR THE SITUATION IS EVEN WORSE.
WHSP
KURŌ-MARU WILL NOT RETURN.
WHAT ?!
SWISH

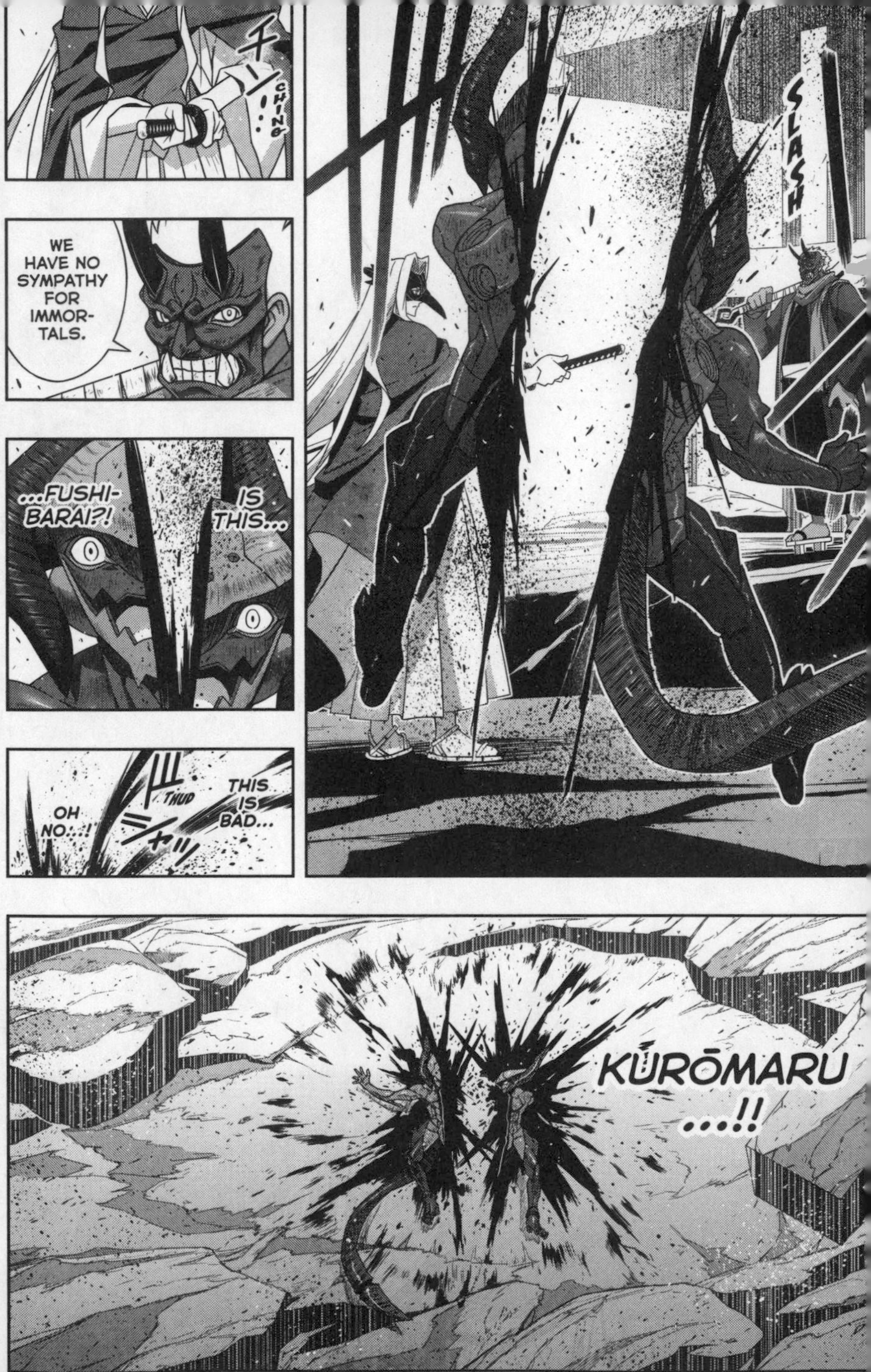
SLASH
CHING
WE HAVE NO SYMPATHY FOR IMMORTALS.
IS THIS...
...FUSHIBARAI?!
THIS IS BAD...
THUD
OH NO...!!
KURŌMARU ...!!

UQ HOLDER!

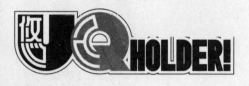

UQ
HOLDER!
ユーキューホルダー!

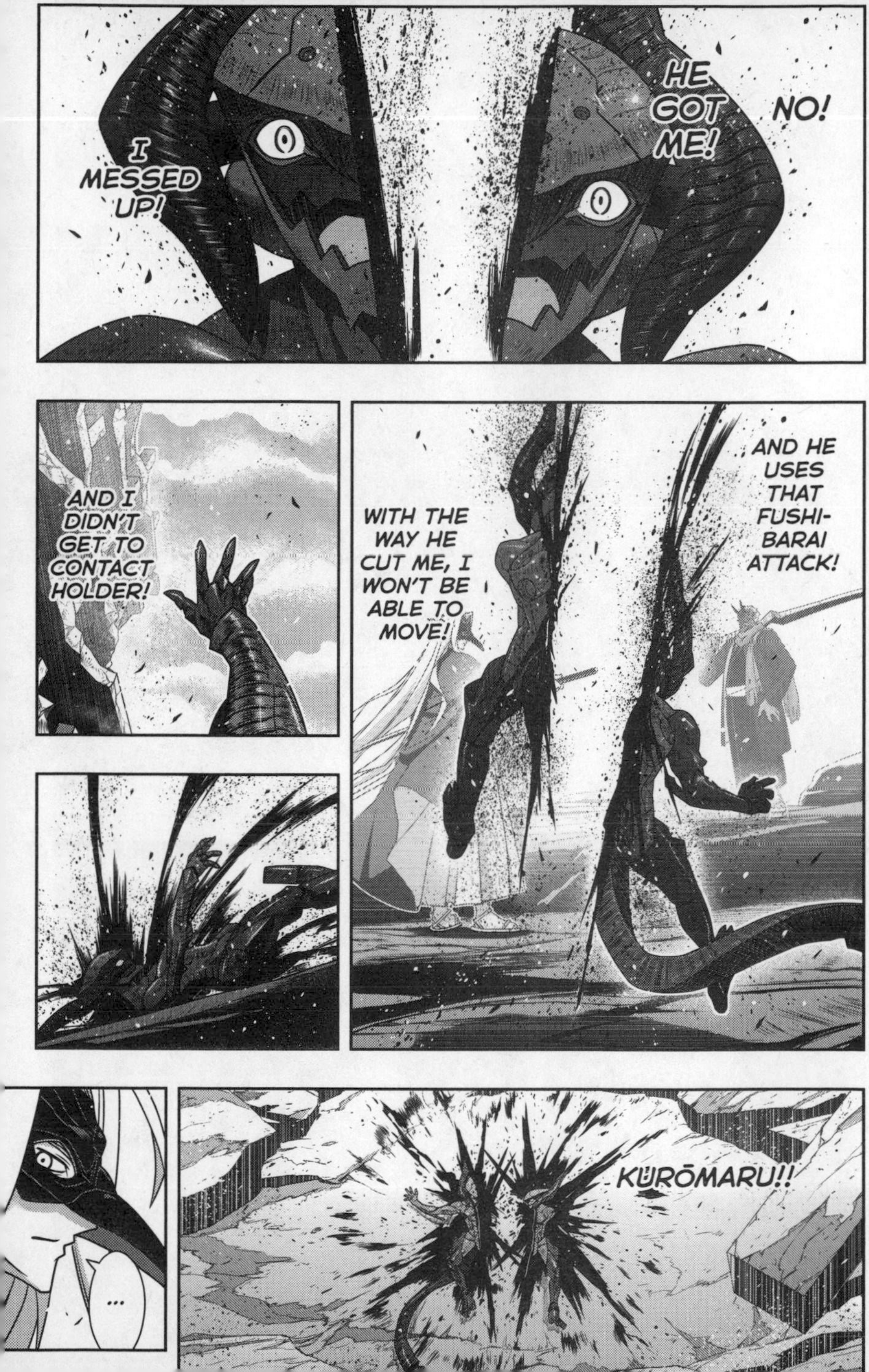
NO!
HE GOT ME!
I MESSED UP!
AND HE USES THAT FUSHI-BARAI ATTACK!
WITH THE WAY HE CUT ME, I WON'T BE ABLE TO MOVE!
AND I DIDN'T GET TO CONTACT HOLDER!
KURŌMARU!!
...

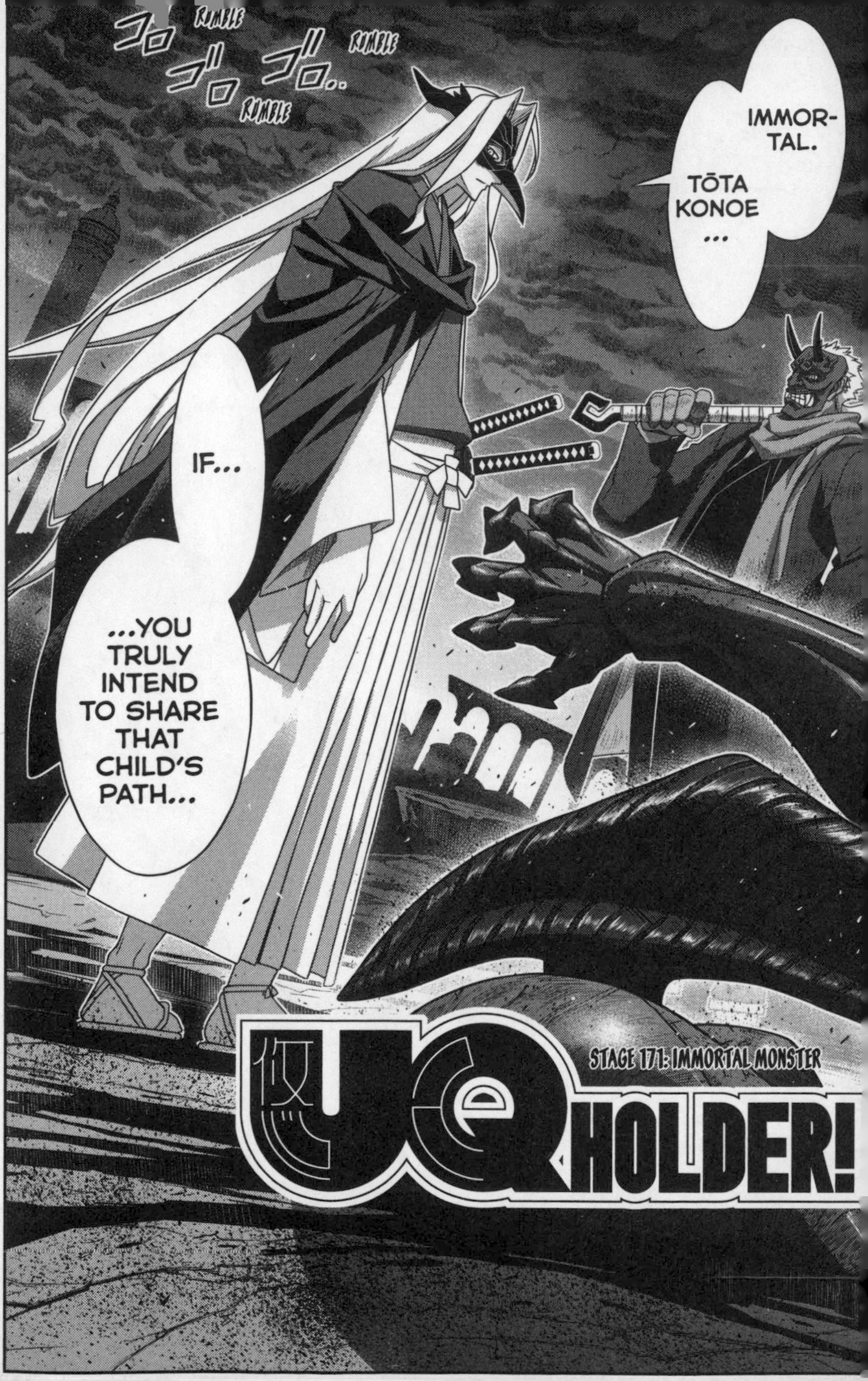
IMMOR-TAL.
TŌTA KONOE ...
ゴロゴロゴロ..
RUMBLE RUMBLE RUMBLE
IF...
...YOU TRULY INTEND TO SHARE THAT CHILD'S PATH...
STAGE 171: IMMORTAL MONSTER
UQ HOLDER!

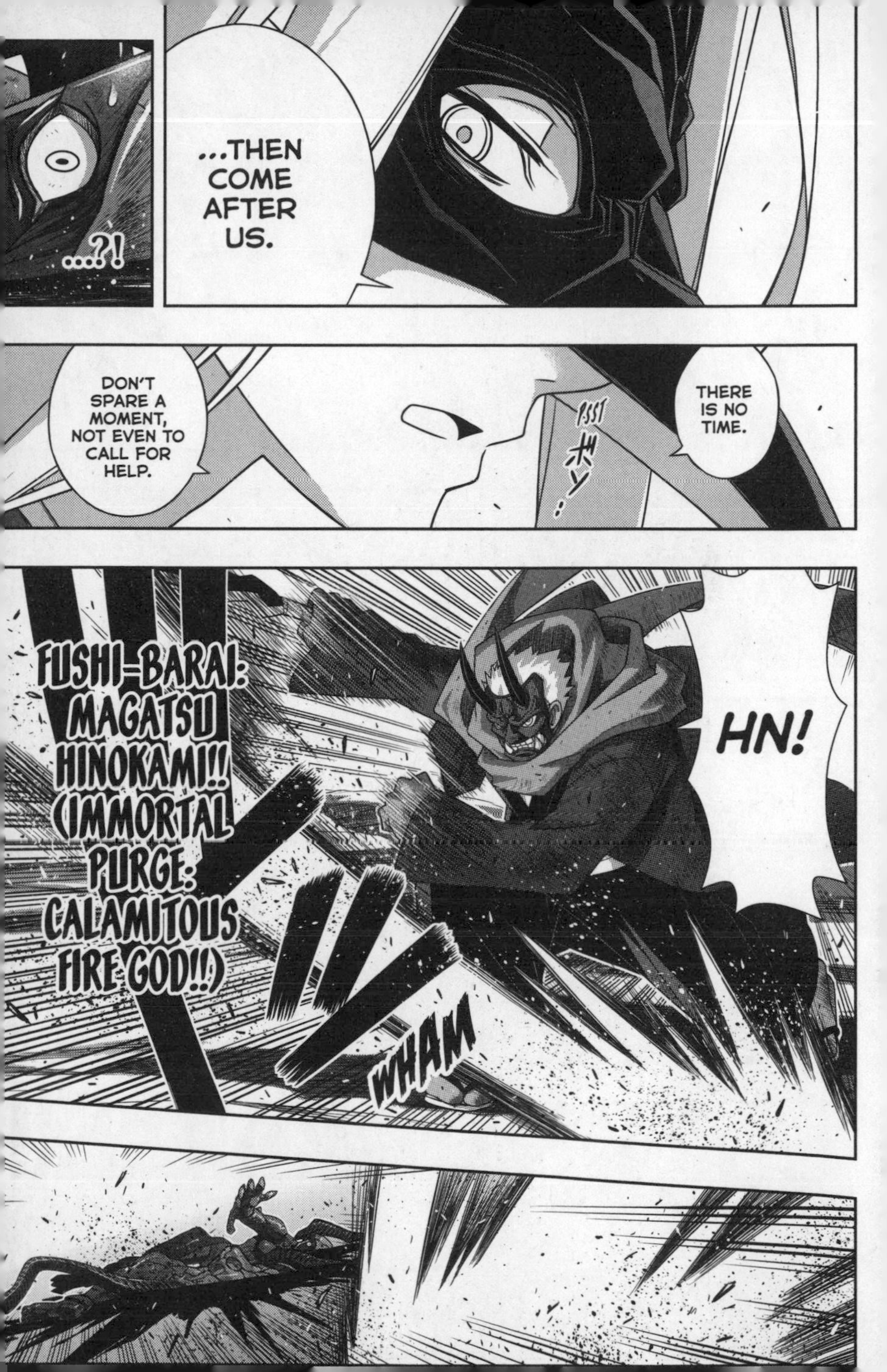
...THEN COME AFTER US.
...?!
THERE IS NO TIME.
P'SST
DON'T SPARE A MOMENT, NOT EVEN TO CALL FOR HELP.
HN!
FUSHI-BARAI: MAGATSU HINOKAMI!! (IMMORTAL PURGE: CALAMITOUS FIRE GOD!!)
WHAM

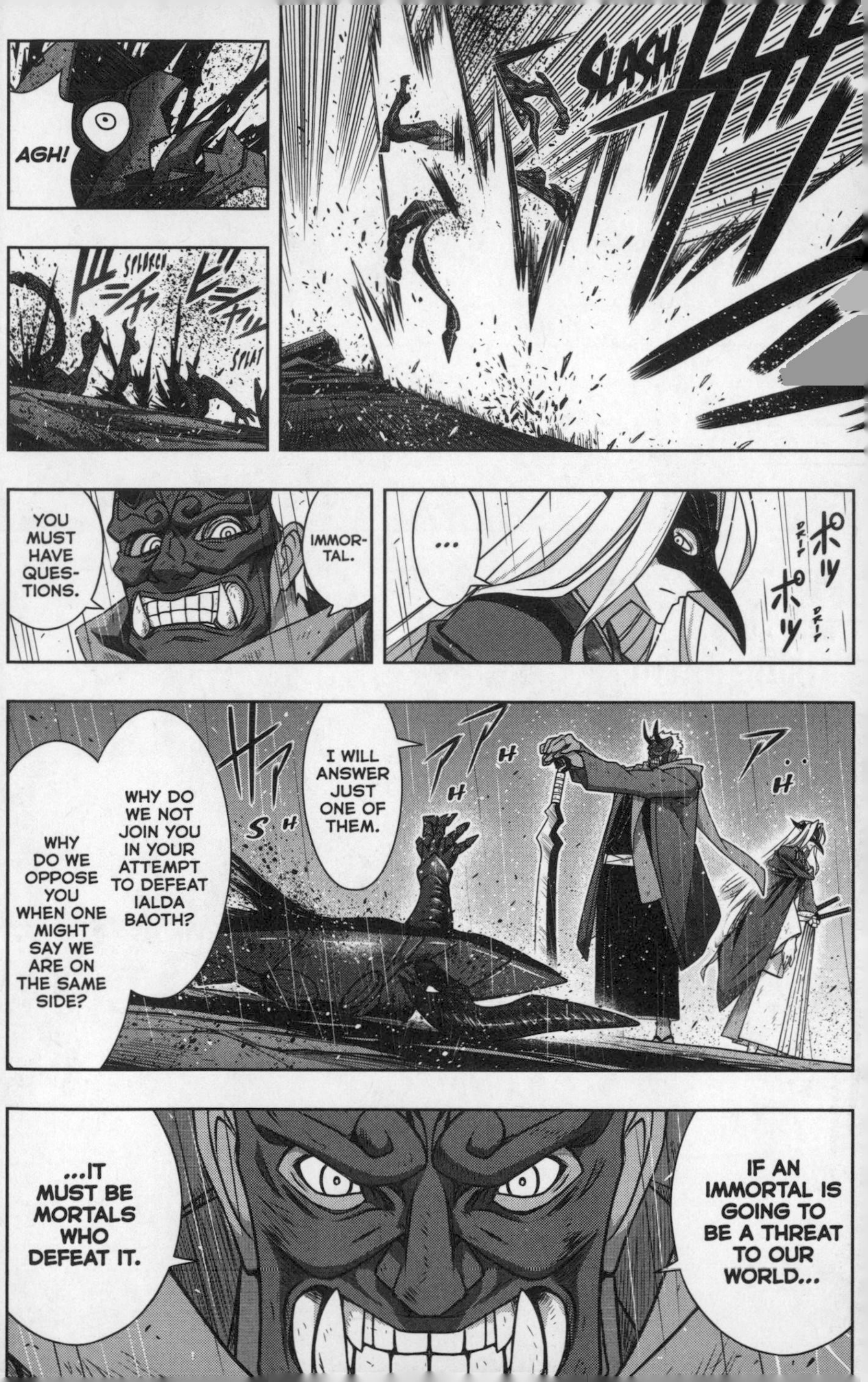
SLASH
AGH!
SPLORCH
SPLAT
...
DRIP
DRIP
IMMORTAL.
YOU MUST HAVE QUESTIONS.
I WILL ANSWER JUST ONE OF THEM.
WHY DO WE NOT JOIN YOU IN YOUR ATTEMPT TO DEFEAT IALDA BAOTH?
WHY DO WE OPPOSE YOU WHEN ONE MIGHT SAY WE ARE ON THE SAME SIDE?
IF AN IMMORTAL IS GOING TO BE A THREAT TO OUR WORLD...
...IT MUST BE MORTALS WHO DEFEAT IT.

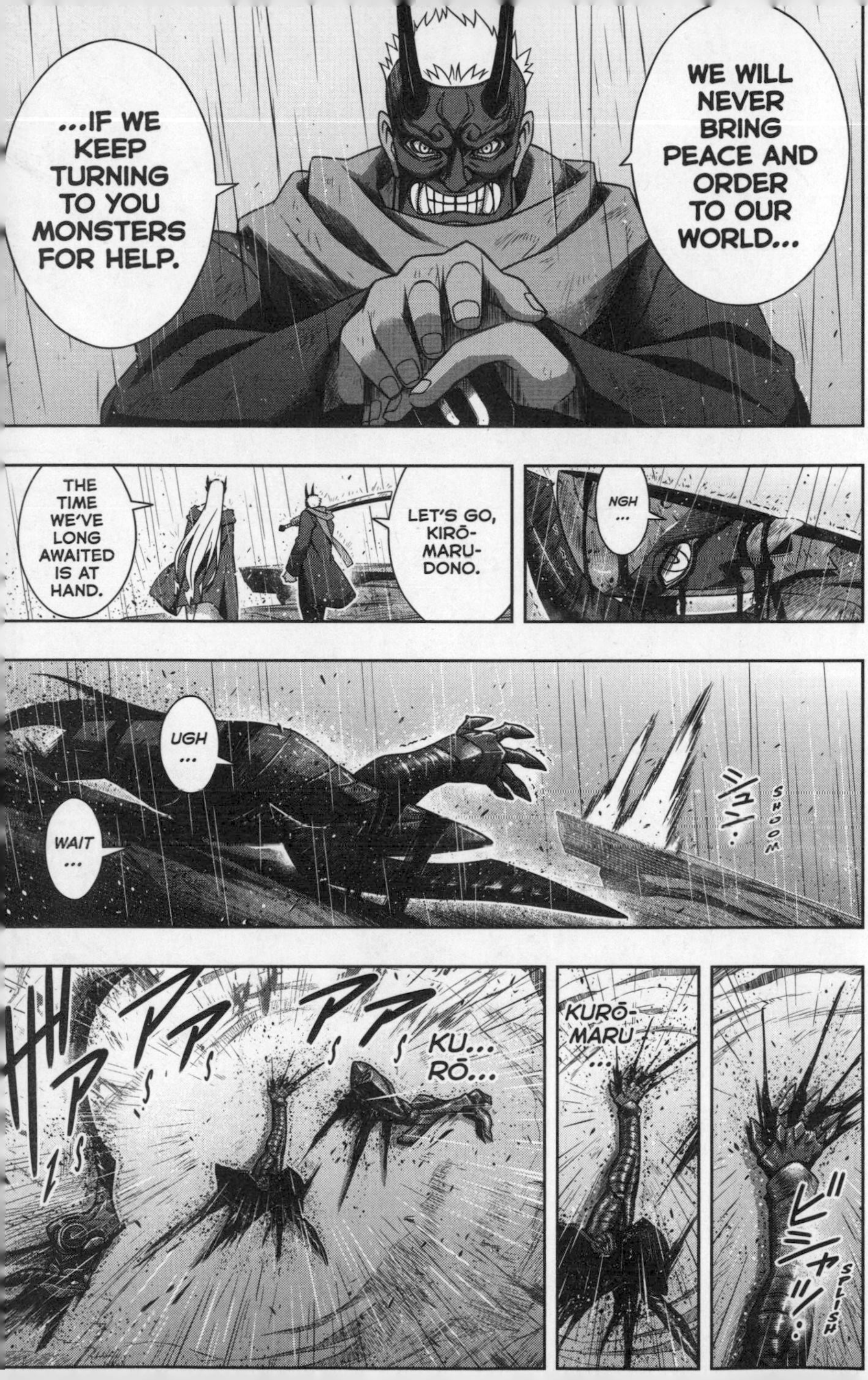
WE WILL NEVER BRING PEACE AND ORDER TO OUR WORLD...
...IF WE KEEP TURNING TO YOU MONSTERS FOR HELP.
NGH ...
LET'S GO, KIRŌ-MARU-DONO.
THE TIME WE'VE LONG AWAITED IS AT HAND.
SHOOM
UGH ...
WAIT ...
SPLISH
KURŌ-MARU ...
KU... RŌ...

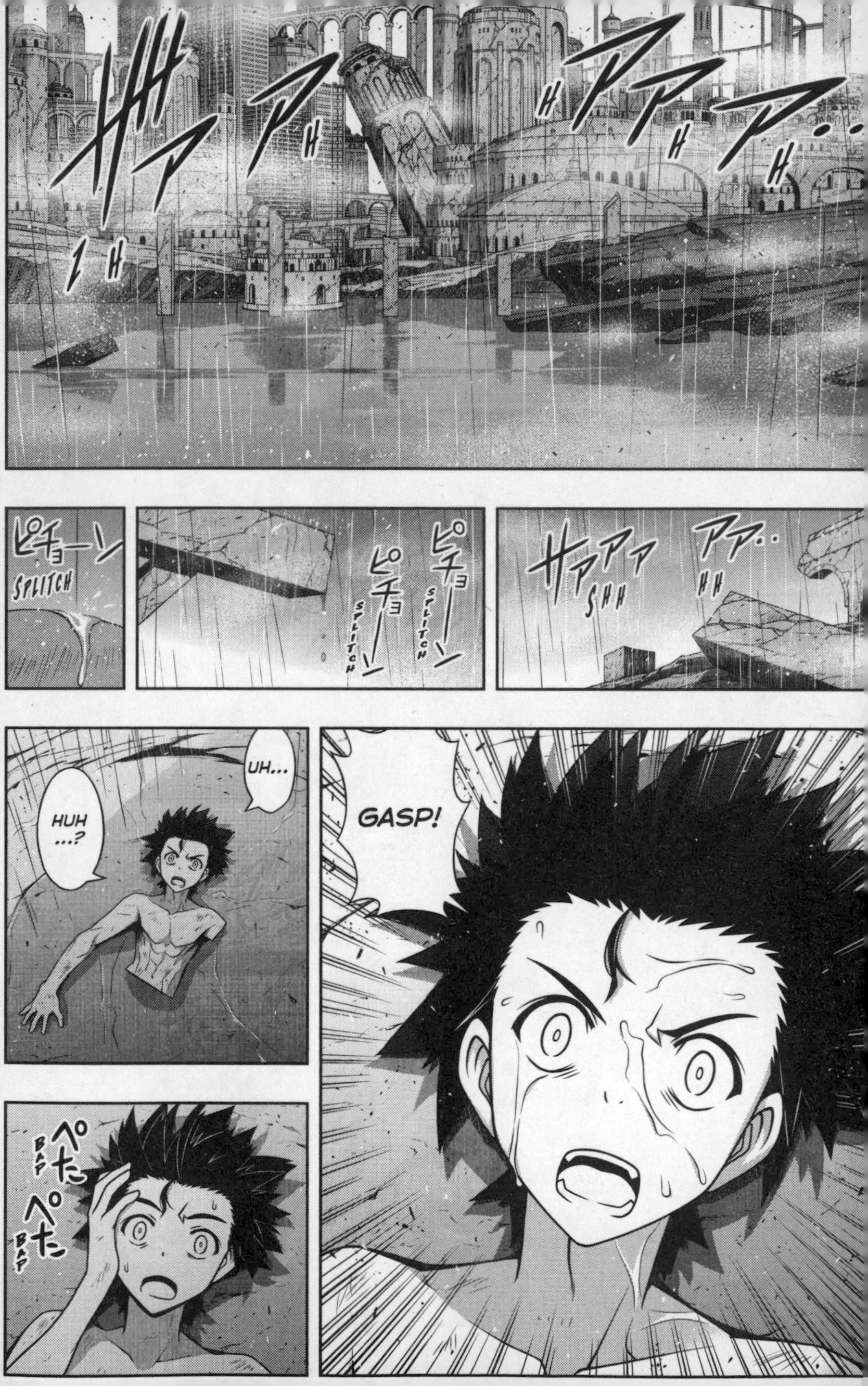
ザァァァァァァァ‥
SHHHHH
サァァァァァ‥
SHHH
ピチョーン
SPLITCH
ピチョーン
SPLITCH
ピチョーン
SPLITCH
GASP!
UH...
HUH ...?
ぺた
BAP
ぺた
BAP

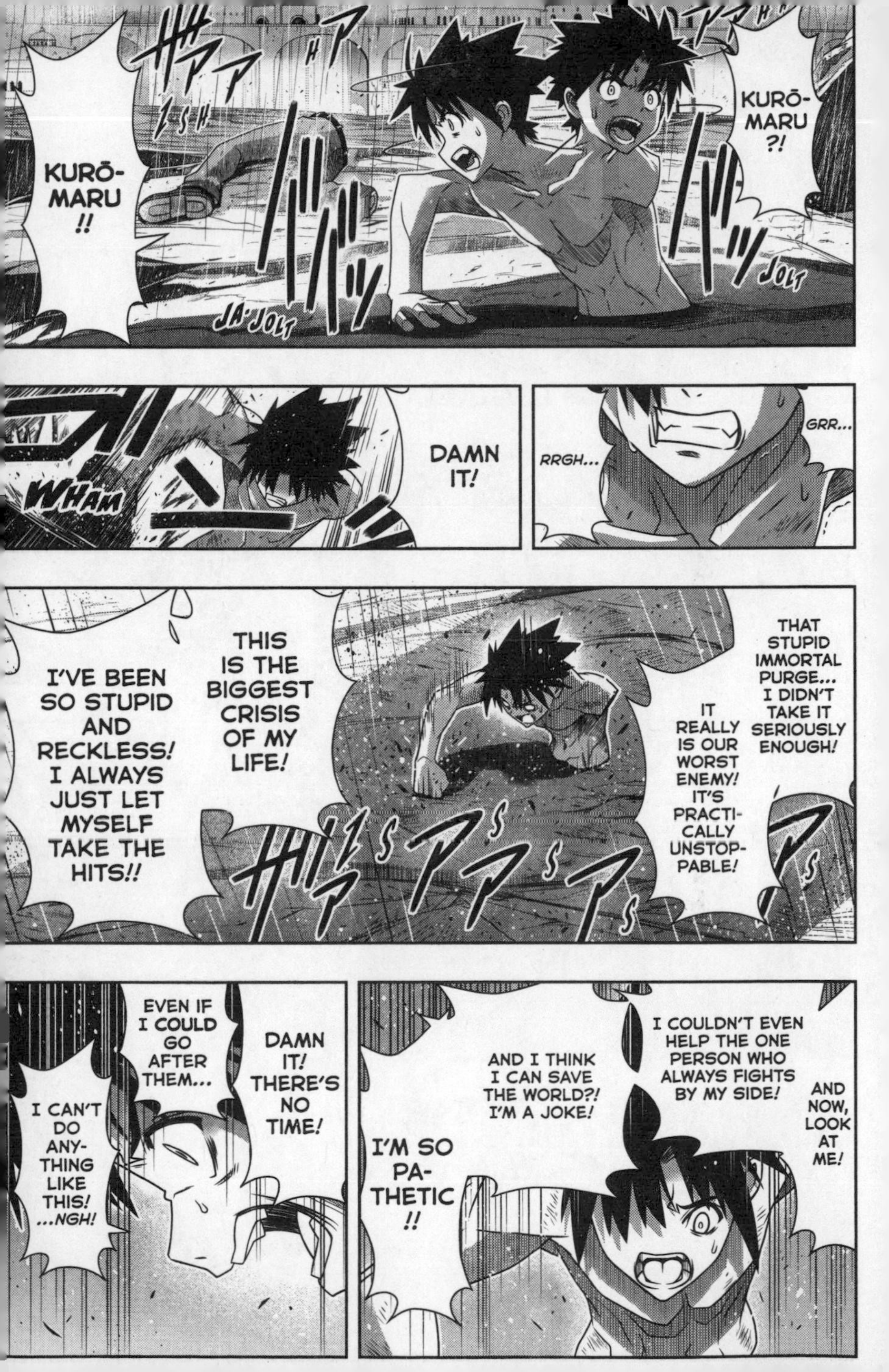

ZSH
KURŌ-MARU?!
JOLT
KURŌ-MARU!!
JA-JOLT
GRR...
RRGH...
DAMN IT!
WHAM
THAT STUPID IMMORTAL PURGE... I DIDN'T TAKE IT SERIOUSLY ENOUGH!
IT REALLY IS OUR WORST ENEMY! IT'S PRACTICALLY UNSTOPPABLE!
THIS IS THE BIGGEST CRISIS OF MY LIFE!
I'VE BEEN SO STUPID AND RECKLESS! I ALWAYS JUST LET MYSELF TAKE THE HITS!!
I COULDN'T EVEN HELP THE ONE PERSON WHO ALWAYS FIGHTS BY MY SIDE!
AND NOW, LOOK AT ME!
AND I THINK I CAN SAVE THE WORLD?! I'M A JOKE!
I'M SO PATHETIC!!
DAMN IT! THERE'S NO TIME!
EVEN IF I COULD GO AFTER THEM...
I CAN'T DO ANYTHING LIKE THIS! ...NGH!

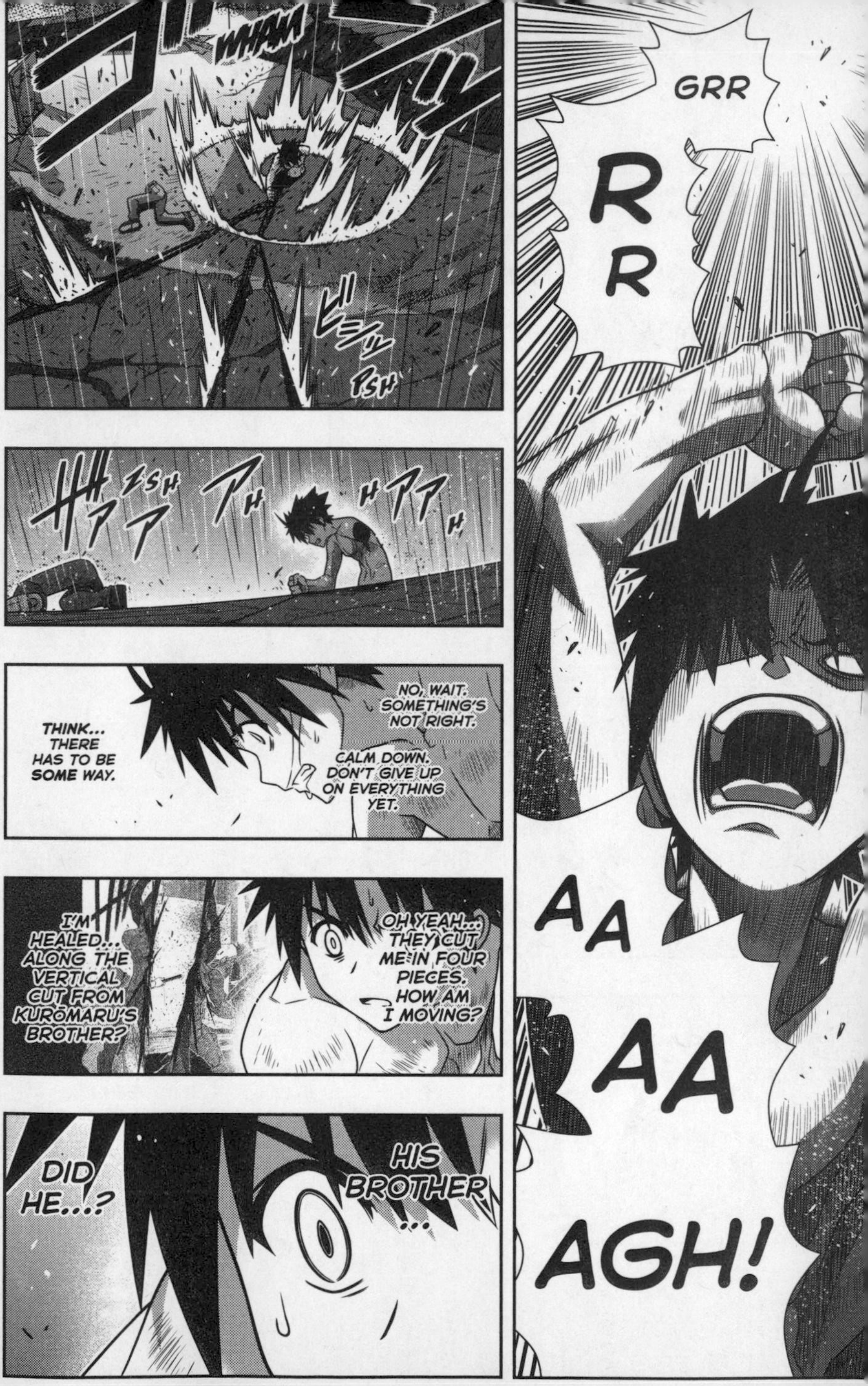
GRR
R
R
AA
AA
AGH!
WHAM
PSH
PSH
NO, WAIT. SOMETHING'S NOT RIGHT.
CALM DOWN. DON'T GIVE UP ON EVERYTHING YET.
THINK... THERE HAS TO BE SOME WAY.
OH YEAH... THEY CUT ME IN FOUR PIECES. HOW AM I MOVING?
I'M HEALED... ALONG THE VERTICAL CUT FROM KUROMARU'S BROTHER?
HIS BROTHER...
DID HE...?

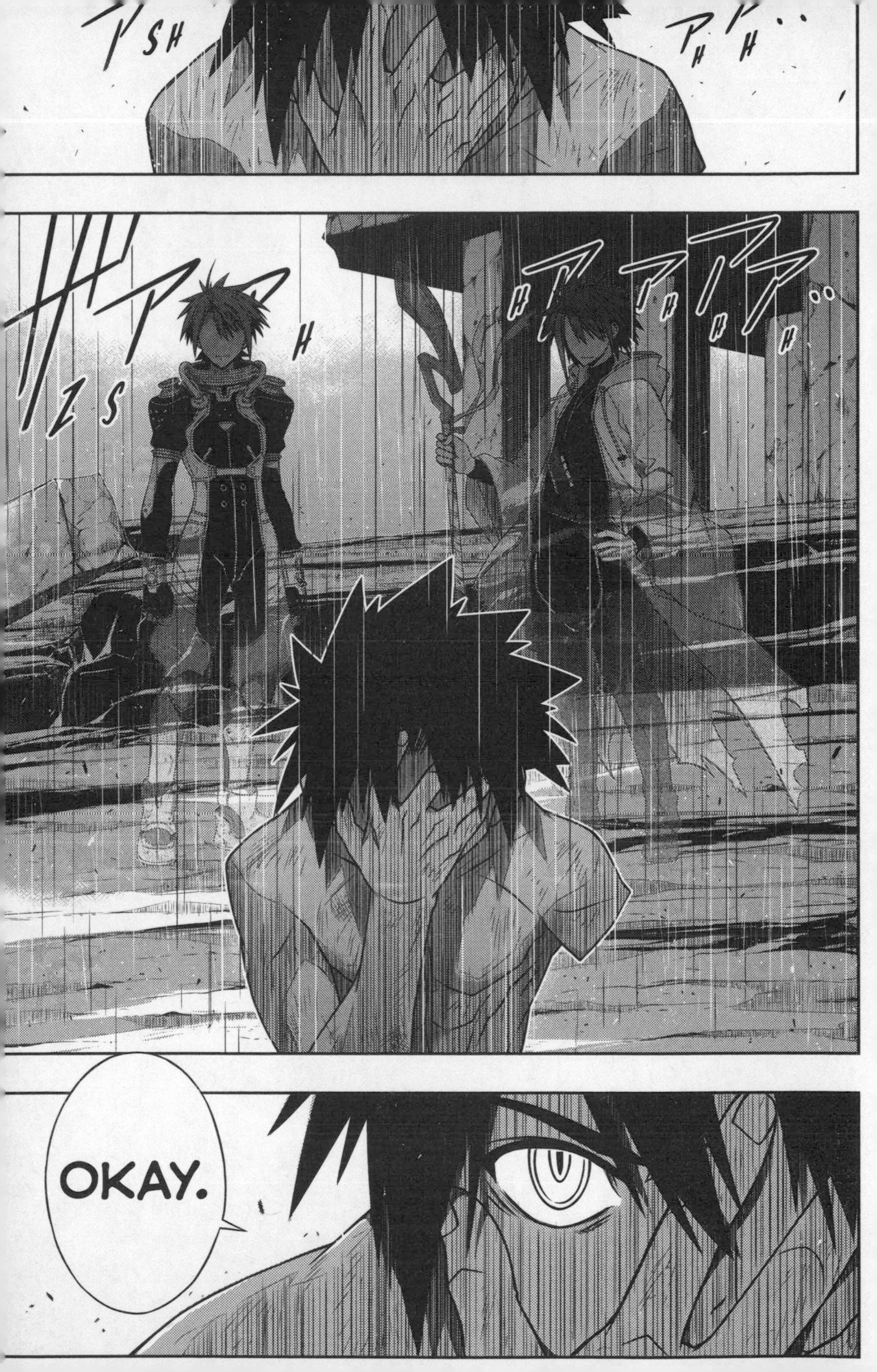
OKAY.

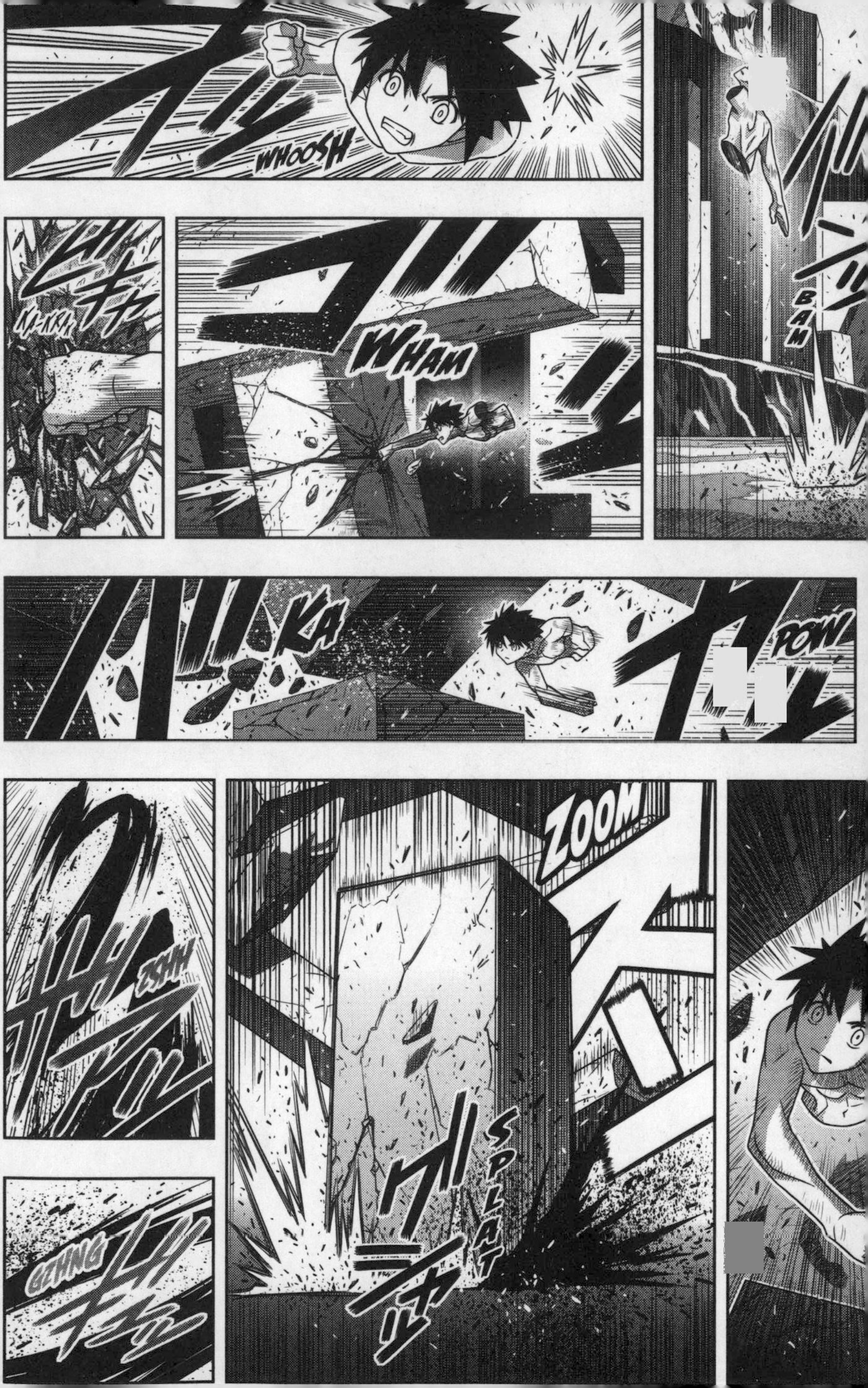
BAM
WHOOSH
WHAM
KA-KRA
POW
KA
ZOOM
SPLAT
ZSHH
GZHNG

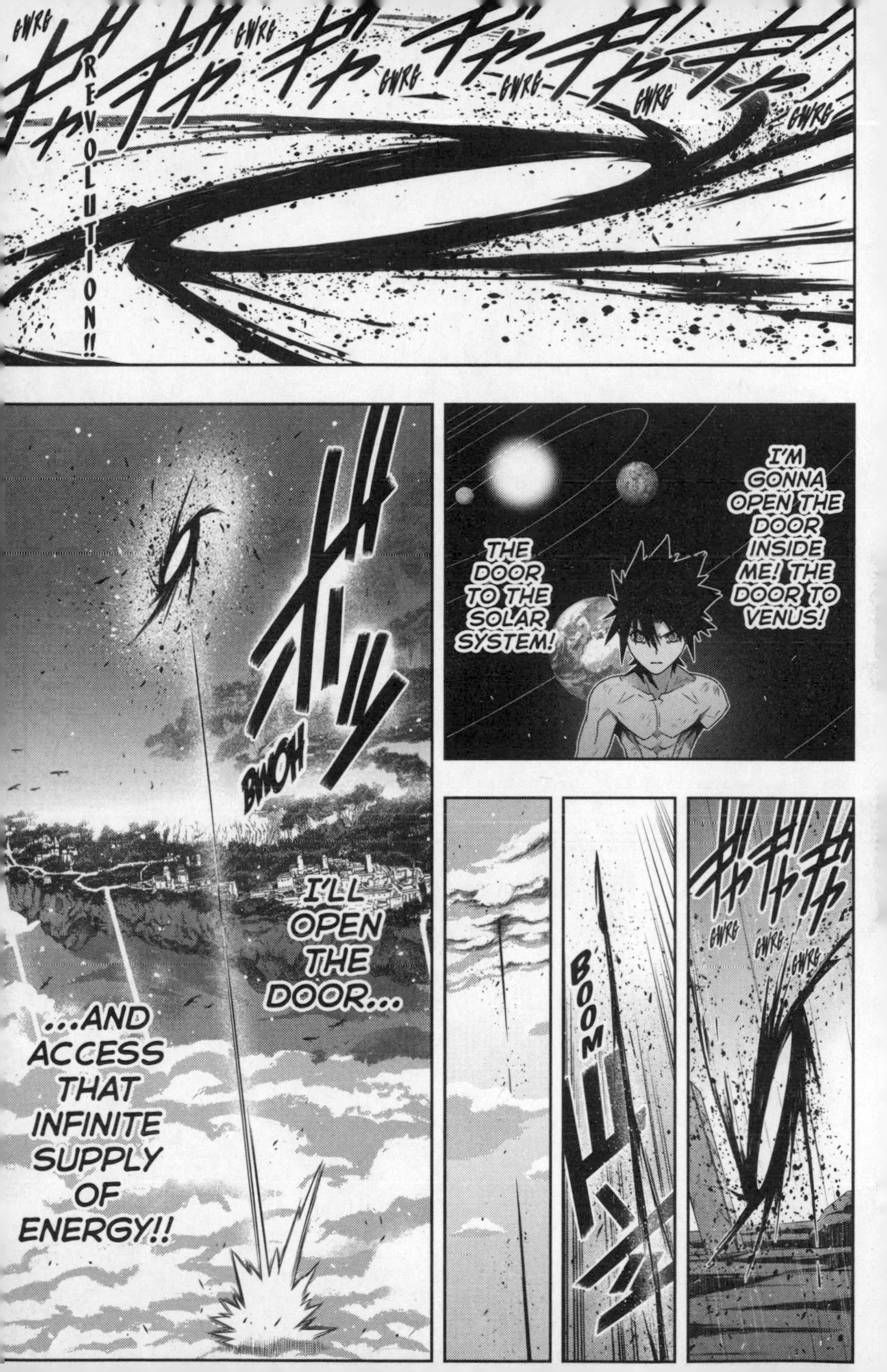
GWRG
GWRG
GWRG
GWRG
GWRG
GWRG
REVOLUTION!!
I'M GONNA OPEN THE DOOR INSIDE ME! THE DOOR TO VENUS!
THE DOOR TO THE SOLAR SYSTEM!
GWRG
GWRG
GWRG
BOOM
BWOOH
I'LL OPEN THE DOOR...
...AND ACCESS THAT INFINITE SUPPLY OF ENERGY!!

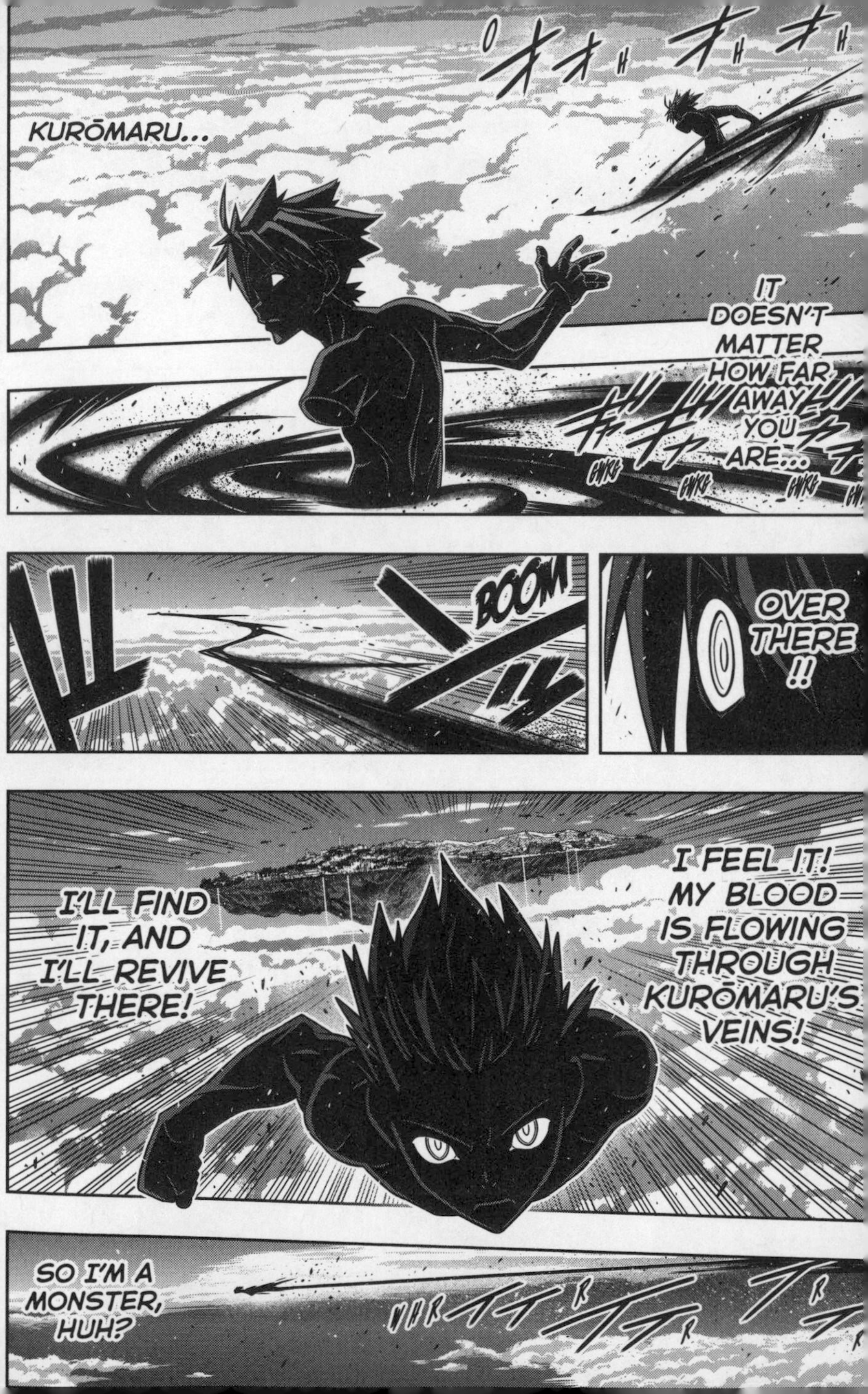

OHH
KURŌMARU...
IT DOESN'T MATTER HOW FAR AWAY YOU ARE...
GWRG
GWRG
GWRG
OVER THERE!!
BOOM
I FEEL IT! MY BLOOD IS FLOWING THROUGH KURŌMARU'S VEINS!
I'LL FIND IT, AND I'LL REVIVE THERE!
SO I'M A MONSTER, HUH?
WHRR

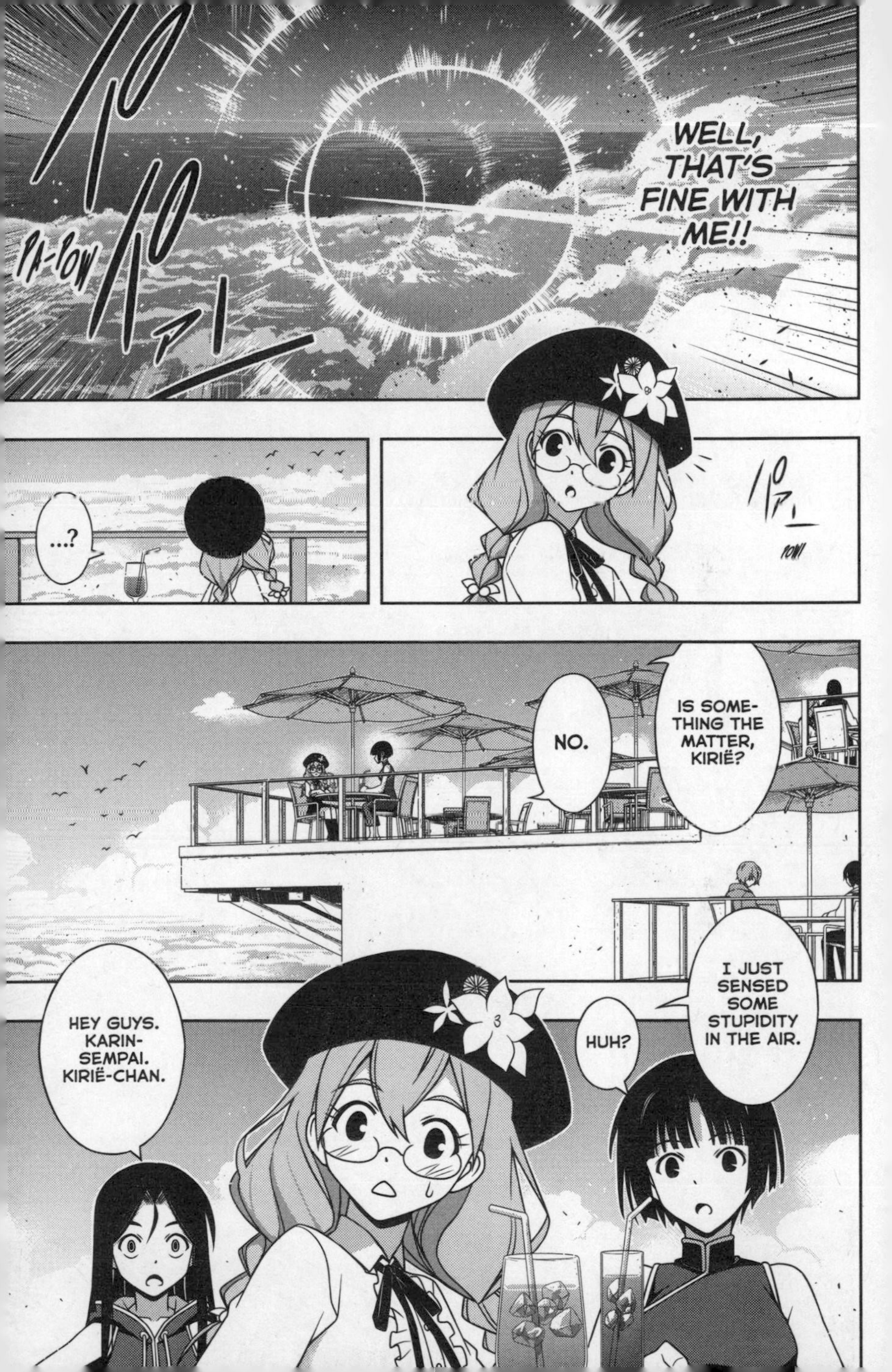
WELL, THAT'S FINE WITH ME!!
PA-POW
POW!
...?
IS SOME-THING THE MATTER, KIRIË?
NO.
I JUST SENSED SOME STUPIDITY IN THE AIR.
HUH?
HEY GUYS. KARIN-SEMPAI. KIRIË-CHAN.

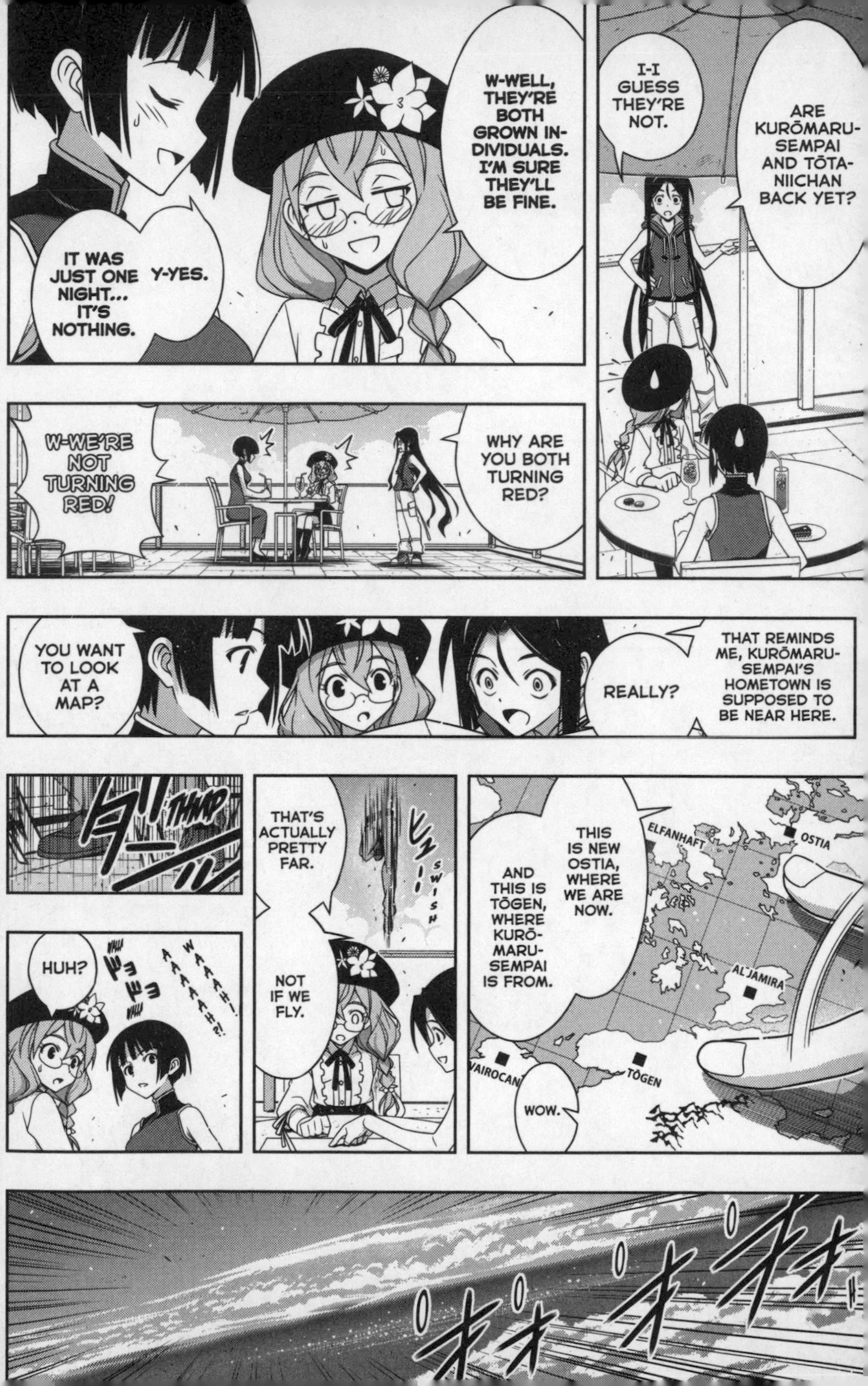
ARE KURŌMARU-SEMPAI AND TŌTA-NIICHAN BACK YET?
I-I GUESS THEY'RE NOT.
W-WELL, THEY'RE BOTH GROWN IN-DIVIDUALS. I'M SURE THEY'LL BE FINE.
Y-YES.
IT WAS JUST ONE NIGHT... IT'S NOTHING.
WHY ARE YOU BOTH TURNING RED?
W-WE'RE NOT TURNING RED!
THAT REMINDS ME, KURŌMARU-SEMPAI'S HOMETOWN IS SUPPOSED TO BE NEAR HERE.
REALLY?
YOU WANT TO LOOK AT A MAP?
OSTIA
ELFANHAFT
AL'JAMIRA
VAIROCAN
TŌGEN
THIS IS NEW OSTIA, WHERE WE ARE NOW.
AND THIS IS TŌGEN, WHERE KURŌ-MARU-SEMPAI IS FROM.
WOW.
THAT'S ACTUALLY PRETTY FAR.
SWISH
NOT IF WE FLY.
THMP
HUH?
WAAAH!
AAAAAAH?!

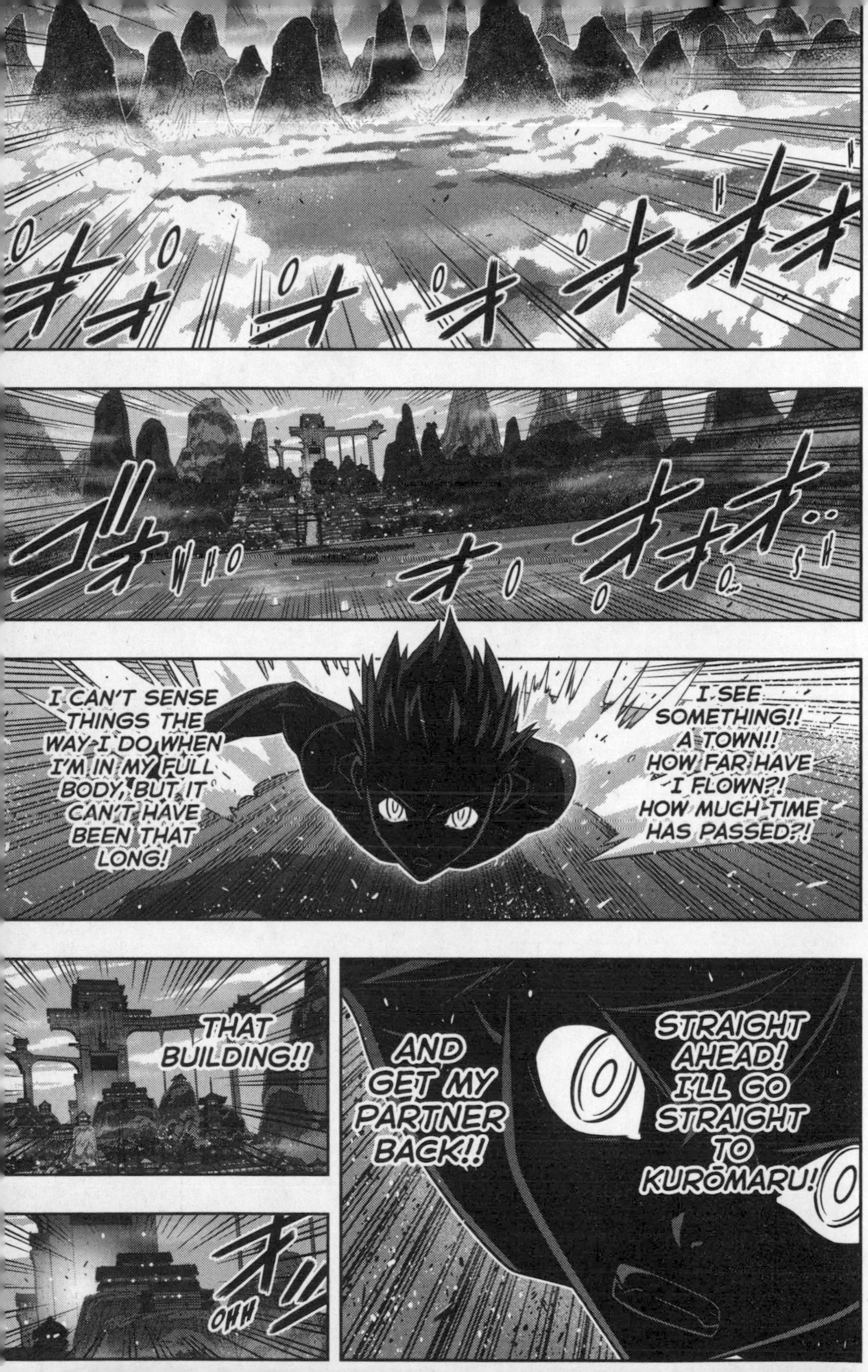

HH
OOOOOOOO
WHO
OOOOOSH
I SEE SOMETHING!! A TOWN!! HOW FAR HAVE I FLOWN?! HOW MUCH TIME HAS PASSED?!
I CAN'T SENSE THINGS THE WAY I DO WHEN I'M IN MY FULL BODY, BUT IT CAN'T HAVE BEEN THAT LONG!
STRAIGHT AHEAD! I'LL GO STRAIGHT TO KURŌMARU!
AND GET MY PARTNER BACK!!
THAT BUILDING!!
OHH

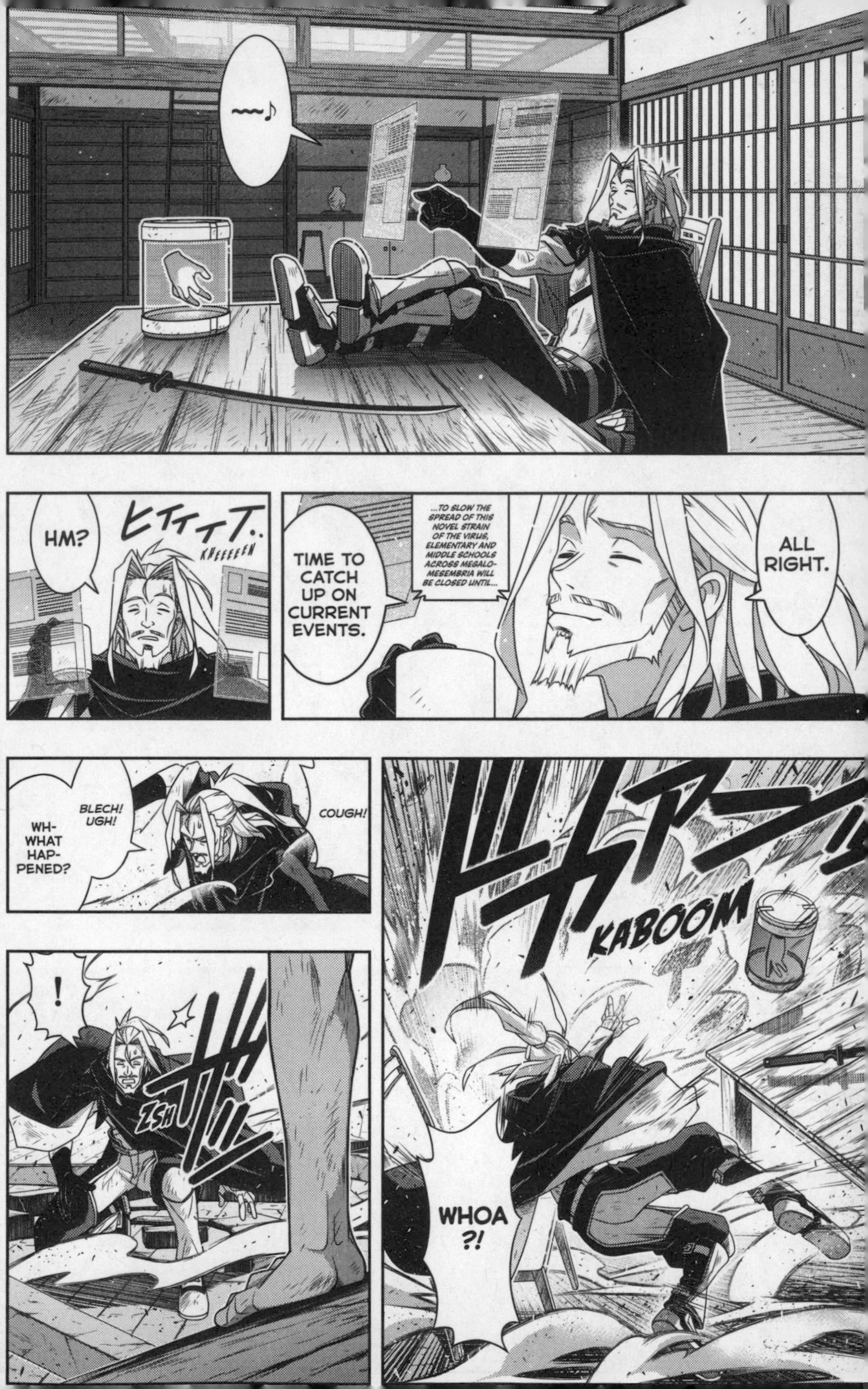

ALL RIGHT.
...TO SLOW THE SPREAD OF THIS NOVEL STRAIN OF THE VIRUS, ELEMENTARY AND MIDDLE SCHOOLS ACROSS MEGALO-MESEMBRIA WILL BE CLOSED UNTIL...
TIME TO CATCH UP ON CURRENT EVENTS.
KHEEEEEN
HM?
KABOOM
WHOA ?!
COUGH!
BLECH! UGH!
WH- WHAT HAP- PENED?
!
ZSH

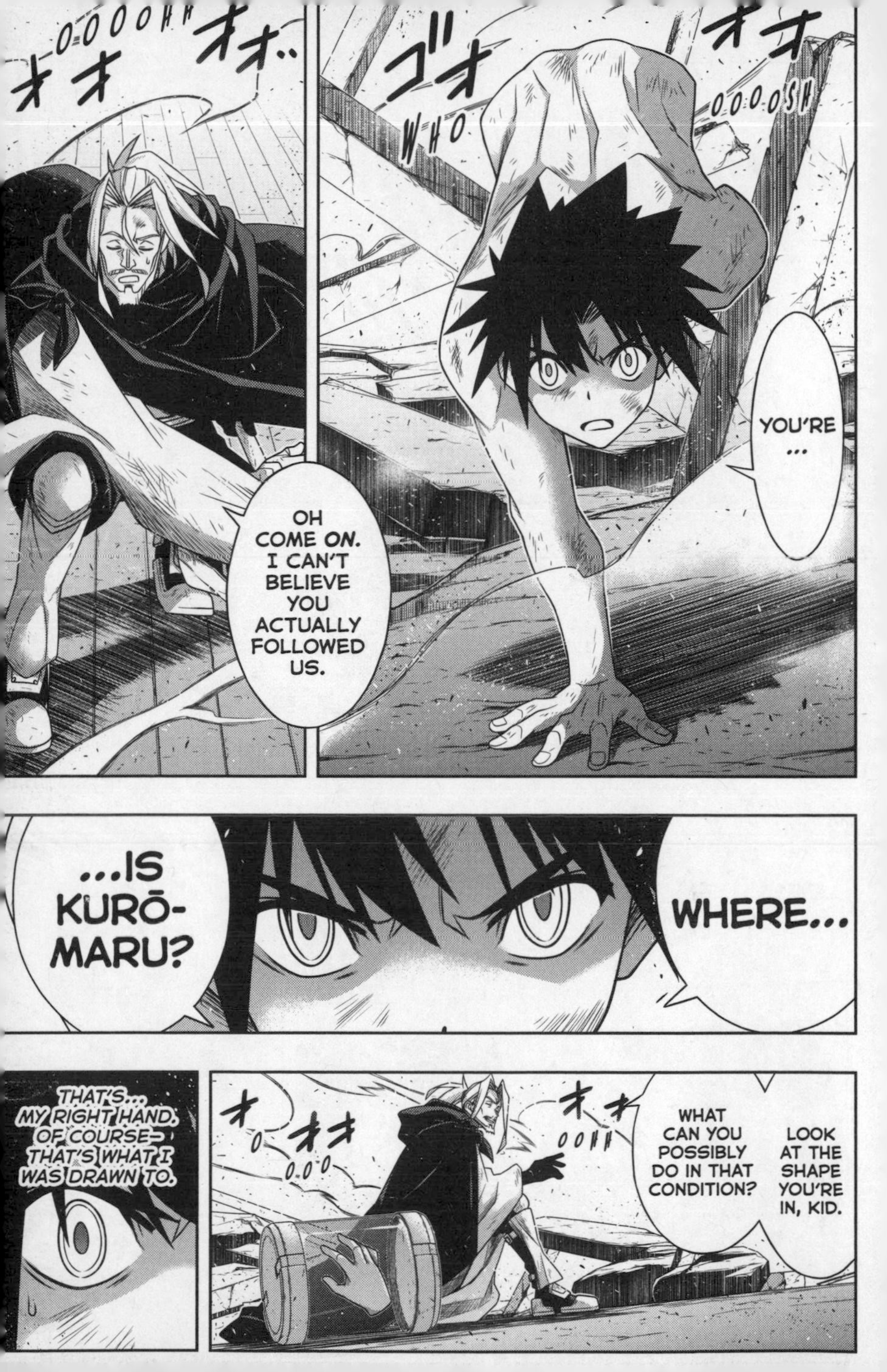
ゴオ
WHO
オオ
OOOOSH
YOU'RE ...
オオオォ
OOOOOHH
OH COME ON. I CAN'T BELIEVE YOU ACTUALLY FOLLOWED US.
WHERE...
...IS KURŌ-MARU?
LOOK AT THE SHAPE YOU'RE IN, KID.
WHAT CAN YOU POSSIBLY DO IN THAT CONDITION?
オオ
OOHH
オオオ
OOO
THAT'S... MY RIGHT HAND. OF COURSE— THAT'S WHAT I WAS DRAWN TO.

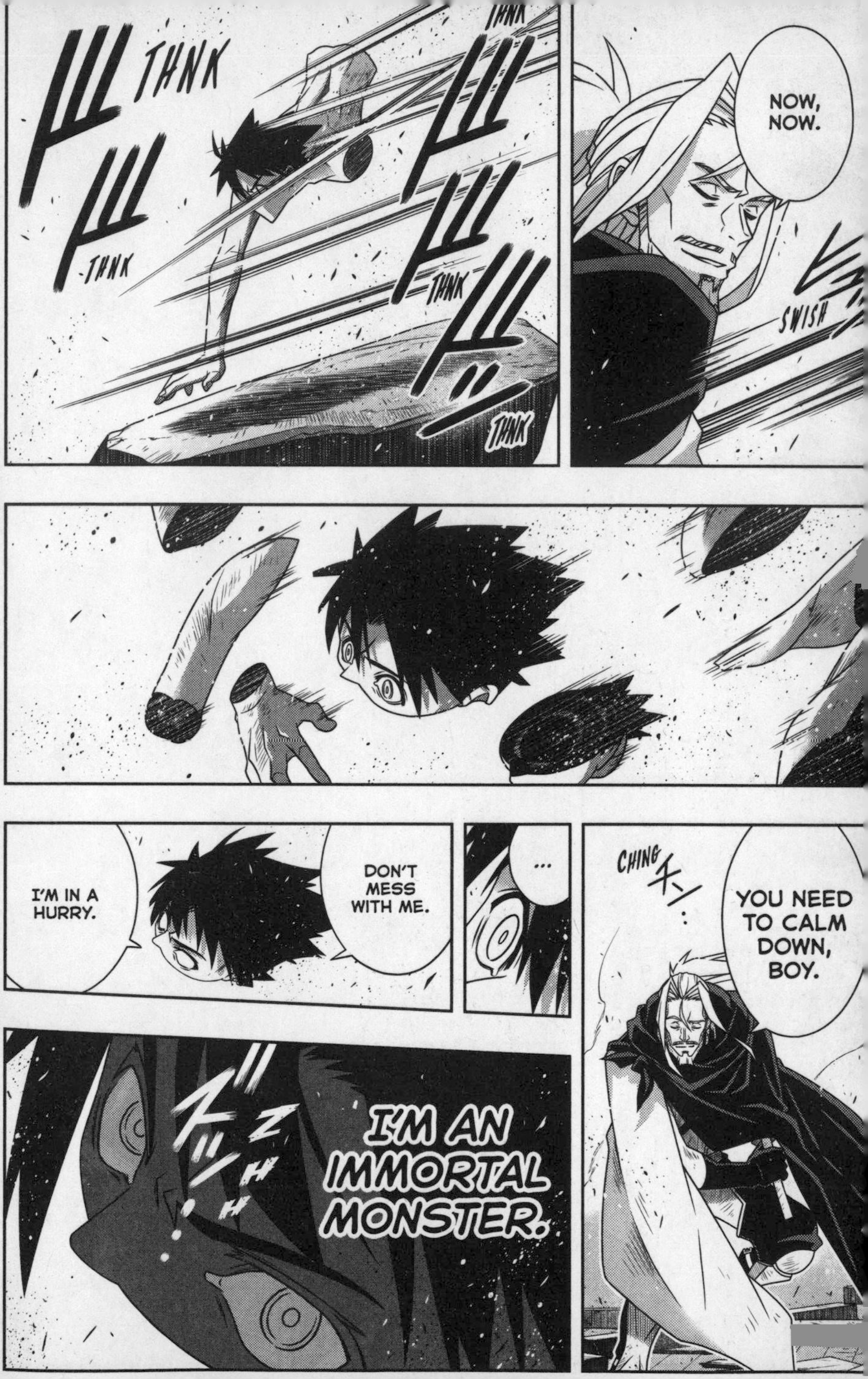
NOW, NOW.
SWISH
THNK
THNK
THNK
THNK
THNK
CHING
YOU NEED TO CALM DOWN, BOY.
...
DON'T MESS WITH ME.
I'M IN A HURRY.
I'M AN IMMORTAL MONSTER.

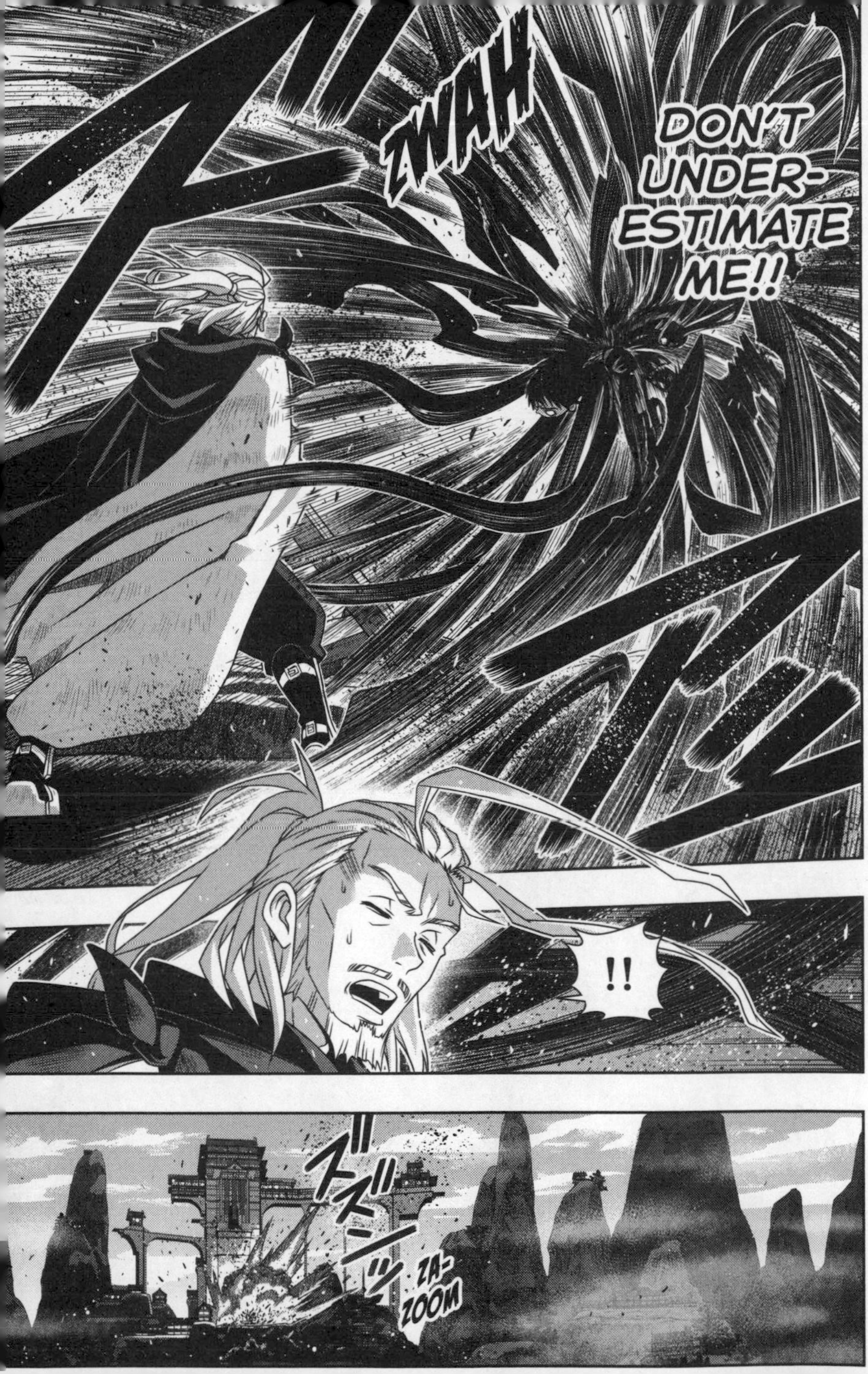
DON'T UNDER-ESTIMATE ME!!
ZWAH
!!
ズズーッ
ZA-ZOOM

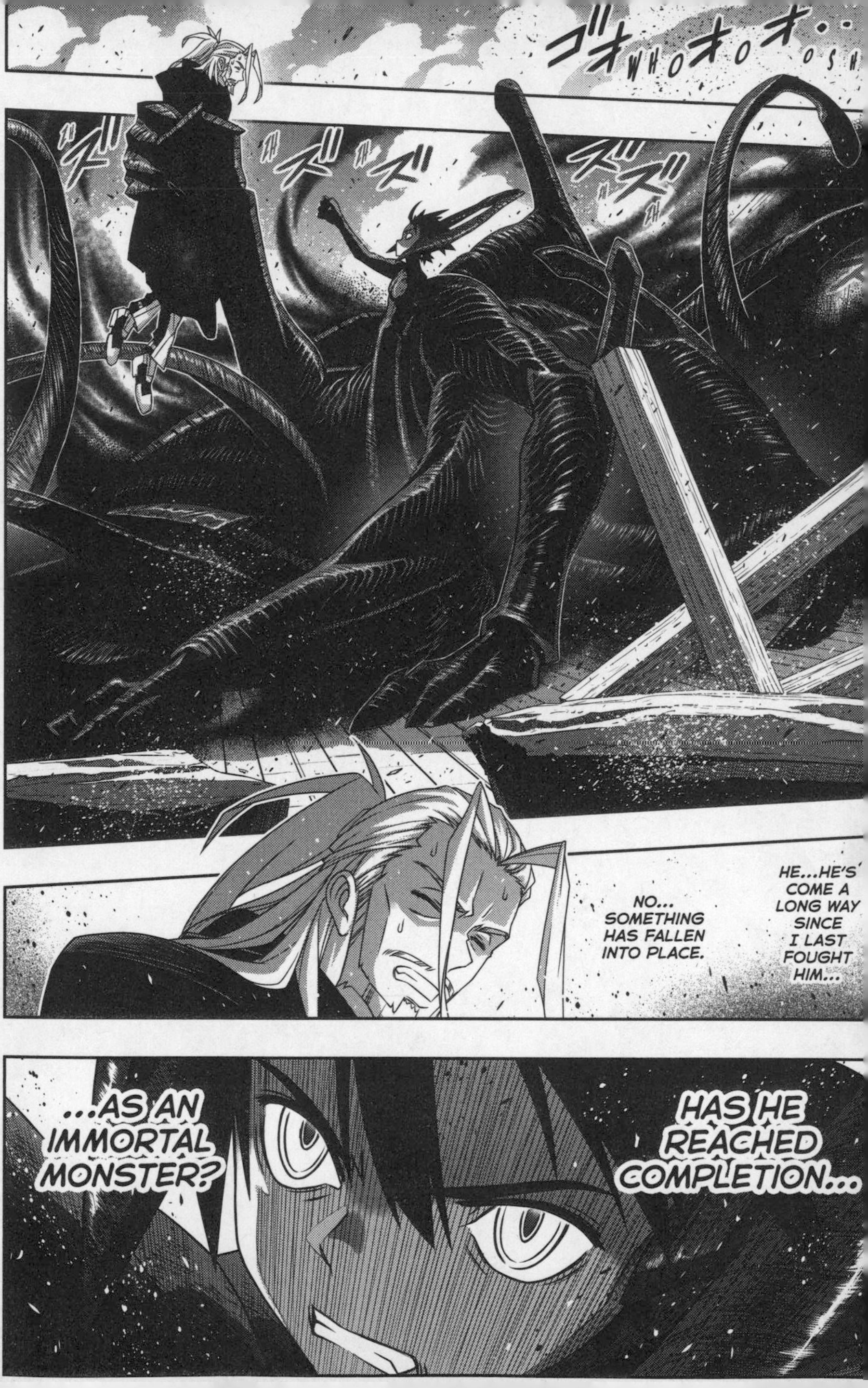
HE...HE'S COME A LONG WAY SINCE I LAST FOUGHT HIM...
NO... SOMETHING HAS FALLEN INTO PLACE.
HAS HE REACHED COMPLETION...
...AS AN IMMORTAL MONSTER?

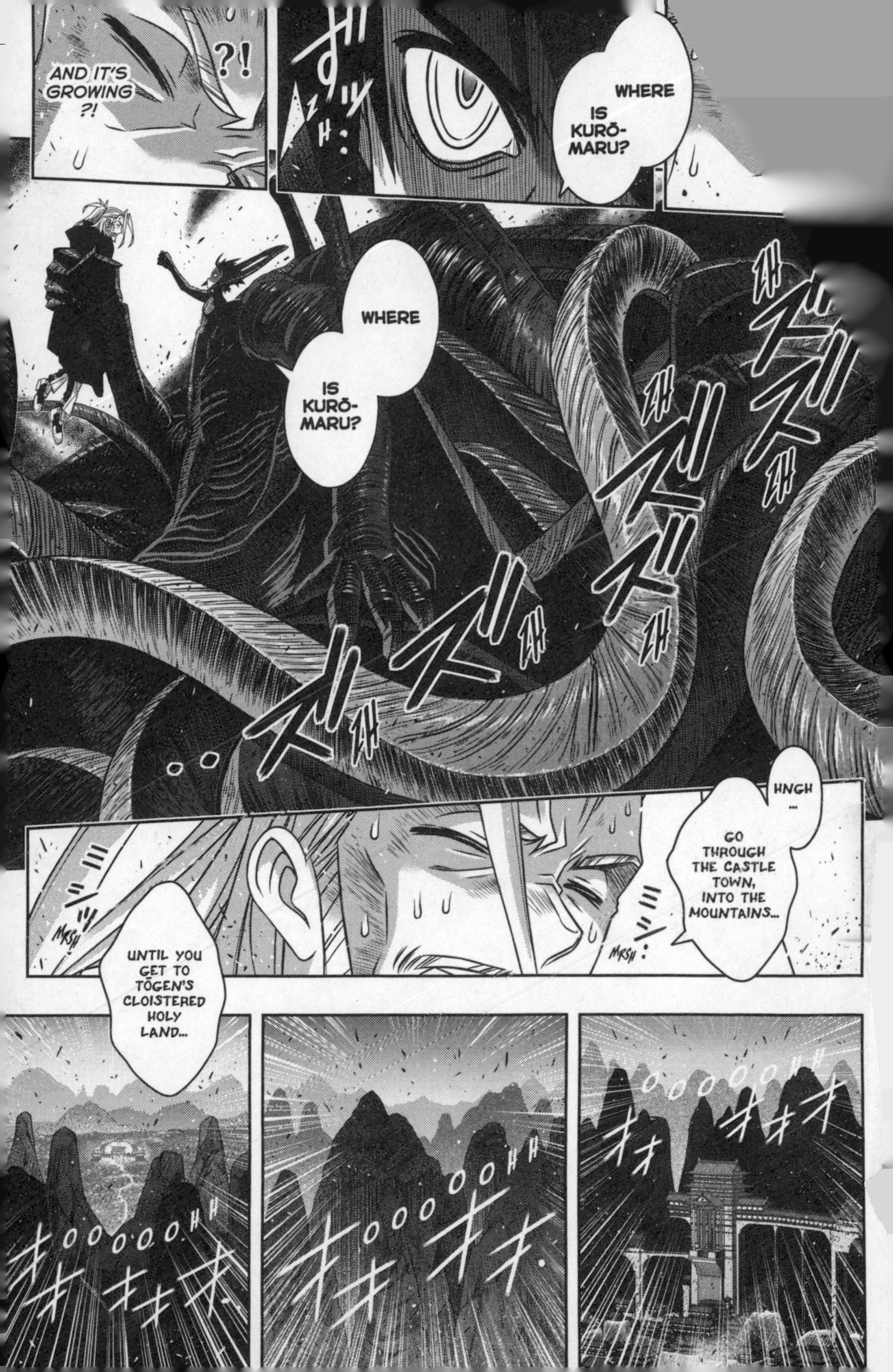
WHERE IS KURŌ-MARU?
AND IT'S GROWING ?!
?!
WHERE IS KURŌ-MARU?
HNGH...
GO THROUGH THE CASTLE TOWN, INTO THE MOUNTAINS...
MRSH
MRSH
UNTIL YOU GET TO TŌGEN'S CLOISTERED HOLY LAND...
OOOOOOHH
OOOOOOHH
OOOOOOHH

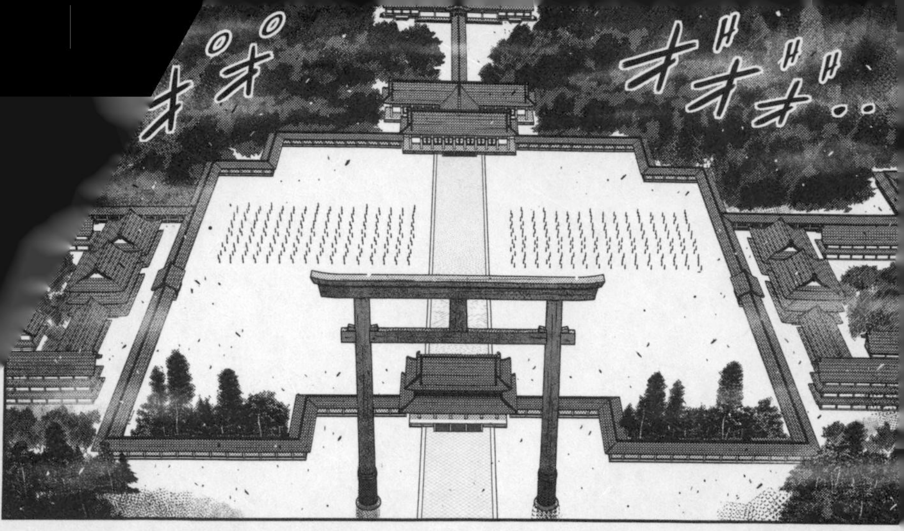
オオオ‥
HHH
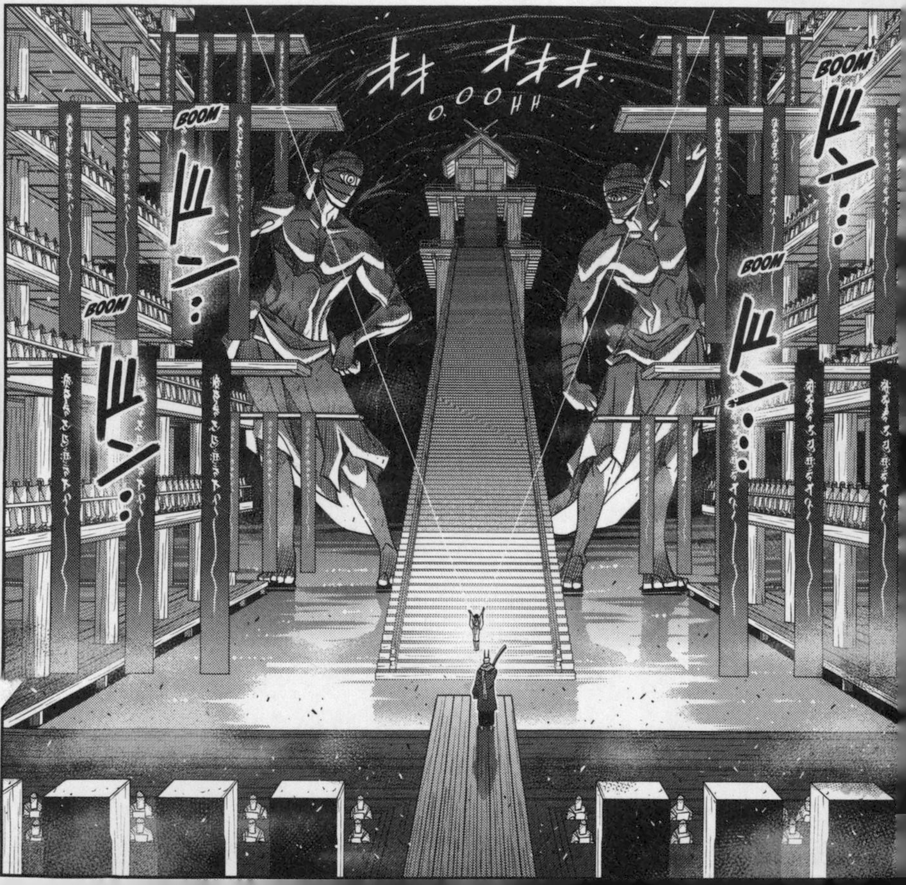
オオ オオオ‥
OOOHH.
BOOM
ドン…
BOOM
ドン…
BOOM
ドン…
BOOM
ドン…

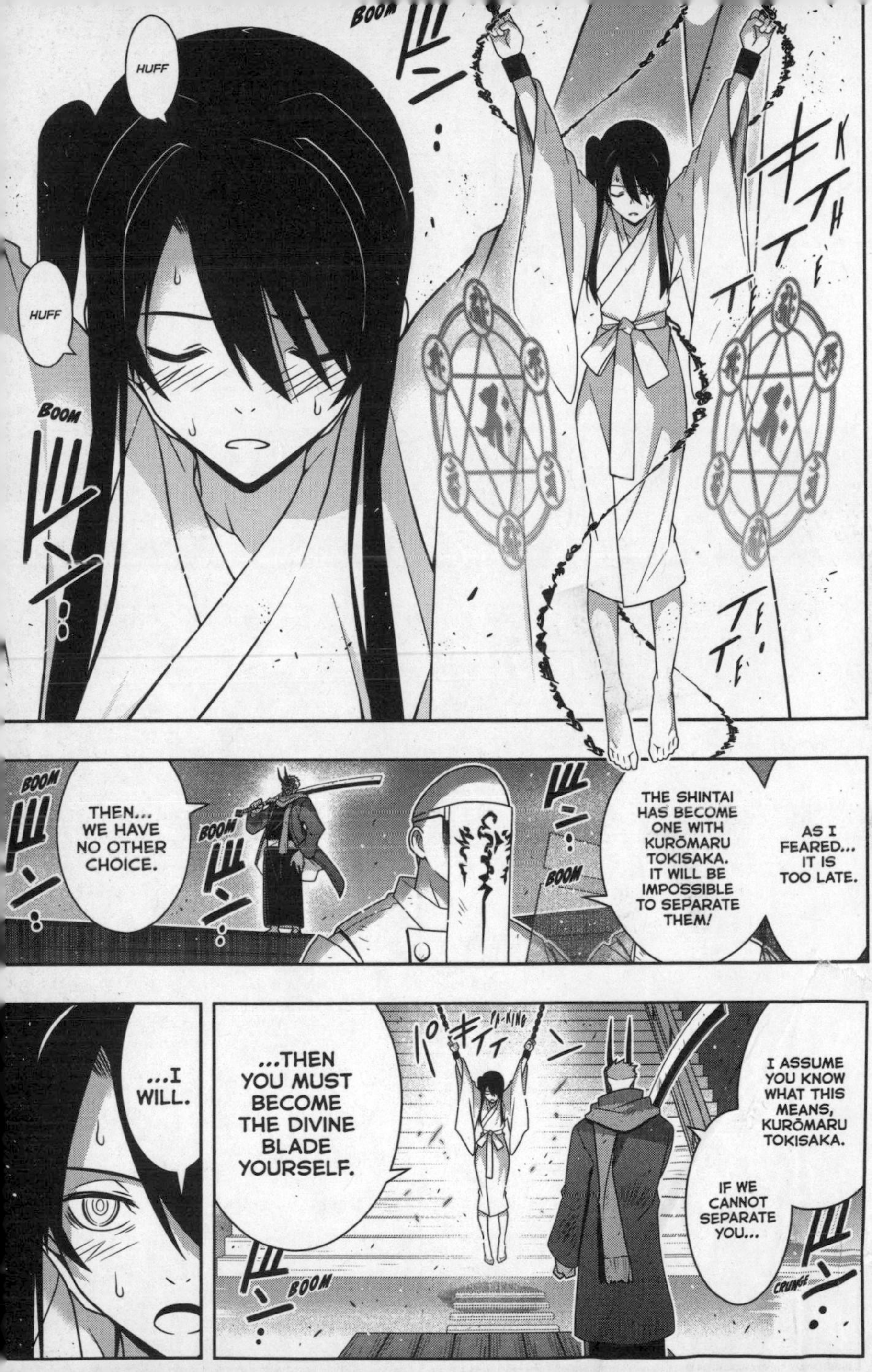
BOOM
HUFF
HUFF
BOOM
AS I FEARED... IT IS TOO LATE.
THE SHINTAI HAS BECOME ONE WITH KURŌMARU TOKISAKA. IT WILL BE IMPOSSIBLE TO SEPARATE THEM!
BOOM
BOOM
THEN... WE HAVE NO OTHER CHOICE.
BOOM
I ASSUME YOU KNOW WHAT THIS MEANS, KURŌMARU TOKISAKA.
IF WE CANNOT SEPARATE YOU...
PA-KING
...THEN YOU MUST BECOME THE DIVINE BLADE YOURSELF.
BOOM
...I WILL.

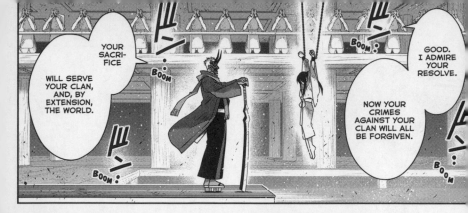

BOOM
GOOD. I ADMIRE YOUR RESOLVE.
NOW YOUR CRIMES AGAINST YOUR CLAN WILL ALL BE FORGIVEN.
BOOM
BOOM
YOUR SACRIFICE
WILL SERVE YOUR CLAN, AND, BY EXTENSION, THE WORLD.
BOOM
YES...
...
THE TRUTH IS, I SHOULD HAVE DIED...
...ALL THOSE YEARS AGO.
...NII-SAMA.
HE'S HARDLY SPOKEN TO ME SINCE HE WAS PUNISHED FOR DEFENDING ME.
BUT I OWE HIM EVERYTHING.
SQUEE
SQUEE

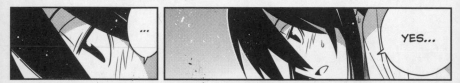

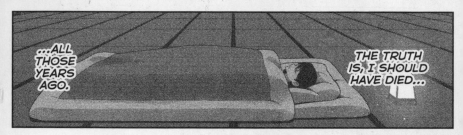

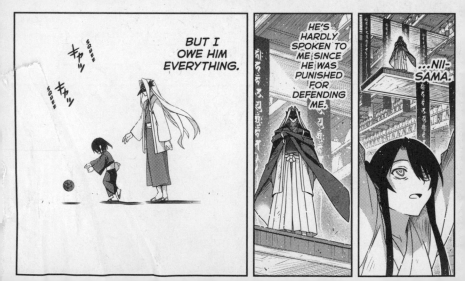

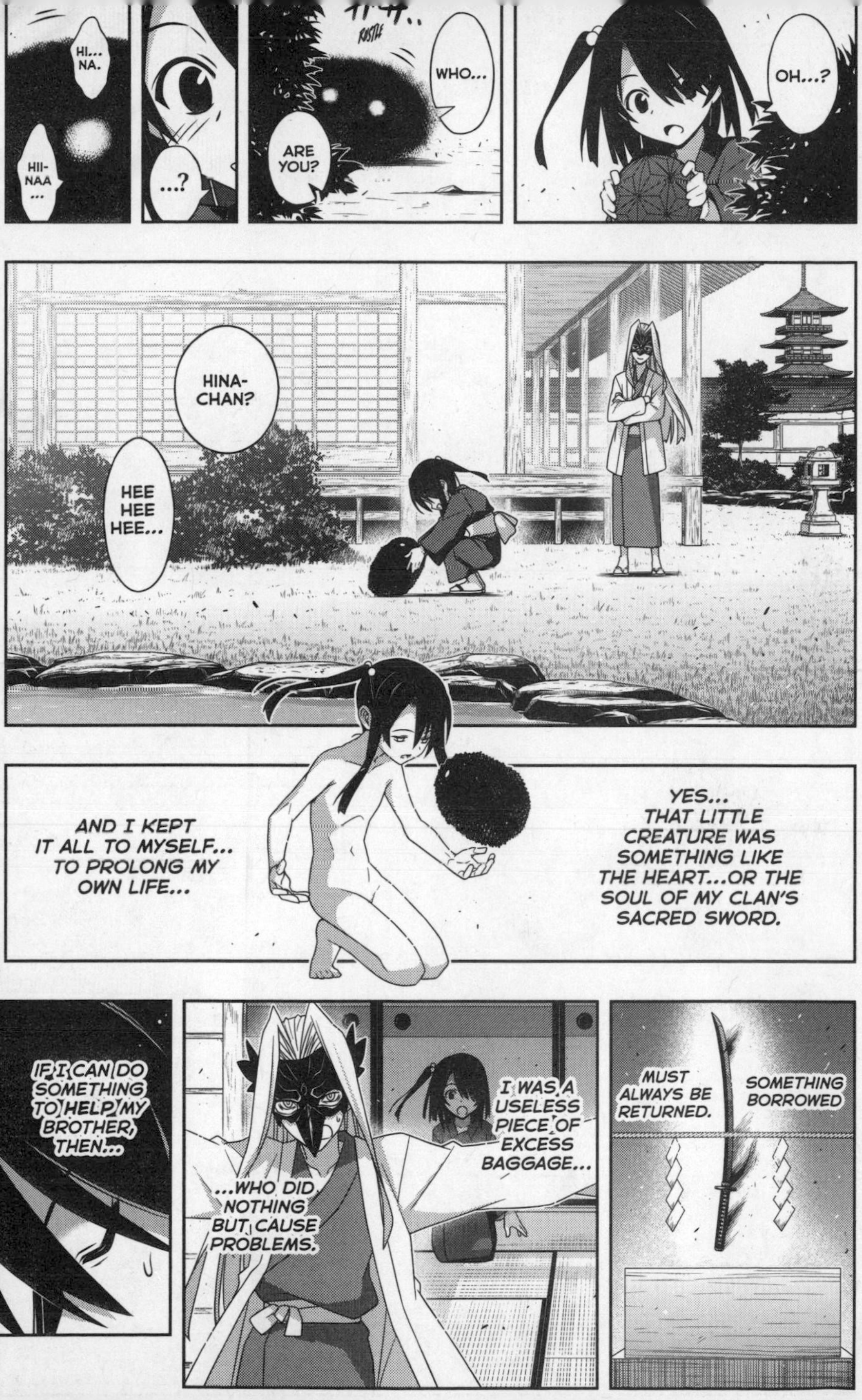
OH...?
RUSTLE
WHO...
ARE YOU?
...?
HI... NA.
HII-NAA...
HINA-CHAN?
HEE HEE HEE...
YES... THAT LITTLE CREATURE WAS SOMETHING LIKE THE HEART...OR THE SOUL OF MY CLAN'S SACRED SWORD.
AND I KEPT IT ALL TO MYSELF... TO PROLONG MY OWN LIFE...
SOMETHING BORROWED
MUST ALWAYS BE RETURNED.
I WAS A USELESS PIECE OF EXCESS BAGGAGE...
...WHO DID NOTHING BUT CAUSE PROBLEMS.
IF I CAN DO SOMETHING TO HELP MY BROTHER, THEN...

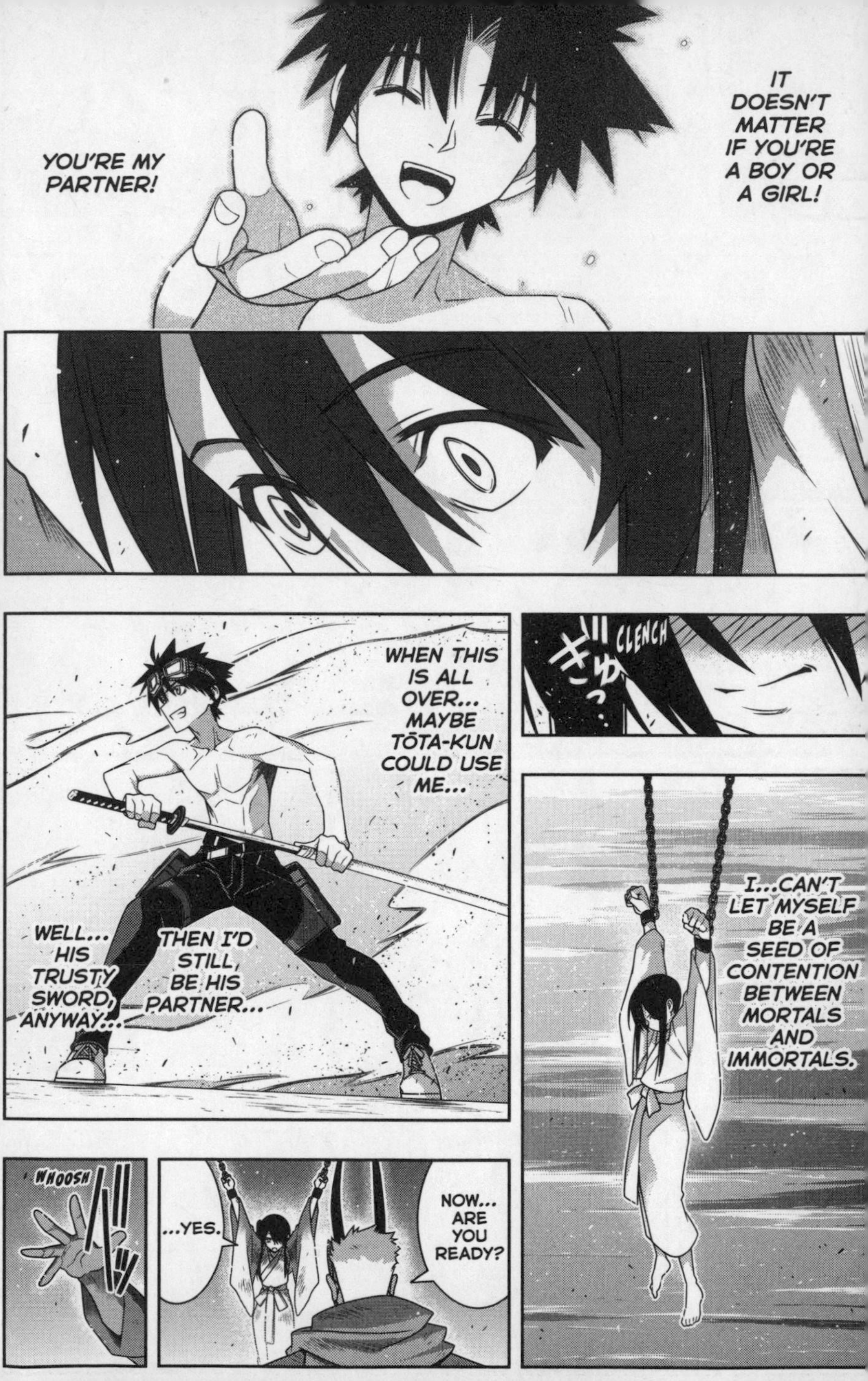
IT DOESN'T MATTER IF YOU'RE A BOY OR A GIRL!
YOU'RE MY PARTNER!
ぎゅっ
CLENCH
I...CAN'T LET MYSELF BE A SEED OF CONTENTION BETWEEN MORTALS AND IMMORTALS.
WHEN THIS IS ALL OVER... MAYBE TŌTA-KUN COULD USE ME...
THEN I'D STILL BE HIS PARTNER...
WELL... HIS TRUSTY SWORD, ANYWAY...
NOW... ARE YOU READY?
...YES.
WHOOSH

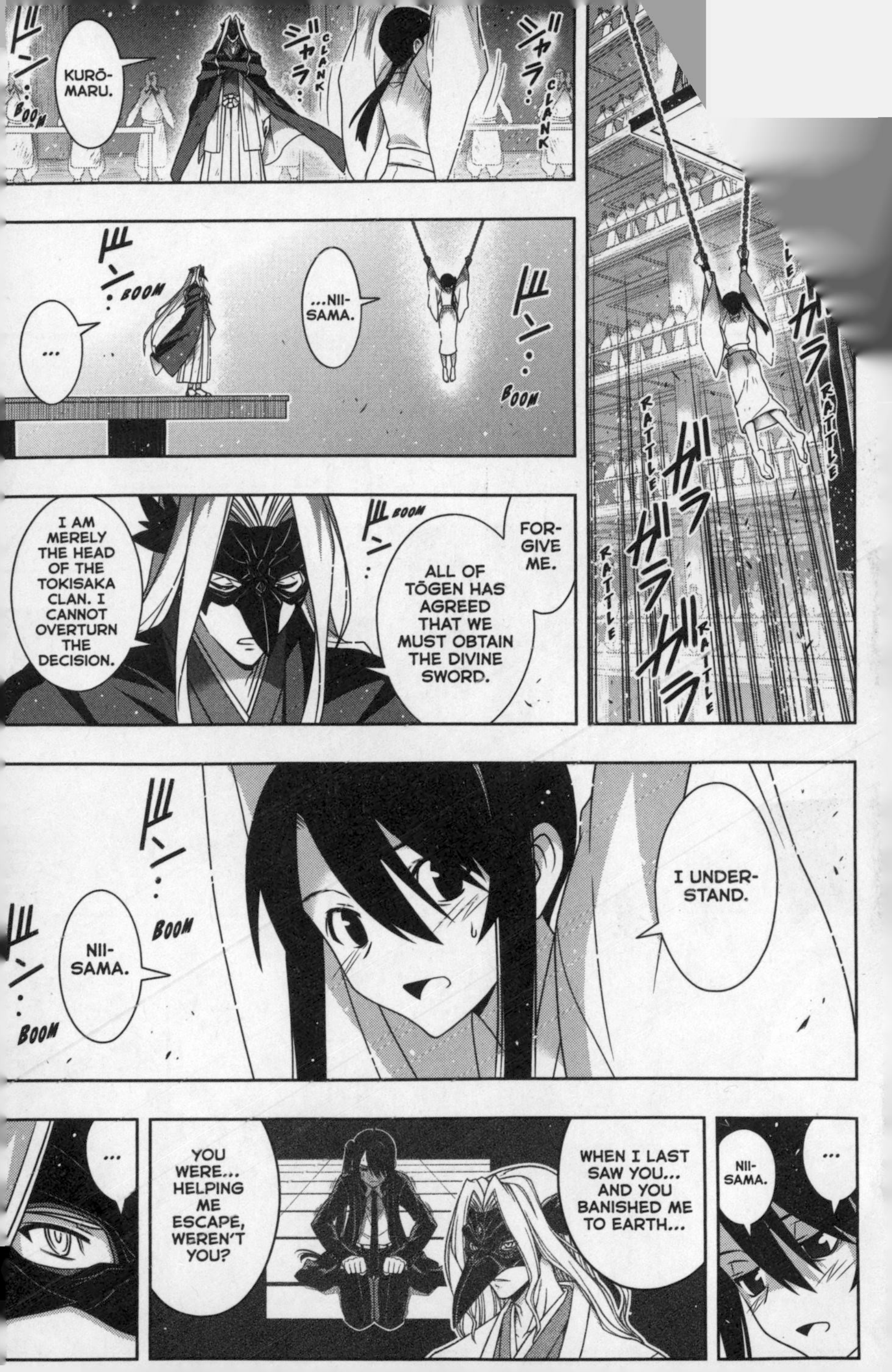
ガラ
RATTLE
ガラ
RATTLE
ガラ
RATTLE
ガラ
RATTLE
ジャラ..
CLANK
ジャラ..
CLANK
KURŌ-MARU.
ドン..
BOOM
ドン..
BOOM
...NII-SAMA.
ドン..
BOOM
...
FOR-GIVE ME.
ALL OF TŌGEN HAS AGREED THAT WE MUST OBTAIN THE DIVINE SWORD.
ドン..
BOOM
I AM MERELY THE HEAD OF THE TOKISAKA CLAN. I CANNOT OVERTURN THE DECISION.
I UNDER-STAND.
ドン..
BOOM
NII-SAMA.
ドン..
BOOM
...
NII-SAMA.
WHEN I LAST SAW YOU... AND YOU BANISHED ME TO EARTH...
YOU WERE... HELPING ME ESCAPE, WEREN'T YOU?
...

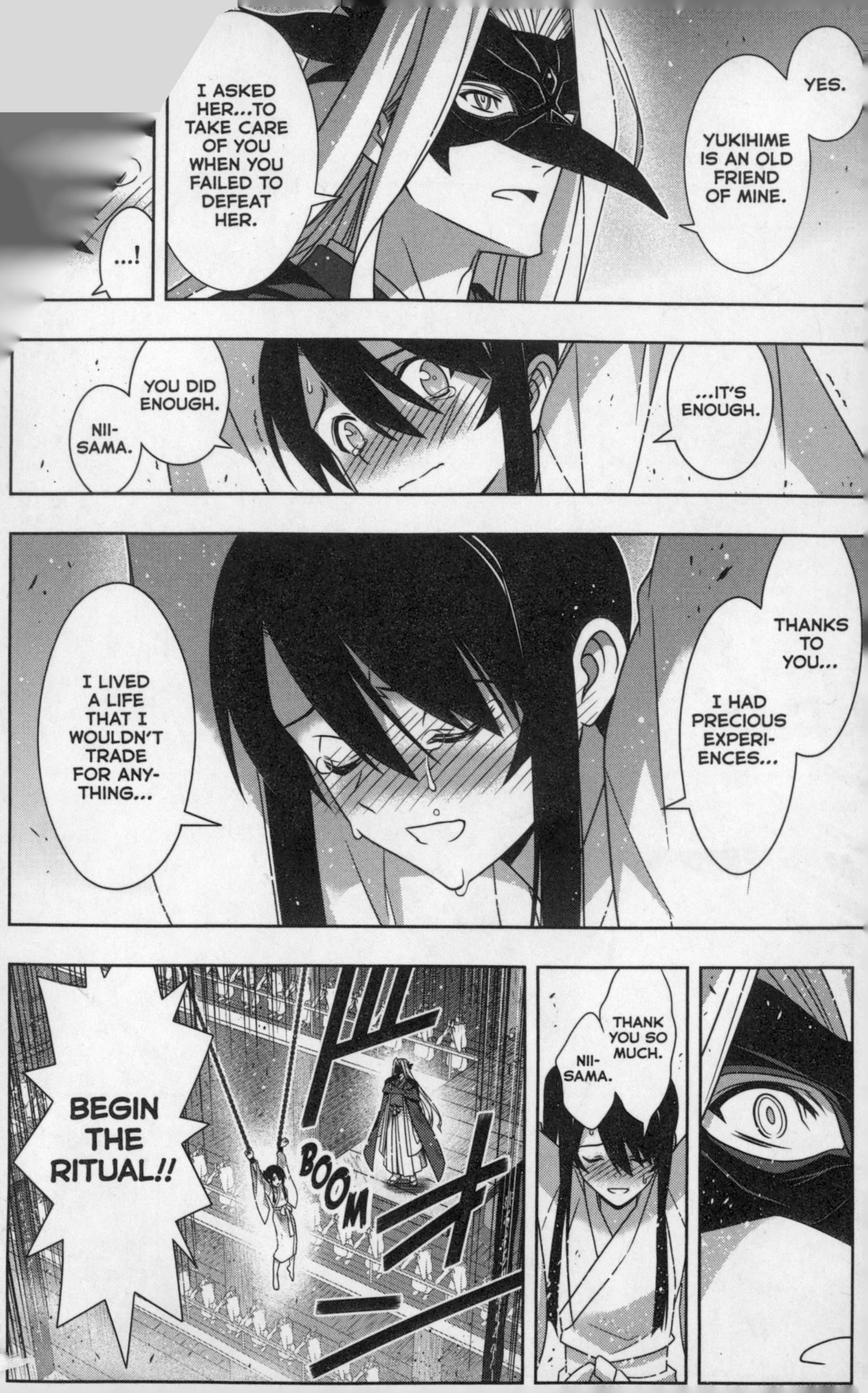
YES.
YUKIHIME IS AN OLD FRIEND OF MINE.
I ASKED HER...TO TAKE CARE OF YOU WHEN YOU FAILED TO DEFEAT HER.
...!
...IT'S ENOUGH.
YOU DID ENOUGH.
NII-SAMA.
THANKS TO YOU...
I HAD PRECIOUS EXPERI-ENCES...
I LIVED A LIFE THAT I WOULDN'T TRADE FOR ANY-THING...
THANK YOU SO MUCH.
NII-SAMA.
BOOM
BEGIN THE RITUAL!!

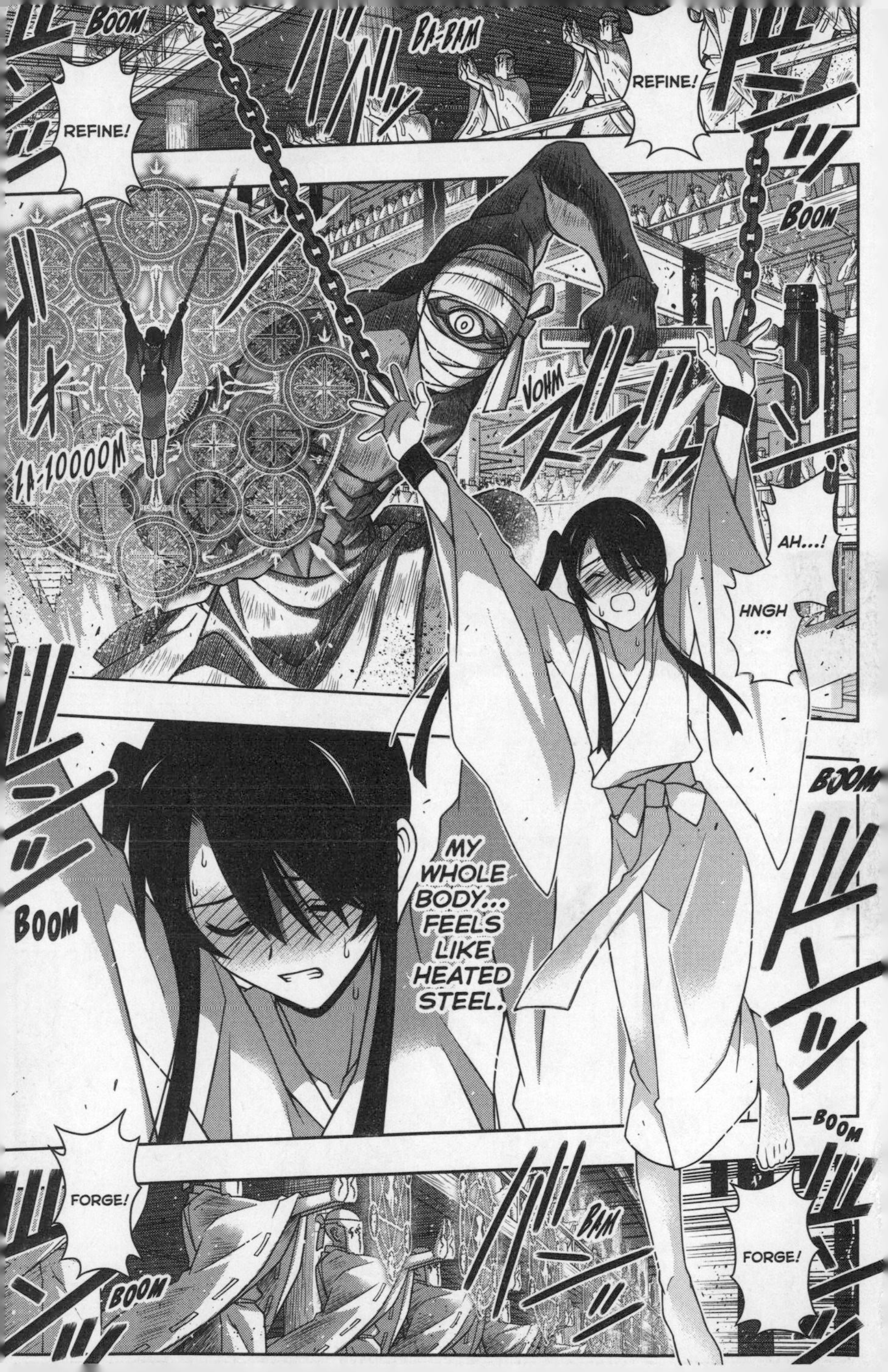

REFINE!
BA-BAM
BOOM
REFINE!
BOOM
VOHM
AH...!
HNGH ...
ZA-ZOOOOM
BOOM
MY WHOLE BODY... FEELS LIKE HEATED STEEL.
BOOM
BOOM
FORGE!
BAM
FORGE!
BOOM

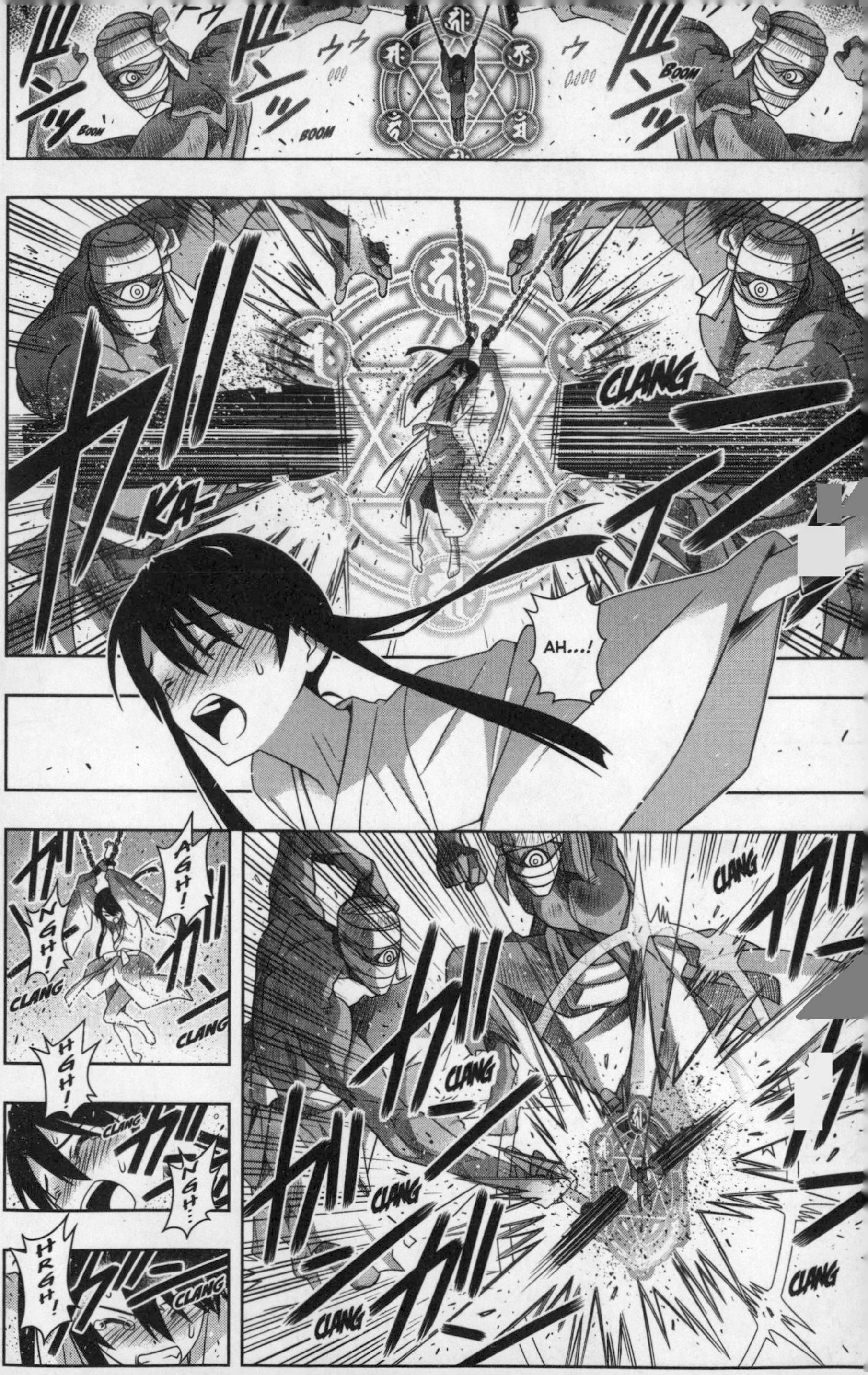
BOOM
BOOM
BOOM
CLANG
KA-
AH...!
CLANG
CLANG
CLANG
CLANG
CLANG
AGH!
NGH!
CLANG
CLANG
HGGH!
CLANG
NGH...
HRGH!
CLANG

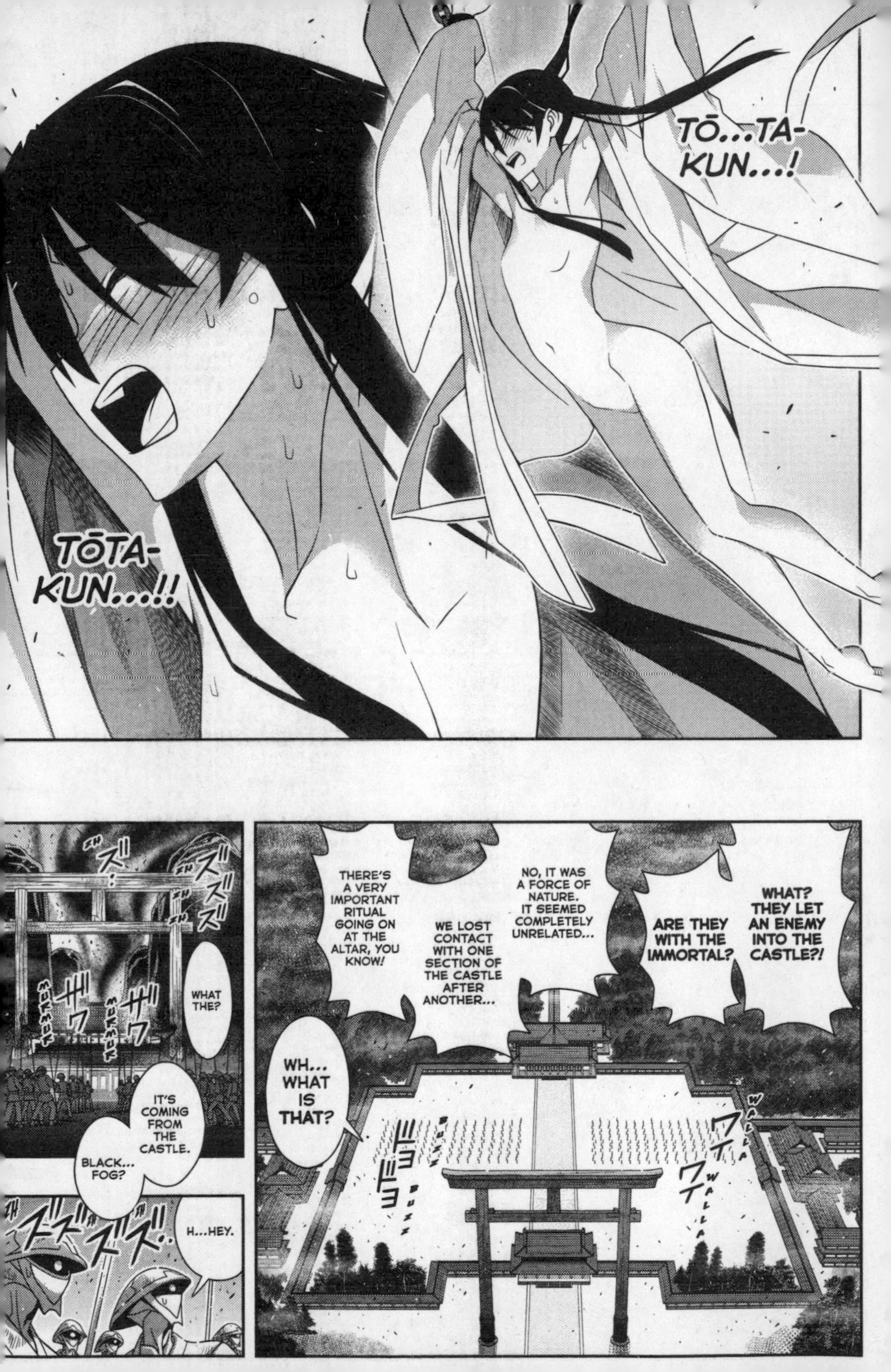
TŌ...TA-KUN...!
TŌTA-KUN...!!
WHAT? THEY LET AN ENEMY INTO THE CASTLE?!
ARE THEY WITH THE IMMORTAL?
NO, IT WAS A FORCE OF NATURE. IT SEEMED COMPLETELY UNRELATED...
WE LOST CONTACT WITH ONE SECTION OF THE CASTLE AFTER ANOTHER...
THERE'S A VERY IMPORTANT RITUAL GOING ON AT THE ALTAR, YOU KNOW!
WALLA
WALLA
BUZZ
BUZZ
WH... WHAT IS THAT?
ZH
ZH
ZH
WHAT THE?
IT'S COMING FROM THE CASTLE.
BLACK... FOG?
H...HEY.

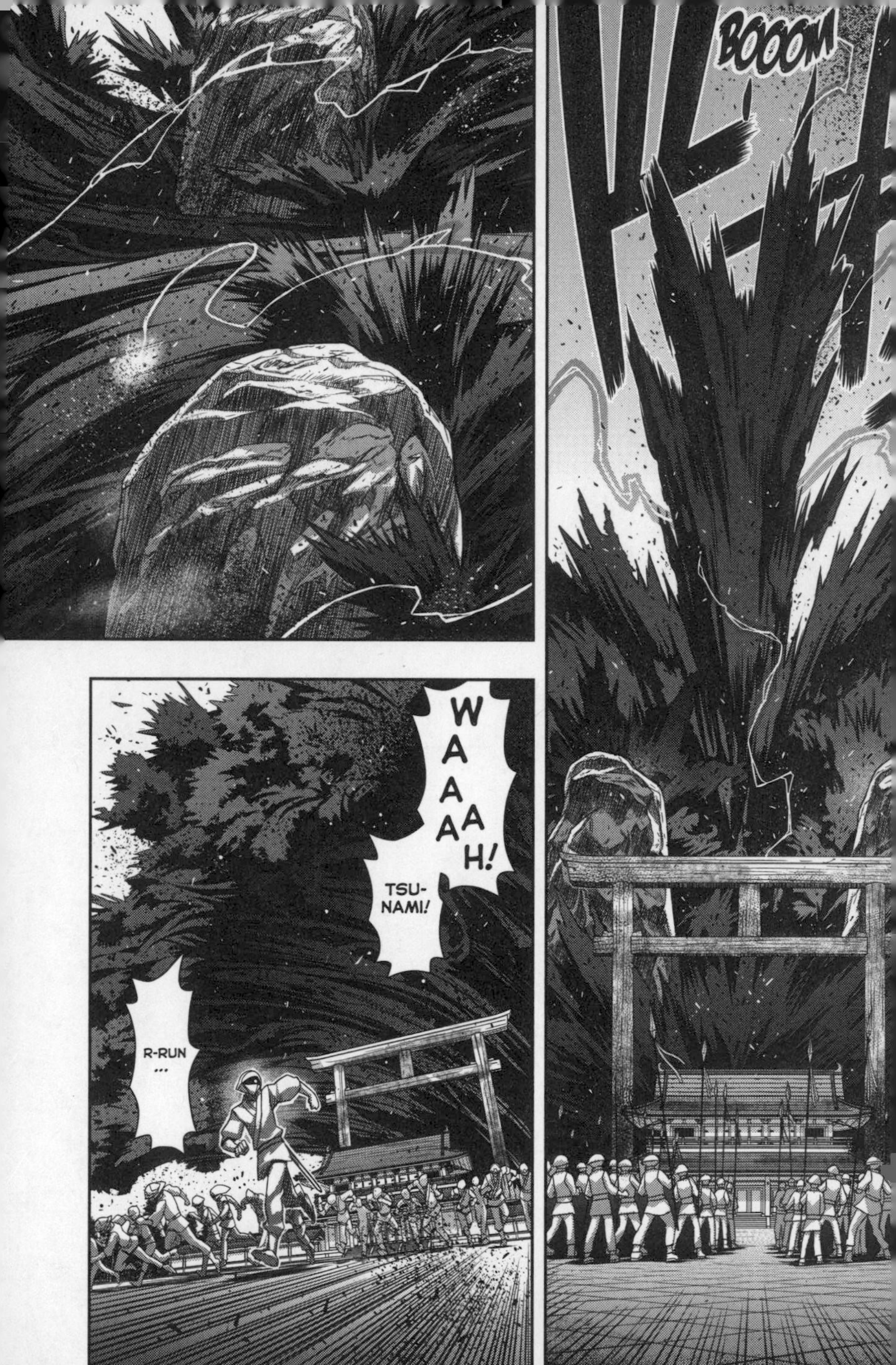
BOOOM
WAAAAH!
TSU-NAMI!
R-RUN...

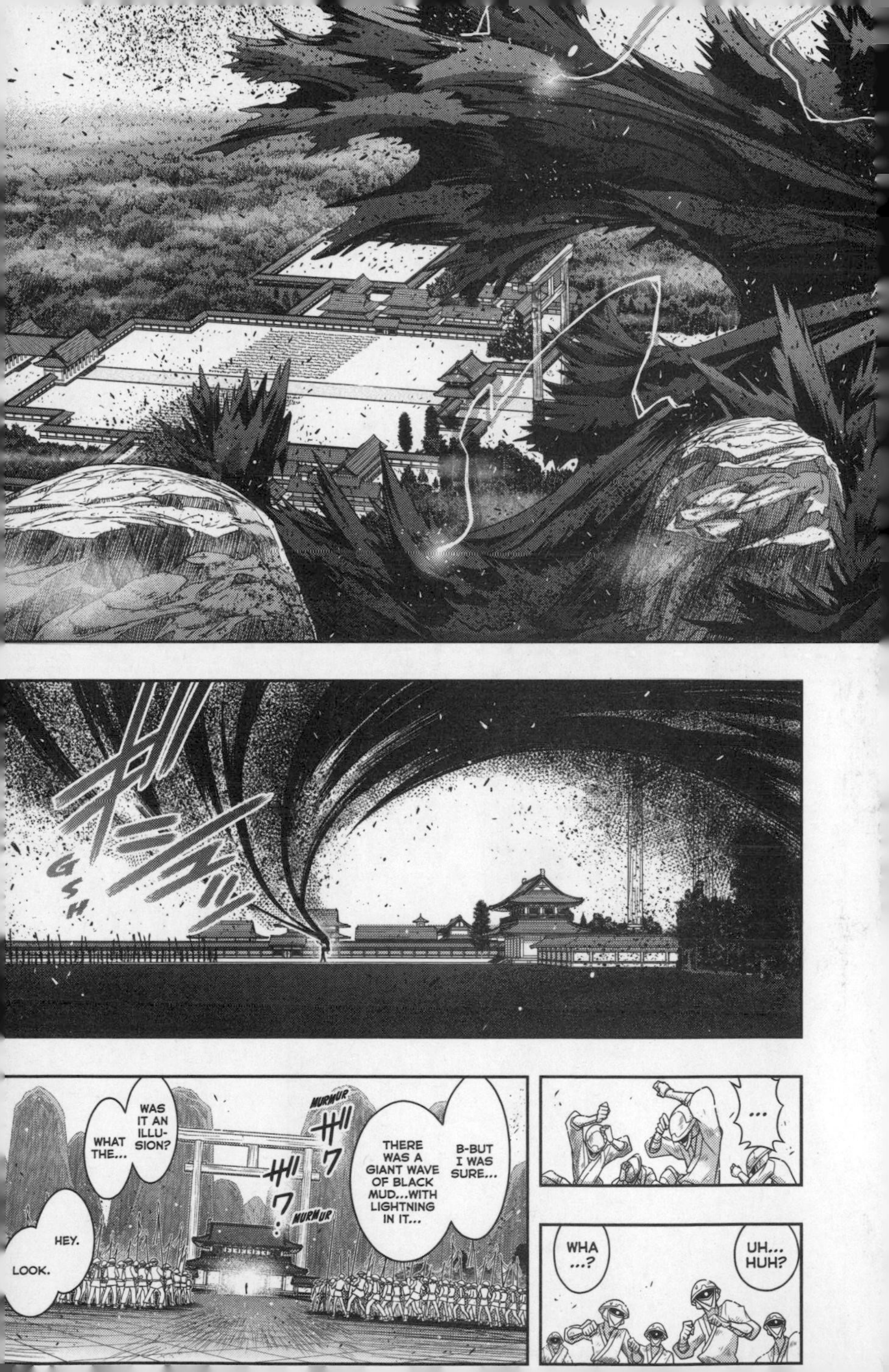
GSH
...
UH... HUH?
WHA ...?
B-BUT I WAS SURE...
THERE WAS A GIANT WAVE OF BLACK MUD...WITH LIGHTNING IN IT...
MURMUR
MURMUR
WAS IT AN ILLUSION?
WHAT THE...
HEY.
LOOK.

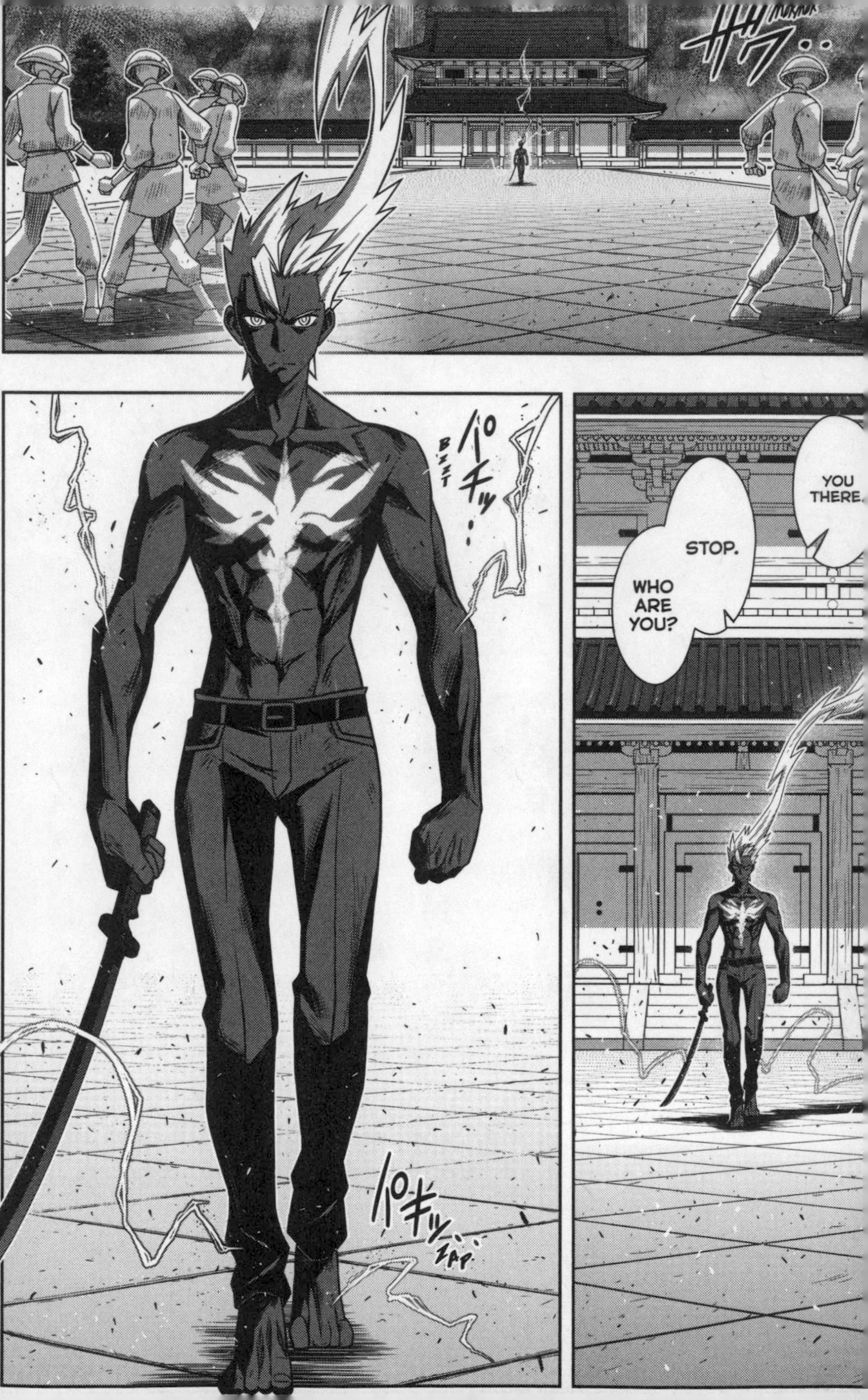
ザワ..
MURMUR
YOU THERE.
STOP. WHO ARE YOU?
パチッ
BZZT
パキッ
ZAP

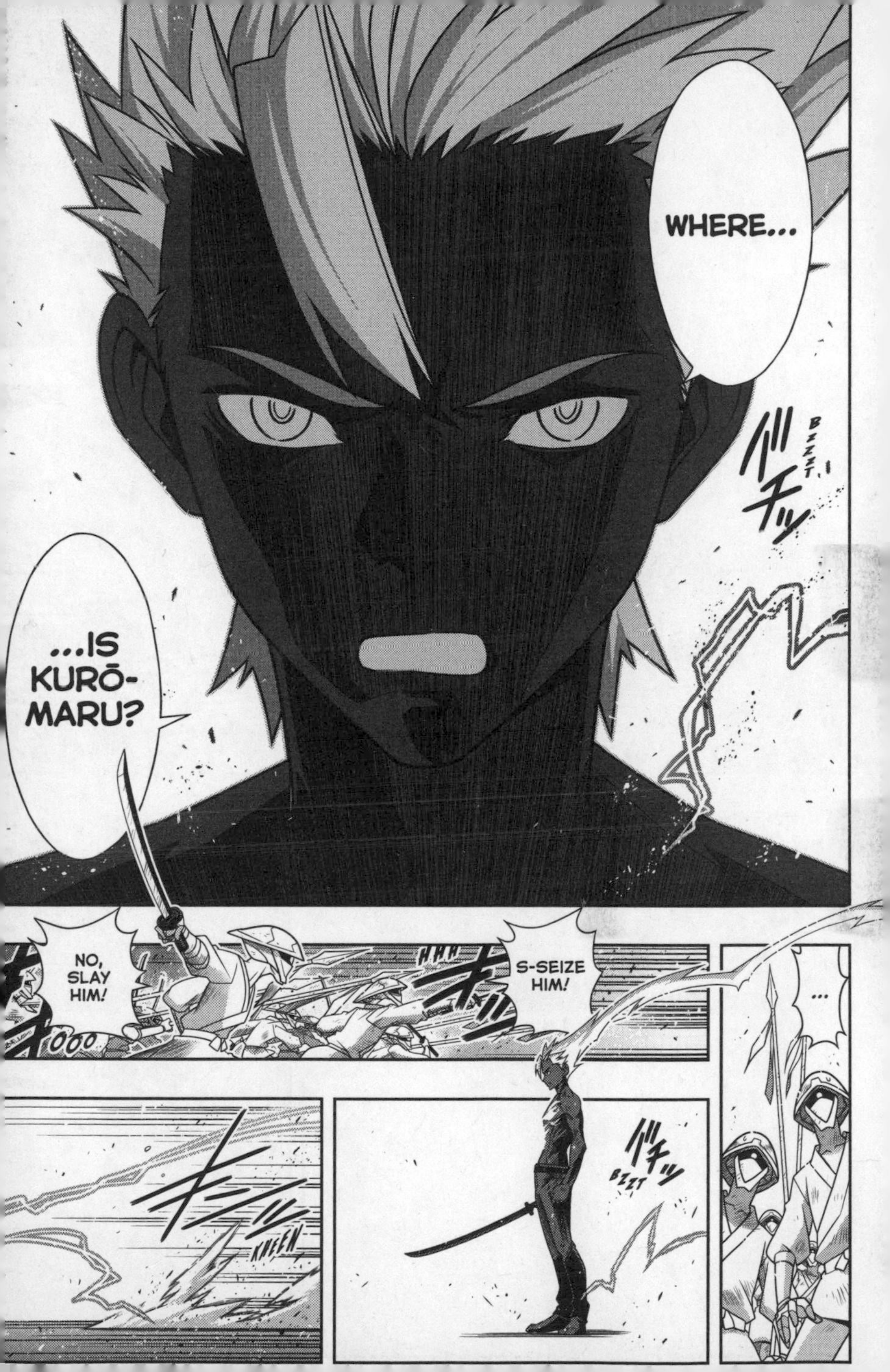

WHERE...
...IS KURŌ-MARU?
BZZT
...
S-SEIZE HIM!
HHH
NO, SLAY HIM!
OOO
BZZT
KNEEN

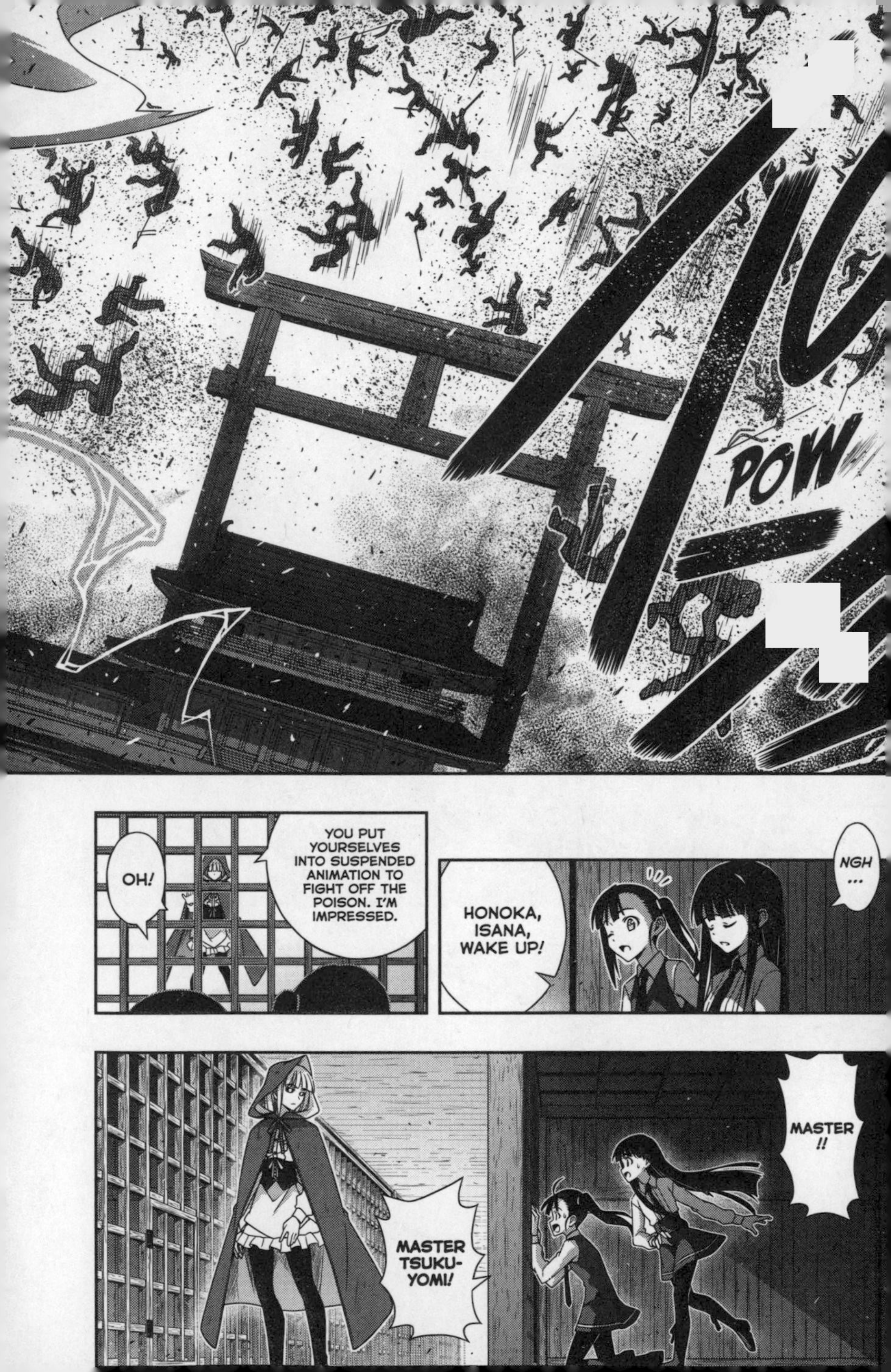
POW
NGH...
HONOKA, ISANA, WAKE UP!
YOU PUT YOURSELVES INTO SUSPENDED ANIMATION TO FIGHT OFF THE POISON. I'M IMPRESSED.
OH!
MASTER!!
MASTER TSUKU-YOMI!

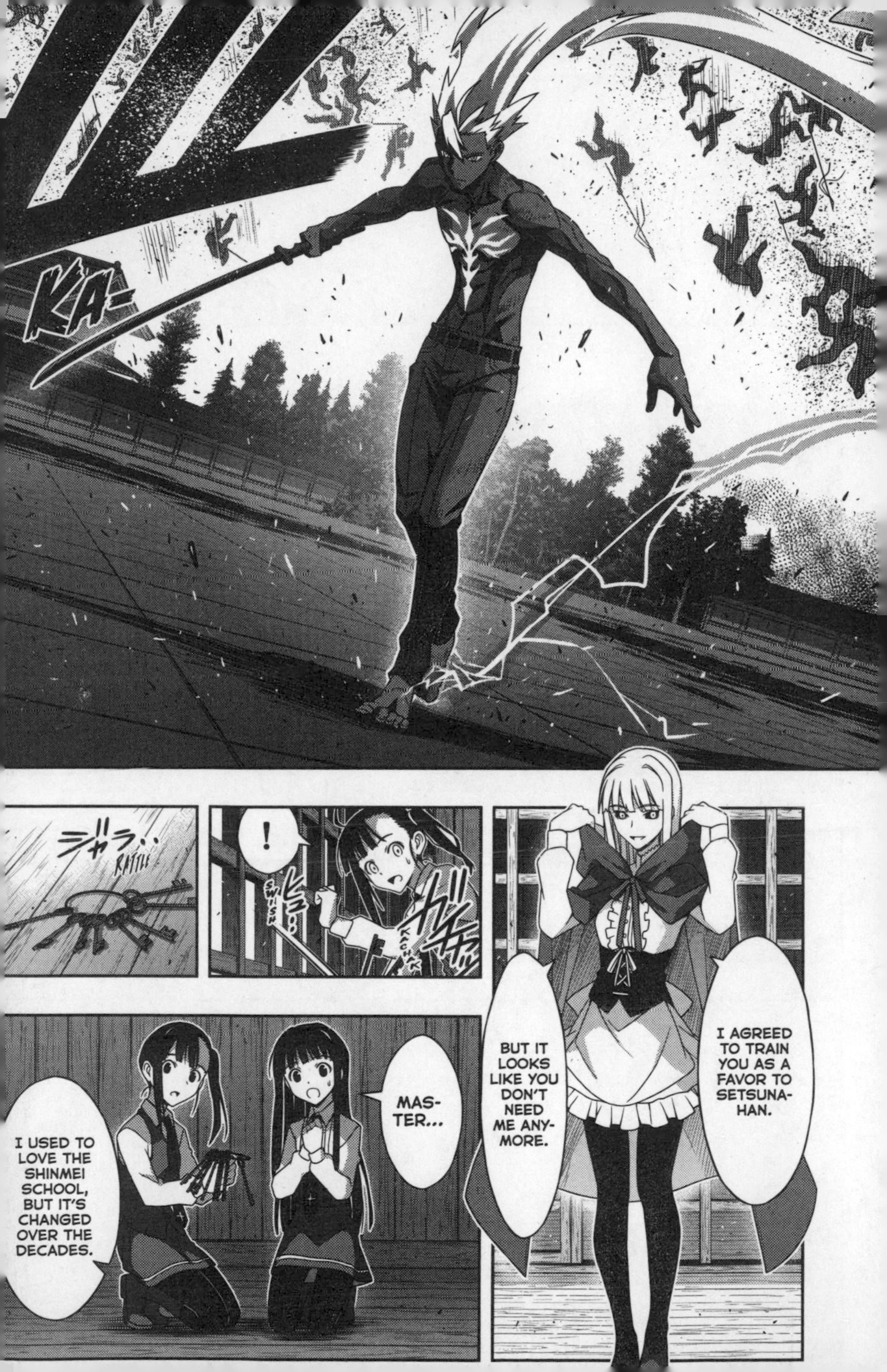
KA-
I AGREED TO TRAIN YOU AS A FAVOR TO SETSUNA-HAN.
BUT IT LOOKS LIKE YOU DON'T NEED ME ANYMORE.
!
SWISH
KACHK
ジャラ‥
RATTLE
MASTER...
I USED TO LOVE THE SHINMEI SCHOOL, BUT IT'S CHANGED OVER THE DECADES.

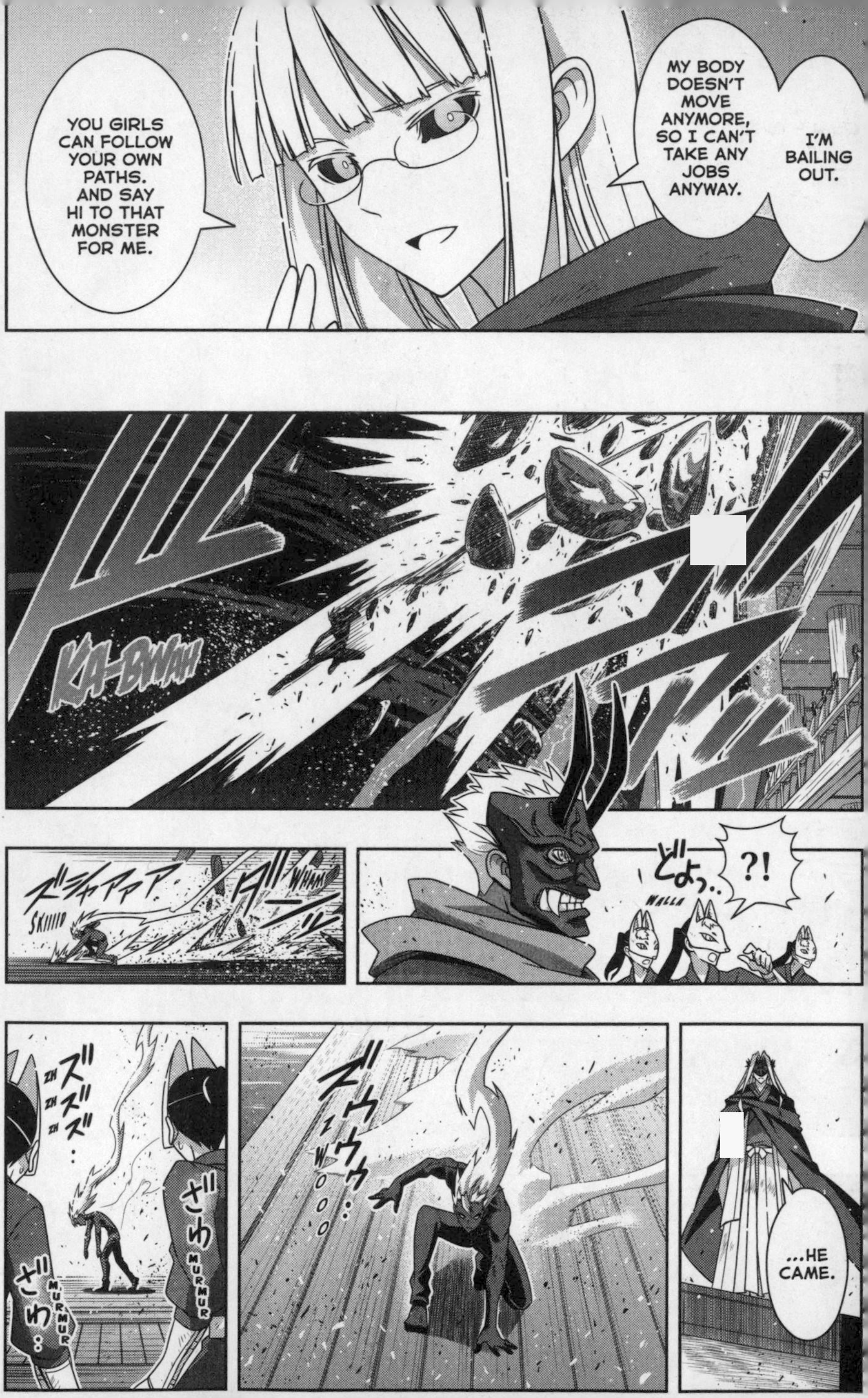
I'M BAILING OUT.
MY BODY DOESN'T MOVE ANYMORE, SO I CAN'T TAKE ANY JOBS ANYWAY.
YOU GIRLS CAN FOLLOW YOUR OWN PATHS. AND SAY HI TO THAT MONSTER FOR ME.
KA-BWAH
どよっ.. WALLA
?!
ズシャアアア SKIIIID
WHAM
...HE CAME.
ズウウウ.. ZWOOO
ズズズ.. ZH ZH ZH
ざわ MURMUR
ざわ.. MURMUR

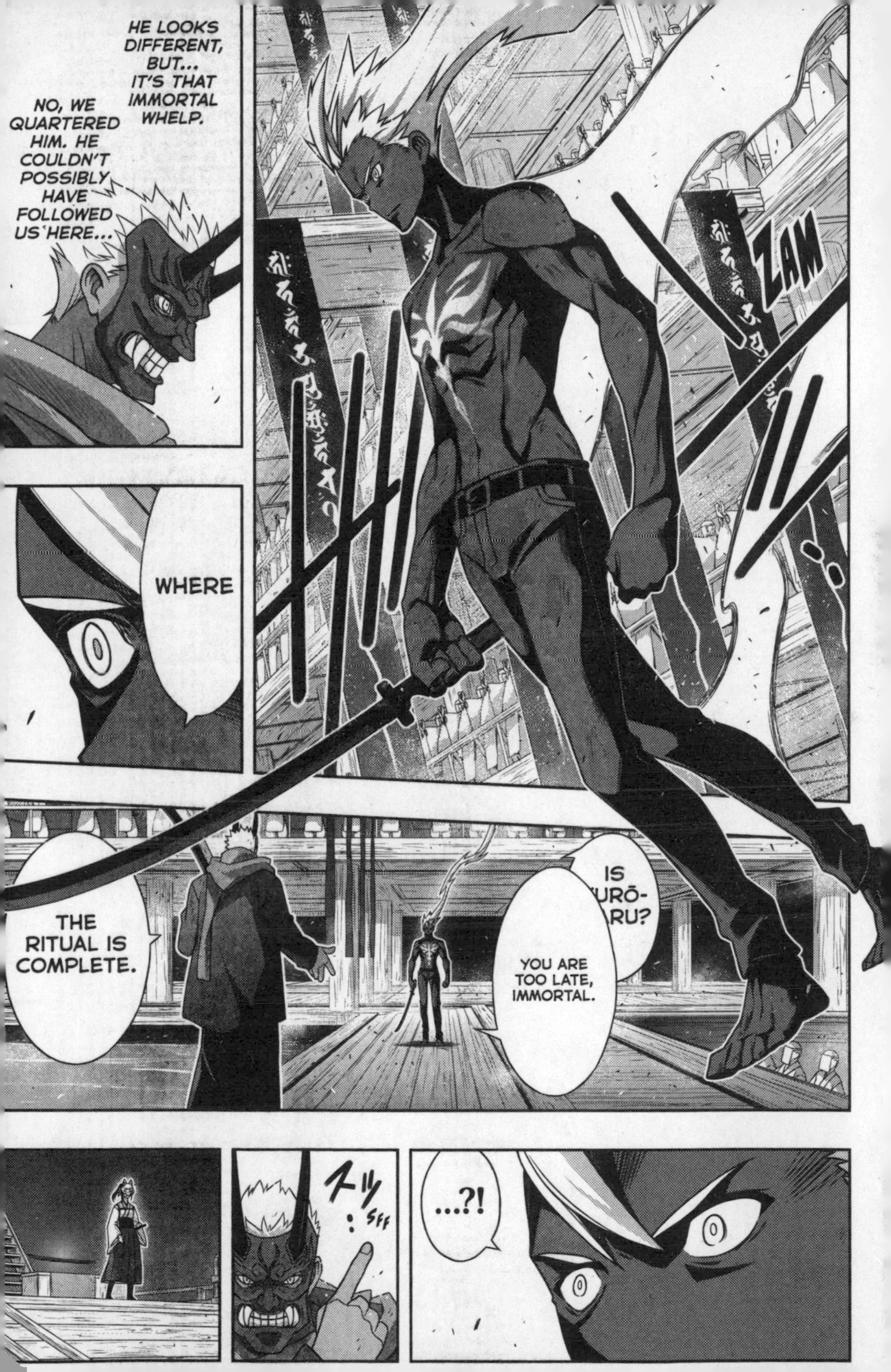
ZAM
HE LOOKS DIFFERENT, BUT... IT'S THAT IMMORTAL WHELP.
NO, WE QUARTERED HIM. HE COULDN'T POSSIBLY HAVE FOLLOWED US HERE...
WHERE
IS
URŌ-
RU?
YOU ARE TOO LATE, IMMORTAL.
THE RITUAL IS COMPLETE.
...?!
スッ
SFF

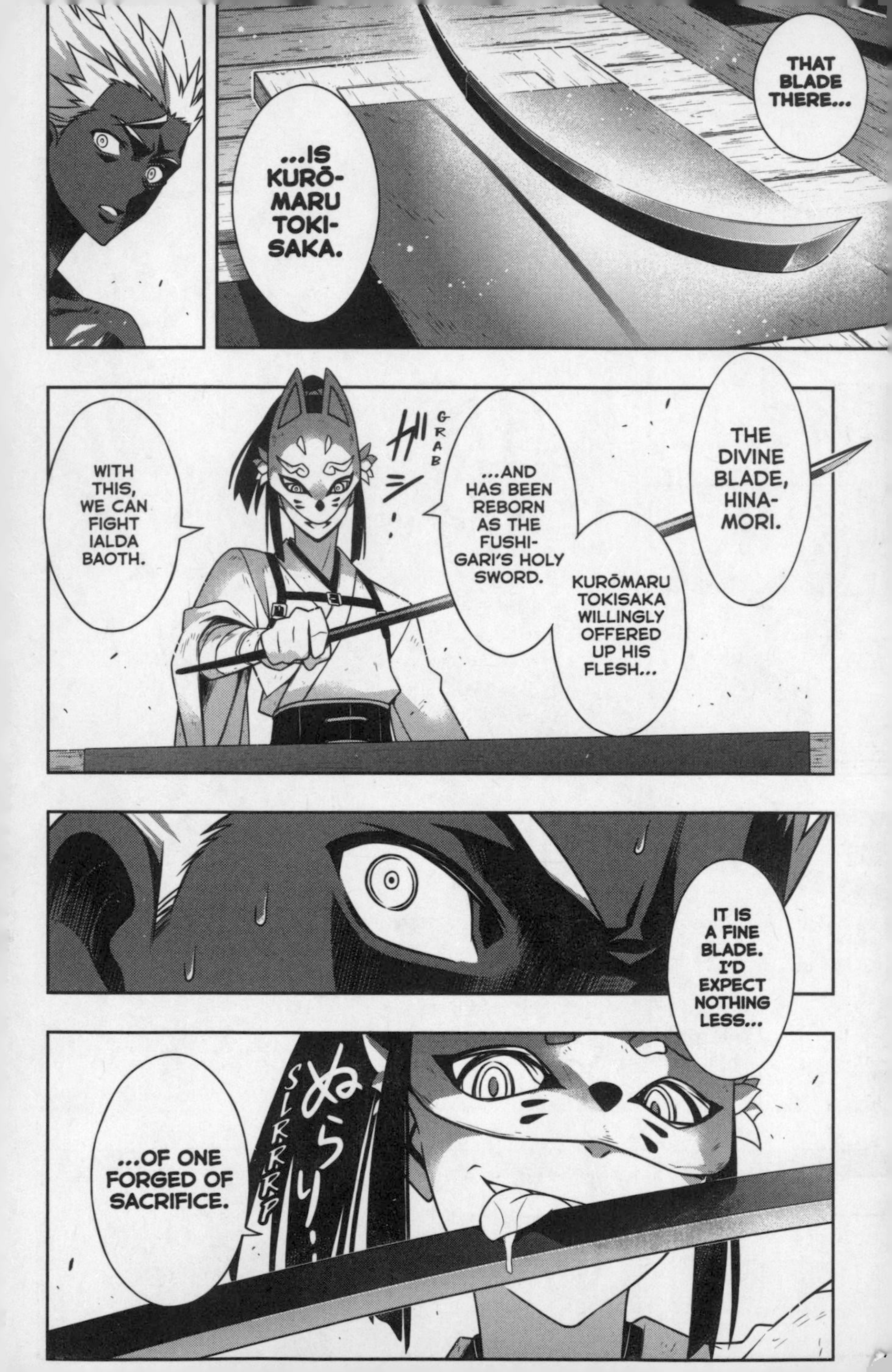
THAT BLADE THERE...
...IS KURŌMARU TOKISAKA.
THE DIVINE BLADE, HINAMORI.
KURŌMARU TOKISAKA WILLINGLY OFFERED UP HIS FLESH...
...AND HAS BEEN REBORN AS THE FUSHIGARI'S HOLY SWORD.
GRAB
WITH THIS, WE CAN FIGHT IALDA BAOTH.
IT IS A FINE BLADE. I'D EXPECT NOTHING LESS...
ぬらり
SLRRRP
...OF ONE FORGED OF SACRIFICE.

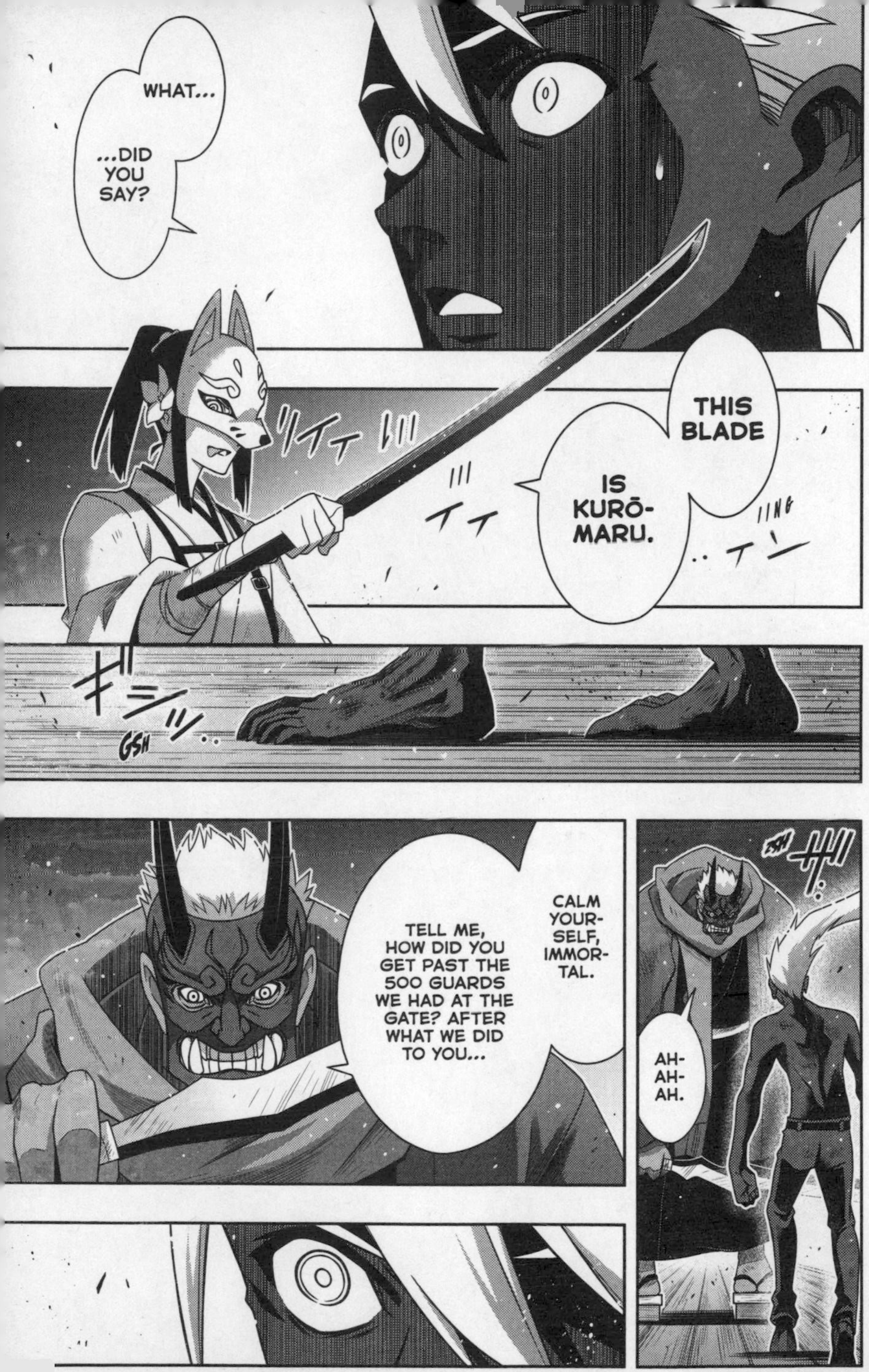
WHAT...
...DID YOU SAY?
THIS BLADE
IS KURŌ-MARU.
IING
GSH
ZSH
AH-AH-AH.
CALM YOURSELF, IMMORTAL.
TELL ME, HOW DID YOU GET PAST THE 500 GUARDS WE HAD AT THE GATE? AFTER WHAT WE DID TO YOU...

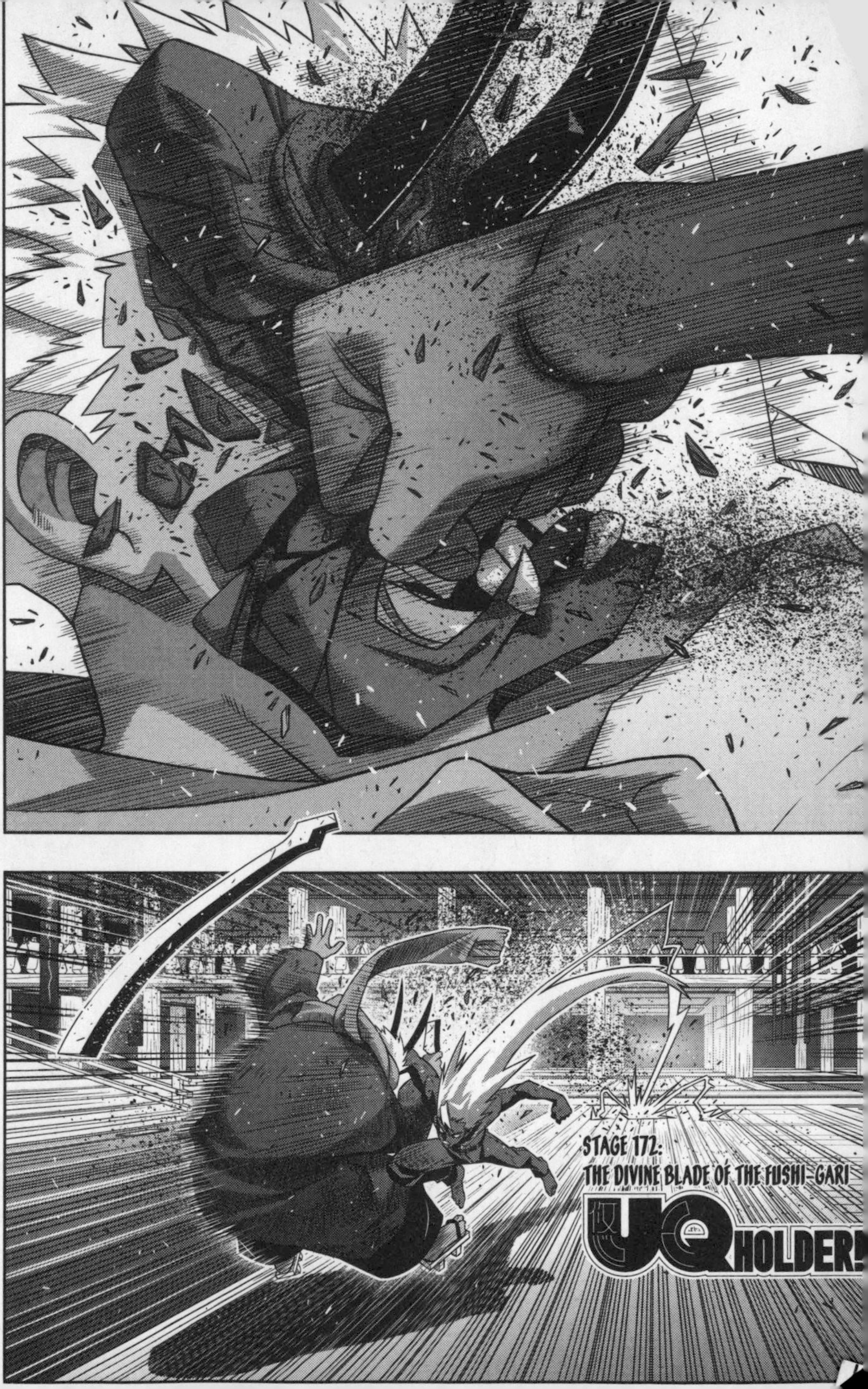
STAGE 172:
THE DIVINE BLADE OF THE FUSHI-GARI
UQ HOLDER!

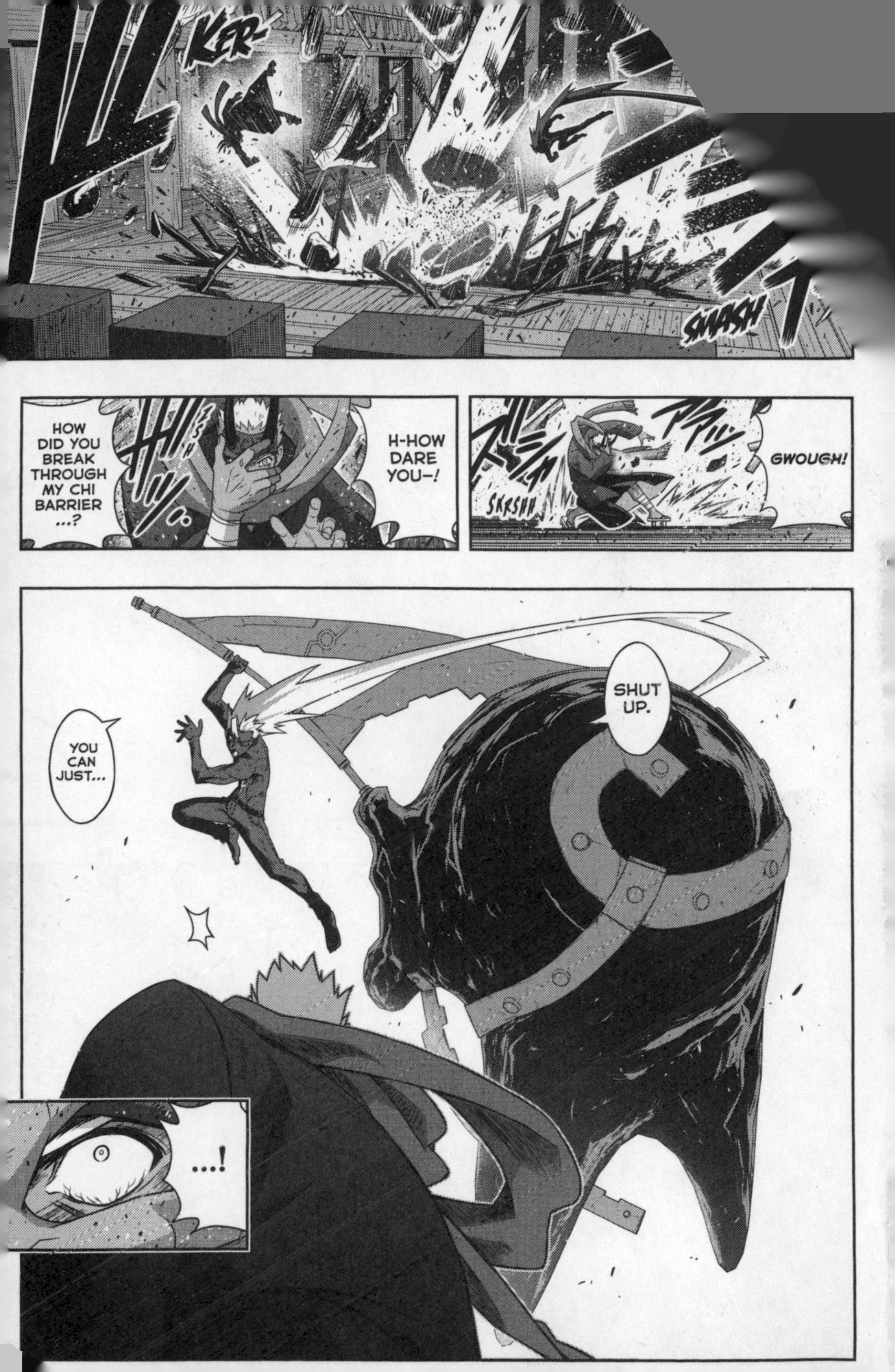
KER-
SMASH
SKRSHH
GWOUGH!
H-HOW DARE YOU-!
HOW DID YOU BREAK THROUGH MY CHI BARRIER ...?
SHUT UP.
YOU CAN JUST...
...!

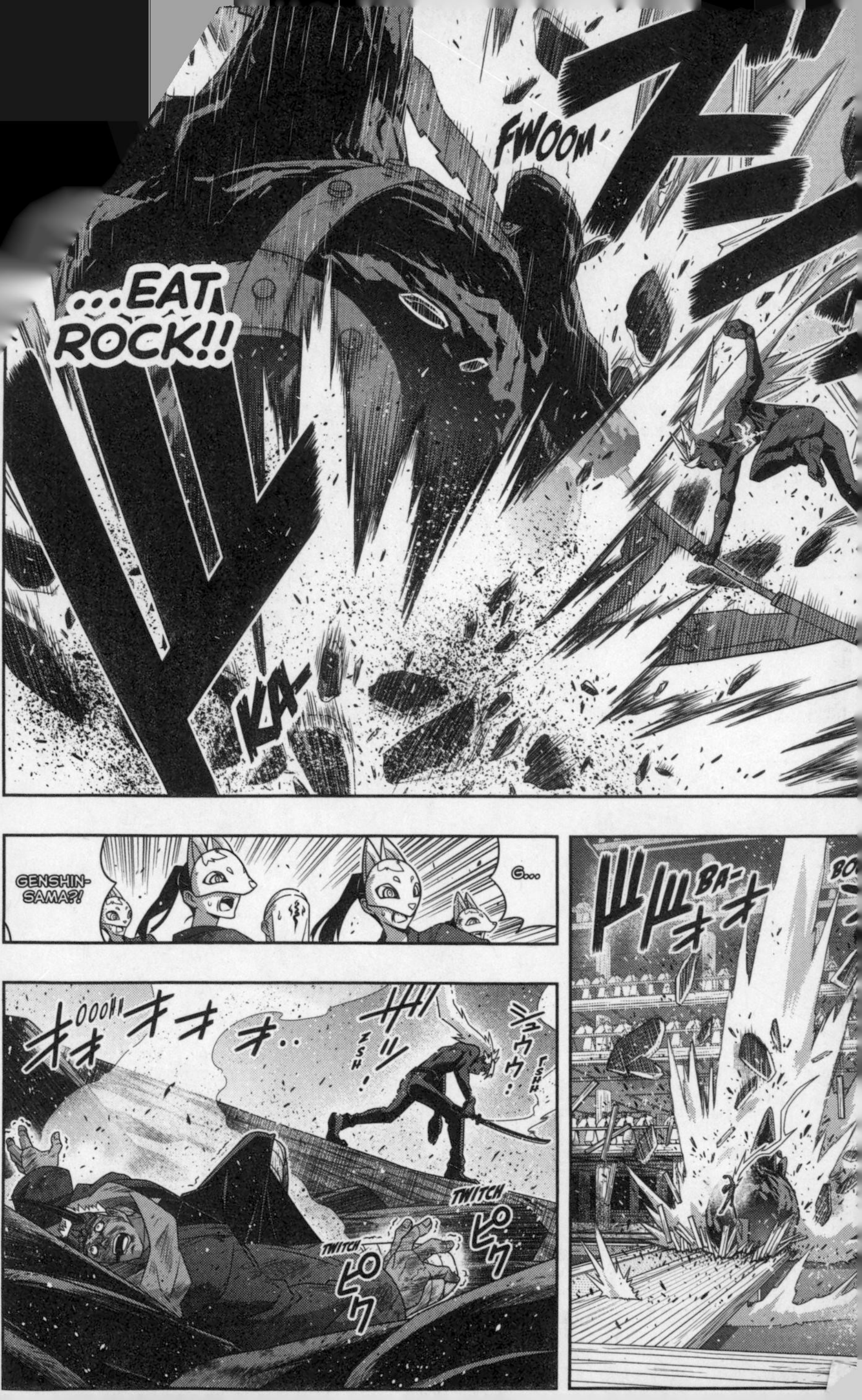

FWOOM
...EAT ROCK!!
KA-
BA-
BO
G...
GENSHIN-SAMA?!
FSHH
ZSH
OOOH
TWITCH
TWITCH

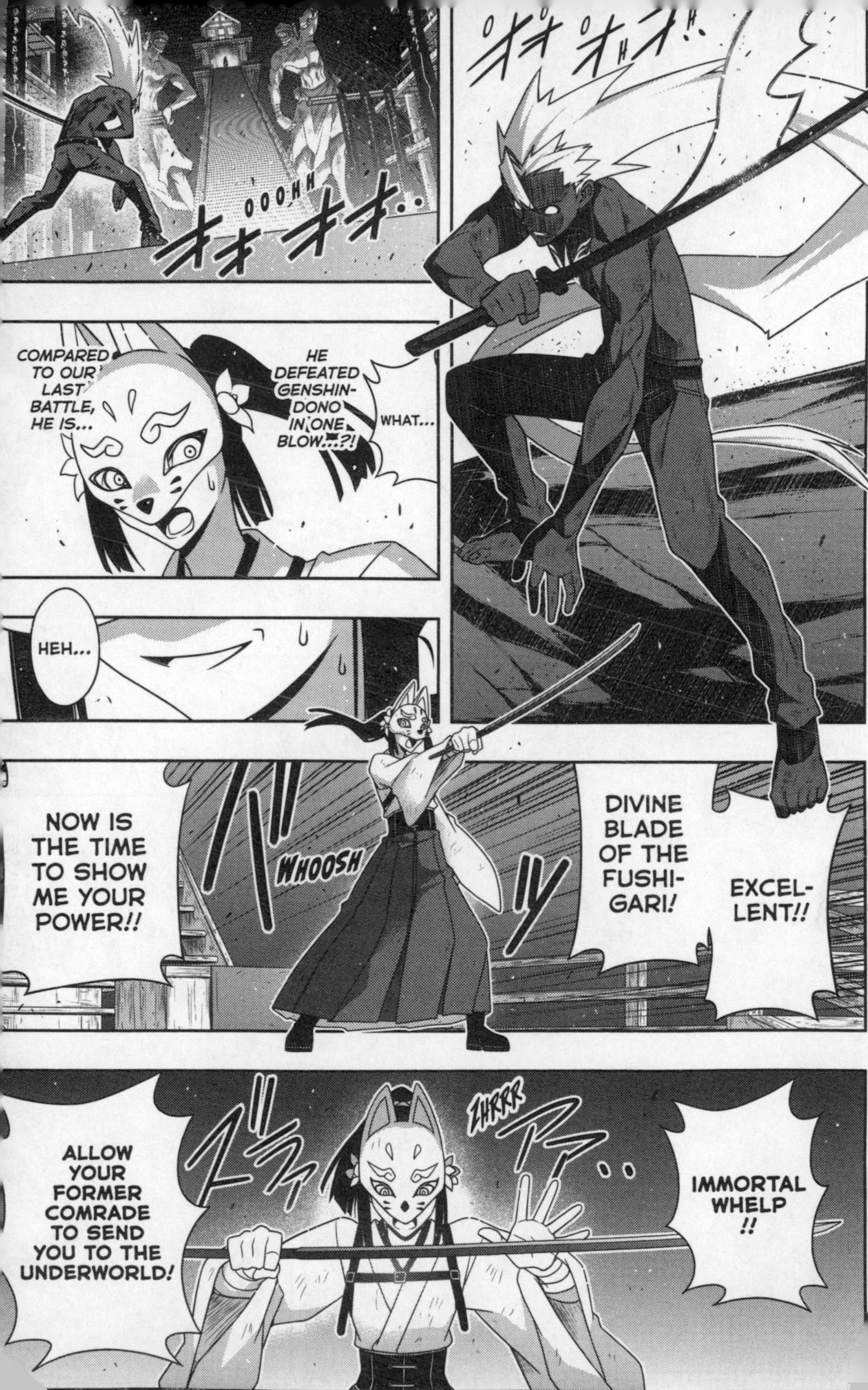
OOOHH
OOOHH
WHAT...
HE DEFEATED GENSHIN-DONO IN ONE BLOW...?!
COMPARED TO OUR LAST BATTLE, HE IS...
HEH...
EXCEL-LENT!!
DIVINE BLADE OF THE FUSHI-GARI!
WHOOSH
NOW IS THE TIME TO SHOW ME YOUR POWER!!
IMMORTAL WHELP!!
ZHRRR
ALLOW YOUR FORMER COMRADE TO SEND YOU TO THE UNDERWORLD!

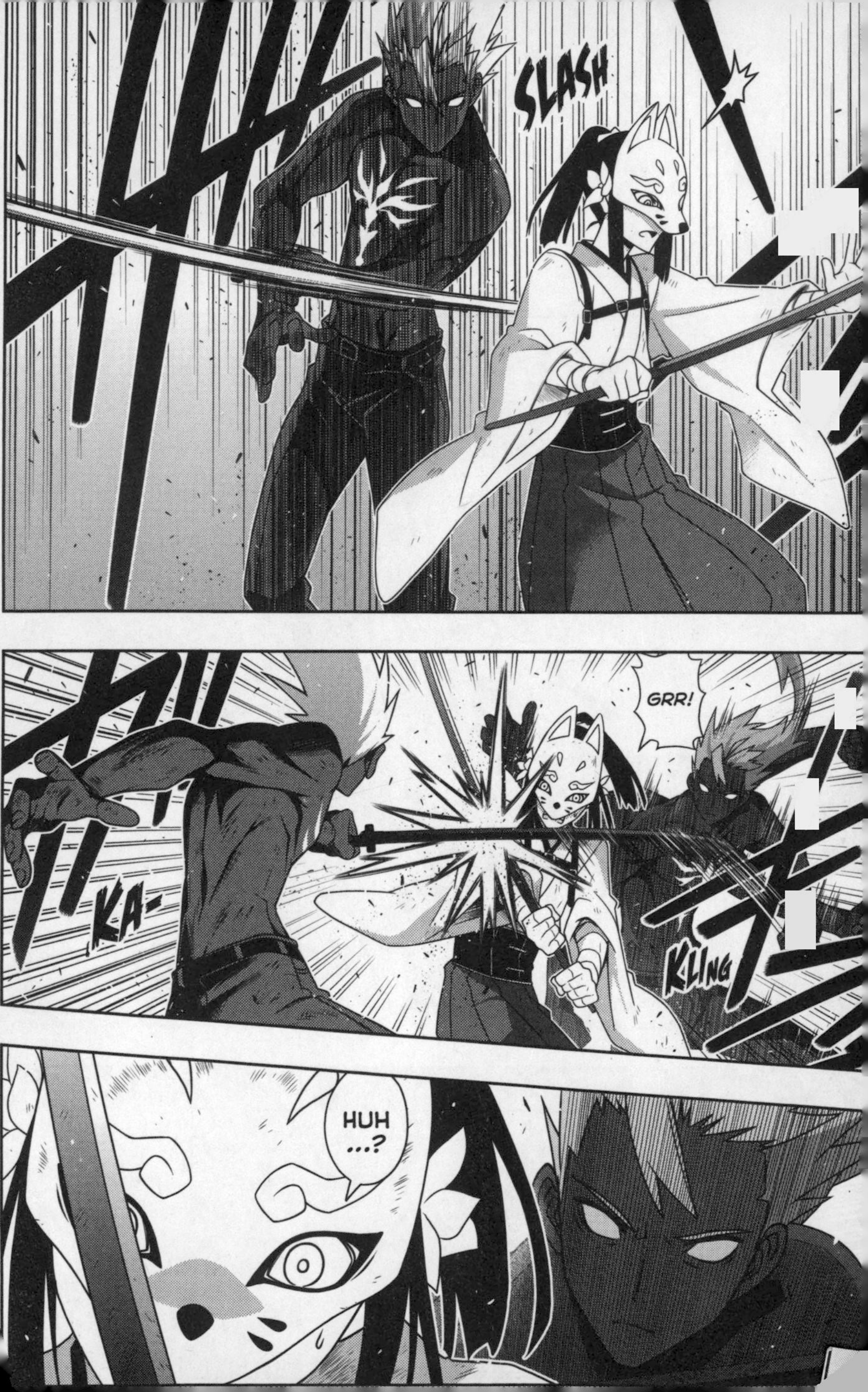
SLASH
GRR!
KLING
KA-
HUH ...?

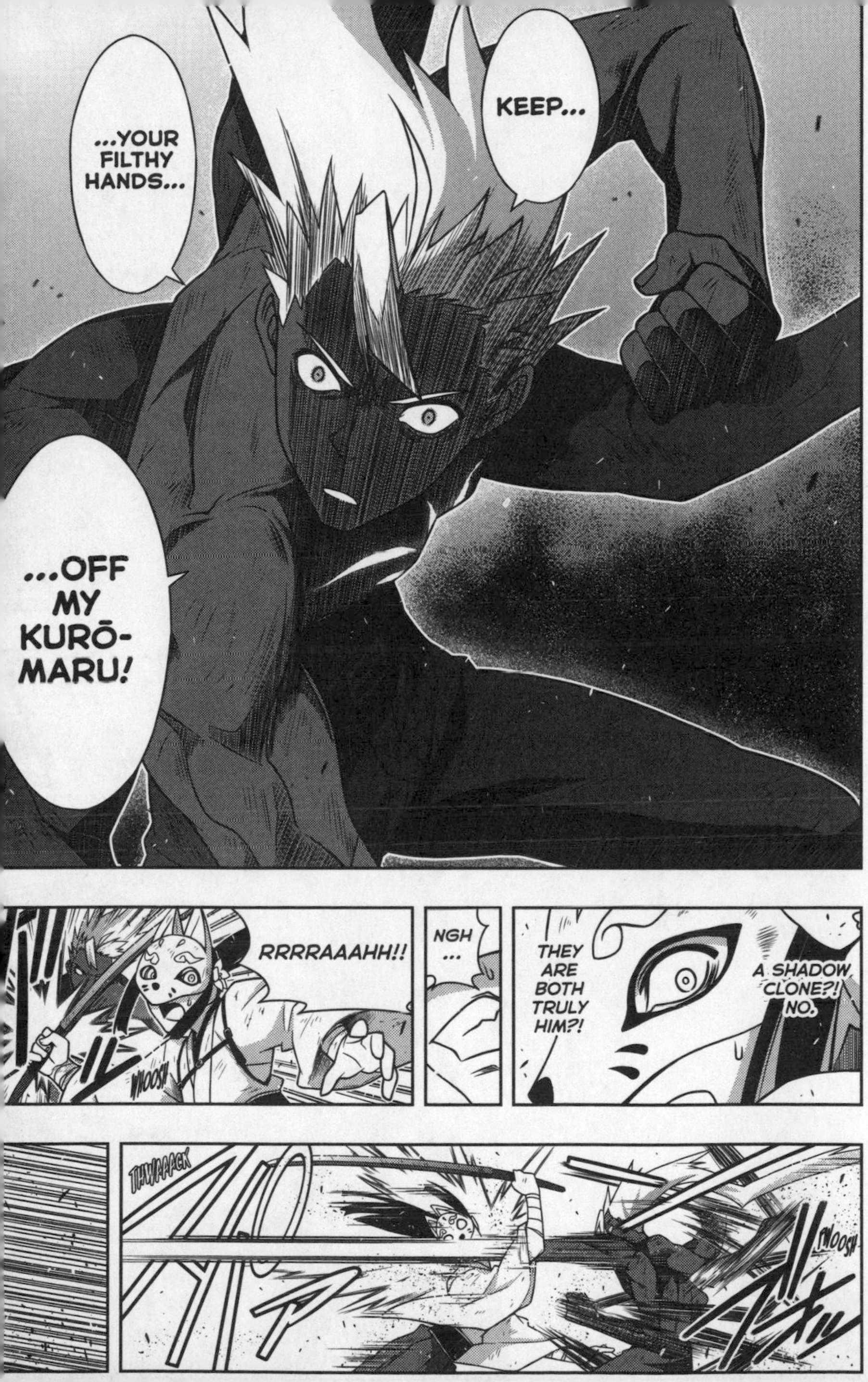
KEEP...
...YOUR FILTHY HANDS...
...OFF MY KURŌ-MARU!
A SHADOW CLONE?! NO.
THEY ARE BOTH TRULY HIM?!
NGH ...
RRRRAAAHH!!
WHOOSH
SWOOSH
THWAAACK

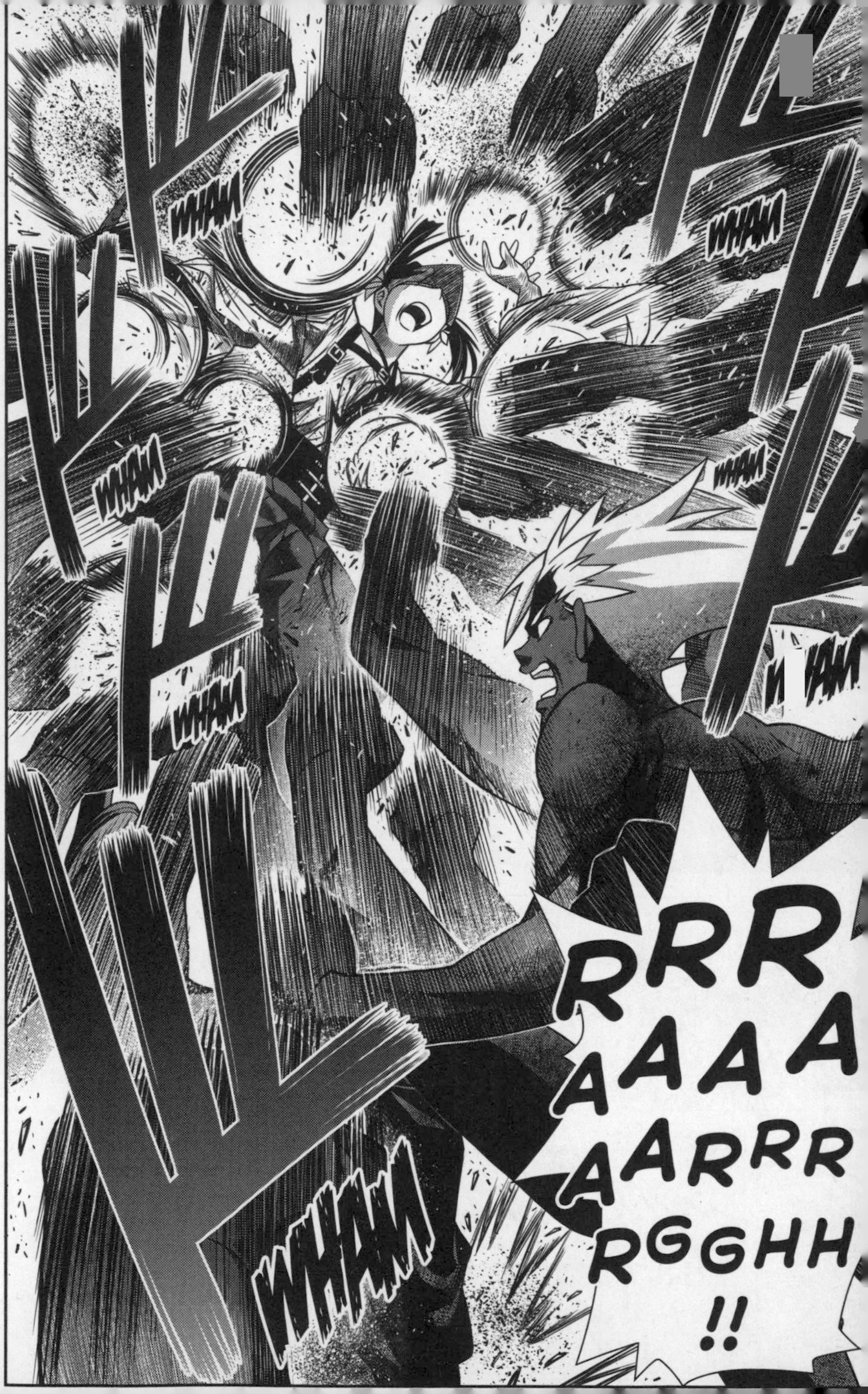
WHAM
WHAM
WHAM
WHAM
WHAM
WHAM
WHAM
RRRAAAAAARRRRGGHH!!

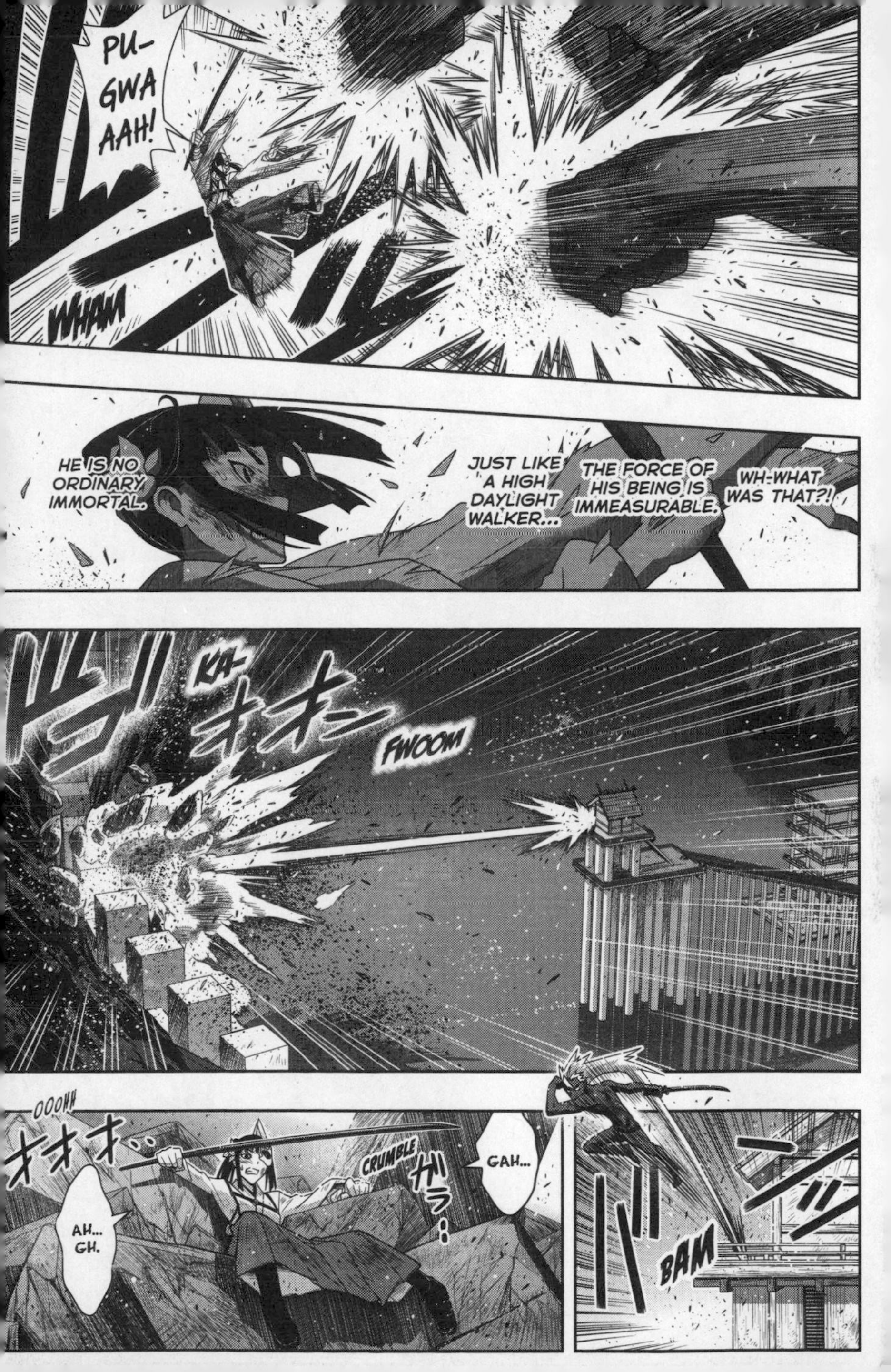
PU-GWA AAH!
WHAM
WH-WHAT WAS THAT?!
THE FORCE OF HIS BEING IS IMMEASURABLE.
JUST LIKE A HIGH DAYLIGHT WALKER...
HE IS NO ORDINARY IMMORTAL.
KA
FWOOM
BAM
GAH...
CRUMBLE
ガラ・
AH... GH.
OOOHH
オオオ・・

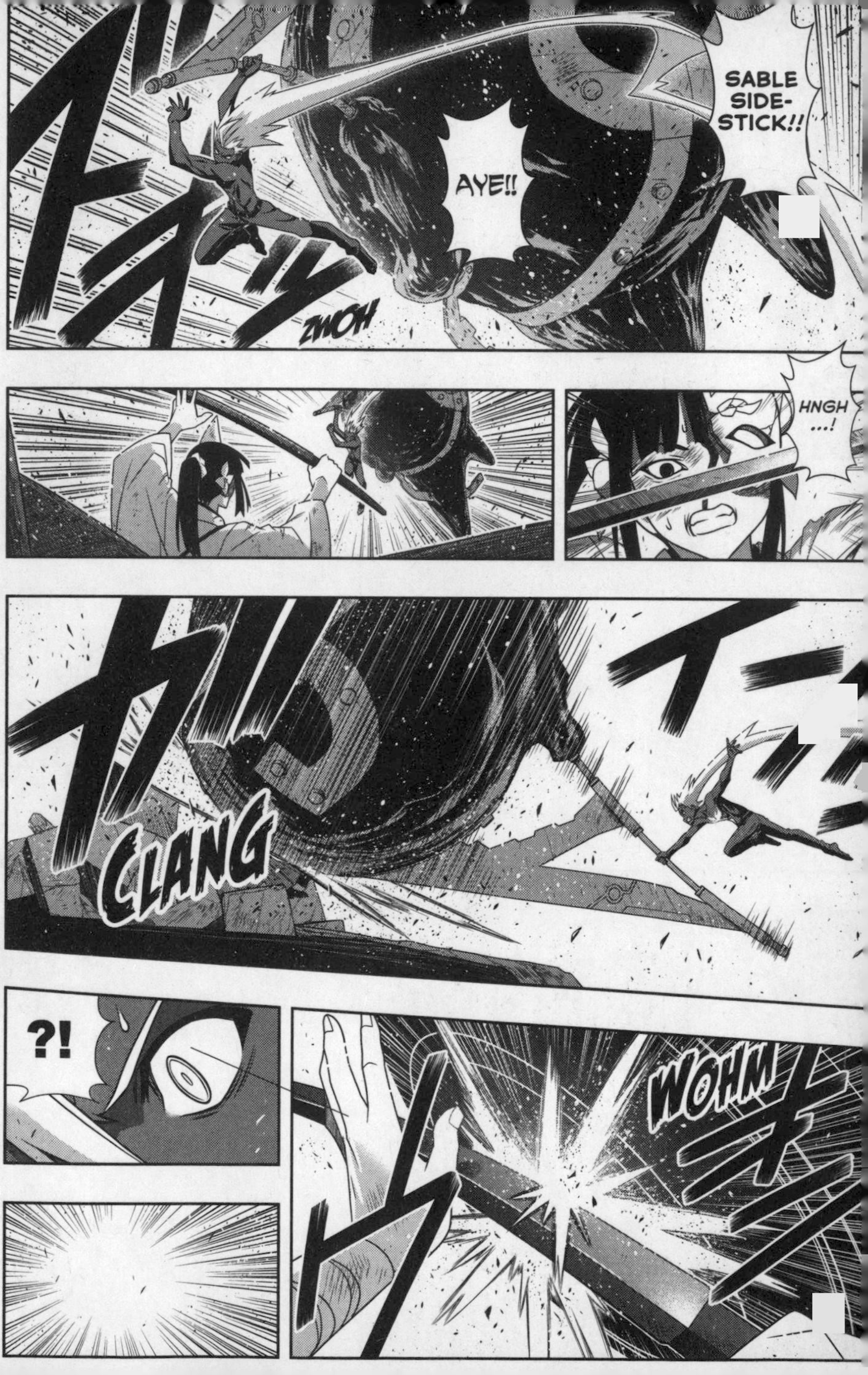

SABLE SIDE-STICK!!
AYE!!
ZWOH
HNGH ...!
CLANG
WOHM
?!

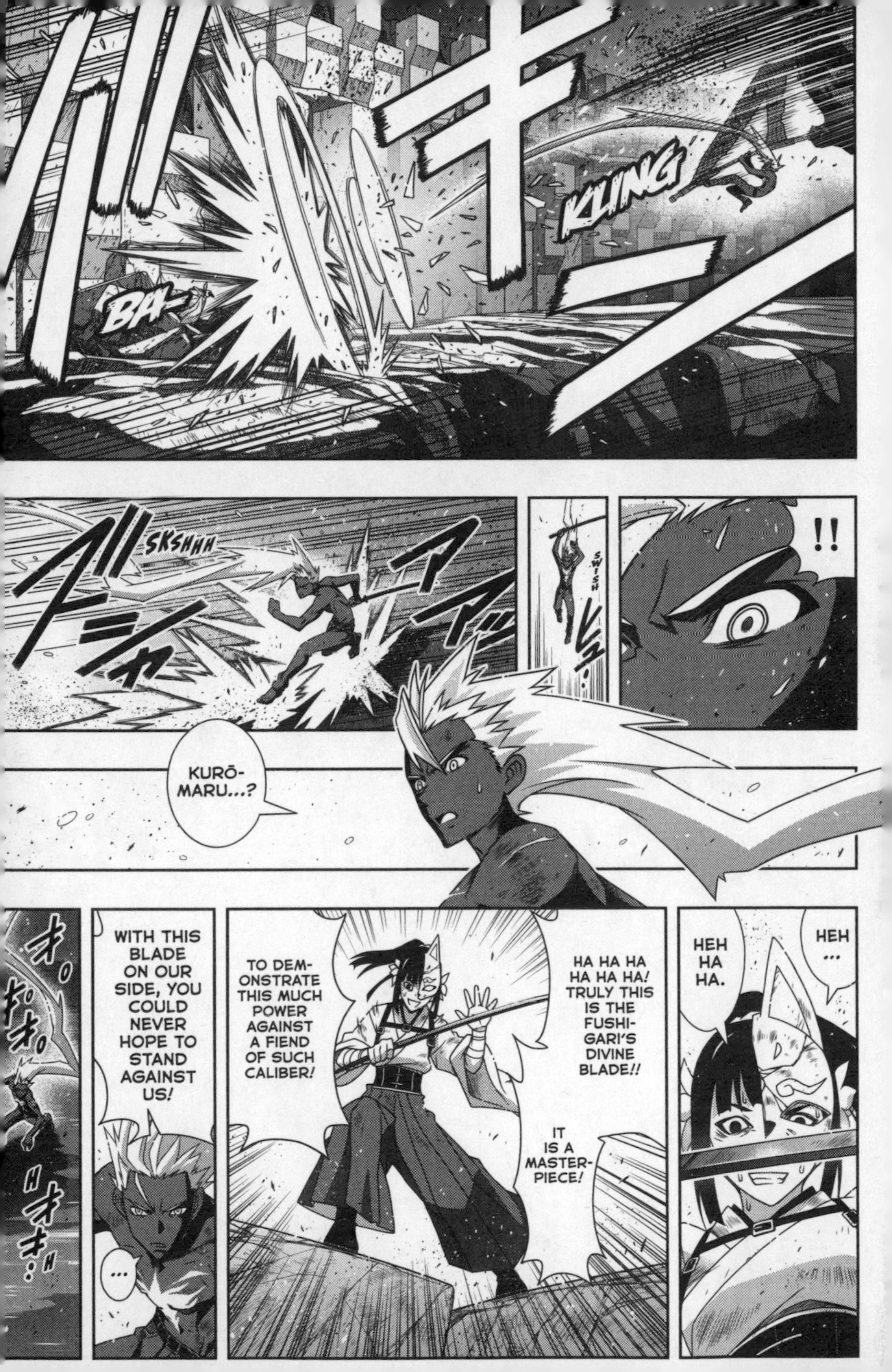
KLING
BA-
!!
SWISH
SKSHHH
KURŌ-MARU...?
HEH...
HEH HA HA.
HA HA HA HA HA HA! TRULY THIS IS THE FUSHIGARI'S DIVINE BLADE!!
TO DEMONSTRATE THIS MUCH POWER AGAINST A FIEND OF SUCH CALIBER!
IT IS A MASTERPIECE!
WITH THIS BLADE ON OUR SIDE, YOU COULD NEVER HOPE TO STAND AGAINST US!
...

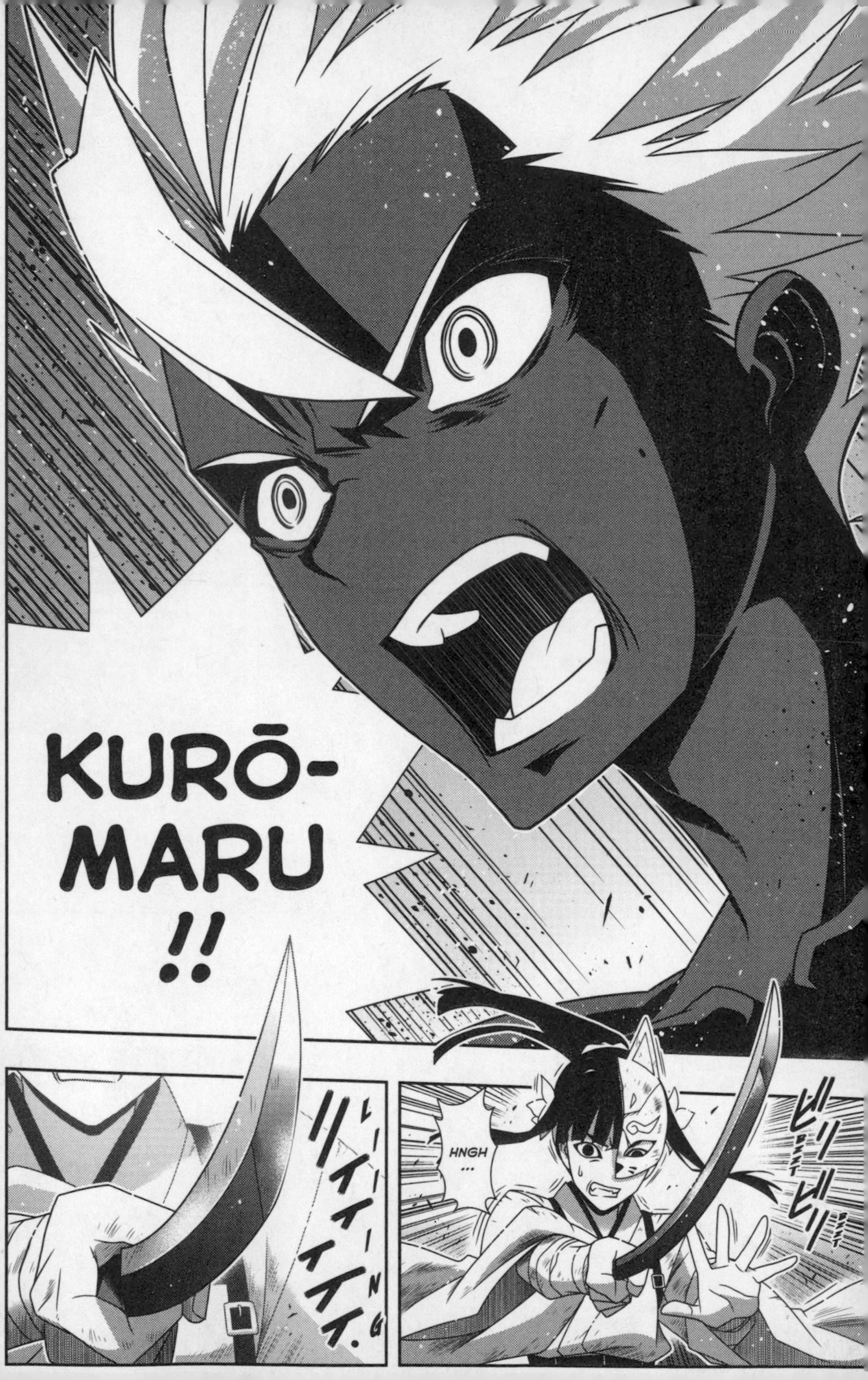
KURŌ-MARU !!
ビリ
BZZT
ビリ
BZZT
HNGH ...
リイィィイイ.
L-I-I-NG

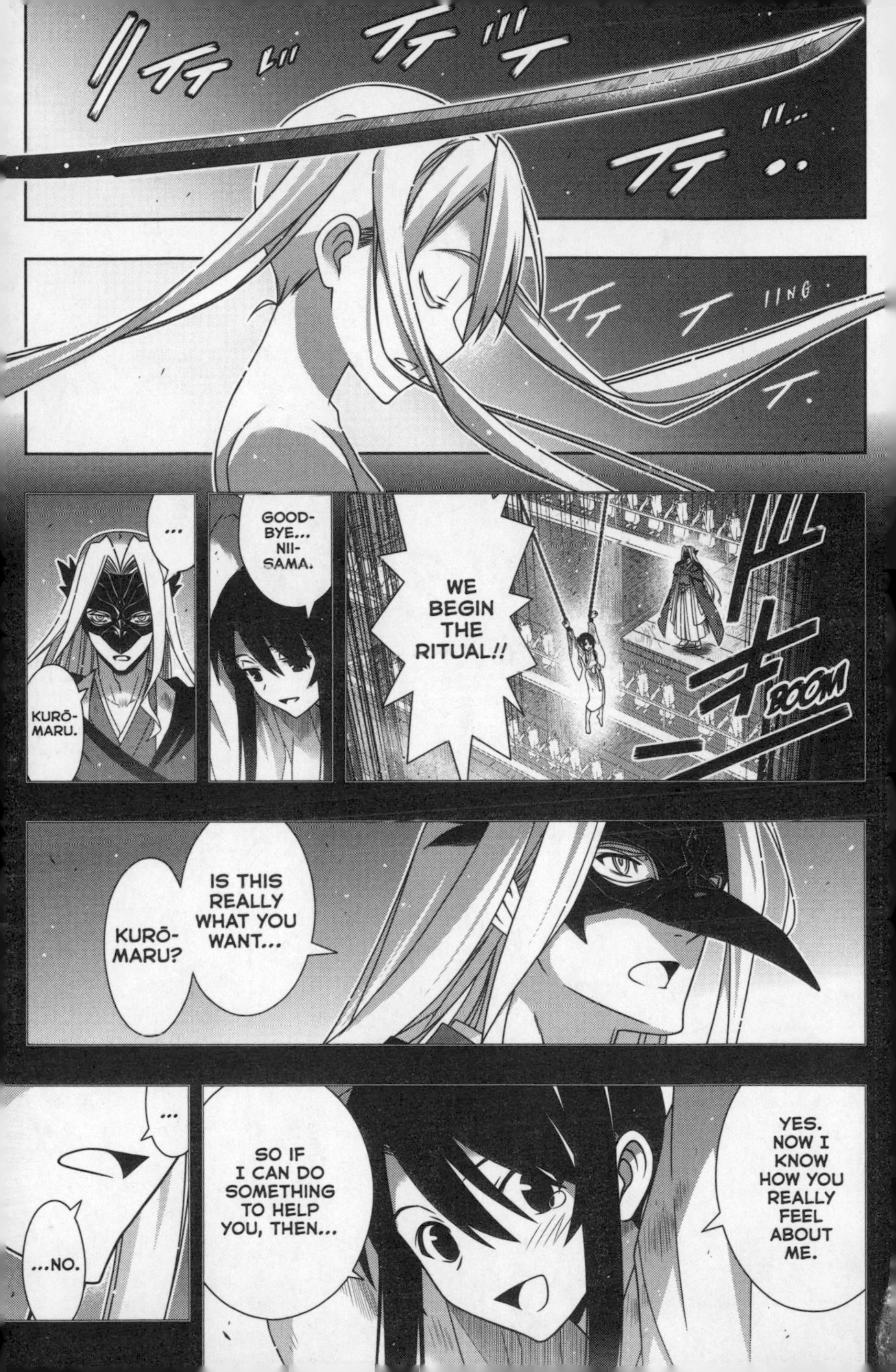
IING
WE BEGIN THE RITUAL!!
BOOM
GOOD-BYE... NII-SAMA.
...
KURŌ-MARU.
IS THIS REALLY WHAT YOU WANT...
KURŌ-MARU?
YES. NOW I KNOW HOW YOU REALLY FEEL ABOUT ME.
SO IF I CAN DO SOMETHING TO HELP YOU, THEN...
...
...NO.

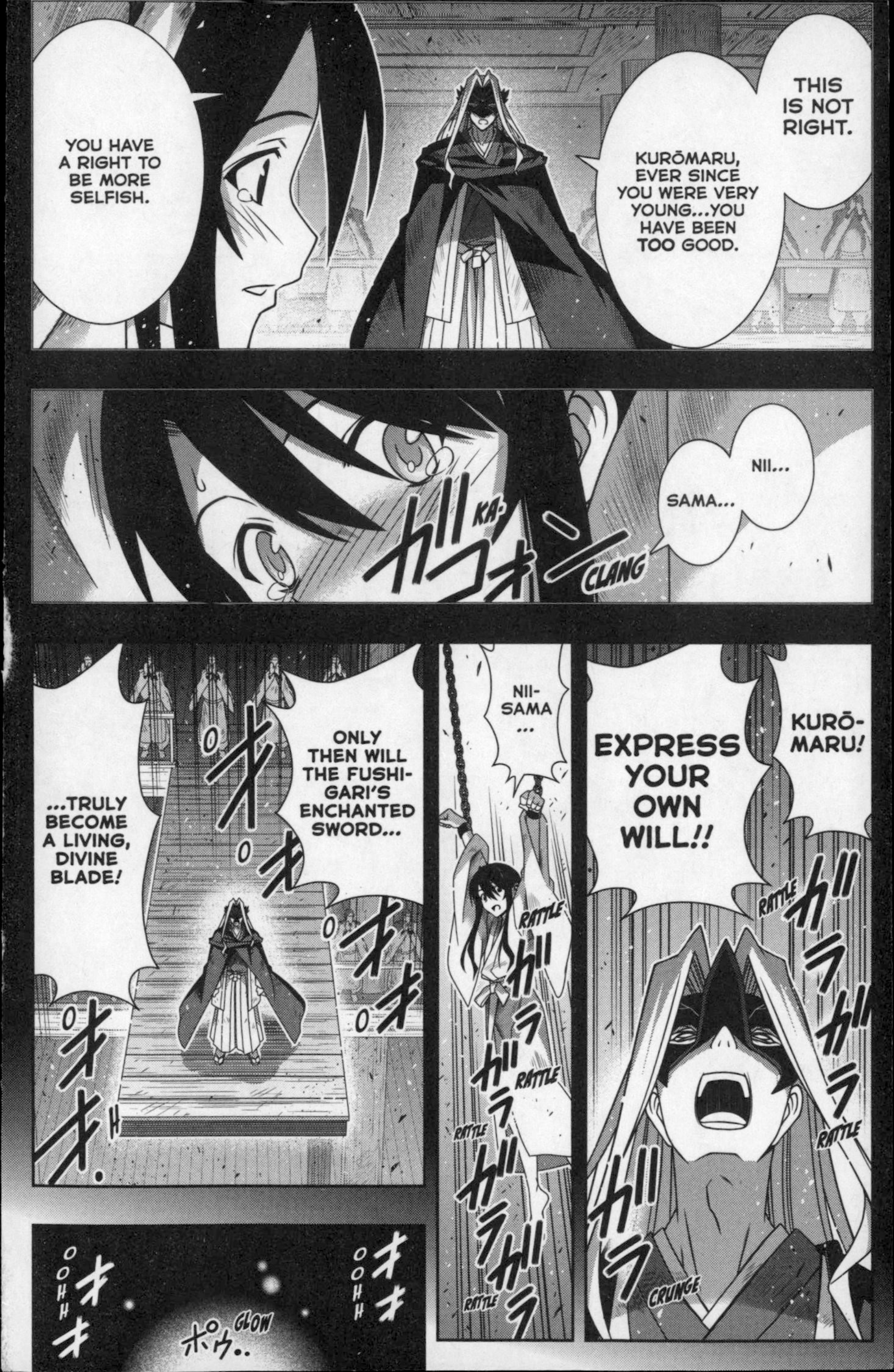
THIS IS NOT RIGHT.
KURŌMARU, EVER SINCE YOU WERE VERY YOUNG...YOU HAVE BEEN TOO GOOD.
YOU HAVE A RIGHT TO BE MORE SELFISH.
NII...
SAMA...
KA-
CLANG
KURŌ-MARU!
EXPRESS YOUR OWN WILL!!
RATTLE
RATTLE
CRUNGE
NII-SAMA ...
RATTLE
RATTLE
RATTLE
RATTLE
ONLY THEN WILL THE FUSHIGARI'S ENCHANTED SWORD...
...TRULY BECOME A LIVING, DIVINE BLADE!
OOOOOH
OOHHH
OOHHH
GLOW

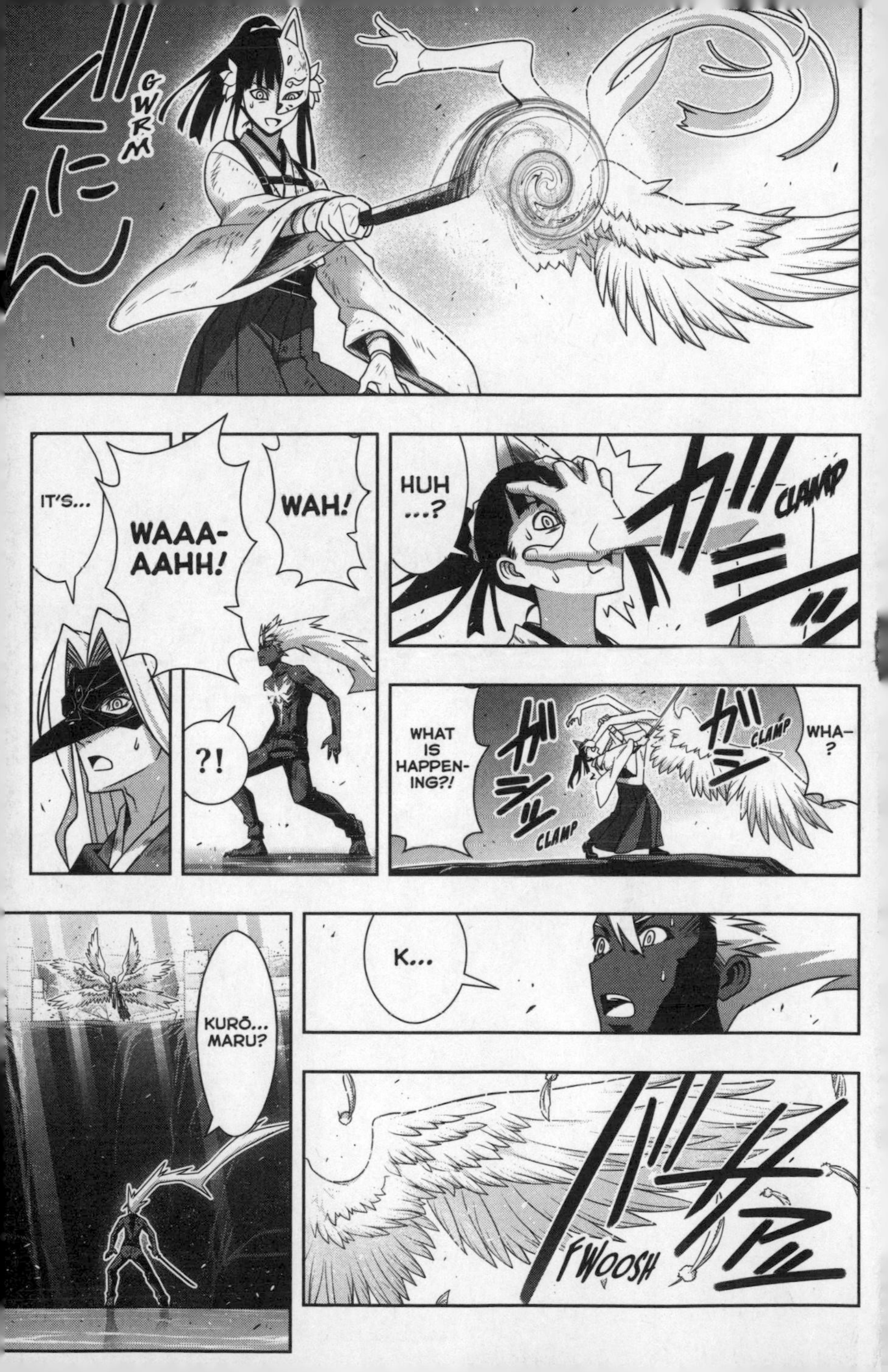
GWRM
HUH ...?
CLAMP
WHA- ?
CLAMP
WHAT IS HAPPEN- ING?!
CLAMP
WAH!
WAAAA- AAHH!
?!
IT'S...
K...
FWOOSH
KURŌ... MARU?

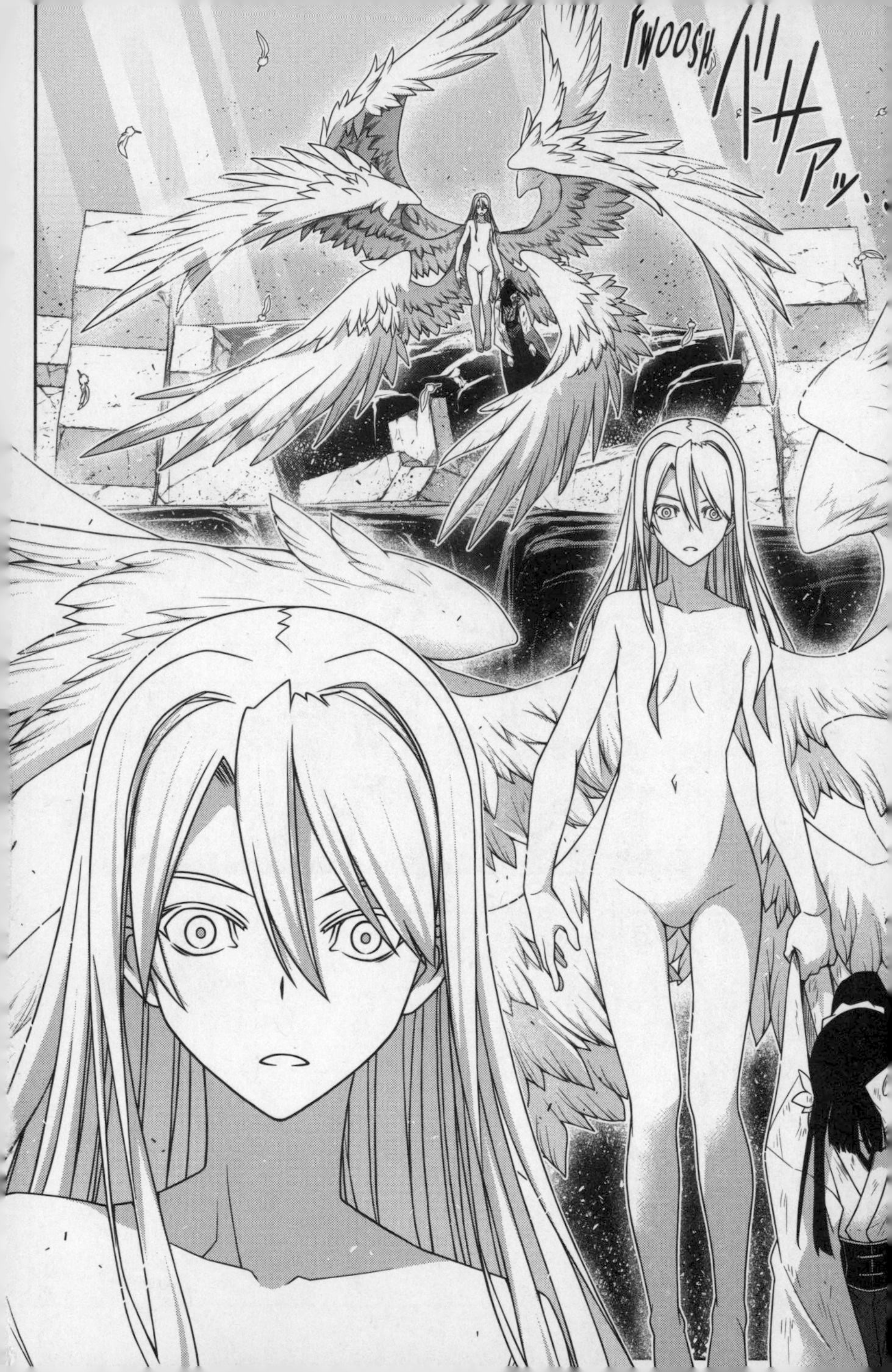
FWOOSH
バサァッ…

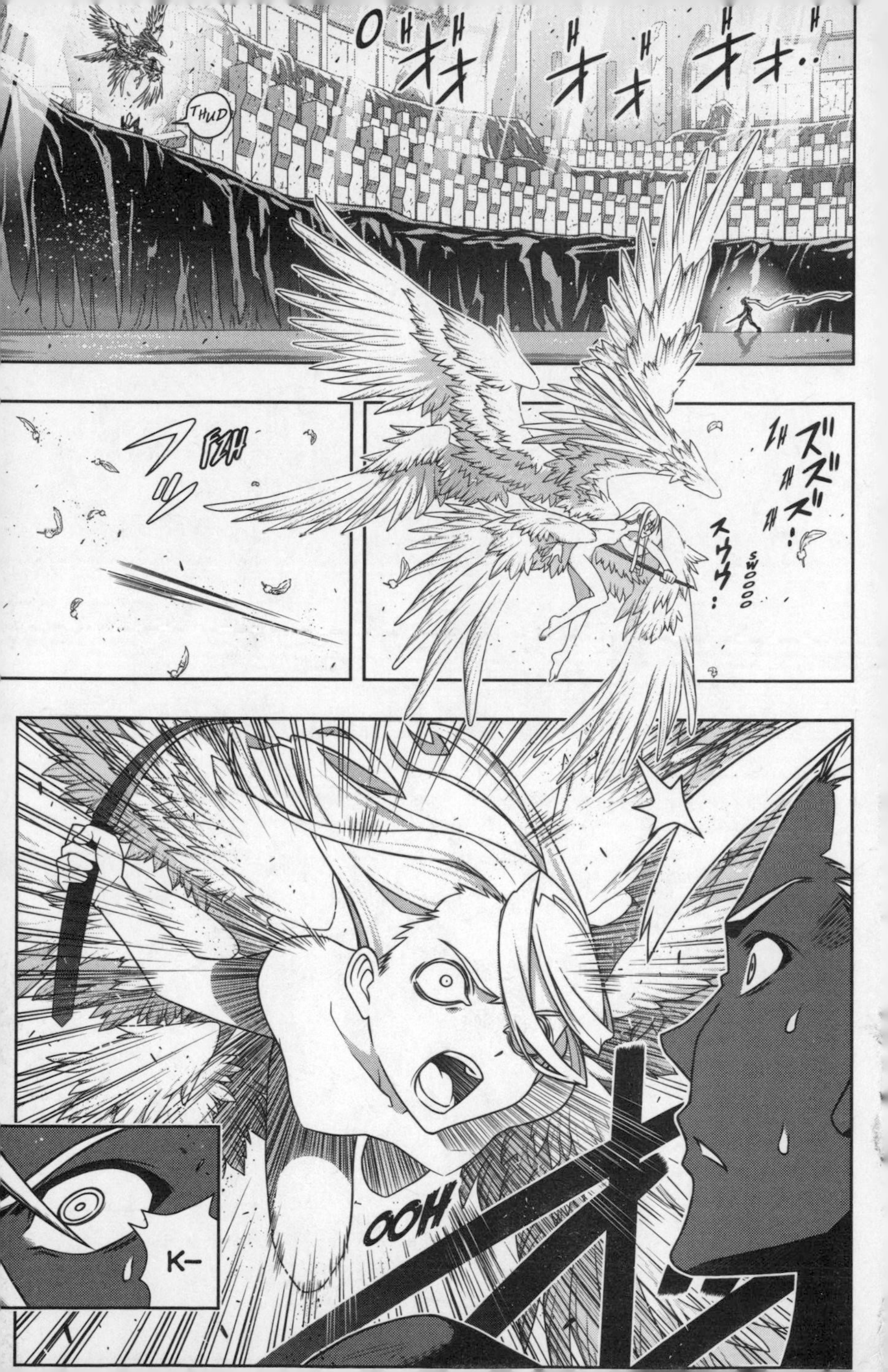

オオオオオオ…
OHHHHHH
THUD
ズズズ…
ZH ZH ZH
スゥゥ…
SWOOOO
フッ
FZAH
OOH
K–

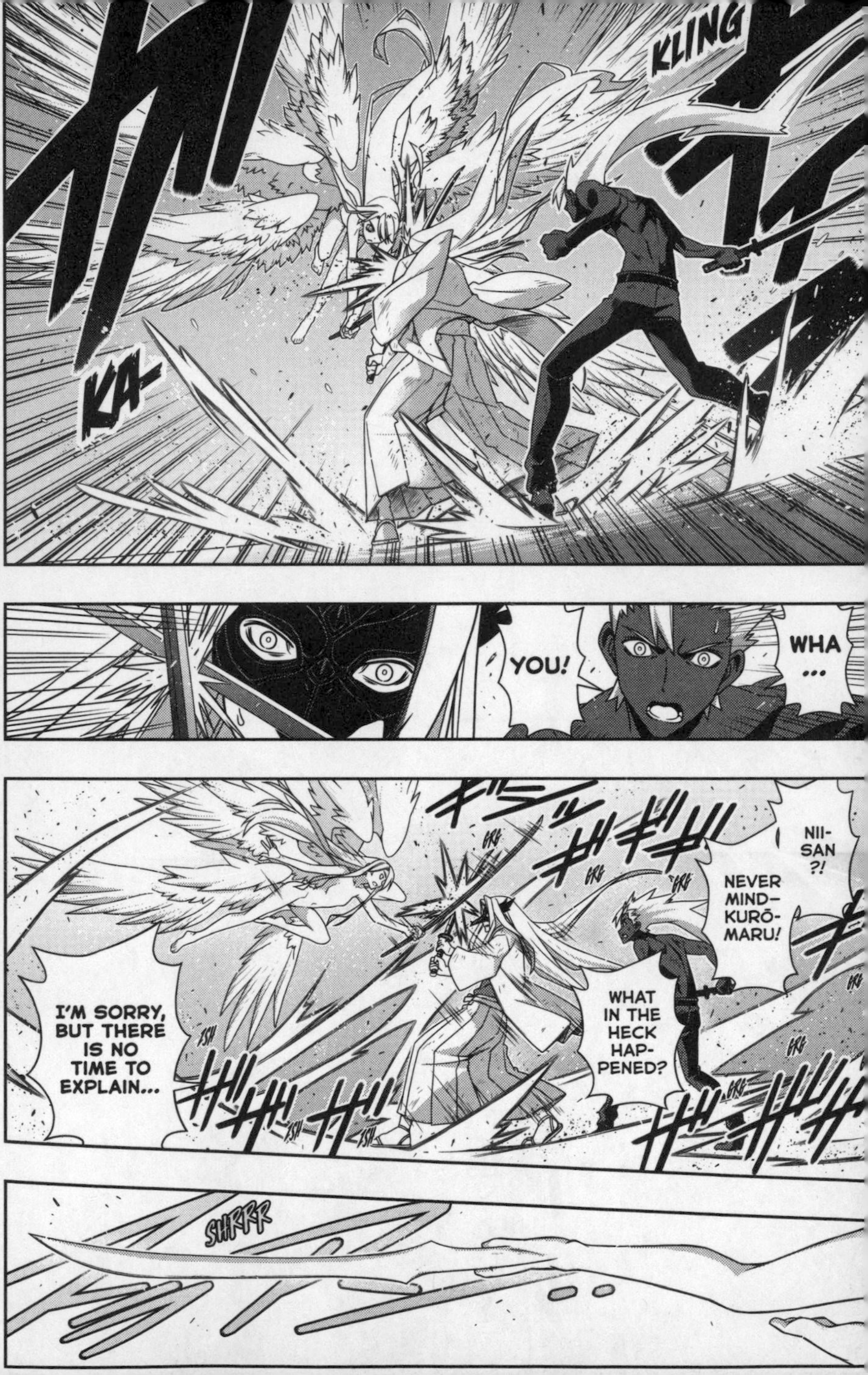
KLING
KA-
WHA ...
YOU!
NII-SAN?!
NEVER MIND—KURŌMARU!
WHAT IN THE HECK HAPPENED?
I'M SORRY, BUT THERE IS NO TIME TO EXPLAIN...
SHRRR

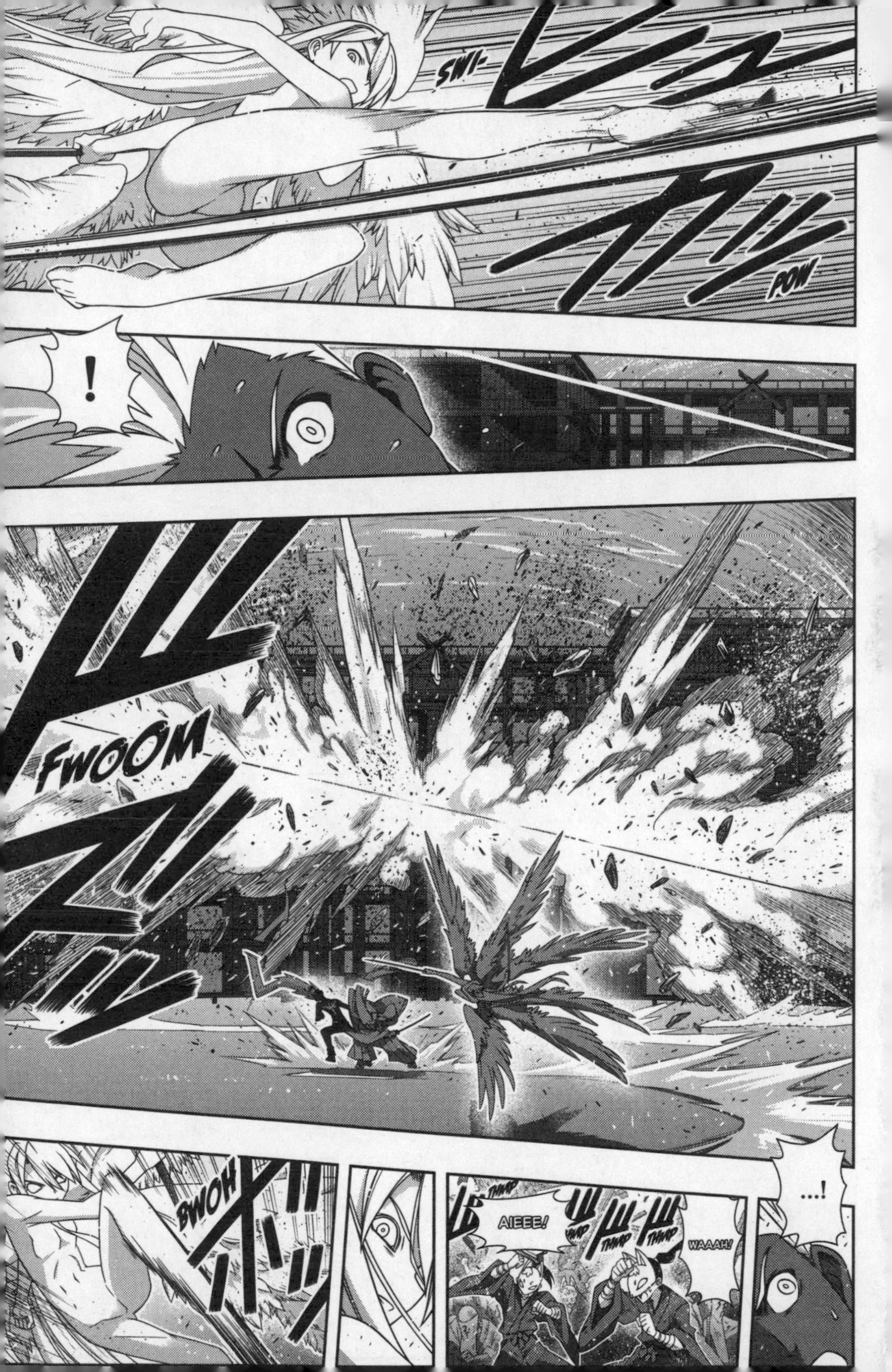
SWI-
POW
!
FWOOM
...!
THMP
THMP
THMP
THMP
WAAAH!
AIEEE!
BWOH

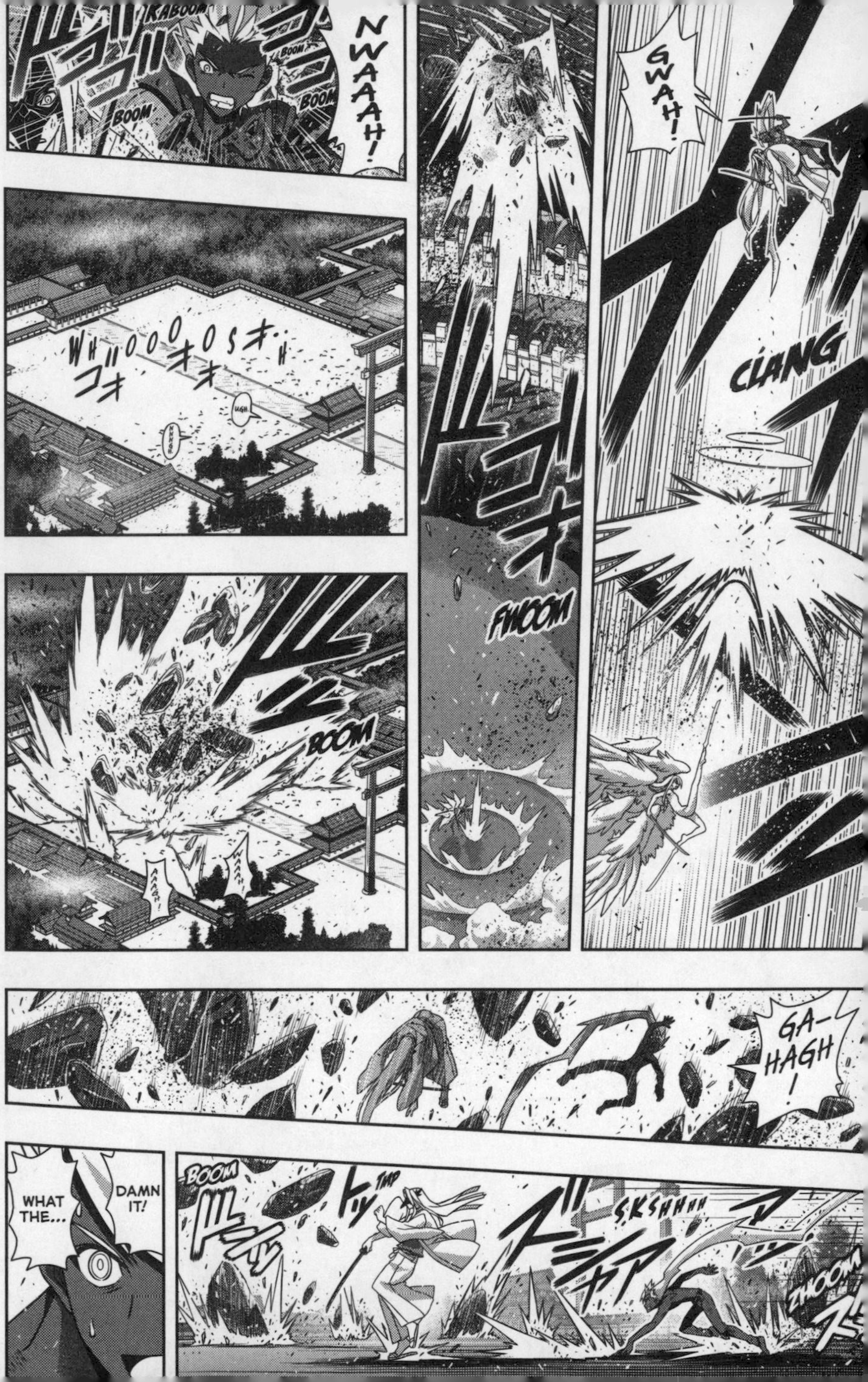

GWAH!
CLANG
FWOOM
KABOOM
BOOM
BOOM
BOOM
NWAAAAH!
WHOOOOSH
UGH
BOOM
GA-HAGH!
BOOM
TMP
SKSHHHH
ZHOOM
DAMN IT!
WHAT THE...

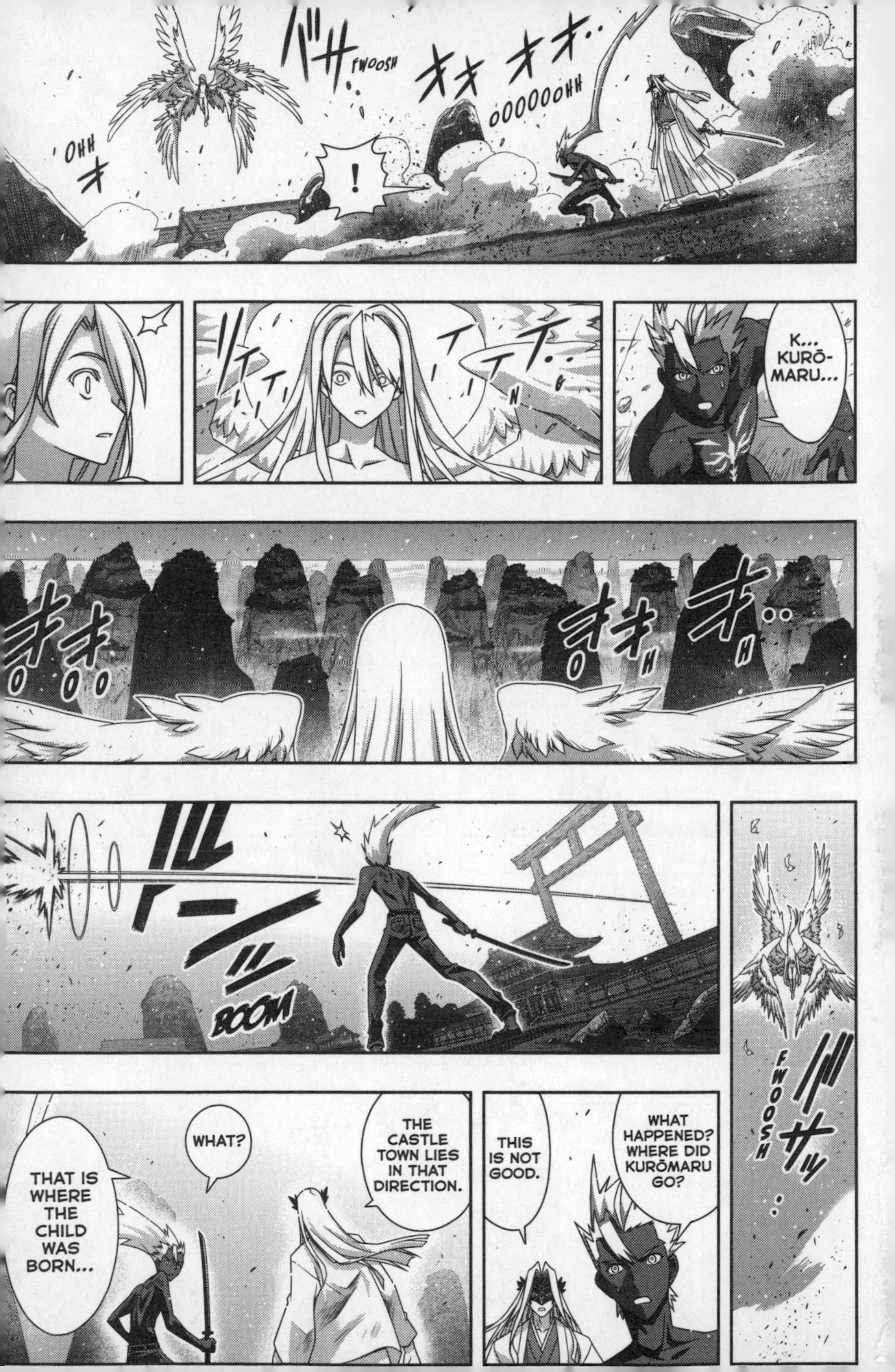
OOOOOOHH
FWOOSH
!
OHH
K... KURŌMARU...
FWOOSH
BOOM
WHAT HAPPENED? WHERE DID KURŌMARU GO?
THIS IS NOT GOOD.
THE CASTLE TOWN LIES IN THAT DIRECTION.
WHAT?
THAT IS WHERE THE CHILD WAS BORN...

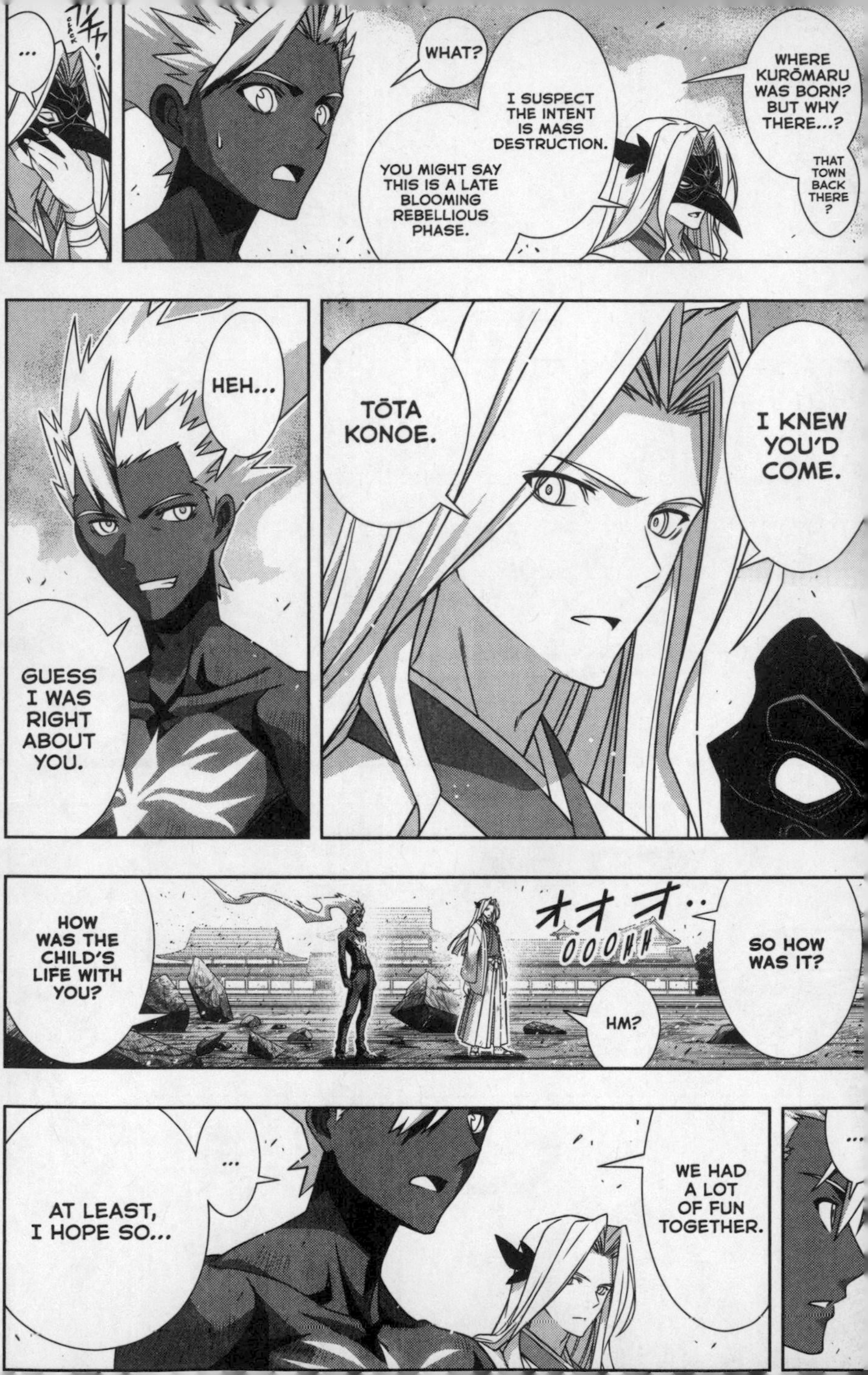
WHERE KURŌMARU WAS BORN? BUT WHY THERE...?
THAT TOWN BACK THERE?
I SUSPECT THE INTENT IS MASS DESTRUCTION.
YOU MIGHT SAY THIS IS A LATE BLOOMING REBELLIOUS PHASE.
WHAT?
CLACK
...
I KNEW YOU'D COME.
TŌTA KONOE.
HEH...
GUESS I WAS RIGHT ABOUT YOU.
SO HOW WAS IT?
HM?
オオオ..
OOOOHH
HOW WAS THE CHILD'S LIFE WITH YOU?
...
WE HAD A LOT OF FUN TOGETHER.
...
AT LEAST, I HOPE SO...

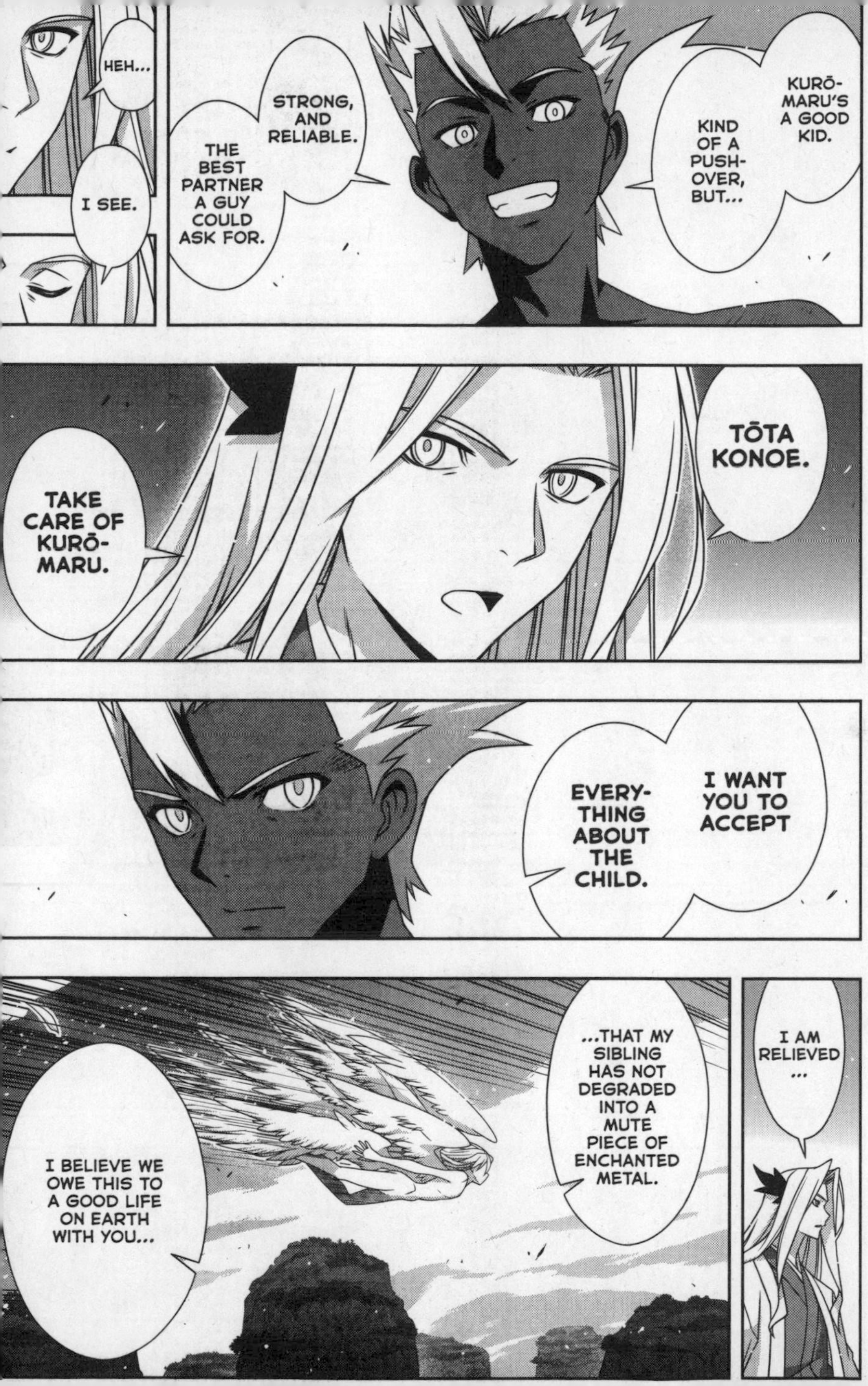
KURŌ-MARU'S A GOOD KID.
KIND OF A PUSH-OVER, BUT...
STRONG, AND RELIABLE.
THE BEST PARTNER A GUY COULD ASK FOR.
HEH...
I SEE.
TŌTA KONOE.
TAKE CARE OF KURŌ-MARU.
I WANT YOU TO ACCEPT
EVERY-THING ABOUT THE CHILD.
I AM RELIEVED ...
...THAT MY SIBLING HAS NOT DEGRADED INTO A MUTE PIECE OF ENCHANTED METAL.
I BELIEVE WE OWE THIS TO A GOOD LIFE ON EARTH WITH YOU...

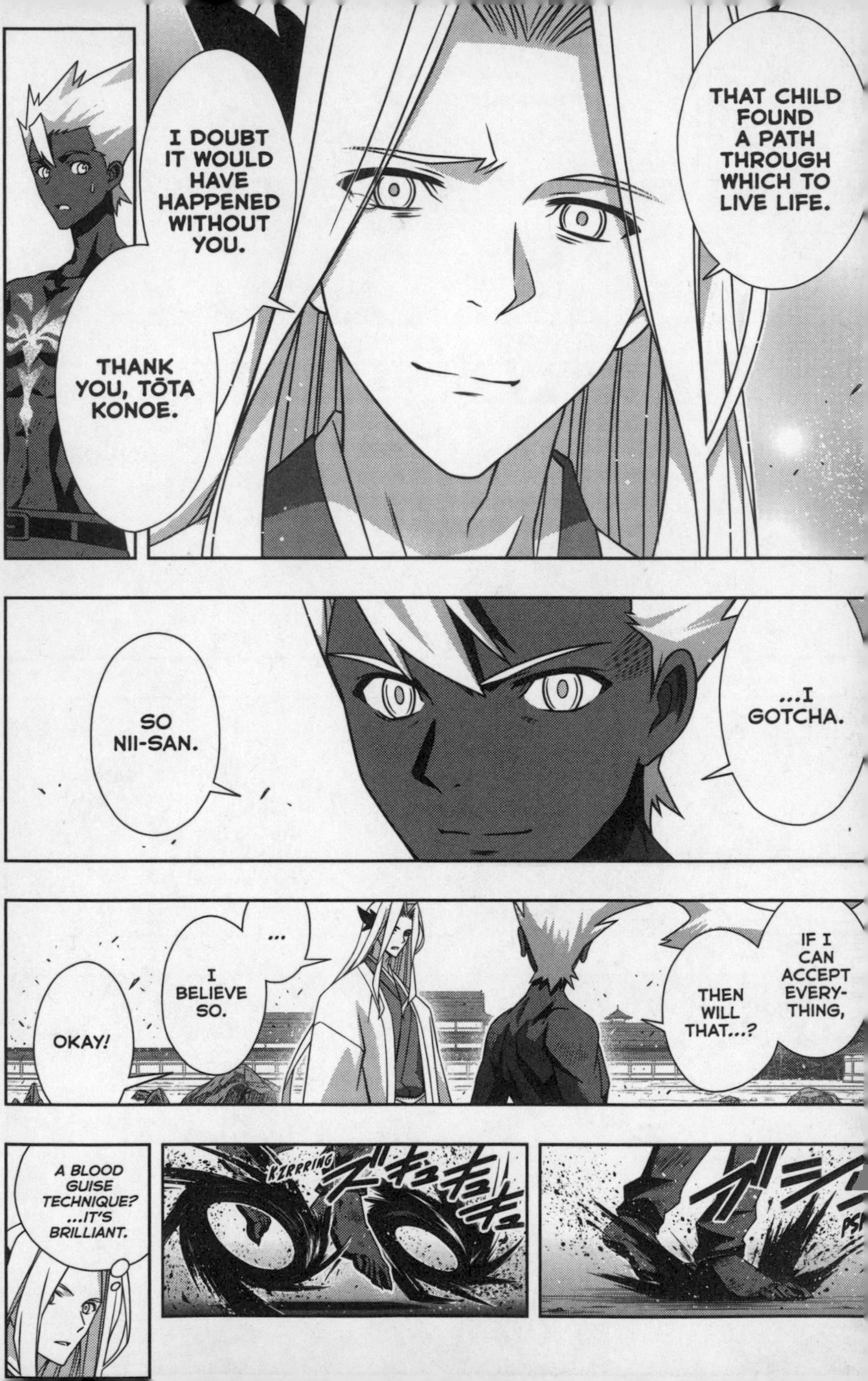
THAT CHILD FOUND A PATH THROUGH WHICH TO LIVE LIFE.
I DOUBT IT WOULD HAVE HAPPENED WITHOUT YOU.
THANK YOU, TŌTA KONOE.
...I GOTCHA.
SO NII-SAN.
IF I CAN ACCEPT EVERY-THING,
THEN WILL THAT...?
...
I BELIEVE SO.
OKAY!
KZRRRING
A BLOOD GUISE TECHNIQUE? ...IT'S BRILLIANT.

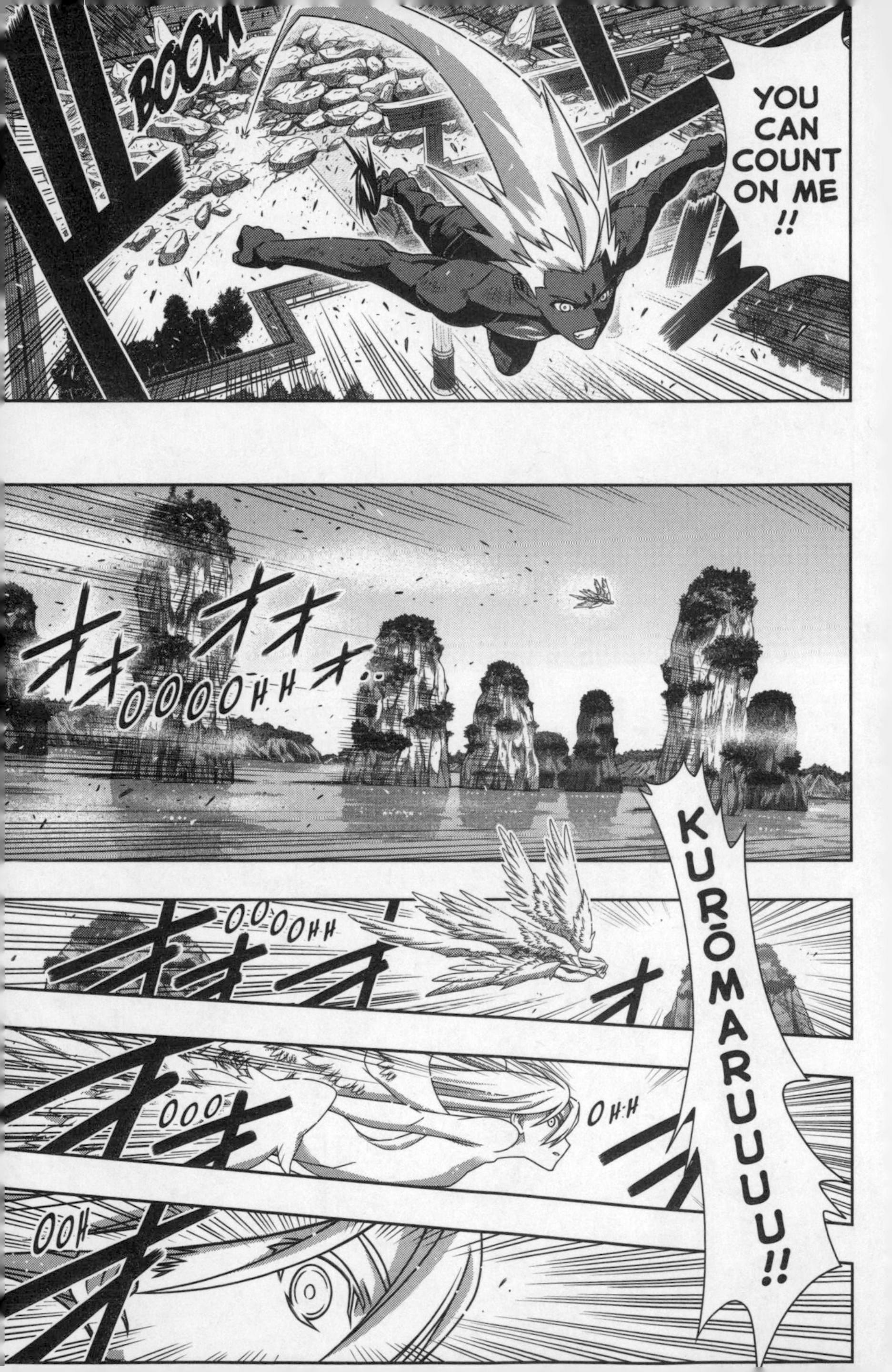
BOOM
YOU CAN COUNT ON ME!!
OOOOHH
KURŌMARUUUU!!
OOOOHH
OOO
OHH
OOH

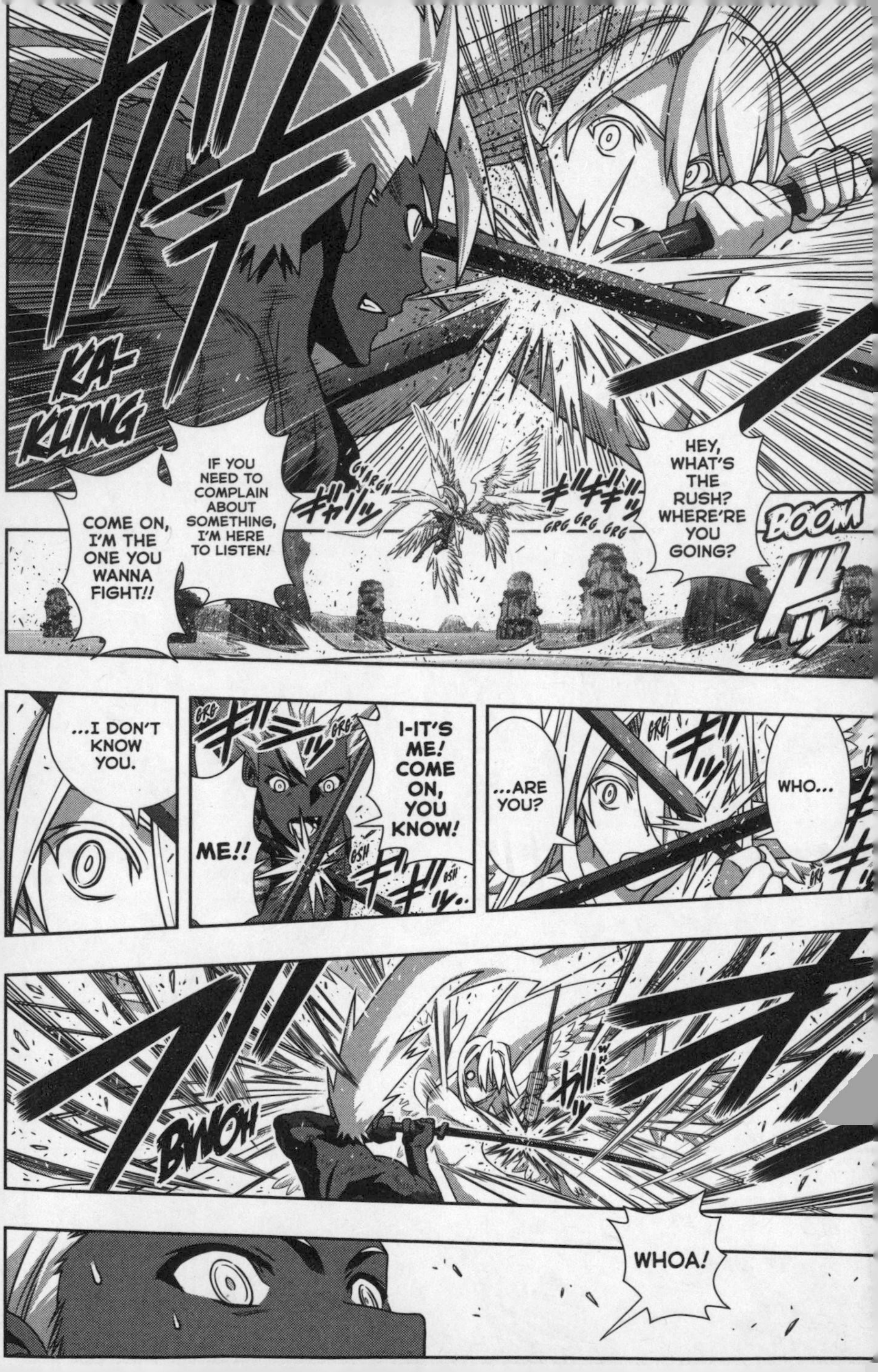
KA-KLING
BOOM
HEY, WHAT'S THE RUSH? WHERE'RE YOU GOING?
GRG GRG GRG
GYARGH
IF YOU NEED TO COMPLAIN ABOUT SOMETHING, I'M HERE TO LISTEN!
COME ON, I'M THE ONE YOU WANNA FIGHT!!
WHO...
...ARE YOU?
GRG
I-IT'S ME! COME ON, YOU KNOW!
ME!!
GRG
GSH
...I DON'T KNOW YOU.
WHAK
BWOH
WHOA!

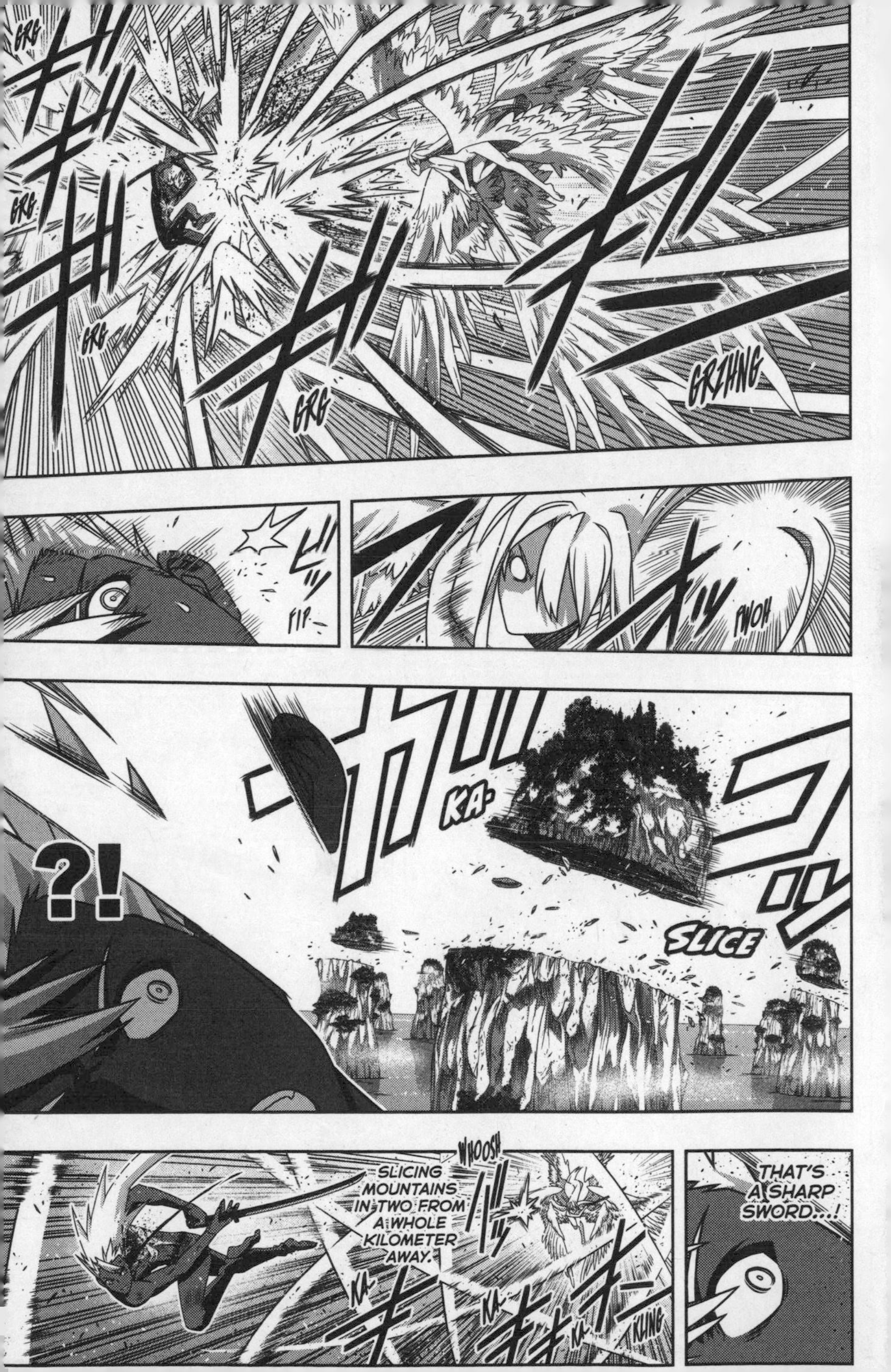
GRZHNG
GRG
GRG
GRG
GRG
FWOH
FIP
KA-
SLICE
?!
THAT'S A SHARP SWORD...!
WHOOSH
SLICING MOUNTAINS IN TWO FROM A WHOLE KILOMETER AWAY.
KA-
KA-
KA-
KLING

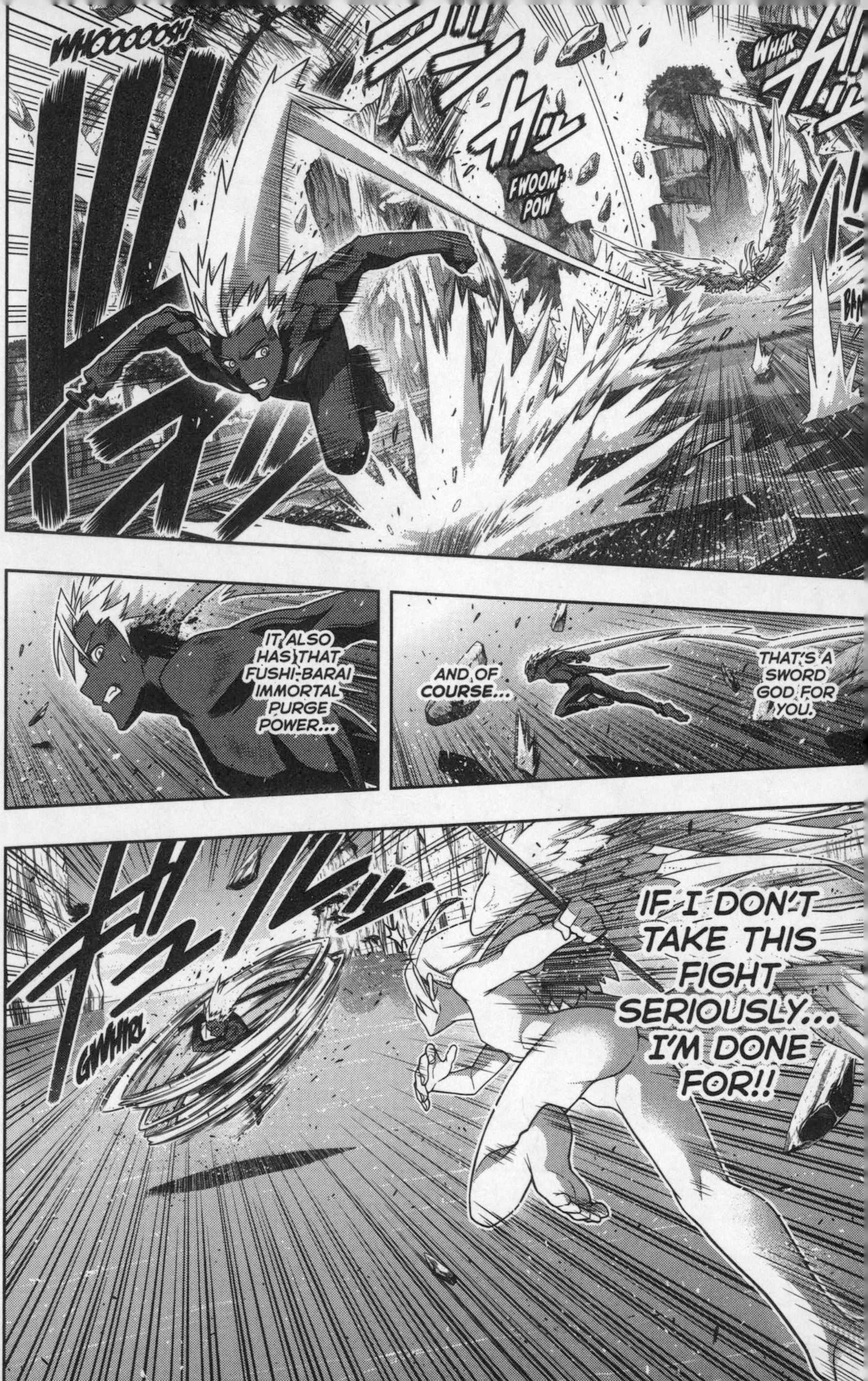
WHAK
FWOOM-POW
WHOOOOOSH
THAT'S A SWORD GOD FOR YOU.
AND OF COURSE...
IT ALSO HAS THAT FUSHI-BARAI IMMORTAL PURGE POWER...
IF I DON'T TAKE THIS FIGHT SERIOUSLY... I'M DONE FOR!!
GWHIRL

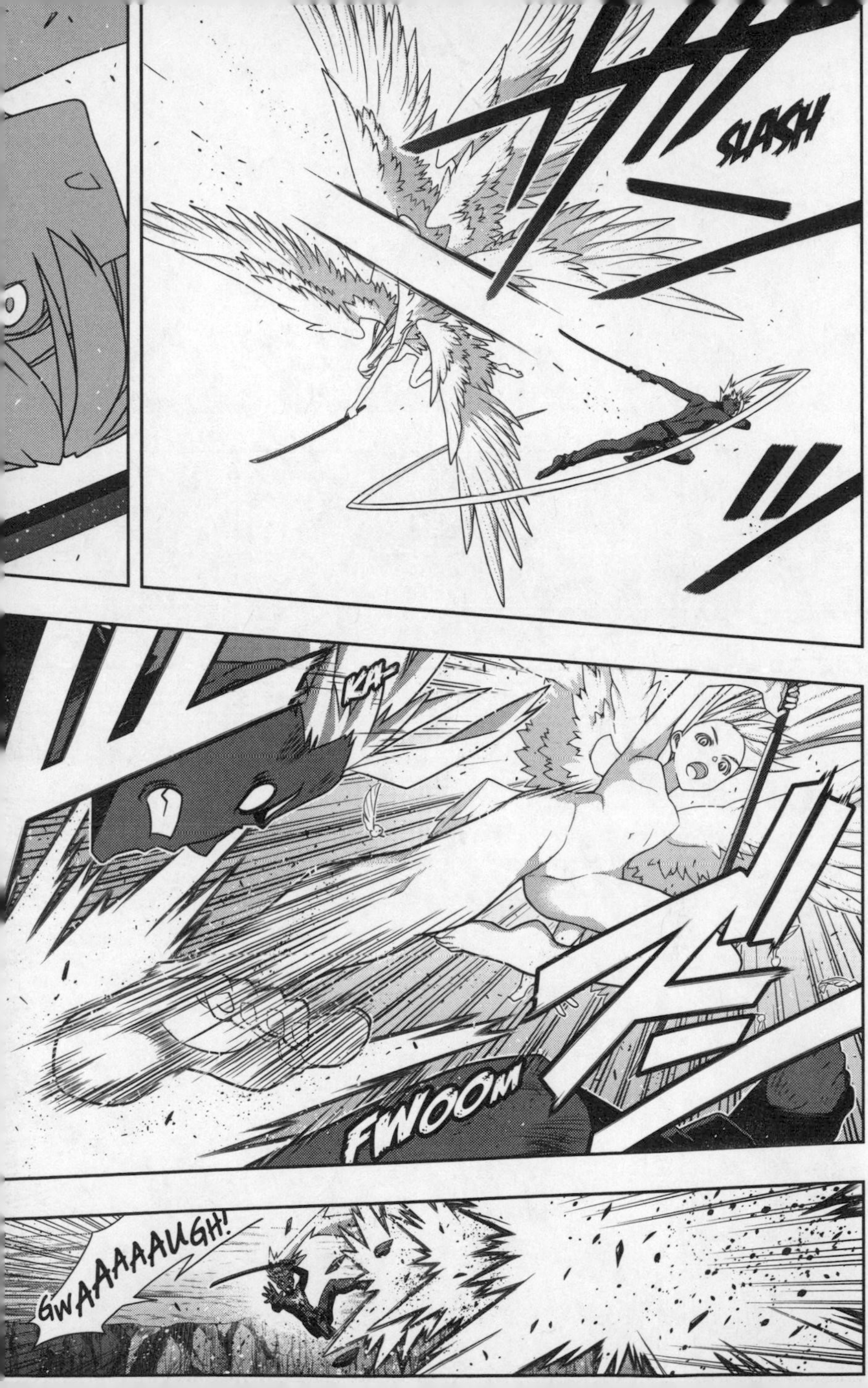
SLASH
KA-
FWOOM
GWAAAAAUGH!

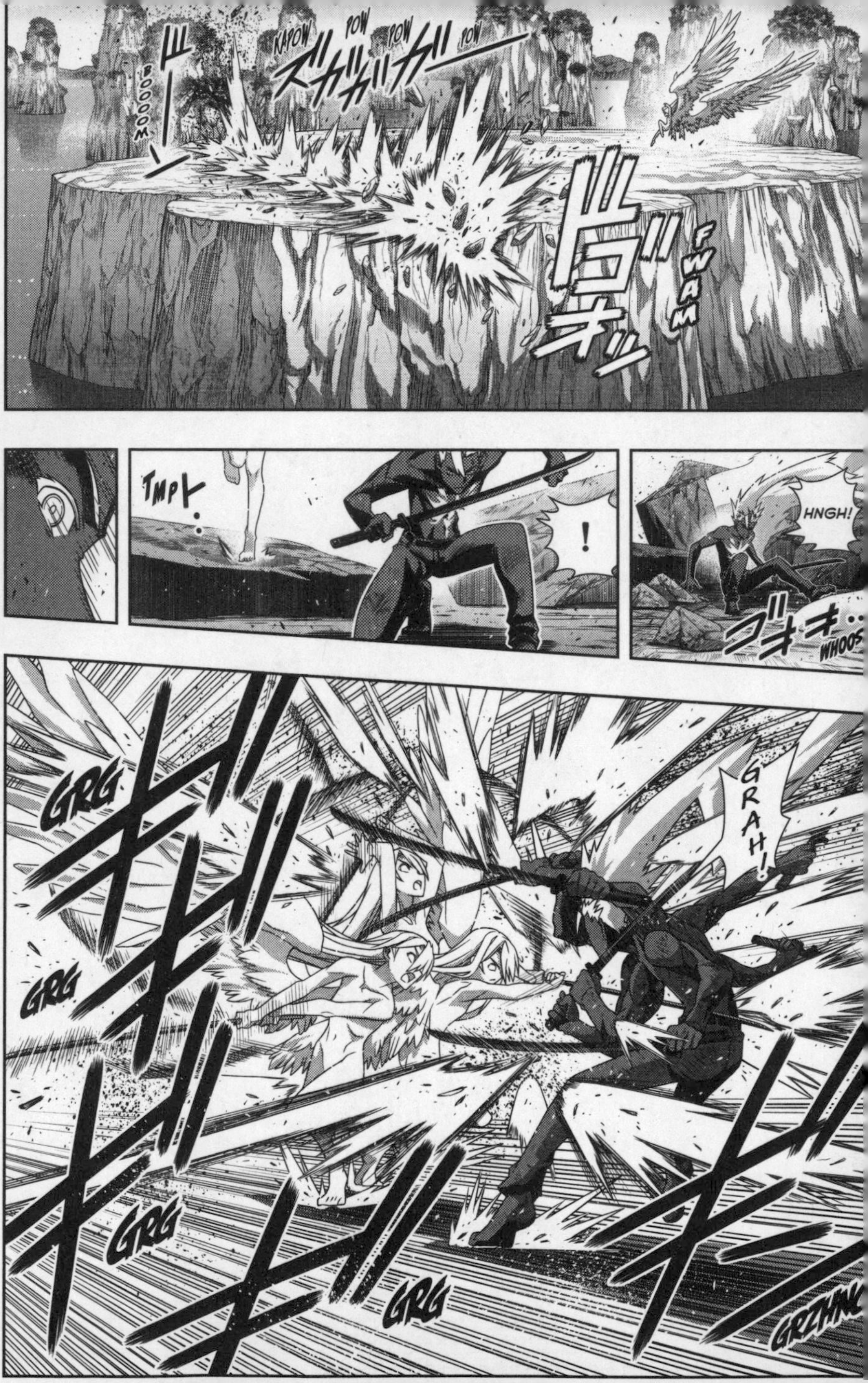
BOOOOOM
KAPOW POW POW POW
FWAM
HNGH!
WHOOS
!
TMP
GRAH!
GRG
GRG
GRG
GRG

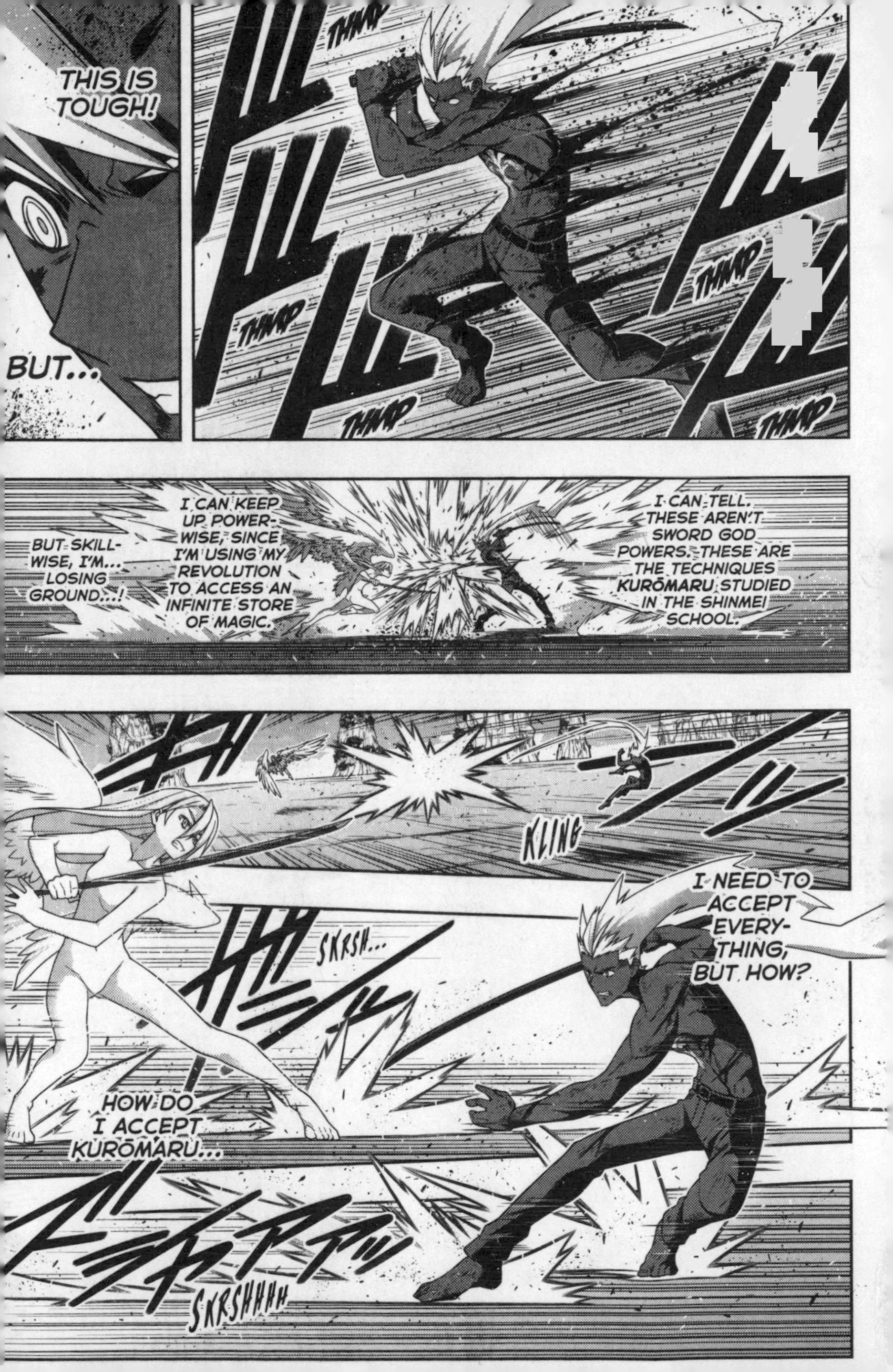
THWAP
THWAP
THWAP
THWAP
THWAP
THWAP
THIS IS TOUGH!
BUT...
I CAN TELL. THESE AREN'T SWORD GOD POWERS. THESE ARE THE TECHNIQUES KURŌMARU STUDIED IN THE SHINMEI SCHOOL.
I CAN KEEP UP POWER-WISE, SINCE I'M USING MY REVOLUTION TO ACCESS AN INFINITE STORE OF MAGIC.
BUT SKILL-WISE, I'M... LOSING GROUND...!
KLING
I NEED TO ACCEPT EVERY-THING, BUT HOW?
SKRSH...
HOW DO I ACCEPT KURŌMARU...
SKRSHHHH

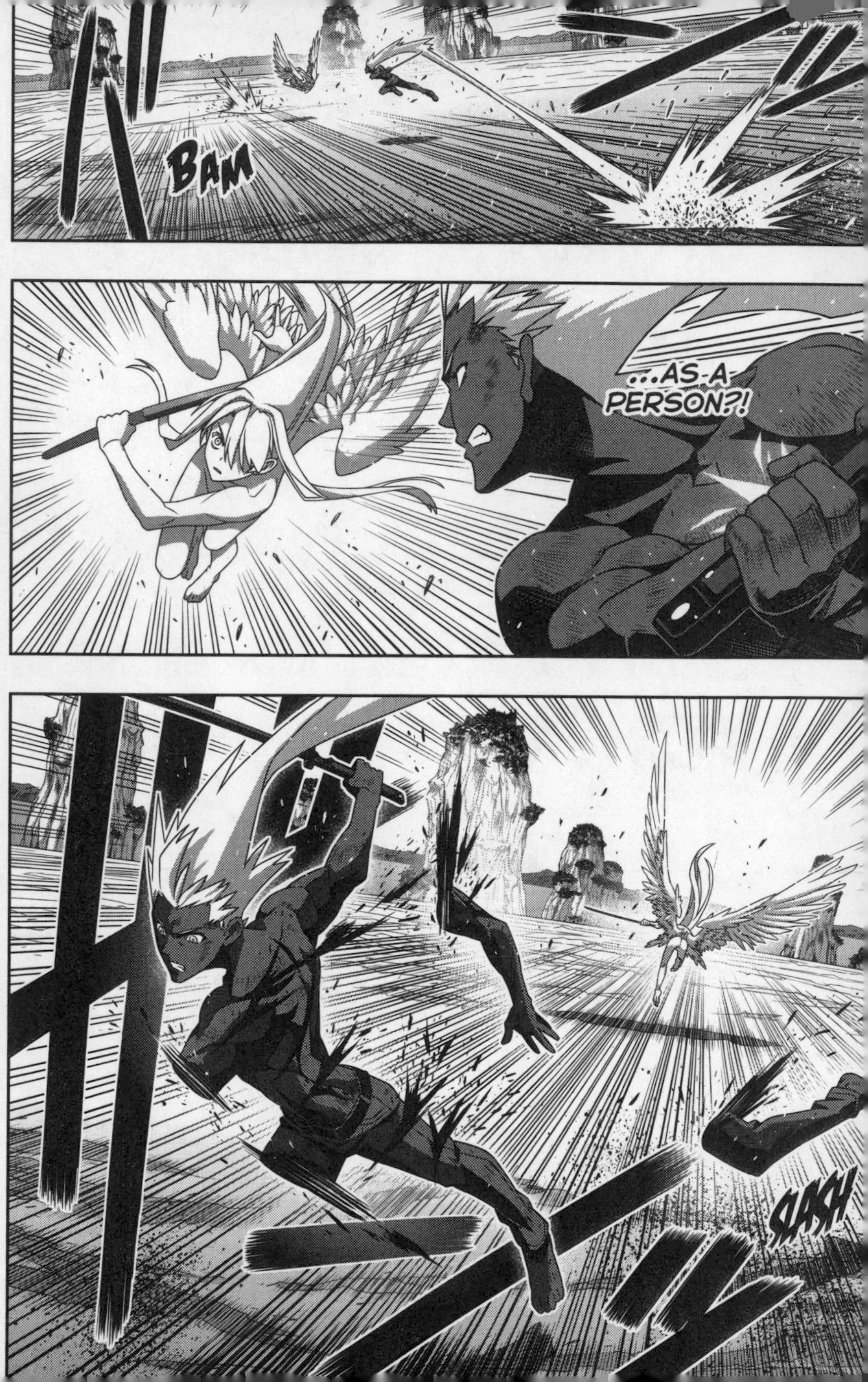
BAM
...AS A PERSON?!
SLASH

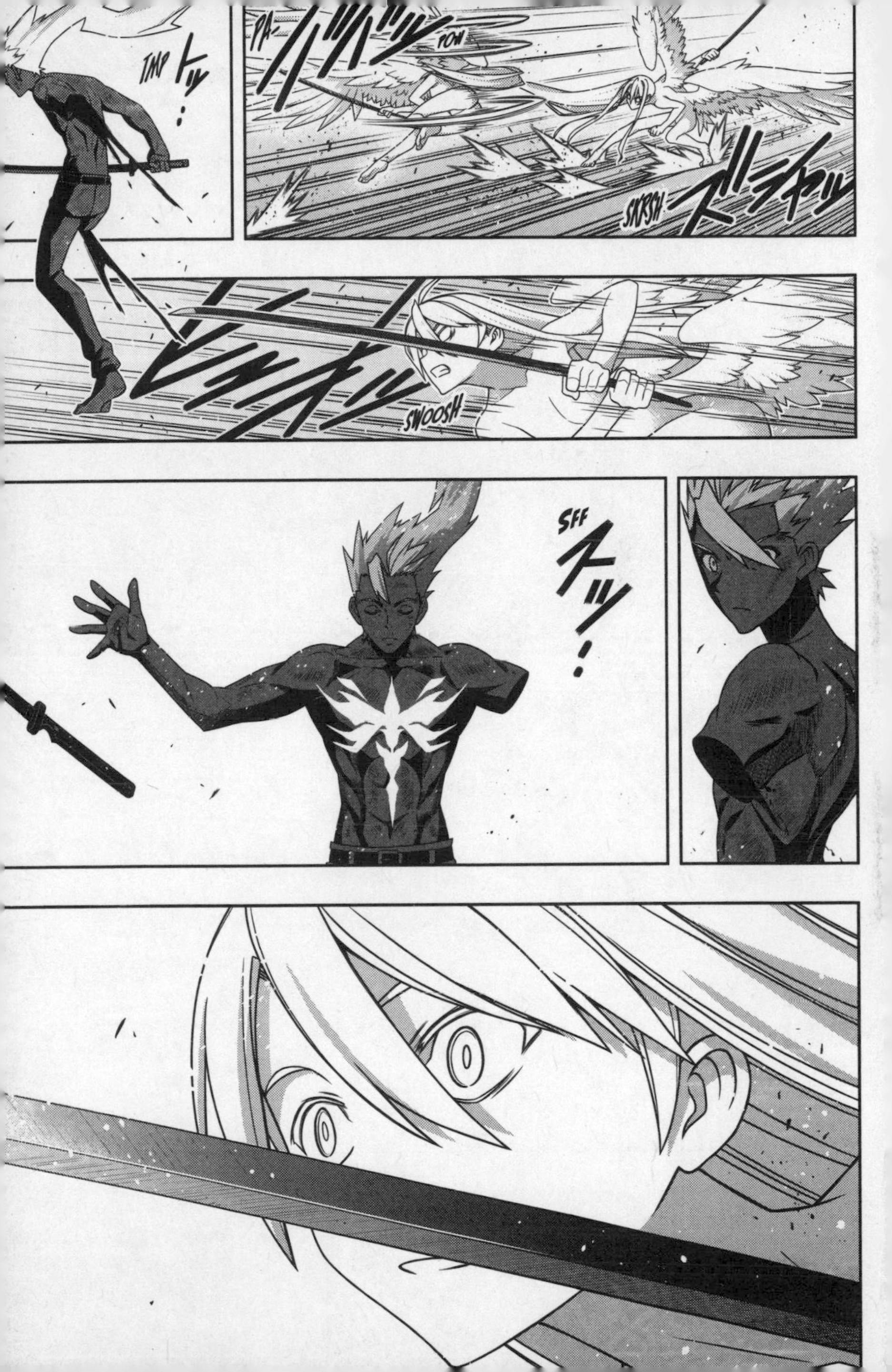
PA-
POW
SKRSH
TMP
SWOOSH
SFF

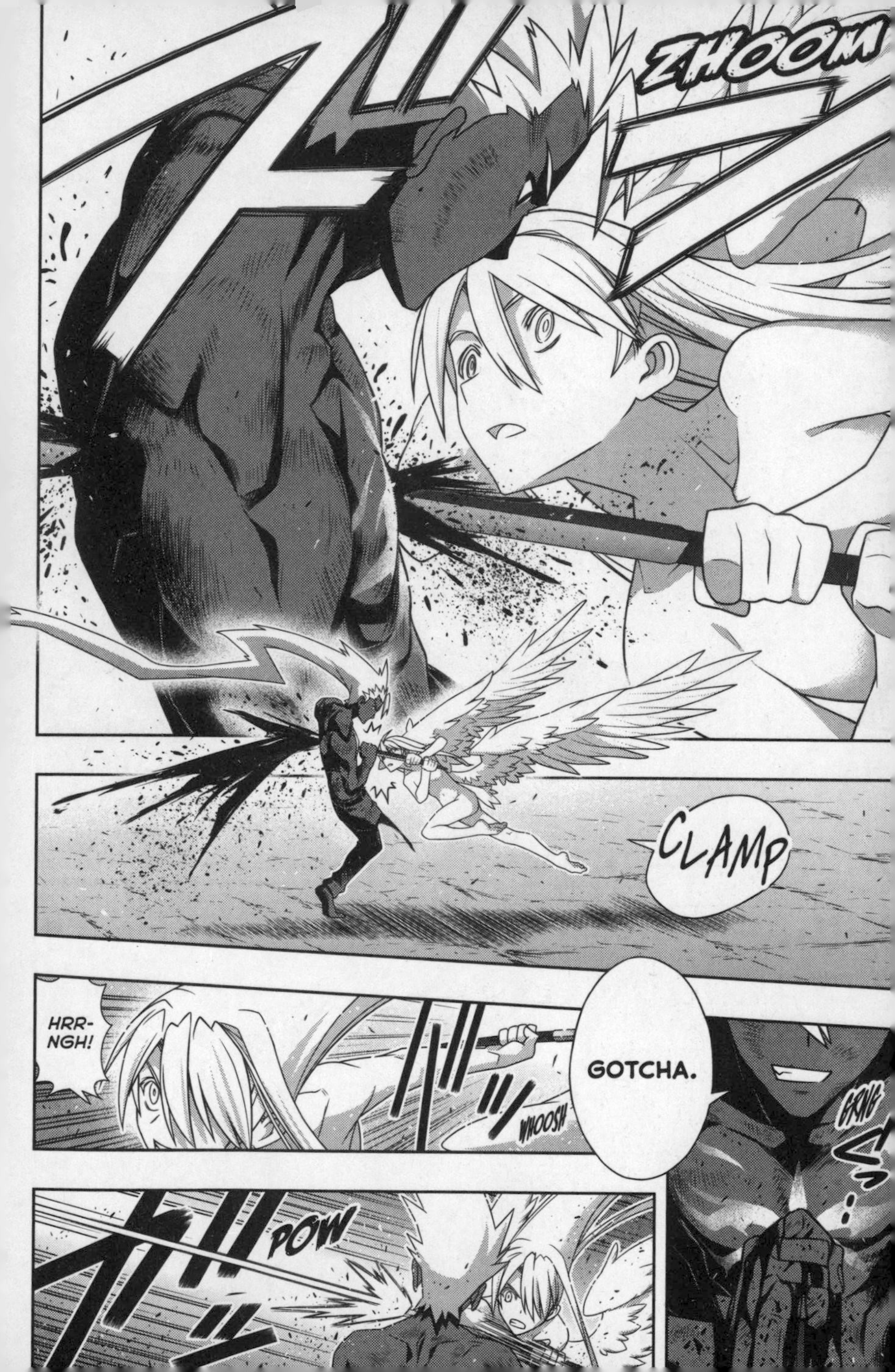
ZHOOM
CLAMP
GOTCHA.
GRNG
HRR-NGH!
WHOOSH
POW

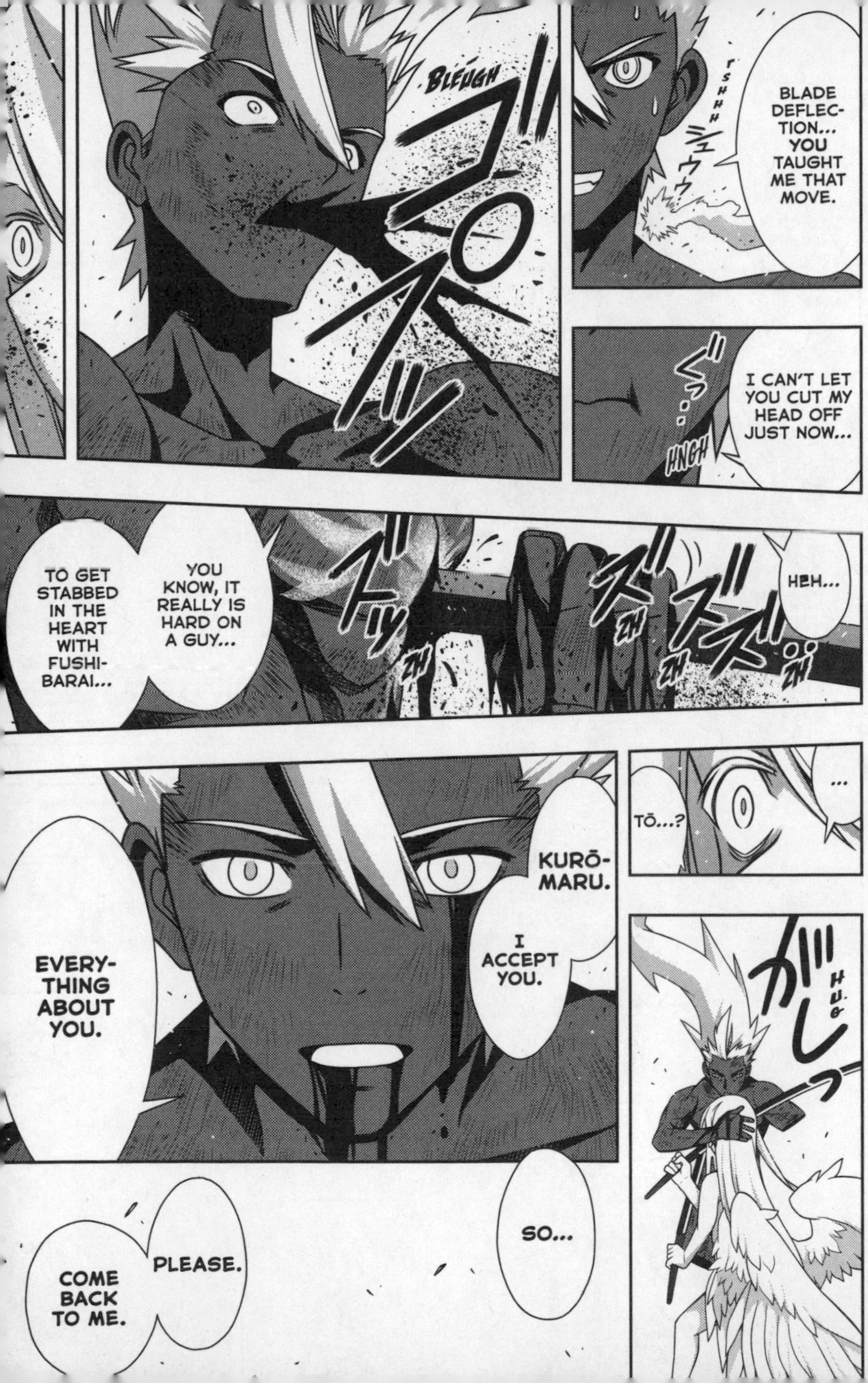
TSHHH
BLADE DEFLECTION... YOU TAUGHT ME THAT MOVE.
HNGH
I CAN'T LET YOU CUT MY HEAD OFF JUST NOW...
BLEUGH
HEH...
ZH
ZH
ZH
ZH
YOU KNOW, IT REALLY IS HARD ON A GUY...
TO GET STABBED IN THE HEART WITH FUSHIBARAI...
...
TŌ...?
HUG
KURŌMARU.
I ACCEPT YOU.
EVERYTHING ABOUT YOU.
SO...
PLEASE.
COME BACK TO ME.

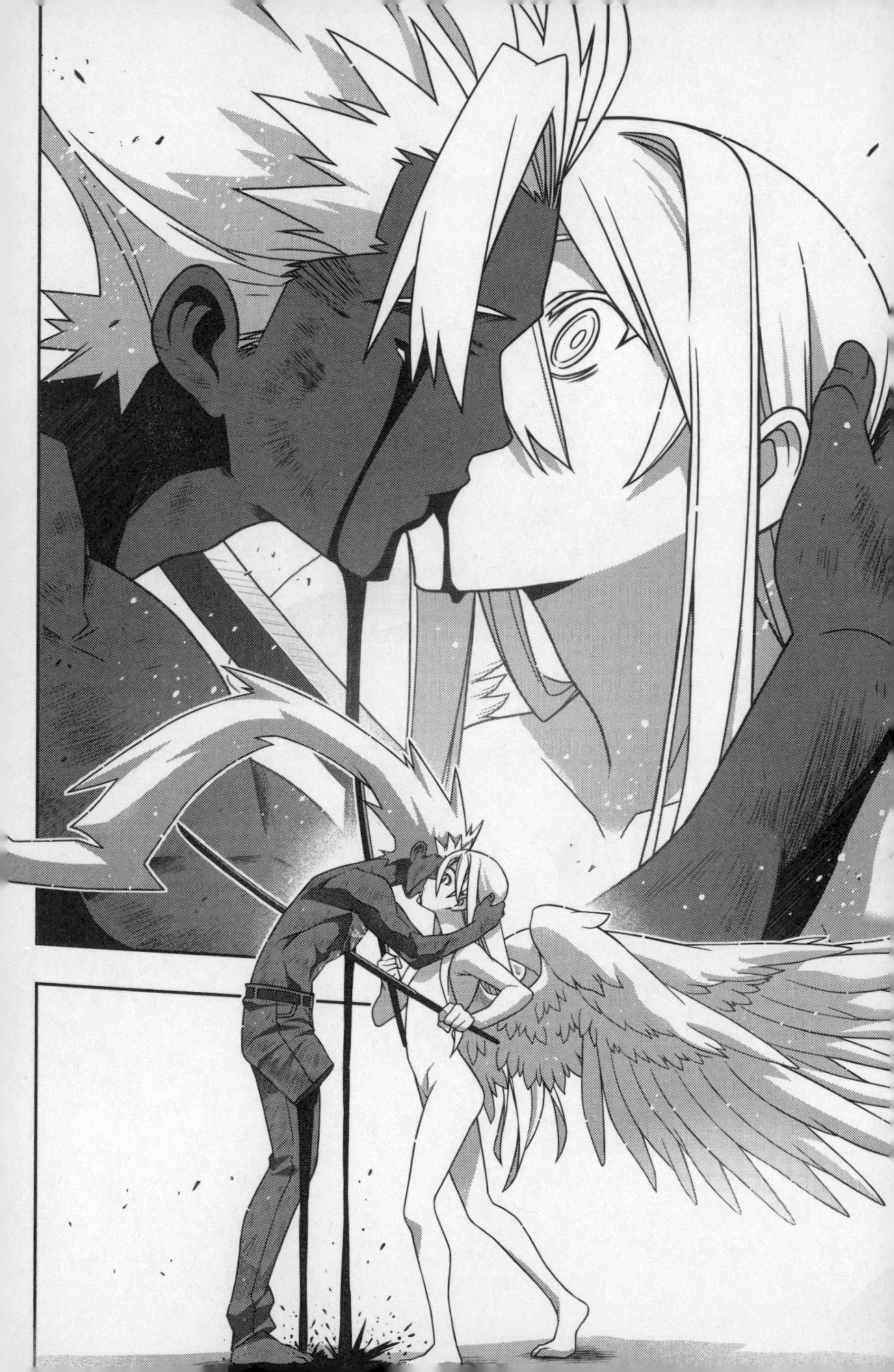

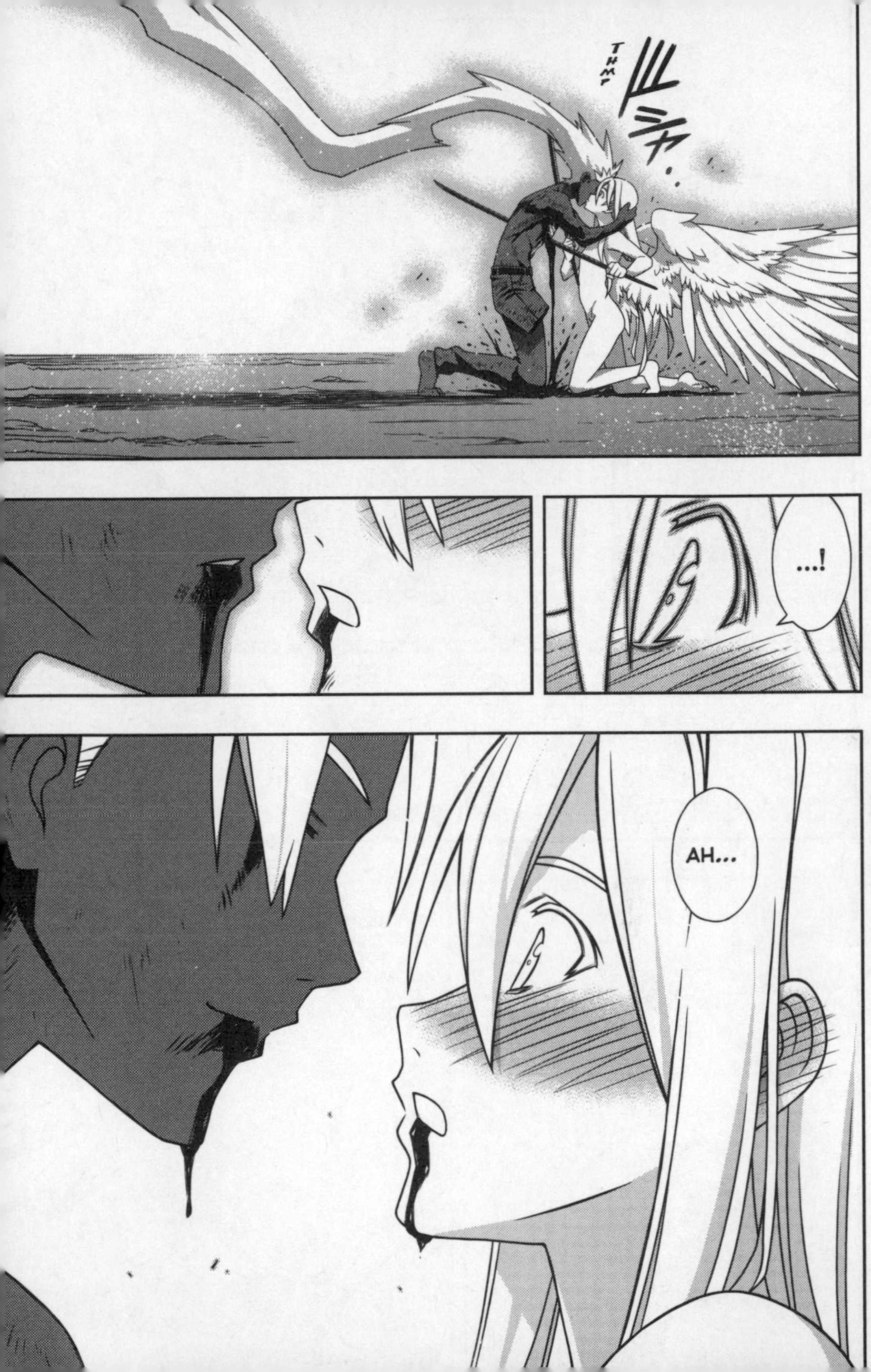
THMP
ドシャ
...!
AH...

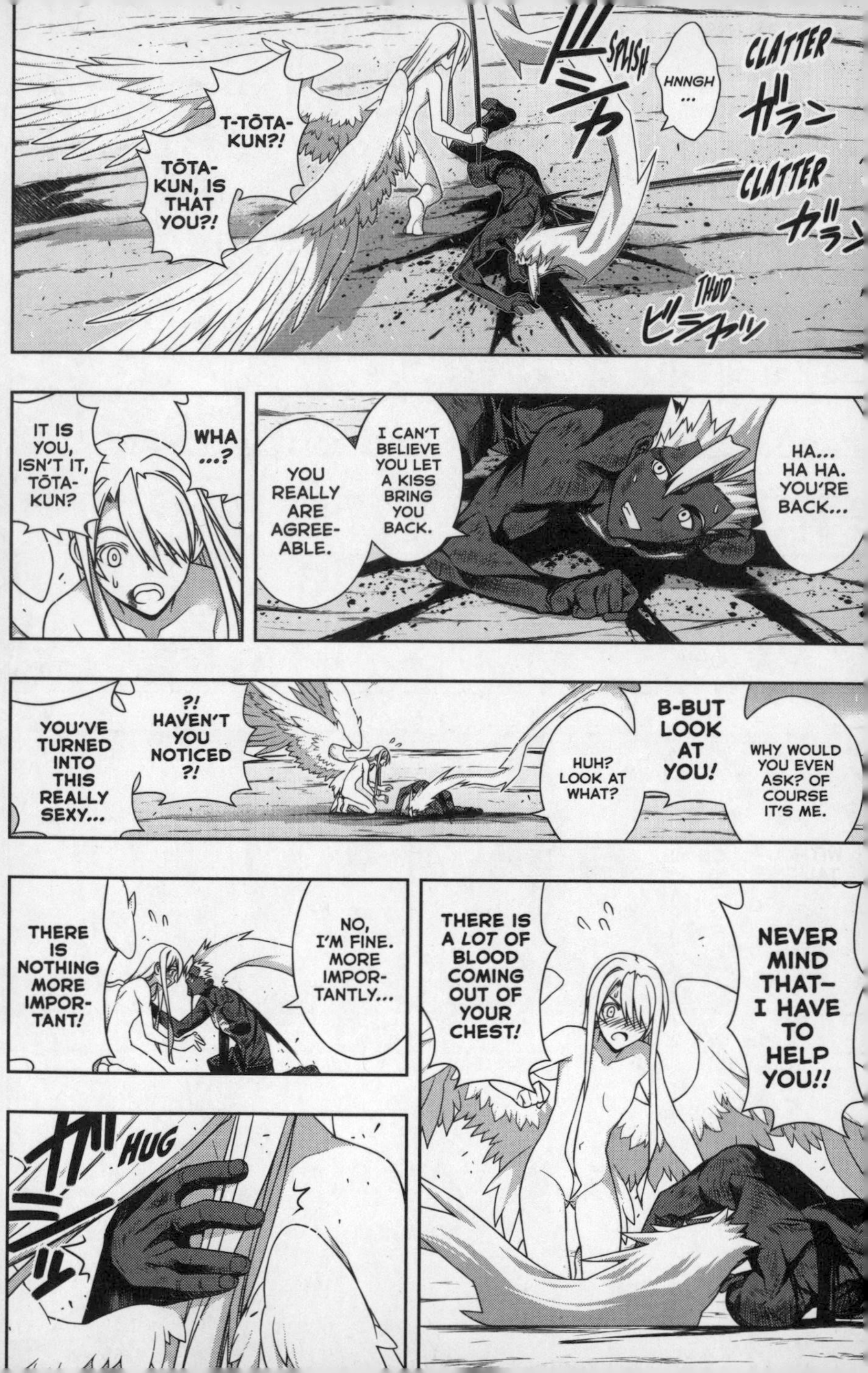
CLATTER ガラン
HNNGH ...
SPLISH
CLATTER ガラン
T-TŌTA-KUN?!
TŌTA-KUN, IS THAT YOU?!
THUD
HA... HA HA. YOU'RE BACK...
I CAN'T BELIEVE YOU LET A KISS BRING YOU BACK.
YOU REALLY ARE AGREEABLE.
WHA ...?
IT IS YOU, ISN'T IT, TŌTA-KUN?
WHY WOULD YOU EVEN ASK? OF COURSE IT'S ME.
B-BUT LOOK AT YOU!
HUH? LOOK AT WHAT?
?! HAVEN'T YOU NOTICED ?!
YOU'VE TURNED INTO THIS REALLY SEXY...
NEVER MIND THAT— I HAVE TO HELP YOU!!
THERE IS A *LOT* OF BLOOD COMING OUT OF YOUR CHEST!
NO, I'M FINE. MORE IMPORTANTLY...
THERE IS NOTHING MORE IMPORTANT!
HUG

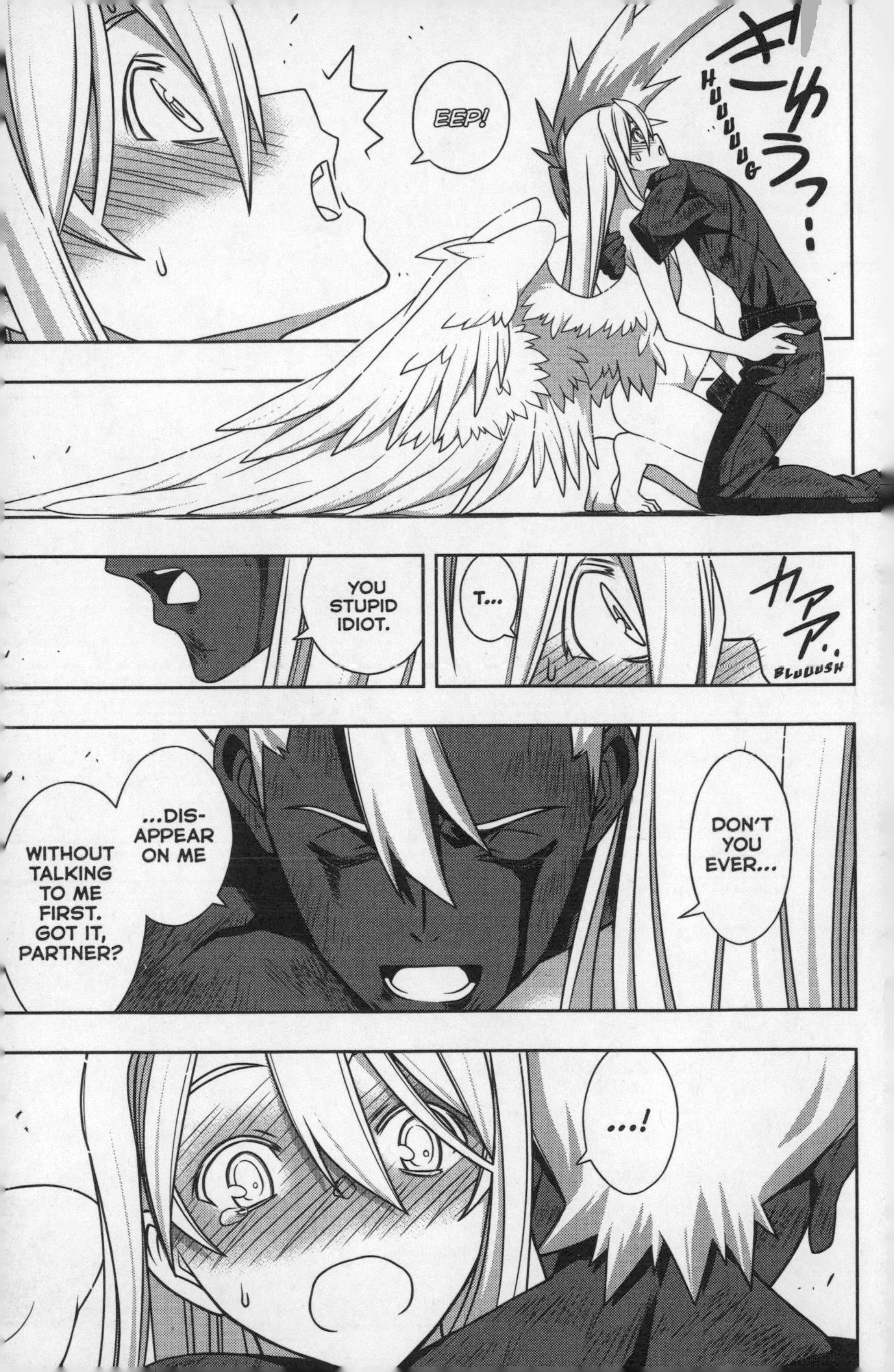
ぎゅうっ..
HUUUUUUG
EEP!
カァア..
BLUUUSH
T...
YOU STUPID IDIOT.
DON'T YOU EVER...
...DIS-APPEAR ON ME
WITHOUT TALKING TO ME FIRST. GOT IT, PARTNER?
...!

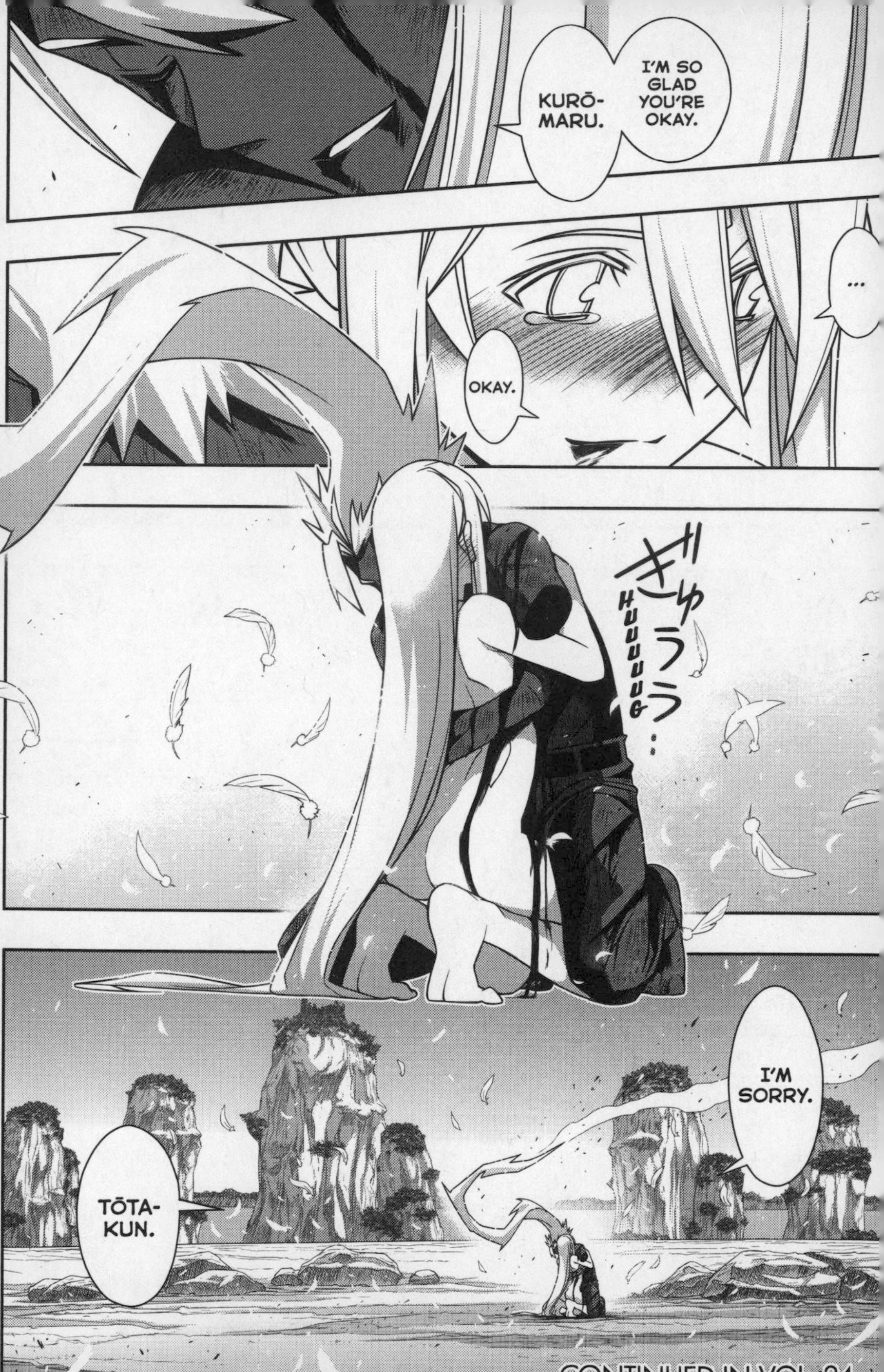
I'M SO GLAD YOU'RE OKAY.
KURŌ-MARU.
...
OKAY.
ぎゅうう..
HUUUUUUG
I'M SORRY.
TŌTA-KUN.

CONTINUED IN VOL. 24

悠 UQ HOLDER!
ユーキューホルダー!

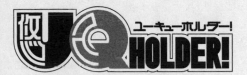

UQ HOLDER!

STAFF

Ken Akamatsu
Takashi Takemoto
Kenichi Nakamura
Keiichi Yamashita
Yuri Sasaki
Madoka Akanuma

Thanks to Ran Ayanaga

Young characters and steampunk setting, like *Howl's Moving Castle* and *Battle Angel Alita*

Beyond the Clouds © 2018 Nicke / Ki-oon

A boy with a talent for machines and a mysterious girl whose wings he's fixed will take you beyond the clouds! In the tradition of the high-flying, resonant adventure stories of Studio Ghibli comes a gorgeous tale about the longing of young hearts for adventure and friendship!

The boys are back, in 400-page hardcovers that are as pretty and badass as they are!

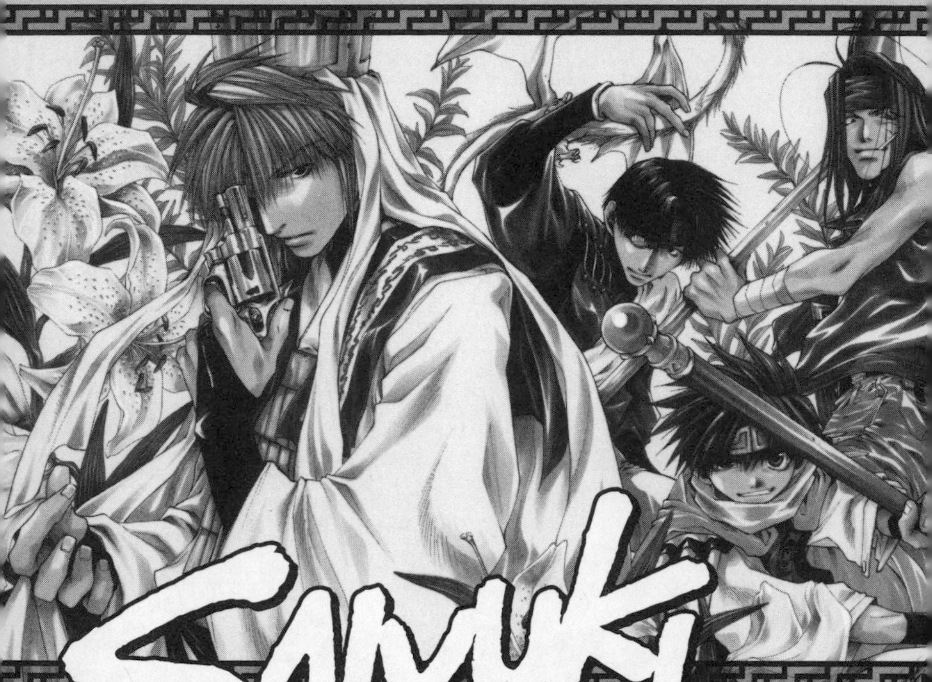

Saiyuki

THE ORIGINAL SERIES

KAZUYA MINEKURA

KC KODANSHA COMICS

"AN EDGY COMIC LOOK AT AN ANCIENT CHINESE TALE." —YALSA

Genjo Sanzo is a Buddhist priest in the city of Togenkyo, which is being ravaged by yokai spirits that have fallen out of balance with the natural order. His superiors send him on a journey far to the west to discover why this is happening and how to stop it. His companions are three yokai with human souls. But this is no day trip — the four will encounter many discoveries and horrors on the way.

FEATURES NEW TRANSLATION, COLOR PAGES, AND BEAUTIFUL WRAPAROUND COVER ART!

THE SWEET SCENT OF LOVE IS IN THE AIR! FOR FANS OF OFFBEAT ROMANCES LIKE *WOTAKOI*

Sweat and Soap © Kintetsu Yamada / Kodansha Ltd.

In an office romance, there's a fine line between sexy and awkward... and that line is where Asako — a woman who sweats copiously — meets Koutarou — a perfume developer who can't get enough of Asako's, er, scent. Don't miss a romcom manga like no other!

KC
KODANSHA
COMICS

The adorable new odd-couple cat comedy manga from the creator of the beloved *Chi's Sweet Home*, in full color!

Praise for Chi's Sweet Home

"Nearly impossible to turn away... a true all-ages title that anyone, young or old, cat lover or not, will enjoy. The stories will bring a smile to your face and warm your heart."

—School Library Journal

Sue & Tai-chan

Konami Kanata

Sue is an aging housecat who's looking forward to living out her life in peace... but her plans change when the mischievous black tomcat Tai-chan enters the picture! Hey! Sue never signed up to be a catsitter! *Sue & Tai-chan* is the latest from the reigning meow-narch of cute kitty comics, Konami Kanata.

KC KODANSHA COMICS

Knight of the ICE

Yayoi Ogawa

Knight of the Ice ©Yayoi Oga...

SKATING THRILLS AND ICY CHILLS WITH THIS NEW TINGLY ROMANCE SERIES!

A rom-com on ice, perfect for fans of *Princess Jellyfish* and *Wotakoi*. Kokoro is the talk of the figure-skating world, winning trophies and hearts. But little do they know... he's actually a huge nerd! From the beloved creator of *You're My Pet* (*Tramps Like Us*).

Chitose is a serious young woman, working for the health magazine *SASSO*. Or at least, she would be, if she wasn't constantly getting distracted by her childhood friend, international figure skating star Kokoro Kijinami! In the public eye and on the ice, Kokoro is a gallant, flawless knight, but behind his glittery costumes and breathtaking spins lies a secret: He's actually a hopelessly romantic otaku, who can only land his quad jumps when Chitose is on hand to recite a spell from his favorite magical girl anime!

UQ HOLDER! 23 is a work of fiction. Names, characters, places, and incidents are the products of the author's imagination or are used fictitiously. Any resemblance to actual events, locales, or persons, living or dead, is entirely coincidental.

A Kodansha Comics Trade Paperback Original

Published in the United States by Kodansha Comics, an imprint of Kodansha USA Publishing, LLC, New York.

Publication rights for this English edition arranged through Kodansha Ltd., Tokyo.

First published in Japan in 2020 by Kodansha Ltd., Tokyo.

ISBN 978-1-64651-235-5

Printed in the United States of America.

www.kodansha.us

1st Printing
Translation: Alethea Nibley & Athena Nibley
Lettering: James Dashiell
Editing: David Yoo
Kodansha Comics edition cover design by Phil Balsman

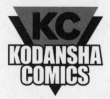

Publisher: Kiichiro Sugawara

Director of publishing services: Ben Applegate
Associate director of operations: Stephen Pakula
Publishing services managing editors: Madison Salters, Alanna Ruse
Production managers: Emi Lotto, Angela Zurlo